Letter and image

LETTER AND IMAGE

by Massin

translated by Caroline Hillier and Vivienne Menkes

VNR **VAN NOSTRAND REINHOLD COMPANY** New York

To Louis Carré,
with my admiration and gratitude.

Van Nostrand Reinhold Company Regional Offices :
New York Cincinnati Chicago Millbrae Dallas

Library of Congress Catalog Card Number 72-114166

Printed and bound in France by Firmin-Didot, Paris - Le Mesnil-sur-l'Estrée - Ivry-sur-Seine.
Published by Van Nostrand Reinhold Company
450 West 33rd Street, New York, N.Y. 10001

Published simultaneously in Canada by
D. Van Nostrand Company (Canada), Ltd.

16 15 14 13 12 11 10 9 8 7 6 5 4 3 2 1

Contents

I Environment

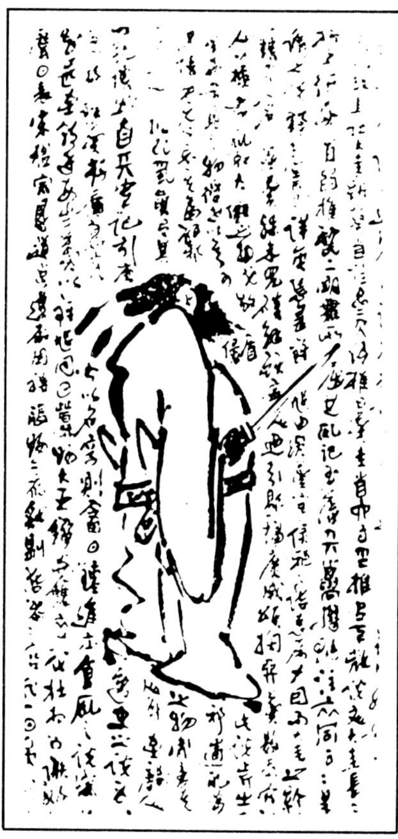

1

The image is the universal language of mankind. It made its appearance on the vaults of prehistoric caves long before men thought of erecting temples or tombs. Thousands of years separate it from writing, the abstract projection of thought.

Writing (or drawing) may well have preceded the articulation of sound. Set in motion by thought, writing is movement, it is accomplished by an act. This act takes visible shape in the tracing of an ideogram; indeed, in the calligraphic writings of the Far East, drawing and writing are so intimately linked that no graphic representation could be achieved without the natural counterpoint of the sign. 1

The image annihilates time and space. It is read instantaneously, and presents an immediate impression of the world. Through the image man recognizes himself; yet its wealth is ambiguous and its power of alienation extreme. The image is a part of truth, always present yet always unobtainable.

Modern mythology proclaims the supremacy of the image. The better to impose its fables and slogans it tries to eliminate the spirit which has animated the letter. Advertising today makes an image of the letter itself.

New York's great artery, Broadway – and its epicentre, 4
Times Square – have the greatest typographical density in the 3
world.

Cinema signs, temples of light, on 42nd Street; the gigantic sign of the Stardust Hotel at Las Vegas, with its 15,000 electric bulbs; that of Macy's in New York ('The World's Largest Store') which covers six stories. An average American can see as many as 1,500 signs a day, the record being held by Las Vegas (by day as well as by night) and Hong Kong. 13 10

Service-stations bristling with poles, pillars and pennants, whose giant labels shout across the sky.

4

HOLY WHEAT BREAD
Kosher-Cola
SINBURGERS
LAST SUPPER MARKET
DANCING
THE UNITED STATES OF AMERICA ONE
FIVE
ONE
ONE DOLLAR FIVE
ONE

2

3

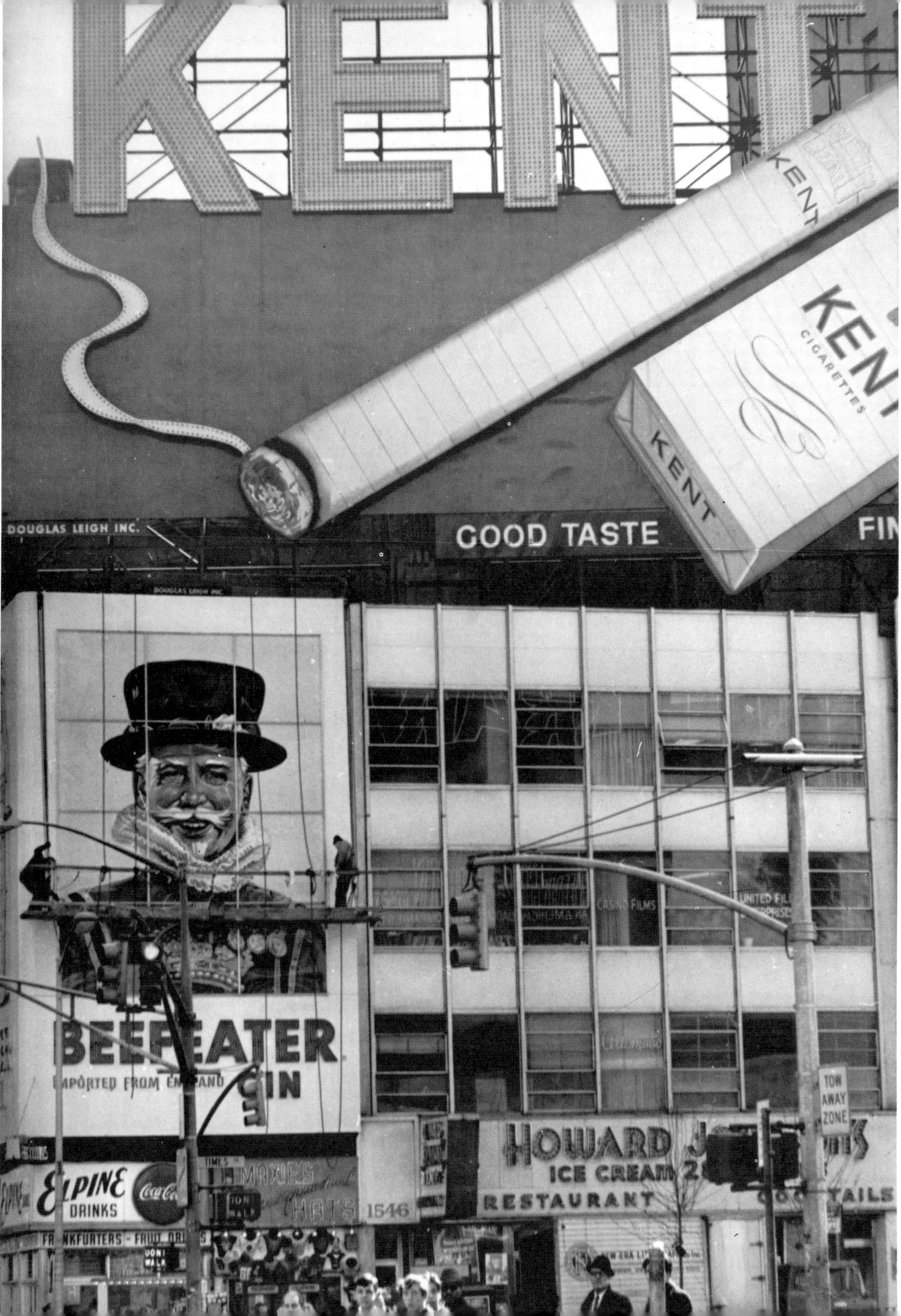

KENT
KENT
KENT
CIGARETTES
KENT
DOUGLAS LEIGH INC.
GOOD TASTE
BEEFEATER
GIN
HOWARD
ICE CREAM
RESTAURANT
TOW AWAY ZONE
DRINKS
Coca-Cola
HATS
1546
FRANKFURTERS - FRUIT DRINKS
DONT WALK

LIQUIDATION TOTALE
AUTORISATION PRÉFECTORALE
ARDY disparait
DÉMARQUES très IMPORTANTES
SUR TOUT le STOCK
DE 20 à 50%
LIQUIDATION TOTALE
PAR AUTORISATION PRÉFECTORALE
ARDY disparait
Rabais DE
50%
SUR TOUT
STOCK
entrée libre
ARDY disparait
LIQUIDATION TOTALE DU STOCK
RABAIS 20 à 50%

5

6

Underground posters looming over drowsing travellers.

Walls which speak and blow bubbles, balloons carrying 12
words into the sky where capricious aeroplanes trace their messages.

Morris pillars in Paris with their playbills, and torn notices 6
with their mysterious slogans. Graffiti.

The forgotten shop signs of the last century.

Market price indicators, packing-cases stencilled with their exotic letters, the fairyland of funfairs.

A grocery with its window chequered by multicoloured notices, the printed-paper walls of the newsagent, the Parisian drugstore's coloured jigsaws, café windowpanes intoning their Gothic script ('banana split', 'ice cream soda'), white-paint scrawls, shop blinds, the outbidding of cut prices, clearance
sales covering the walls with posters. 5

7

AU MANDARIN
18, Avenue de l'Opéra, 18
Étrennes Japonaises

Le Quina anti diabetique
ROCHER
est le remède préconisé par le médecin pour guérir le diabète.

12f 50 JOSEPH 12f 50 (Pas de succursale.)

Migraines, Congestions
HÉMORRHOÏDES
Et nombreuses maladies qui en dérivent, guéries par la
POUDRE LAXATIVE ROCHER
Flacon 2 f. 50 contre mandat
Adresse: ROCHER, 1, rue Perrée (Temple) PARIS
Eviter les contrefaçons en demandant dans toutes les pharmacies
LA POUDRE ROCHER (Papier gris)
MARQUE R. F.

CONVULSIONS
PRÉSERVATIF ET GUÉRISON immédiate par l'emploi du
Collier de la Bonne Mère
R. BRULLIARD
20, rue Lamartine, 20

HYGIÈNE MAISON DARBO MÉDECINE
PARIS.— 86, PASSAGE CROISEUIL.— PARIS
Spécialité de ceintures pour dames

12f 50 FONDATEUR DE LA CORDONNERIE FRANÇAISE 12f 50

COMPTOIR FINANCIER DU NORD
3, Boulevard Denain, Paris
8e ANNÉE
Avances sur Titres — Ordres de Bourse
Au comptant et à terme.

P. ARNOULD
14, boul. Poissonnière, 14
ÉDITEUR de la PETITE BIBLIOTHÈQUE PORTATIVE

Ernest CARCASSONNE
TAILLEUR
104, Rue Richelieu, 104
PARIS

AU PRIX UNIQUE DE 12f 50
154, RUE MONTMARTRE

ORGUES d'ALEXANDRE Père et Fils
106, Rue de Richelieu, 106
PARIS
DEPUIS 100 FRANCS JUSQU'A 6,000 FRANCS
NOUVEAU MODÈLE D'ORGUES
A MAINS DOUBLÉES
3 ANS DE CRÉDIT
Envoi franco illustré du Catalogue sur demande

GARDEN HORTICULTEUR - IMPORTATEUR
Collection complète d'Orchidées
4, Rue Auber Paris.
Envoi franco du Catalogue

ORIOL ORIOL ORIOL
70 Rue Amelot

A. STORP
121, rue Saint-Lazare, 121
FLEURS NATURELLES

TOUT-PARIS
Suivis d'un DICTIONNAIRE DES PSEUDONYMES
LA FARE, 21, RUE FONTAINE SAINT-GEORGES, 21, ET CHEZ LES LIBRAIRES

AU MANDARIN
18, AVENUE DE L'OPÉRA
ÉTRENNES JAPONAISES

LES ÉLÉGANTES CHAUSSURES DU RACING CLUB se trouvent 30, RUE VIVIENNE, 30

ENTREPOT GÉNÉRAL DE TOUTES LES EAUX MINÉRALES

Les Nouvelles MACHINES à Coudre Modèle "NEW HOME" Type (STANDARD)

ORIOL
LA MEILLEURE EAU DE TABLE

CÉLÈBRES MACHINES A COUDRE FRANÇAISES VIGNERON

F. Rigollot
Dans toutes LES PHARMACIES
PAPIER RIGOLLOT
24, AVENUE VICTORIA PARIS

AU MANDARIN
18, Avenue de l'Opéra
ÉTRENNES JAPONAISES

AMEUBLEMENTS
126, rue de Rivoli, 126
PARIS

VÊTEMENTS EN CAOUTCHOUC
MAISON MAGER

LES MEILLEURES MACHINES A COUDRE DU MONDE SONT LES "H. VIGNERON"

BRETELLE AMÉRICAINE
BREVETÉE
Diplôme d'honneur
134, RUE DE RIVOLI
Paris

BORDEAUX
GRAND HOTEL RESTAURANT DU CHAPON FIN
EXTRÊME CONFORT - TABLE SUCCULENTE - CAVE RENOMMÉE

The giant price-tickets of supermarkets, painted walls, parti-coloured houses, hippy messages, 'we love you', oblong obituary notices, car number-plates, street-plans.

Newspapers, shops, prospectuses, tracts, posters, prescriptions, mail, telegrams, books, dictionaries, year books, theses, instructions for use, maps, personal column ads, 'lonely hearts' columns. Teleprinters, comic strips, tokens, tickets and bank notes, ornamental menus, windows of bookshops and estate agents. And all the neon lights which run, the words which blink, the letters which climb up signs or tumble down them. Publicity vans, walking publicity, sandwich-men and paper carriers which walk along in step with their owners.

The mysterious arithmetic that covers railway goods-vans, the racing of numbers on meters.

The Cuban pavilion at Montreal, subversive, dramatic, entirely typographical – walls, floor, ceiling.

Signposts with their many arms, all the placards which hang over the street, which rear out from walls, shop-fronts, gables, doorways, and which streak across waste-spaces, climb up buildings. The little advertisements 'don't be a figure of fun learn to dance!' hanging from drainpipes in Paris, slot-machines, pintables, letter-boxes, tattered advertisements fluttering in the wind, slogans running along the pavement, administrative notices, electoral manifestos, National Lottery stands, timetables, street signs and 'stick no bills'.

8

9

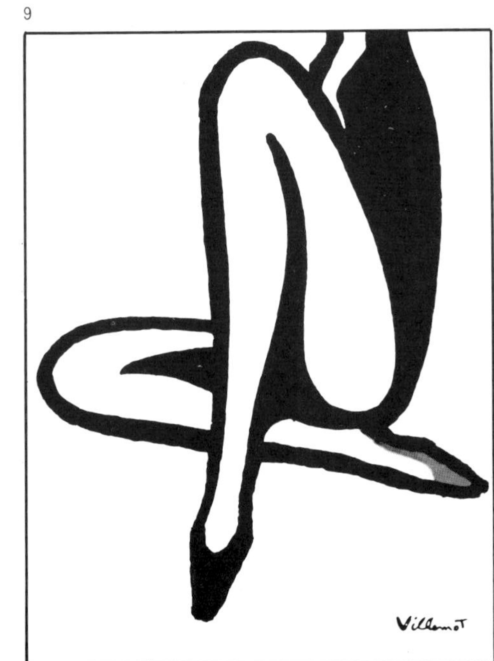

10

13 ▶

11

12

MOTEL
MOTEL
Del Rey
VACANCY
NO
RKING
ANY
IME
HAM AND EGGS 65
VACANCY
ENTRANCE
ENTRANCE

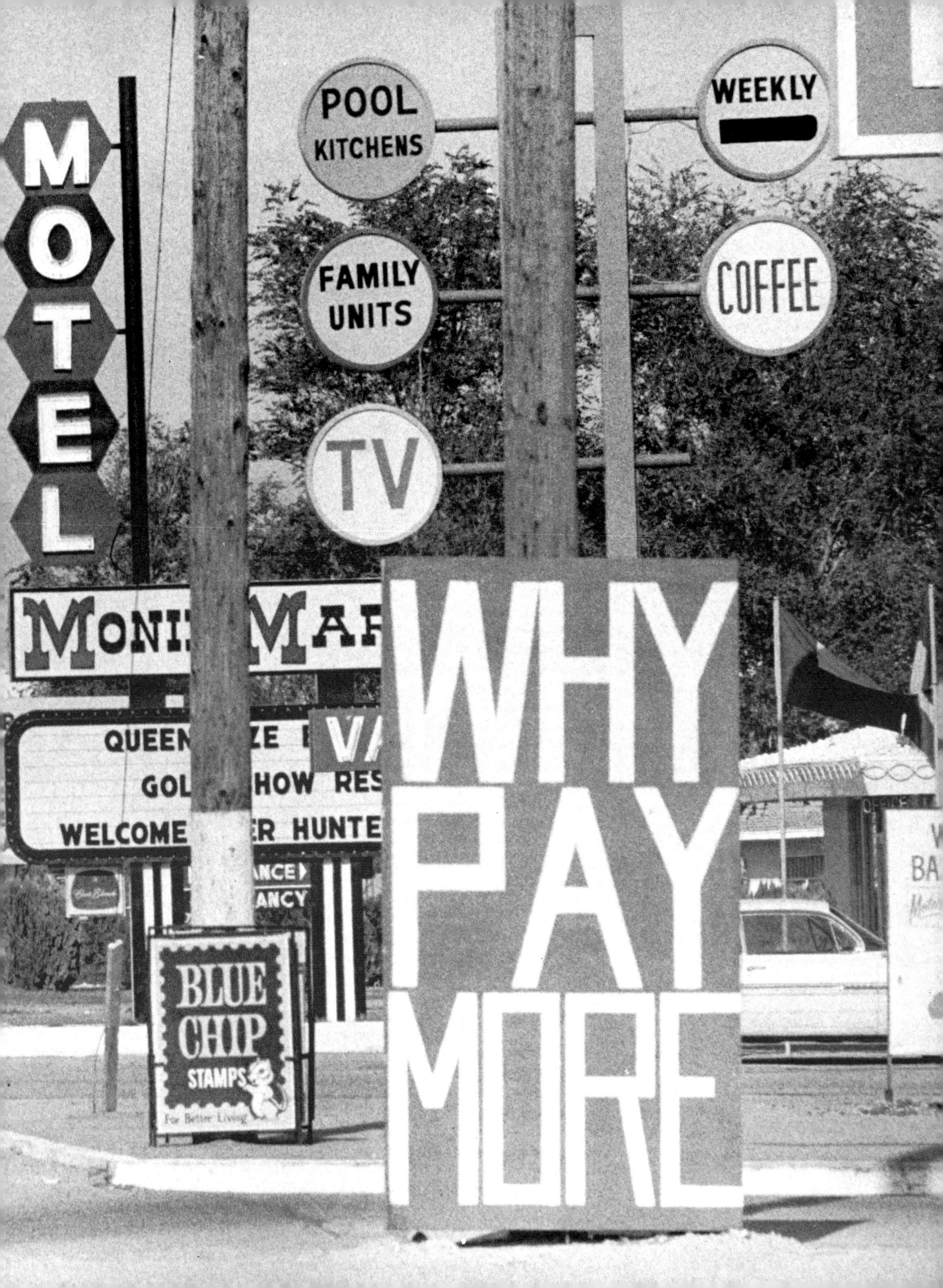

MOTEL
POOL
KITCHENS
WEEKLY
FAMILY
UNITS
COFFEE
TV
WHY
PAY
MORE
QUEEN
WELCOME
BLUE
CHIP
STAMPS
For Better Living

REAL ESTATE

INGHAM — State College early American colonial rms., sturdily built 1912 & the fresh as a daisy, cab. fully built extra charm in arge livrm., sitting rm., 5 rms., all the charm of the sex Village area, numerous ideal for the exec. or prof. al man, or large fam. with olonial taste. By appointment only $38,500. Mr. Maloney REALTY, 186 Union Fram. 875-0681.

INGHAM's public transport and shopping is only 2 from this stunning 8 rm. colonial in Hollisten, drms., multiple baths, first n. rm., huge formal dining appliance ultra modern Hot water oil heat, many live extras. $3200 takes over mortgage. An unbelievable at $26,900. A. SIMEONE TOR. 991 Route 9, Natick. Open Sun.

INGHAM—8-rm. ranch in llent condition on a beautiful wooded ½ acre lot, 24' family room, 1½ baths, porch, den, 3 bedmodern eat-in kitchen, room, fireplace and garage mortgage; $159 mo. P.I.T. extras. Fine value at R. T. WARREN, INC. TORS, Route 9 at Route Framingham, 235-3331 or

INGHAM—Eldorado ranch wooded ½-acre cor. lot size bdrms., 2½ ceramic baths, all applcs. in kitchen, dining, frpl. liv. rm., pan. rm., wall to wall carpeting rms., 2-car gar., outdoor with privacy fence. $32,900. CHARLES STEWART, Realty at Sea 'N Surf. Rte. 126, Framingham.

BDRM. colonial reproduction nestled on 1¼ acres of treed land, 10 minutes from World, custom built ago, tool shed attached to garage, beamed ceiling room with bay window. ½ baths, separate 12 x 25 $21,500. FHA approved. ESTATE CORP. OF ICA, Rte. 9, Natick. 237-655-4806.

INGHAM—A Fountainwood 3 generous bdrms., frpl. form. din. rm., balcony overlooking lge. pan. fam. baths, full basmt., wall carpeting thru-out including bdrm. gar. $27,700. LES STEWART, Realtors at Sea 'N Surf. Rte. 126, Framingham. 237-873-9722.

INGHAM—$36,000, new colonial with 4 large bdrms., 5 bdrms., 2½ baths, sized kit. king-sized din. beamed ceilings first family rm., paneled doors wall to wall carpeting. COUNTRYSIDE REALTORS. CE 5-5734 or 873-Rte. 9, Framingham.

INGHAM—New colonial on acre lot in a professional four large bedrooms, 2½ family room with fireplace floor, porch, dining room, family kitchen. Ready your choice of decor. Near church and buses. Only R. T. WARREN, INC. TORS, Route 9 at Route Framingham, 235-3331 or

INGHAM — In immac this 7-rm. raised ranch is beautifully treed & landscaped lot. Lge. frpl. liv. kit. with bit.-ins, 1½ 3 bdrms., 22x30' pan. 2-zoned f.h.w. ht. 1½ gar. Immed. occup. realistically priced at only $34,500.

INGHAM CENTER — Last by owner, priced for fast don't pass up this chance to buy on a custom built home in a top neighborhood. 3 bdrm. house with features: central air-cond., acre wooded lot, beamed ceilings, new carpet, panel & brick walls, frpl. & gracious entry, low 30's. Call now. 879-0916.

INGHAM—Picture pretty colonial ranch on ½-acre treed lot, 3 lge. airy bedrooms, 1½ baths, 18-ft. family room, packed kitchen, spacious dining room, living room, wall carpeting, porch and garage, special corner spot $22,900. Call TOWNSEND ELLETT INC., 875-5343 or

INGHAM — $31,200 — Long ranch, just oozing charm, wide board floors, fantastic decorated, beautiful shrubs, flowers, outdoor privacy. All other homes on worth from $28,000-$40,000 make this unusual offer. Call SAWYER & CO. RE. 235-1583. Rte. 9, Natick. Tel. Member MLS.

INGHAM—Ranch with full ment setting on beautiful lot, features most attractive living room with fireplace, bedrooms, modern kitchen, porch, family room and garage. Excellent condition. G.I. FHA min. down, occupancy. Only $22,000. WARREN, INC. REAL Rte. 9 at Rte. 126, Fram-235-3331 or 875-5203.

INGHAM Magnificent, impressive, lovely, etc. only a few of the words to describe our 2-yr.-old colonial, there are too extras to describe here, kit., children, must seen to be appreciated. Big 2½ baths, lg. eat-in you are ready to buy now a chance of your lifetime the home of your dreams, occup. Own.

INGHAM — $26,900, new 7-rm. garrison colonial, 4 bdrms., f.h.w. ht. 1 paneled family room, wooded lots, betterments immediate occupancy SIDE REALTY REALTORS, CE 5-5734 or 873-7443.

INGHAM, $20,500. split entry ranch, 3 firepl. liv. rm., modern kitchen, formal dining, play rm., planned bsmt. corner lot, close to all LAYTON REALTY. 20 Cochituate rd.

INGHAM—$20,500, popular—shaped 7-rm. mod. ranch, 3 bdrms., full bsmt., all baths, fin. family rm., w.w. carpet, ex. nr. everything. COUNTRYSIDE REALTORS.

INGHAM—Yg. 6 rm. ranch nicely wooded lot, 3 bedrms, all. Garage. Convenient to ping. Asking $18,500. You'll hurry! Call STATE PARK Rt. 20, Fram.-Natick.

INGHAM — This can be 8 rooms, 4 bdrms., on en-filled street, that goes n-of baths, sep. din. rm., kit., lge. pan. playroom, wooded lot, 2 zone heat, low 30's, 879-0591.

INGHAM, $26,900 — New with spacious liv. formal dining, appliance filled kitchen, upstairs oversized gar., full bsmt. on only. LAYTON REALTY, 20 Cochituate Framingham. 873-9797.

INGHAM—$18,900. custom cape w. car. gar., natural area, walk to schools, kid. children, area, 2 twin lge. liv. rm., deluxe fam. 2 unfin. bdrms. with f.h.w. JANE WALKER REALTOR 872-5061.

INGHAM—Off Concord St. house, 3 bedrms. each with nice & clean. price $15,400. From Holbin HORNE REALTY 875-0681.

INGHAM — $22,400, new 64 ft.

HUDSON — Open house today 11 a.m.-5 p.m. Drive out and see these fabulous new homes in a marvelous loc., nr. town park and all facilities. Few minutes from Mass. Pike and Rte. 495. You'll see a wide variety of styles including ranches, split levels, capes, colonials and raised ranches. Ready for immed. occupancy. Featuring 3 or 4 bdrms., multiple baths, full bsmts., fireplaces, family rms., gar., plastered walls, f.h.w. heat, finished streets, lge. lots, and landscaping are all included. There are no extras. Prices start at only $18,500. GI no money down, little down for others. Drive out today. DIRECTIONS: From Rte. 9 or Rte. 20 drive North on Rte. 85 to downtown Hudson. Watch for Open Houses signs and turn left on Hapham st. Continue west by town park and famous Hearthstone Farms to Chapin rd. Turn sharp left to Open House. 2-3 of a mile. We look forward to serving you. For further information, phone CE 5-2390, 653-3000 or Community Office Phone 562-5452. MARTIN CEREL REALTOR, Inc. New England's Largest Home Sales Organization, Rt. 9, Natick. Open daily to 9 p.m.

HYDE PARK — Milton line. Charming custom built tri level on Brush Hill side of Fairmount Hill. Shade & beaut. landscaped lot on quiet circle, lge. patio & sun porch, 3 bdrms., 1½ baths, eat-in kit., din. rm., pan. fam. rm., den with built in tv & hi-fi, pan. cellar with bar & garage. Low interest take-over avail. Only $25,500. Owner 361-3723. Principals only!

HINGHAM—$6500 and up. Choice ½ acre lots, beaut. neighborhood, covered with gorgeous natural pines. Limited fall offer—to 30 days only. We will also custom build. Raised 7-rm. ranch, $35,000; 8-rm. colonial with family rm., 2 frplcs., 2½ baths, $39,500. WILLIAM F. DOWNES & CO., 749-0333.

HINGHAM, new sparkling 8-rm., 4 bdrm. C.E. garrison colonial with family rm. extras including 1st flr. paneled family rm., formal din. rm., formica kit. cab., kitchen with dishwasher, frpl. livingrm., formal dining rm., 1½ ceramic baths, 2-car gar., ½-acre lot. $29,900. Exclusive. HINGHAM REALTY ASSOC., 749-3660.

HOLLISTON. $2500 & assume 5¼% mtg. on 7-rm. split level on ½ acre lot, full bsmt. & garage. P.I.T. $163 per month. FRANK WALKER, REALTOR, 235-1578, 653-8240.

HYDE PARK, St. Joseph's—5 yr. old Garrison Col., 3 bdrms., 1½ baths, frpl. livingrm., beaut. fenced in grounds, a real dream home with many extras! Low 20's. MAC PHEE, 323-7747.

HUDSON—4-year-old, 3 bedrm. ranch, alum. storm windows, screens, porch, 1½ baths, dishwshr. & disposal, part. fin. basmt., sewer, newly painted. Owner transf. $18,500. 562-7323.

HINGHAM—4-bdrm. brick cape, resid. area, close to school & bus stops, large living room, tile bath, garage. Call 749-0247.

HYDE PARK—6-rm. home, 2 full baths, modern kitchen, tremendous sized living rm.; the handiest location in the city; $18,900. GNB REALTY. EM 4-1921.

HUDSON — Contemp. 7 rm. ranch, 1 full and ½ half baths, town water & sewerage, nr. schls. & stores, lge. lot, priced for quick sale at $21,400. Call after 5 p.m., 562-6419.

HUDSON — 4-yr.-old, 3-bedrm. ranch, alum. storm windows, scr. porch off lge. kit. New d&d, partially finished basmt., sewer, newly painted. Owner transf. $18,500. 562-7328.

HYDE PARK — Yng. mod. 7-rms., 4 bdrms., 1½ baths, fin. bsmt. $21,000. FHA appr. KAR-DON. FA 5-5892.

HANOVER — 7-rm. split entrance, attach. garage, 3 bdrms., firepl., 1½ baths, excel. loc. $19,800. TA 6-2021.

HULL—Beach front 5 bdrm. furn. home with 3rd flr. apt. can be converted to yr rnd. home. Asking assessed value. 332-4927.

HOLBROOK — Lakeview 10,000 sq. ft. lot, 3 bdrms., 2 small studies, fin. playrm., enc. breezeway, gar. $17,500. Owner 963-3823.

HYDE PARK-ROSLINDALE Line 2 fams., 5-6, 2 steam ht. gas., nr. trans. $19,500. EM 1-5050 or EM 1-3377.

HINGHAM, col., $18,900—3-bdrm. tree studded ¾ acre. gar. excel. cond. Open house Sun. 2-5. 149 Cushing st. 749-3252 eves.

HYDE PARK—Mod. 2-fam., in exc. area, nice st., all 5-5, 3½ plus sun porch; 2-car gar.; $25,000 O'LEARY REALTORS 524-3420.

HAMILTON: Bright, spacious 4-bedrm., 3 yr. old colonial. Choice neighborhood. $28,900 Owner, 468-3483.

HOLBROOK—2 fam., 7 & 4, sep. ht., excel. cond. center of town. $23,000. 963-3261.

HYDE PARK — 6-rm. cape, 3 years young, loaded with extras. Call owner EM 4-2434.

IPSWICH — 8 rm. col. ranch, 4 bedrms., 2½ baths, 2 car gar., fully equip. kit. $27,400. Owner, 356-5974. principals only.

JAM. PL. — Arborway Area—Charming older type 6-rm. single, 3 bdrms., formal size din. rm., & kit. with frpl., 1¼ lavs., garage, yard with pool. No bldg. lot. Owner sacrificing at $23,900. T. K. FALLON CO., Rltrs., 522-6100.

JAMAICA PLAIN — Perkins st. area, 3 fam., colonial, lge. rms., freshly painted in and out, new tiled bath, panel, kitchen on 1st fl. for buyer, price $23,900. ST 2-7424, eves. and Sun.

JAMAICA PLAIN — Jamaica Pond, 3 fam., 5-8-8, 3 baths, all in excel. cond., very clean and modern, nice yard, near everything, asking $22,900. GI or FHA buyer 3% down. NICHOLS REALTOR 323-7500.

JAM. PL. Mary Curley Sch. Area—3 fam., 6-7 rms.; owner's apt. has mod. kit. & 2 baths, fireplace in liv. rm. fine loc., handy for rr. trans., schools & shops. Call $19,500. T. K. FALLON CO., 522-6100.

JAM. PL.—3-family, 4-5-5, good income, freshly painted, spotless throughout; close to trans., schools & churches; this house is realistically priced at $18,900. FALLON, 522-6100.

J. P.—White City—3 or 4 bdrms., 2½-yr.-old single, alum. sidings, first flr. den, new oil burner, exc. loc., only $16,500. Call $18,500. O'LEARY REALTORS, 524-3420.

JAMAICA PLAIN — Pond area, converted 2 fam., 6 & 6 rms., corner lot with driveway for 4 cars, frpl., comb. windows. Call owner, JA 4-0402.

JAM. PLAIN. Sgle. house, 11 rms., 2 kits., 2 frpls., 2½ baths, parking. Nr. trans. & shopping. $17,500.

JAM. PLAIN—Pond side, 2 fam., 5-5, conv. loc., nr. stores & trans. $24,900. MacMILLAN REALTORS, JA 2-2286.

JAMAICA PLAIN — 2 fam., 5-5 rms., bath, tile each, apt. each near. Owner, 323-8090.

J.P. — 2 fam., 4-5 rms. each, very good cond., sep. htrs., good loc. $35,000. Excel. KEHIAN REAL ESTATE, 522-3341.

J.P. — Pond Sec. — Col. 2-fam. 5-5, recep. hall, pors., h.w. ht. by gas, c.h.w. Owner, 323-8690.

JAMAICA PLAIN—2-fam., 4½-2½ rms. extra lot of land. conv. loc. $16,000. 298-1188.

KENNEBUNK PORT, MAINE—unique col. homestead, nr. village, 10 rms., hip., mod. kit., old-fashioned barn, work shop and playhouse. 2-car gar., lawn and garden. $55,000. WILDES REAL ESTATE. 207-967-3537.

LEXINGTON—Ranch with economic air, near center; flagstone entrance hall leads to spacious living and dining room. Kitchen has plenty of cabinets; 3 bedrooms lend themselves to charming furniture arrangements; 2 baths, playroom, garage. $38,900. LELAND RLTY., 862-8000.

LEXINGTON—Lovely brickfront ranch, lg. frplcd. liv. rm., hostess din. rm., spacious cab. kit., frplcd. fam. rm., 3 double bdrms., 2-car gar., beautiful grounds, excellent location. E. J. REALTY, REALTOR. 862-8438.

LEXINGTON — Contemporary 8-rm. tri-level, free standing firepl. liv. rm., formal din. rm., eat-in kitch., d&d, 3 bdrms., family rm., 2½ baths, 30,000 sq. ft. lot overlooking scenic valley. In the $30's. Exclusively with P&K Realty, 862-5075.

LEXINGTON—$25,500—Attractive family home in perfect cond., lge. liv. rm., formal din. rm., 4 or 5 bedrms., 1½ baths, gar. near trans. & shopping. E. J. REALTY, REALTOR. 862-8438.

LYNNFIELD — Warm, comfortable 4-bedroom garrison with den and porch in a most desirable area; 2½ baths, family room with fireplace; landscaped corner lot, in prestige neighborhood; $34,500. Dial 245-7878; RICHARD D. SIMMONS INC., Realtors.

LEXINGTON — Well built oversized cape in Manor sec.; fp. 25 ft. livrm., formal dinrm., eat-in kit., pnld. den leading to lge. deck, 3 bdrms., 1½ baths, fp. bsmt. rumpus rm., 1 car gar., lovely tree-shaded lot, conv. to trans., stores and Rt. 128; low $30's. Owner, 862-7428.

LEXINGTON — Open 1-5, new community of homes, new elementary school. access. to everywhere, 7 & 8 rms. splits and colonials. Dir. Concord av. or Waltham st. to cor. of Pleasant st and Rt. 2. LA 7-8483.

LEXINGTON—Upper $20's Better than new Raised Ranch, frpl. livrm., dinrm., 3 bedrms., 2 full baths, fam. rm., laundry rm. gar. JOSEPH TOOMEY, REALTOR. THE TOWN REALTY 861-9090. 862-1431.

LEXINGTON — $42,000 Choose your own decor. Attractive Colonial. Split, 4 bdrms., 2½ baths, lge. frpl. livrm., frpl. fam. rm., w. sep. wooded lot. THE TOWN REALTY, 861-9090. 862-1431.

LITTLETON — Split entry ranch, 3 bedrooms, living room, screened sun porch, 2 baths, 1 acre lot; price $21,900. BARTKUS REAL ESTATE, Littleton Common. 486-3000.

LYNNFIELD — 6-rm. cape; mid teens; mod. bath & kit., liv. rm., din. rm., master bdrm.; lovely fenced yd., comb. winds.; ideal starter home for retired couple; low taxes. Owner, 334-3794.

LITTLETON — Ranch, 3 bedrooms, fabulous family game room, trees, reduced to $18,500. BARTKUS REAL ESTATE, Littleton Common. 486-3000.

LINCOLN — Contemporary, Colonials and ranches; every listing avail. in town is handled by this office; Price range $34,000 to $125,000. H. H. TETREAULT REALTOR. 259-8909.

LEXINGTON—8-room older colonial with 2-car garage, large glassed-in porch, plenty of trees, spacious rooms, dead end street. Priced in lower 20's. Call New-Associates, 1763 Mass. av., 862-8400.

LEXINGTON — 6% takeover mort., lge. 7-room split level, exec. area, exclusively yours. $31,900. 329-1102. 274-1205.

LEX.—Look at 133 Maple st. 2 bdrm. ranch, gar., takeover 5½% 25 yr. mtg. $2800 down. $15,900. LEXINGTON REALTY.

LYNN — Lakeshore pk. lg. fenced-in yd. 5½-rm. bung. alum. sidg. & wind. $18,700. Own. 593-8928.

LEXINGTON — Snuggled in trees, 3-bdrm. young cape, 1½ baths, garage, sewer; lowest $20's. Call BATTLE GREEN R.E., 861-0312.

LEX.—$26,500. 3 br. ranch, like new. ROBERT G. POIRIER & SON. 861-0576. 703 Mass. av.

LOWELL, Belvedere — 4 bdrm. home very good cond.; $14,500. GERSH REALTY, 687-1501.

LITTLETON, Mass., lake front 4-rm. house, lake. $11,500. Call eves. HU 6-3849.

LEXINGTON—$36,900, 4 bdrm. gar. Exclusive. ROBERT G. POIRIER & SON. 861-0576.

LEXINGTON — $17,900 firm, good condition. ROBERT G. POIRIER & SON. 861-0576.

MELROSE—The Harvest Moon shines through the trees and over the first Country Club Fairway on an exquisite colonial home... bedrooms 2 baths plus 2 tiled lavatories... First floor den... music room or solarium with window walls. ... two-car garage ... all-electric kitchen. ... Call now. ... ROBERT STONE INC. 665-4260.

MELROSE—Home & investment. 3-fam. 5-5-5, with 3 steam oil htrs. and enclosed sun porches. ... Call ... R.O. ROCKWELL CO.

MILTON — Quincy and vic. We have listed all types of homes within the area. Colonials, Capes, Ranches, Tri-Levels. Priced from the high teens to the $50's. For more inf. please call GREENLEAF REALTY. 479-1178.

MARBLEHEAD—Waterfront-sgle. residence or unit income property. ... Call ... anytime.

MALDEN, $16,500 — "Best Buy" majestic colonial set on a lovely tree-studded lot ... MORIARTY & MURPHY. 395-6960.

MELROSE — Happy Birthday! Just 3 years old. This ranch is a decorator's showplace. ...

MORTGAGE takeover, no credit checks ... WILLIAMS ASSOCIATES, REALTORS, 438-6880.

MELROSE—extra special!!! 12 rm. formal residence for the senior executive. ...

MALDEN, $14,200—"Young cape" West End loc. ...

MEDFORD — Excellent location, reasonably priced in most desirable Lawrence Estates, frpl. liv. rm., fam. size din. rm. enhanced with rich gumwood, heated sunrm., screened porch, 3 lge. bedrms., lge. yard with country setting, excellent value, $24,900. LA 4-3456. MORIARTY & MURPHY, 395-6960.

MILLIS—Lovely 7 rm. cape on nr. acre heavily wooded lot, frpl. liv. rm., formal din. rm., 1½ baths, twin sized bdrms., lge. fam. rm., 1½ baths, lg. rm., heat, alum. comb. winds. & drs., shrouded very, very low $20s. PHILIP SCOTT REAL ESTATE, INC. Westwood, 762-4570.

MILTON—Immac. 8 rm. Canton ave. Ranch, in new cond. and loaded with extras, 1½ baths, 2-car att. garage, 1 acre, $30,500. Call EXECUTIVE ESTATES REALTORS, your key to happiness in Milton, Quincy and Braintree; Jed De Rusha, Manager. HU 3-4744; eves. VI 6-1736.

MELROSE—1st offering, charming 7-rm. cape ... cheery rms. Widow moving ...

MALDEN — If you see me you will buy me. ... LINCOLN REALTY, 389-7550.

MEDFORD, Somerville line—Berwick rd. sec. St. Joseph's Parish lovely 2 fam. ... $28,500. Call 623-2300. Exclusive with Bremis.

MALDEN, Library Sect., Nr. Sq. lge. colonial type 2-fam. 5-6 rms., sep. auto. h.w. htrs. ...

MEDFORD—New 2-family home. ...

MELROSE — 4-bedroom colonial with tremendous sunroom ... GEORGE CRANE, REALTOR, 438-2850.

MEDFORD—Open house. 1-6 Sun. ...

MEDWAY — 5 yr. old, 7 rm. ranch ... Medway. 533-6265.

MELROSE—Mellow 7-room colonial ... ROBERT STONE INC. 665-4260.

MEDFORD—Lawrence Memorial Hospital is but a few blocks ...

MATT.—Immac. 8 rm. bungalow ...

MEDFORD—2 fam., 5-6, mother will be so happy in this immaculate home. ... MORIARTY & MURPHY, 395-6960.

MALDEN — 3 fam. 4-4-4, large rms. ...

MELROSE, Best East Side Location ... 665-4260.

MALDEN—$16,500 ...

MEDFORD, Governor's av. area ... MORIARTY & MURPHY, 395-6960.

MEDFORD—Colonial, four 2d flr. rms. ... GEORGE CRANE, REALTOR.

MELROSE—Embank. ranch, lge. livrm. ...

MELROSE—8-rm. colonial ... WILLIAMS & LOVEJOY, Realtors.

MELROSE—Open house Sunday. 2-5 p.m. ... Mr. Carvalho, 868-7387.

MALDEN—3-rm. embankment ranch ... Call Sunday. 321-3585.

MEDFORD — Low $20's, 6-rm. single ... 396-5134 ...

MARSHFIELD—7-rm. year-round Dutch col. has frplcd. liv. rm., 2-car gar., lge. lot, nr. beach, nr. everything; $22,900. Sea 465 Ocean st. or owner, 834-7119.

MEDFORD—Single, 6¼ rms., & glassed por., fenced yd., level lot, gar., immed. vac. Only $17,900. Mr. Dennehy, Agt. SHERMAN R. E., 396-9134; 395-3861.

MEDFORD—Hillside, 2 fam., aluminum siding, mod. baths, cab. kit., walk in closets, lge. yard, very good cond. Price $24,500. 190 ...

MATT.—Ormond st., excel. 2 fam. of lge. 6 & 6 rms., 3 bdrms., each apt. family size kit., 2 car gar., owner asking only $31,900. FALLON CO. 522-6100.

MATT. — Exceptionally clean 3 fam. of 5-4-4, sep. htrs., frnt. & back pchs. FHA or GI. Only $18,500. T. K. FALLON, CO. Call 522-6100.

MILTON—Sparkling 7 rm. Gar. 3 bdrms., fam. rm., 1½ baths, low $30's ... CY 6-1841 or TA 5-7615 Agt.

MELROSE—Upper teens for this convenient col. ... WILLIAMS ASSOCIATES.

MATTAPAN, St. Angela's Par. 3 fam. 5-5-5 ... 522-6100 ...

MEDFORD—2 fam. 5-4-3, 2 sep. htrs. ... DONOUGH & SONS. 83 Lambert st., Medford, 395-5507.

MEDFORD—Nr. square 11 yr. old, 6-rm. colonial ...

MIDDLEBORO — Income prop., bsmt. cond. ...

MELROSE—2-fam., 4 & 4; priced to sell quickly $17,000. WILLIAMS & LOVEJOY, Realtors.

MEDFORD—Lynn st., nr. Linden sq. Stand. 2 fam. ...

MELROSE—Somerville line ...

MEDFORD, North — Brick front ...

MALDEN — (Ldn) nice loc., Dutch col. 6 rms. ...

MEDFORD, WEST — Mystic Lakes area ... $30,900. ROBERT E. ...

MARBLEHEAD, Clifton — 8-rm. colonial, 4 bedrms., 2-car garage ... CASSIDY & CO., 598-4300.

MEDFORD, Brooks estate—9 rm. single ... GEORGE R. STONE CO. REALTORS. TR 6-4710.

MEDFORD—2 fam., 5 & 3, sep. heaters, nr. schls. ...

MEDFORD—Ranch, mod. 6 rms. ... Mr. SHERMAN RLTR.

MEDFORD — 4 rm. brick cape ...

MEDFORD—Custom brick raised ranch ...

MEDFORD, South—2 fam., 4-4 ...

MARSHFIELD — Humarock. 2 fam. house & store ...

MALDEN—Belrock; 3 fam. ...

MEDFORD—Nr. sq. 11 yr.-old colonial ...

MALDEN—4 rm. single, extra nice ...

MEDFIELD—New & few ...

MELROSE—2-family, ...

MATTAPAN — Off Cummins highway ...

MEDFORD—Malden line, brand new ...

MALDEN — 6 rm. single ...

MALDEN — 3-fam. 5-5-5 ultra mod. baths ...

MEDFORD — West; 2-fam., 5-5 ...

MATTAPAN, 2 fam., 7-8 rms. ...

MALDEN, Belmont Hill-Stand. 2-fam. ...

MALDEN — Maplewood, 6-rm. cape ...

MEDFORD—Open house Sunday ...

MALDEN—7-rm. col. ...

MEDFORD—Cummings Hwy., well ...

MARBLEHEAD—Clifton col., 6 rms. ...

MATTAPAN, Hyde Park Line—Cape, 6 rms. ...

MALDEN—8 rms. 2-fam. ...

MARBLEHEAD—3-bedrm. ranch ...

MILTON — Brand new 4 bedrm. colonial ...

MALDEN—Maplewood, 6-rm. col. ...

MALDEN, $13,500—Small 2-family ...

MEDFORD—Large single, large lot ...

MELROSE—3 or 4-bedrm. homes ...

MELROSE, nr. Lynn Fells Pkwy. ... WALSH, 396-0080.

MALDEN—2 family, 5-6, sep. ... WALSH 396-0080.

NO. READING—All brand new homes! 4-rm. expan. cape, $16,700. Just 2 left! Split entr. 6 lge. rms., alum. siding, gar. & future firepl. fam. rm. $23,900! Georgian col., 7 rms., aluminum siding door to porch, overlooking beautiful wooded lot, fin. fireplace fam. rm. $25,900! Like something different? Lge. 6-rm. ranch, sunken liv. rm., fam. size dream kit., din. rm. has glass sliding doors onto por., 3 twin size bedrooms, lge. gar. ... HASHEM REALTORS, 172 Main st., Rte. 28, 944-3949.

NEWTON—Partial brick colonial, 7 rooms, 2½ baths ... WESTWARD HOMES, INC.

NO. READING—10-rm. col. ... HASHEM REALTORS, 172 Main st., Rte. 28, 944-3949.

NEWTON CENTRE—French Normandy elegant slate roofed brick beauty ...

NORWOOD — Fantastic buy ! ! $22,900. Young picturesque rambling ranch ...

NATICK, $23,900 — Split level with a 5½% mortgage takeover. ...

NATICK, East, $17,900—Ranch ...

NATICK — 4 bedrm. ...

NEW TO MARKET — Oversized 24-ft. frpl. liv. rm. ...

NATICK—New top notch exec. area ...

NEWTON—Brae Burn area ...

NATICK — 5 rm. brick cape ...

NO. READING—1½ yr. old, 6-rm. split entr. ...

NORWOOD—An attractive 7-rm. cape ...

NEW TO MKT. 60 ft. custom ranch ...

NEW HOMES—West of Boston. $16,990 to $33,900, ranches, capes, splits ...

NEWTON (Waban) away from traffic ...

NEWTON CENTRE—Owner ...

NORWOOD—$21,900 ...

NEWTON CTR.—Best buy ...

NEWTON CENTRE — A great house for large family ...

NEWTON—Exceptional 4 bdrm. ...

NATICK — New executive ...

NORWOOD—Lge. colonial, overlooking lake ...

NEWTON—Mid 30's spac. "Picture book cape" on lovely quiet street, 6 rms., 2 full baths, eat in kitchen. ... MARIAN T. SWARTZ REALTORS.

NEWTON CTR. — Special, $34,900 ...

NEWTON CENTRE—Crystal Lake area ... JOHN T. BURNS & SONS INC.

Natick South — 7 rm. Georgian ...

NEW TO MKT. $17,900 ...

NEWTON CORNER spotlessly kept ...

NEWTON CENTRE, owner ready to sell ...

NATICK—Spacious 8-rm. ranch ...

NEEDHAM—Just listed ...

NORTH READING, ranch ...

NEWTON CTRE—Town house ...

NATICK SOUTH—Lovely South Natick ...

NEEDHAM—Beautiful young split entry ...

NATICK—Newton line ...

NEWTON—Brae Burn area ...

NEWTON—WABAN, ranch ...

NEWTON—West Newton Hill ...

NEEDHAM—Master built colonial ...

NO. READING—Zoned for bus. ...

NORWOOD—Walk to everything ...

NEWTON—Horace Mann Schl. ...

NORTH READING — New split entry ...

NEWTON, WHITE COLONIAL ...

NEW 7-rm. embankment ranch ...

NATICK—6-rm. modernized older home ...

NEWTON CENTRE — Terrific value ...

NEWTON—Brae Burn area ...

NATICK — 3 bdrms. ...

NATICK — $13,900 ...

NEWTON—9 sunny rms. ...

NEWTON—Mod. 11-rm. Colonial ...

NORWOOD — 6 rm. ranch, 3 bdrms., w.w. carpet., Tappan range, disp. & d.w. Owner. 762-2567.

NEWTON—8 rm. col., 1½ baths ...

NATICK — 6 rm. ranch ...

NORWOOD, MEDFIELD ...

NORWOOD—5-family ...

NORWOOD—6-rm. ranch ...

NEWTON — 2 fam. ...

PEABODY — Convenient to everything ...

NORWOOD — $21,900 ...

PEABODY — Near schools ...

NORWOOD — split entry ...

PEABODY — $17,900 — Split-entrance Ranch ...

PEABODY, West—Open house ...

PEABODY — Wanted garage ...

PEMBROKE, cape exc. cond. ...

PEABODY — Finest area, Pilgrim Heights ...

PRIVATE PARTY wishes late model house ...

PEABODY — 6-rm. ranch ...

PEABODY — 7-rm. brick front ...

PEABODY — A new 8-rm. garrison ...

PEABODY, West ...

PEABODY — 6 rm. garrison ...

PEABODY — Lowell st. ...

QUINCY—Milton line ...

QUINCY — $13,900 ...

QUINCY—Furn. Brk. Pkwy. ...

QUINCY — 1st time advertised ...

QUINCY—Wollaston ...

QUINCY, Montclair ...

QUINCY — Bungalow ... Priced for quick sale. ...

QUINCY—7-rm. single ...

QUINCY—5 rm. cape ...

QUINCY—Dup 5-5 ...

QUINCY — 5 rm. bungalow ...

QUINCY—West, $19,500 ...

QUINCY—$29,500, 6 rm. ...

QUINCY—2 family ...

QUINCY—$22,900 ...

QUINCY—2 family ...

QUINCY—$9600 ...

QUINCY, Wollaston ...

QUINCY—$17,900 ...

QUINCY — 2 fam. 5-7 ...

QUINCY — 8 rm. ...

READING—Just listed ...

READING, North ...

READING—New custom ...

RANDOLPH — $11,800 ...

RANDOLPH — 6 rms. ...

ROSLINDALE, Sacred H ...

READING—Great living ...

READING, older ranch ...

READING—Open house ...

ROSLINDALE — Excel. ...

RANDOLPH — New to ...

READING—Starter ...

ROSLINDALE — ...

ROSLINDALE, Holy ...

READING—6 rm. ...

READING — Under ...

ROSLINDALE — ...

15 *b*

And all the 'danger' notices, or 'fragile', 'wet paint', 'emergency exit', 'police', 'wait', 'cross', 'no parking', 'Sunday parade', 'no entry', not to mention all those eye-level prepositions: 'in', 'out', 'up', 'down', 'pull', 'push' . . .

The sense of sight is nearly ten times more sensitive than the other senses; from the twenty-six letters of the alphabet, the number of possible combinations is 620, 448, 401, 733, 239, 439, 360,000. Or, as Cocteau said, 'The greatest literary masterpiece is no more than an alphabet in disorder'.

16

II The symbolic letter

17

The letter is the vehicle of printed communication. Lost within the word, carried along with the flow of the narrative from page to page, barely glanced at by hurried and impatient readers, the essential job of the letter is to be as unobtrusive as possible. Perceptible, but invisible, silent, and yet a mental projection of speech, a letter on paper has only the weight of ink. Yet one only has to pause for a moment in the slightly illogical process of reading, dissect the construction of the sentence and untie the links of a word, to get at the letters. The liberation of the letter, which Marinetti and the 'spatialist' poets so much desired, has its beginnings in the stammers of childhood and can already be seen in medieval manuscripts.

Carved, painted, cut, or moulded in lead, and, finally, photographed, impervious to everyday wear-and-tear and to the erosion of the centuries – although vulnerable to fashion – the letter has always been an object of veneration. Knowledge begins with letters; power is upheld by them; through them man knows himself; they enable him to hand on his legacy to posterity.

Born on the shores of the Mediterranean – and nowhere else – and linked to a form of civilization fashioned by Aristotle and Plato, the letter inscribed its definitive expression on the marble of the Trajan column. It was to survive centuries of invasion and conquest, bear witness to the adventures of the spirit, take its part in the exercise of power or associate itself with expressions of faith; by the time the shape of the letter was fixed, in Germany, Italy and France, it was already part of history. The adept inserted it in a fine tracery of lines; added the arcs and interlacing of the mystical golden number; constructed round it the scaffolding which contented their spirit and gave it the majesty of a building or the cold beauty of a statue.

18

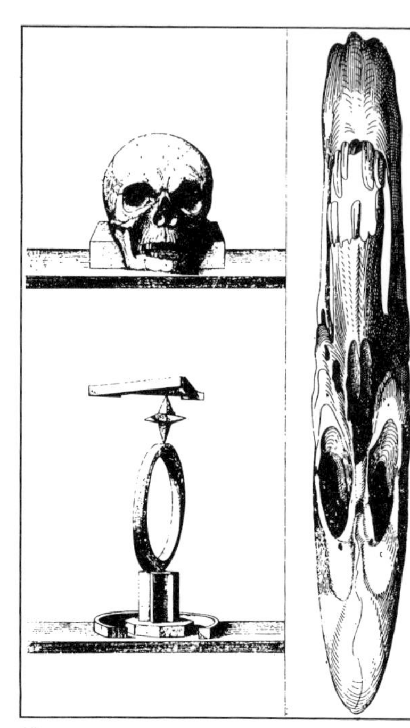

19

Removed from the milling throng of words and separated
from its semantic implications, the letter becomes an entity in
itself. Thrown into perspective, making play with light and
21 shade, cleverly distorted, it draws the eye to its own aesthetic
values.

The role of the letter during the Talmudic period is well
known; it was both talisman and possessor of miraculous
powers. Its magical properties were used by the Caballa and
in medieval alchemy. This omnipotence lasted right up to the
time of Descartes and informs those allegories which, as in the
work of Holbein or in the computations of Father Kircher,
project on to the array of human vanities the image of philoso-
phical doubt (as opposed to the divine truth). In these juxta-
positions of emblems the letter plays its role, whether as part
of acrobatic figures or shown in an extension of itself, the open
19 book. Letters stand beside the skull and the hour-glass, with
the compass and the astrolabe, with the lute and cross-hilted
dagger.

20

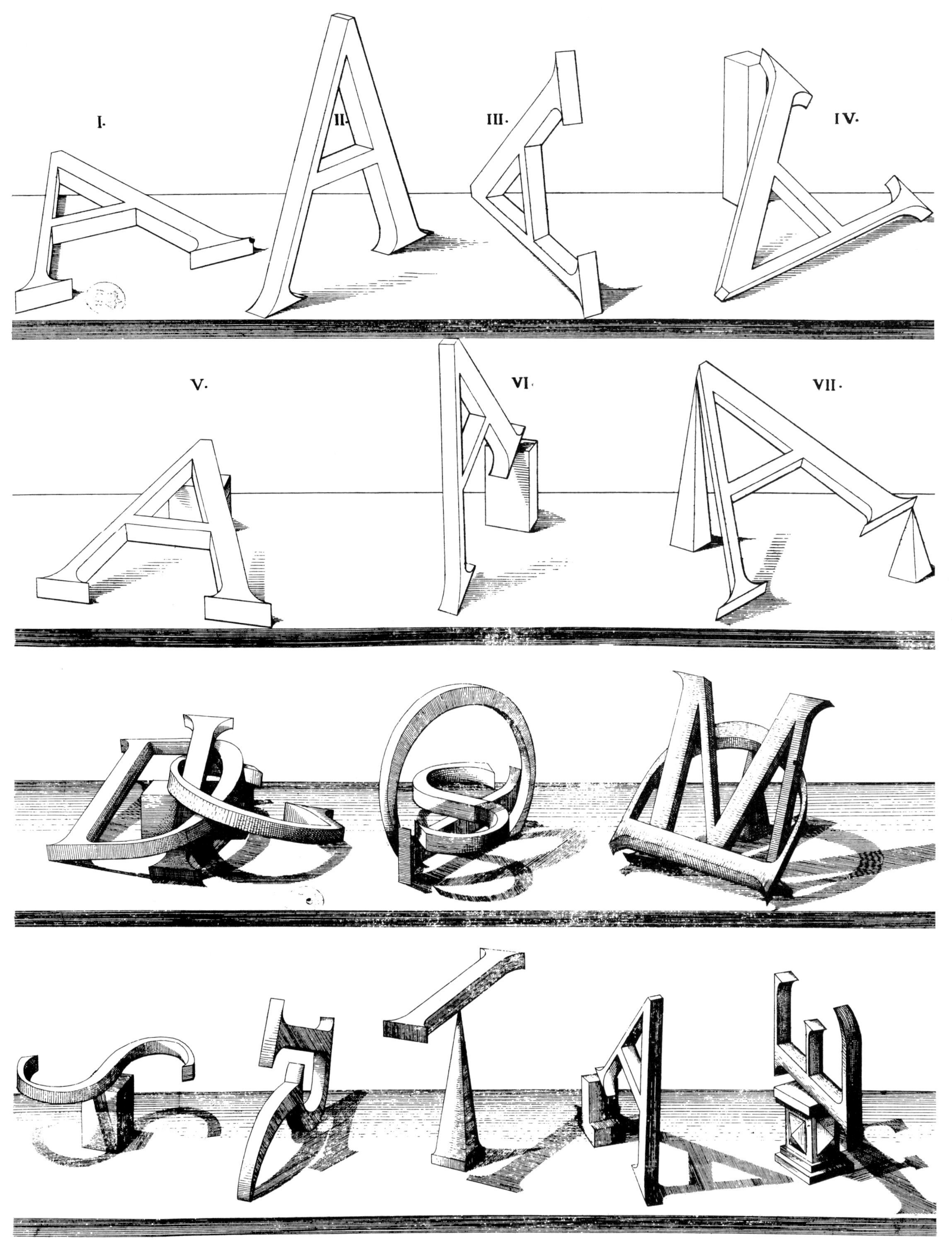
I.
II.
III.
IV.
V.
VI.
VII.

We no longer have these arrays of objects in which the sacred and the profane, the real and the abstract are blended in an atmosphere of poetic symbolism. And the exponent of letters
17 today follows designs amongst which metaphysical enquiry or even, simply, aesthetic delight, play little part.

It was the growth of commercial advertising during the last century, which gave rise to that flowering of signs which still hang their gilded wooden letters from the balconies of London and Paris. But Grandville could still imagine an
20 exhibition at the Louvre where letters were shown beside *tableaux vivants* (a foretaste of pop art), while previously Paul Valéry had not felt himself above inscribing on the pediment of the Palais de Chaillot the greatest graffiti the world has seen. And if the workmen putting the finishing touches to the
26 metalwork of a steamer proudly pose behind the letters which identify her – *France* – it is not so much on account of their gleaming workmanship but because these letters will for years afterwards symbolize their country wherever they go across the sea, and because this prestigious unit of the merchant navy is in that instant wholly summed up by these few signs.

22 Letters standing on the bare ground, among pigeons, or descending the steps of a Hindu temple, or on camel-back against a backdrop of pyramids: these advertisements of a Pakistani airline show, with sophisticated intent, the same approach, the same inspiration, which the workmen in the previous example unwittingly chose. The letter is valued for itself.

22

23

24

25

Sandwich-men are words in motion, living advertisements, 31
travelling slogans. They stem from the same root as the
'letter man' conceived by Geoffroy Tory in the sixteenth 35
century in an allegory which has its source in mythology and esoterism. In both cases, the man makes a support for the letter; in the case of the sandwich-man the letter stands within a prescribed area, which does however have its own power of movement. One no longer meets in the streets these strange pedestrians who promenaded their boredom within the heavy confines imposed by 'publicity' for the idle rich of the *Belle Epoque* to stare at. It was a barbarism similar to the type of slavery in which prisoners or galley slaves were branded with numbers, with giant distinguishing marks – usually of a defamatory kind – and which makes sportsmen wear initialled helmets and singlets which are also the stamps of ownership.

Rooted to the spot like a totem pole behind his copies of the
News of the World, stressing with his megaphone hand the 33
terrible official news of the outbreak of war which the wind flattens to his stomach, does this London newspaper seller realize how long and weary the road will be until the armistice is declared? Modern herald of a drama with the whole world for its stage, does he take in the special role in which he has suddenly been cast, and forsee the storm which these eleven letters will unleash?

In various parts of the world where revolution breeds, the letter composes slogans and becomes the emblem of the struggle of workers, trades-unionists and students. Enclosed

26

27

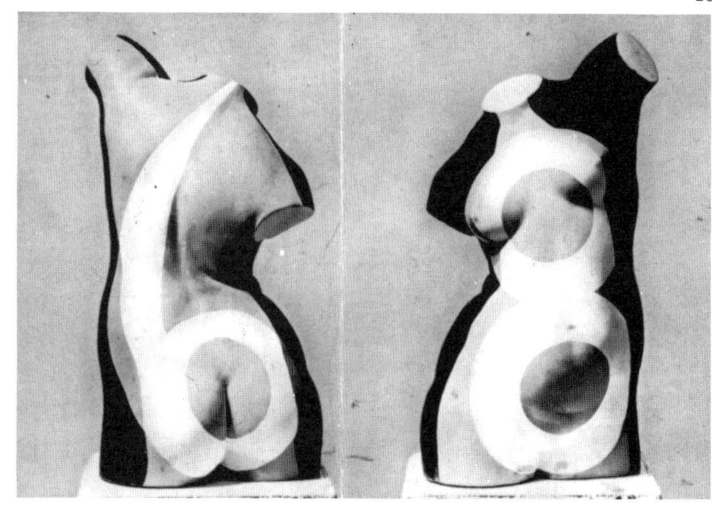

28

CITROËN-CLICHY
1000Fr MINI
5e SEMAINE DE
CONGÉS POUR LES
-21
ITROËN
NANTERRE
ENTATION GENERALE
SALAIRES
NOS 40H
RETRAIT
60 ET F55 ans
BERCOT
N
N T E R R E
C I T R

30

31

32

33

in cardboard boxes, having voluntarily subjugated their fleshly appearance to the abstract reality of the sign, the militant students of May '68 restored to the letter its magic 29
and ancestral power. They also brought to light its full ambiguity: the feigned liberty which is abolished by the significant constraint of the word.

It is only politicians (or the force which emanates from their doctrines) who can rival directors such as Eisenstein in the art of handling crowds. In the past, during big Nazi parades, thousands of torches brandished in the night sky of Nuremberg traced the words 'Heil Hitler' in flames. In Moscow and 25
Peking, soldiers, athletes and militants form with their bodies words which express the official joy that presides over Party celebrations. Recently, too, in Cambodia, a spectacle was put on for General de Gaulle, who was welcomed by crowds a thousand strong who made with their bodies separate words and different sentences, according to a cleverly thought-out overall plan.

Following the letter which walks in the street, comes the letter which dances on paper. True, large-scale photography, 34
distorting the scale of things, (one of the tricks of pop art), quite transforms these *homunculi*, fugitives from an 1840 rebus, of which we will see other examples later. They are not a solitary example, and are in fact of a type of figure very widely

34

used at that time, in the guise of entertainment. The rebus was often conceived as literature for the illiterate: it is therefore the popular, or primitive aspect of such a use of letters which is of interest to us here. If some thousand readers of Thackeray, in his *Book of Snobs,* and of Balzac, in his *Petites Misères de la vie conjugale (The Troubles of Married Life),* could see at the beginning of each chapter letters in the shape of people, how many hundred thousand other, less demanding readers, had the chance to see each day on calendars, or in comic papers and catalogues, similar examples of living letters. Even more numerous were the spectators – thanks to the mass media
36/40 again – who, in *Goldfinger* and *From Russia with Love* could see letters projected onto human bodies (Brian Gysin, also, projected his calligraphs on to the face of the writer William
27 Burroughs). And the poster for the later *Casino Royale,* a sort of pastiche of the James Bond films, alludes to these projections.

A generation elapsed between this poster and the invitation
28 illustrated by Max Ernst which uses the same theme: surrealism has become so much a part of current life that one is no longer surprised at anything – least of all at the unusual. (If women today wear vividly coloured dresses and scarves, it is a debt they owe to the Fauve painters.) However, it is doubtless not due to Roger Blin's superb use of a paint bomb in the production of Jean Genet's *Paravents* that this has become the favourite weapon of anarchists and political rebels. 'He who loves, writes on walls,' said Cocteau. From the catacombs of the first Christians to our walls today, covered in chalk, charcoal and

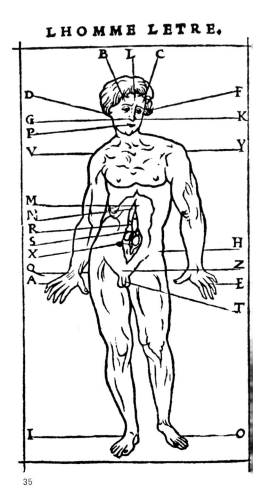

LHOMME LETRE.

35

crayon, messages inspired by love and hate have mingled in a maze of inscriptions which fight for space with the mosaic of advertisements. The relic of some electoral meeting, a *Non*
written up on a Paris wall prettily mitigates its refusal with a 42
smiling face in its central letter. The author of this naive and poetic inscription must have been enchanted by his invention, because he repeated it in different parts of the same district.

Four hundred years earlier, Geoffroy Tory was no less
pleased by the same discovery, which he had just made, and 43
which he describes in a book whose title *Champ Fleury* (The Field of Flowers) makes us think of paradise.

The artists of the Renaissance were, as is well known, painters, engravers, geometricians, architects, writers, theorists at one and the same time. They tried to master all that was known at that time (Rabelais – doctor, writer, philosopher – is a case in point). It is therefore not surprising to find mathematics so closely bound up with their art, and especially with their graphic and typographic expression. In fact all artists of

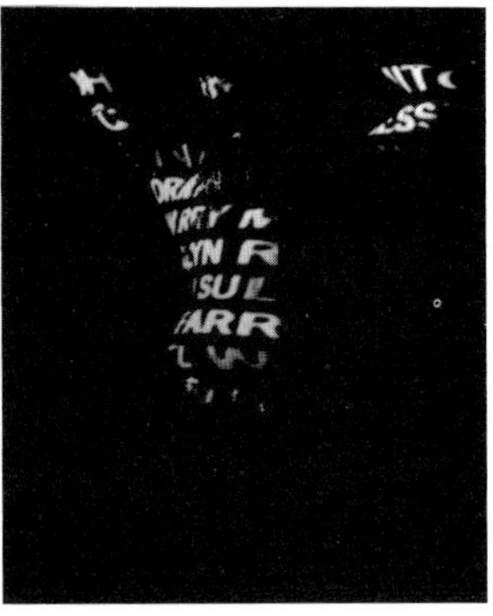

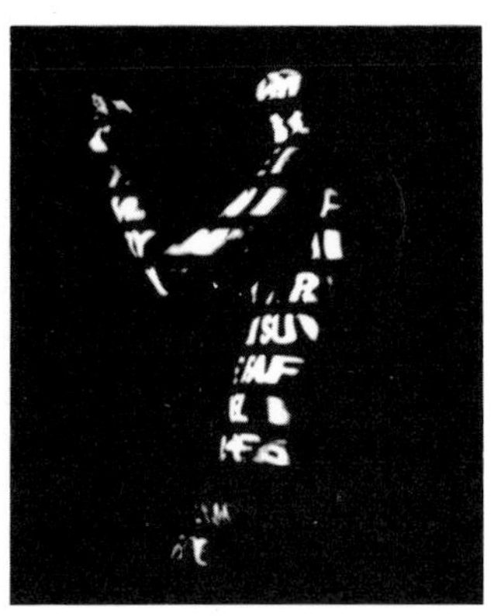

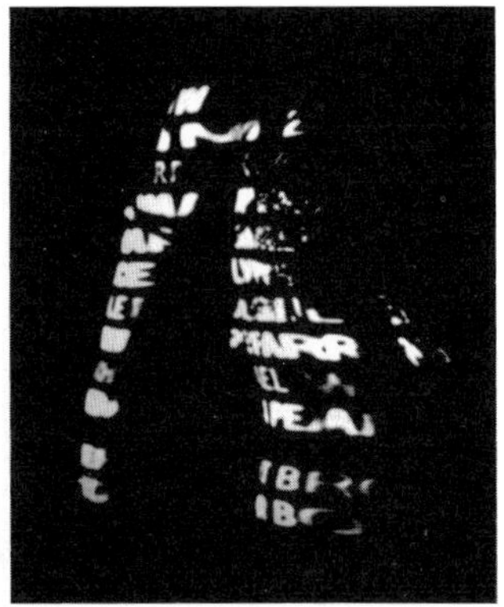

36/40

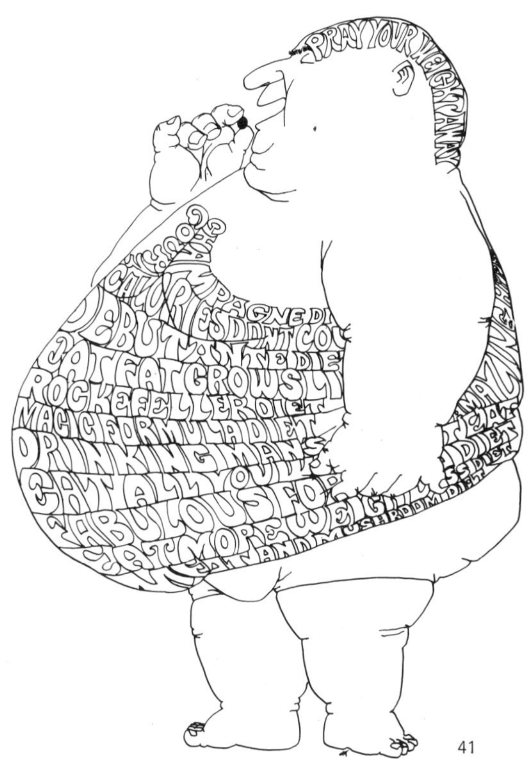

41

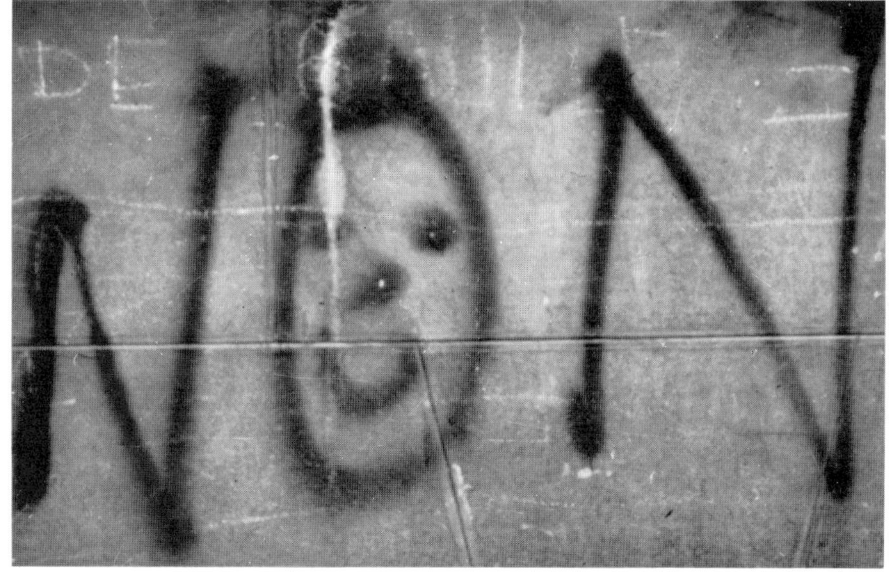

42

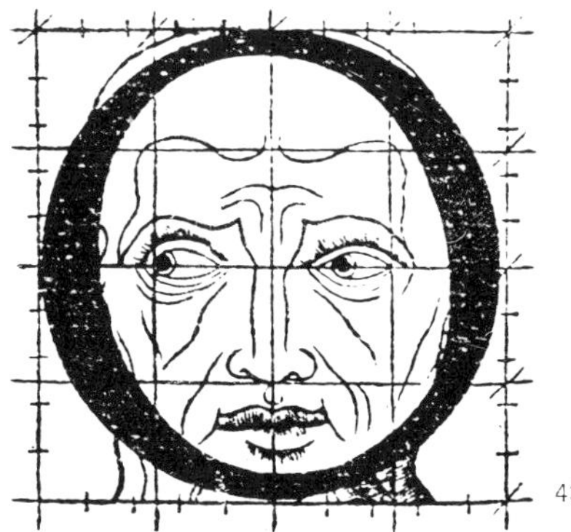

43

the time, Dürer in Germany, Leonardo da Vinci, Pacioli and Vincentino in Italy, Tory and Le Bé in France, were steeped in the Pythagorean tradition and made the proportions of letters conform to architecture and geometry. Most of them wrote treatises in which they expressed their theories and their ideas, which differ very little from one author or country to another: besides having a common source of inspiration, they had at that time no scruples about copying a neighbour, and it is difficult, for instance, to see what distinguishes the theories of Brother Luca Pacioli, author of the *Divina Proportione*, from those of Leonardo. On the contrary, in his *Champ Fleury* (1529) Geoffroy Tory pays homage to Vitruvius, 'prince of writers on architecture and buildings', who tried to determine, before he died, the proportions of the human form by means of geometry. But what makes the *Champ Fleury* an outstanding book and confers originality on its author is Tory's discovery that all the letters of the Latin alphabet can be reduced to the proportions of the human face and body. 'I know no author, whether Greek, Latin or French, who gives the proportion of letters as I have done, for which reason I call it my invention, since I conceived and learnt of it rather by divine inspiration than from any writing or hearsay.' Moreover, letters are for Tory 'so naturally well proportioned that like the human body they are composed of members, that is to say of measurements, of points and lines consisting of equal and unequal divisions . . .'

It is true, as Gustave Cohen, who reprinted the work four hundred years after its original publication, wrote, that Tory inherited from Dürer and in particular from Leonardo 'this tendency to see and seek everywhere, in their humblest forms, the sign of man, the hand of God and the marvellous unity of the universe'.

help!
BLAT
PHOOEY
H2O
NO2
VROOM
HELP!
RAT TAT TAT
COUGH
DONG
HONK
BOOM
UGH
COUGH
SLAM
ZOOM
COUGH
COUGH
help!
ZAP
HONK
cough
POW
ZOW
help!

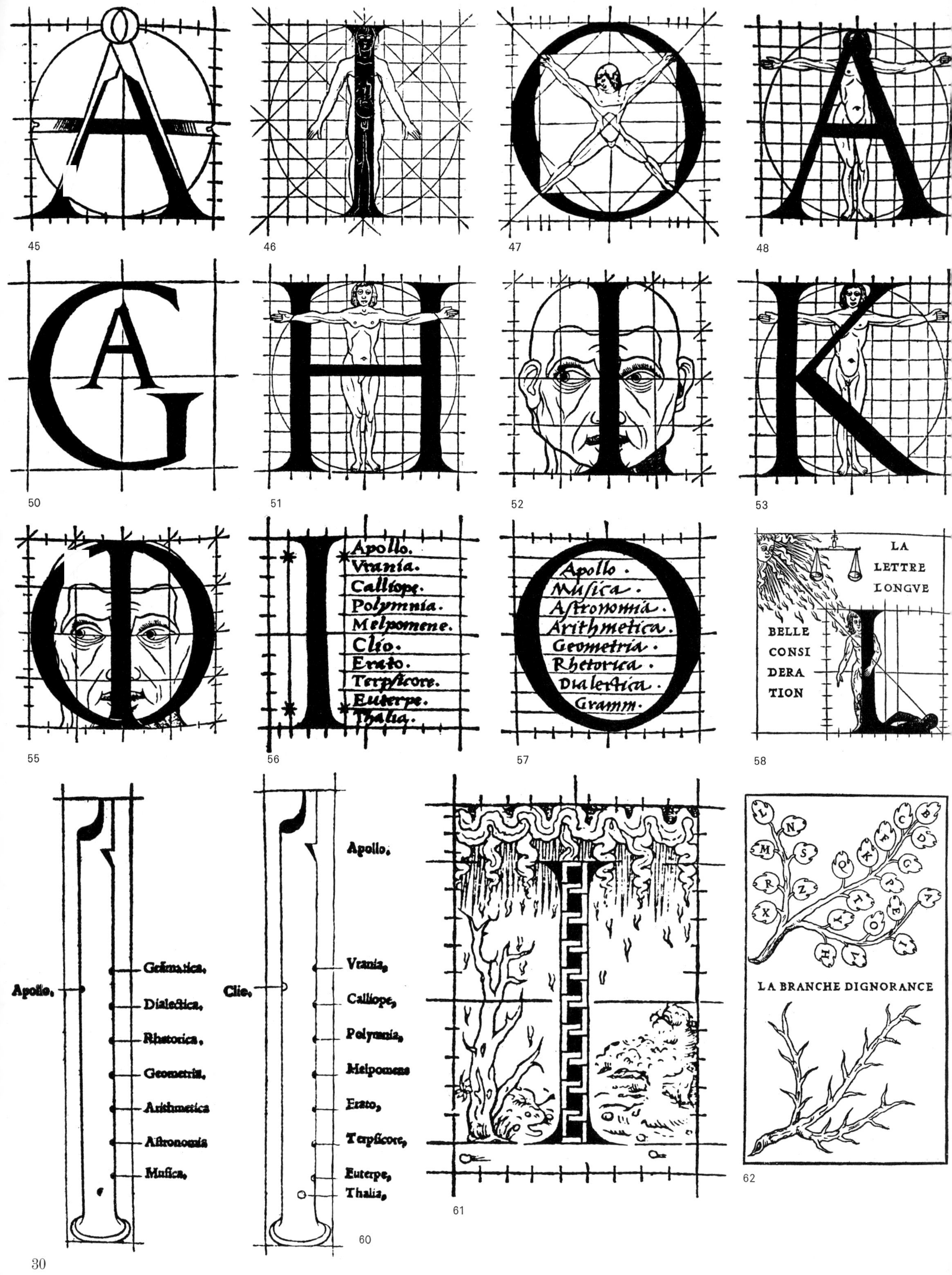
Apollo.
Vrania.
Calliope.
Polymnia.
Melpomene.
Clio.
Erato.
Terpsicore.
Euterpe.
Thalia.
Apollo.
Musica.
Astronomia.
Arithmetica.
Geometria.
Rhetorica.
Dialectica.
Gramm.
LA LETTRE LONGVE
BELLE CONSI DERA TION
Apollo,
Grāmatica,
Dialectica,
Rhetorica,
Geometria,
Arithmetica
Astronomia
Musica,
Apollo,
Clio,
Vrania,
Calliope,
Polymnia,
Melpomene
Erato,
Terpsicore,
Euterpe,
Thalia,
LA BRANCHE DIGNORANCE

45 46 47 48

50 51 52 53

55 56 57 58

60 61 62

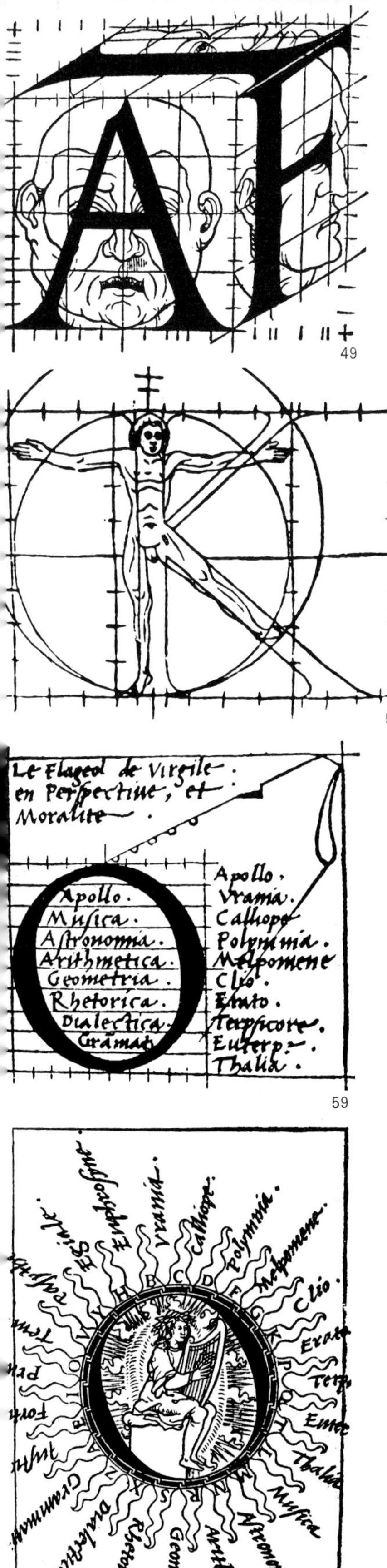

49
54
59
63

Yet Tory goes one step further: he enclosed in the letter O, 57
with its perfect circle, the seven liberal arts, and gave to I,
another basic letter, the task of representing the nine muses. 56
Finally, encouraged no doubt by the daringness of his invention and quite undeterred by any acrobatic figure, he combined
these seven liberal arts and the nine muses in the design of a
flageolet (a kind of flute with seven holes) which, seen from 59
behind and in perspective, resembles both a standing O and a
recumbent I. Combining the straight line and the circle,
these two letters symbolise the two generative organs; from
this union, under the sign of the goddess Io, are born all the
letters of the alphabet . . . Finally, freehand and with the help
of a compass, Tory arranges the twenty-three letters of the
alphabet as it then was round a central O representing a sun, 63
whose twenty-three rays are the nine muses, the seven liberal
arts, the four cardinal virtues and the three graces.

Twenty-three letters are considered in the *Champ Fleury*, commented on and described in detail with a meticulous care that is somewhat reminiscent of a scientist with his microscope; some are particularly worthy of note.

The letter A 'has its legs stretched out and spread wide, 48
like a man's feet and legs when he is walking along'. Moreover, the transversal bar of the A 'exactly covers man's genital
member to denote that modesty and chastity are to be desired
above all things in those who seek access and entry to the
world of letters, to which the A is the doorway, being the first
letter in all alphabets'. Elsewhere Tory builds the A with a
ruler and compass which represent the king and queen 45
respectively.

The letter D is like 'the stage of a theatre, such as that which I saw in a city near Avignon on the Rhône' . . . This stage, which has its 'front edge in a straight line and the back in a round half-circle can be very easily seen as a letter D'.

The letter H represents 'the body of a house, in that the part below the transverse line which I have called central and diametrical is to contain the lesser rooms and chambers. And the part above is thus for the greater rooms or greater and middle-sized rooms'.

The letter I: 'I cannot proceed further without mentioning 61
that our letters owed their invention to divine inspiration.
Certainly, at the beginning of the eighth book of the Iliad,
Homer, king of Greek poets, told how once upon a time
Jupiter declared that if he wished he could pull towards him
by means of a golden chain, all the other gods, and even the
earth and the sea as well'. If we imagine this golden chain
hanging down from the sky to reach our feet, we can see that it
is in 'length and breadth comparable in proportion and sym-
metry to the letter I . . .' This theme of a golden chain runs
through all Tory's work, sometimes linked to other allegories,
such as that of the golden branch 'which has twenty-three 62
leaves which mysteriously symbolize the twenty-three letters

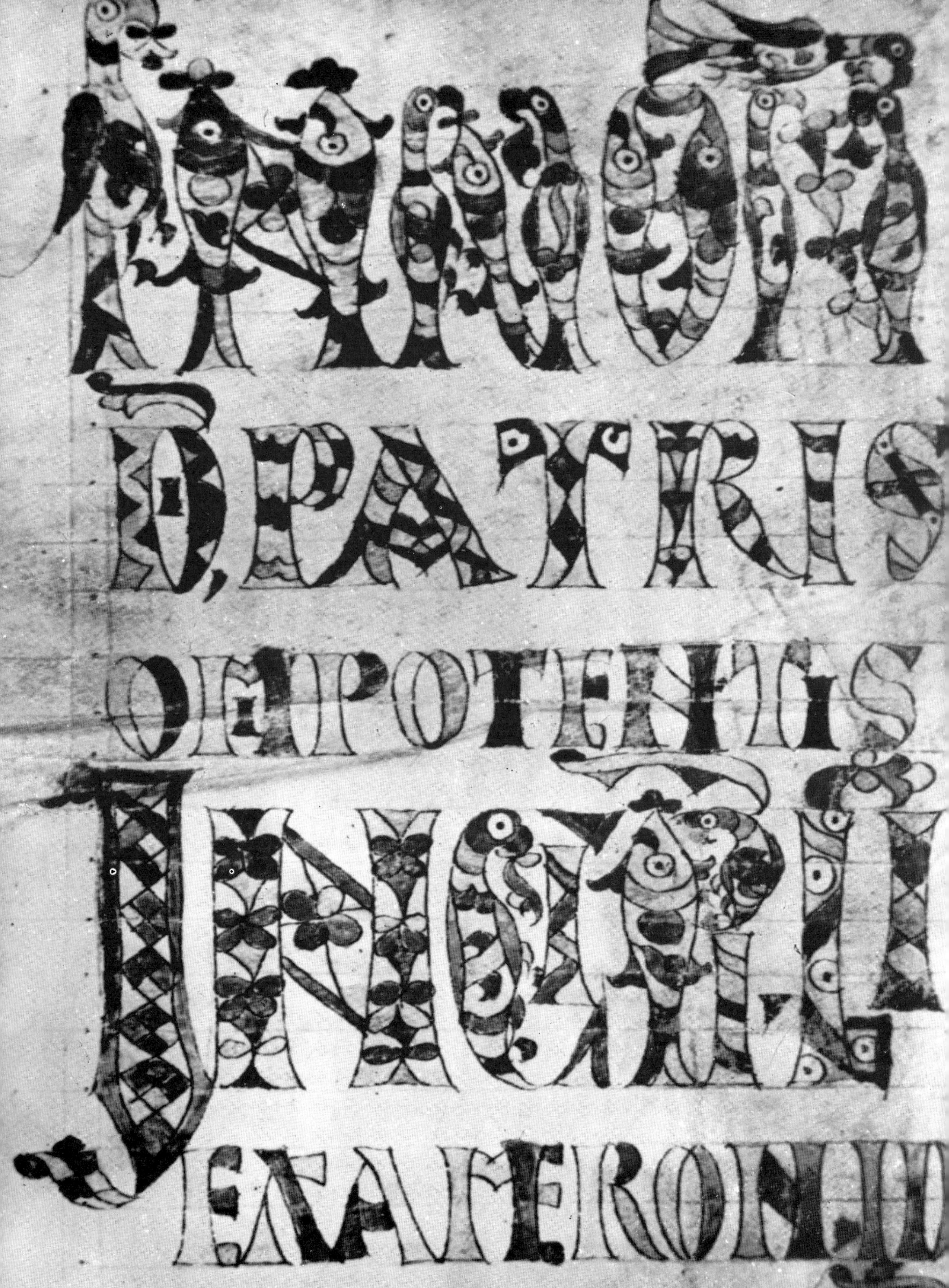

64

65

66

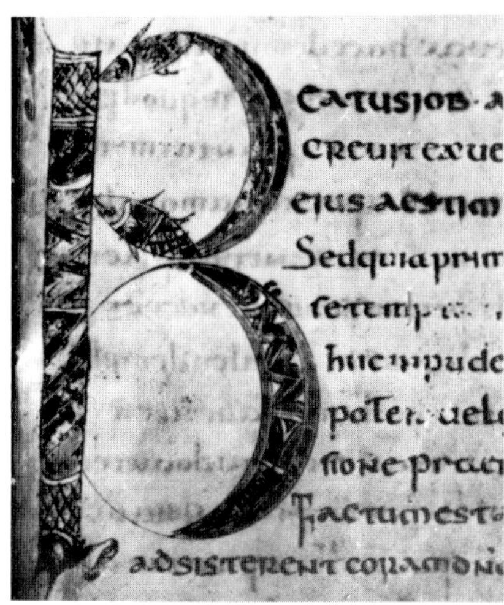

67

68

of the alphabet'. This last image, borrowed from Virgil, shows the influence of the classics and Italy on Tory. 'I have seen the Coliseum more than a thousand times', he says. And the Coliseum had, when it was still whole, the shape of the letter O, 'round outside and inside oval shaped'.

The letter L is illustrated by another allegory, of the sign of 58
Libra. It is shaped like the human body and its shadow, 'the sun being in the sign of the Scales'. The letter M however, has a more prosaic interpretation: it is 'like certain men, who are so fat that their belts are larger than the height of their body'.

But it is Q which gives rise to the most amusing comparison. After having noted that 'this letter Q is the only one of all the letters which steps out of line downwards', for which no one, Tory says, had been able to give him a good reason, he continues by saying: 'I have so pondered and puzzled on these so-called ancient letters, that I have discovered that Q steps out of line because it is never written in any word without its companion and good friend U, and to show that it desires this letter always to follow it, it stretches out its tail below to embrace it . . . '

To pronounce the letter S, is 'to hiss, as powerfully as a red-hot iron when it is plunged into water'.

Finally, the letter Y, like the 'vanities' painted by the contemporaries of Tory, is the sign of pleasure and virtue.

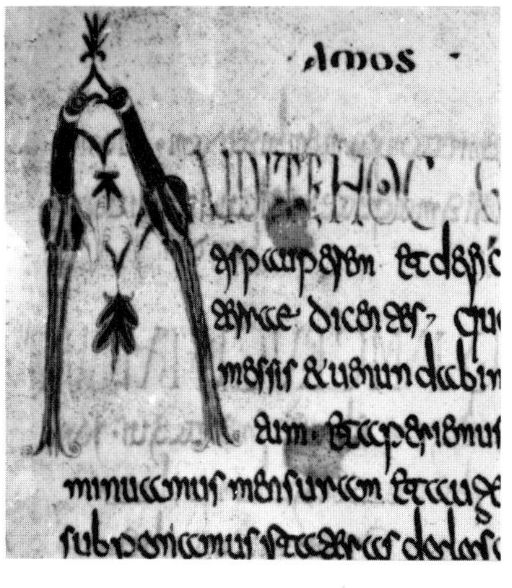
69

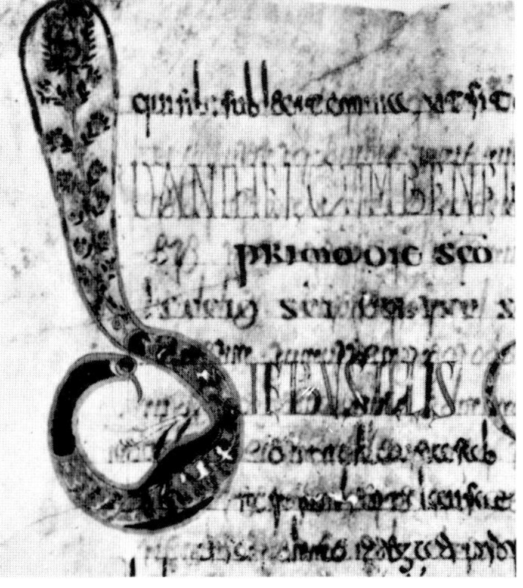
70

71

72

73

74

75

76

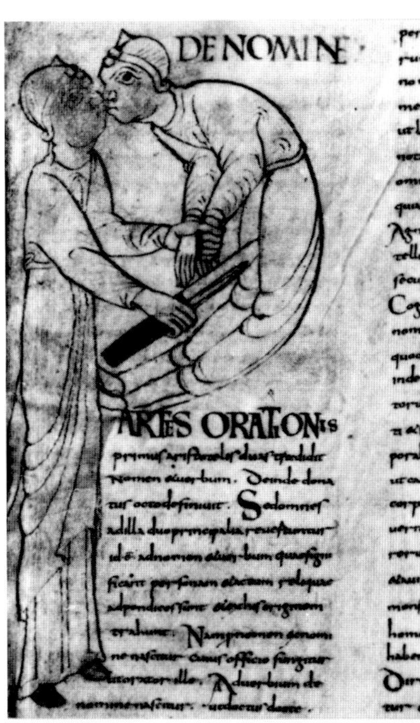
77

78

79

Conscious of the originality of his approach and of the dialectical excesses to which it might lead him, Geoffroy Tory forestalled the criticisms that might be aimed at him. 'I have no doubt that detractors and tiresome people will sneer at it', he prophesied; but that did not stop him writing his 'fantasy and speculative work, to be of pleasure and service to good students'.

Sworn enemy of pedantry, Tory equals Rabelais (who was possibly born in the same year as him) in gaiety, good humour and pertinent wit. Here, for example, is how the first book of the *Champ Fleury* begins: 'On the morning after Twelfth night, after having partaken of a restful sleep, and my stomach having digested, lightly and joyously, the fact that it was now 1523, I began to ponder as I lay in bed and go back over various things in my memory, thinking a thousand inconsequential thoughts, both light and serious, and so doing I remembered an antique letter I had drawn long ago . . .'

Indeed, this key book is of far more interest than a mere sample alphabet (even if the *Champ Fleury* was only that, it would still be attractive enough in conception and presentation). In addition to its philological interest – it gives valuable indications of the spelling and pronunciation of the time – and the graphical notation of accents, apostrophes and the cedilla, which it introduced, the *Champ Fleury* has played a considerable part in the evolution of French typography. It was, in fact, during the ten years after its publication that roman characters were definitively substituted for the bastard Gothic ones (which are so close in style to manuscript writing) and also superseded the italic letter made fashionable by the Aldine editions.

Apart from different versions of sans-serif type, all descended from the German Bauhaus school which itself developed from the medieval Gothic tradition, the majority of countries which today use the Latin alphabet have found nothing else to offer in the way of typographical print other than Garamond. Which, imbued as it is with the spirit of the Renaissance, was designed in 1545 by Claude Garamond – who was, in fact the pupil of Geoffroy Tory.

80

81

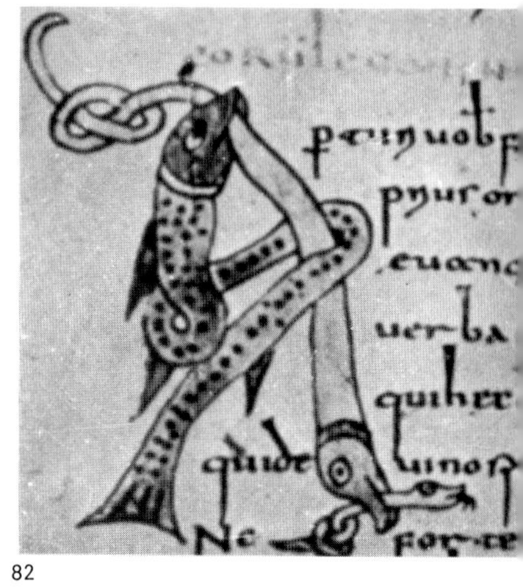

82

83

84

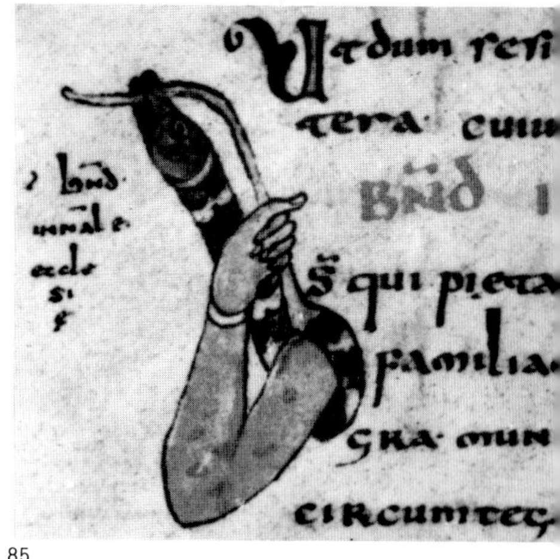

85

87

88

89

92

93

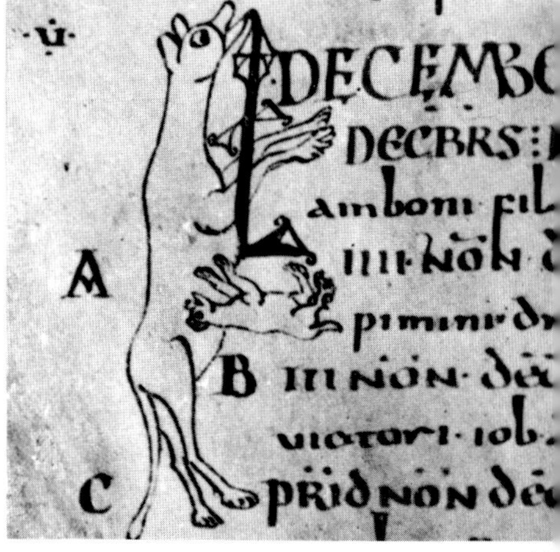

94

The most important contemporary typographical innovation, that of the Univers letter designed by Adrian Frutiger, is once more reminiscent in design, style and weight, of the Bauhaus school. True, the programme and aims of the Weimar school (which was later transferred to Dessau) and its promoters were no less ambitious than those of the artists of four centuries before: a new Renaissance was to be celebrated in all aspects of design, whether it was a case of constructing a chair or fashioning a new typographical fount. However, even taking into account that the rise of Nazism accelerated the break-up and dispersal of the Bauhaus group, it does not seem that this enterprise ever succeeded in giving to its creations any character or style other than the intrinsically Germanic. (For the rest, apart from a few architects of very strong personality, the most gifted artists, such as Klee and Kandinsky, could not long submit to the constraining intellectual discipline imposed upon them.) We have need, today, of a second Geoffroy Tory.

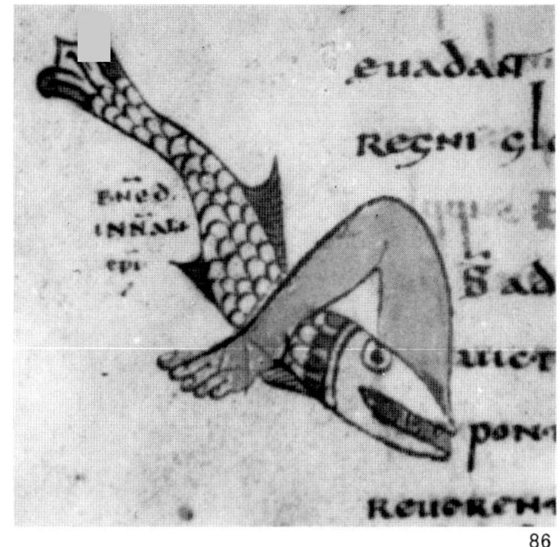

86

90

91

95

96

97

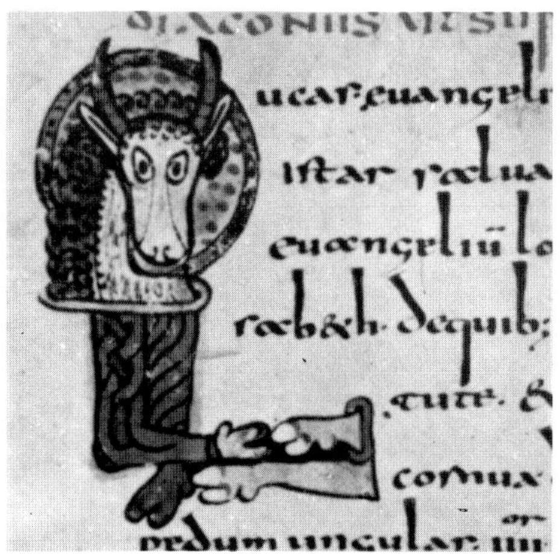

98

99

102

103

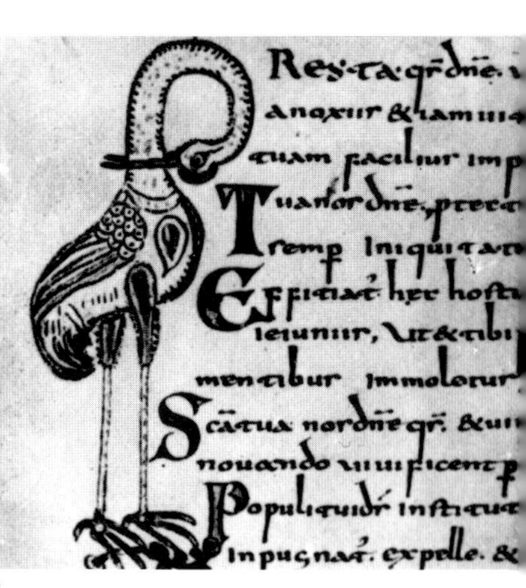

104

107

108

100

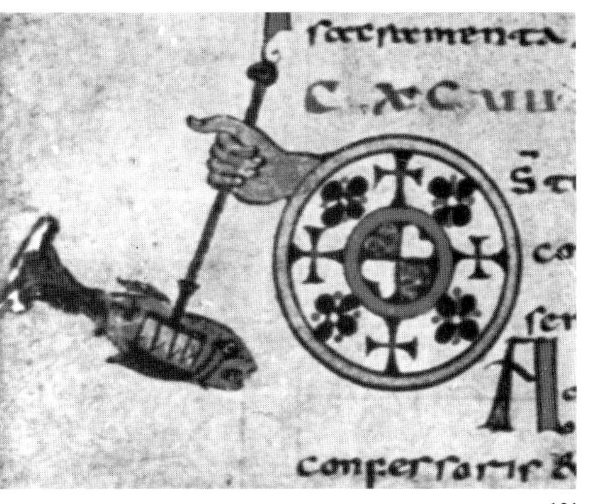

101

105

106

109

The animated letters which adorn numerous Carolingian manuscripts are descended from two different traditions: that of the illuminated letter which combines various Mediterranean influences and which, with its predilection for abstract tracerty and arabesques, sacrifices everything to a geometrical pattern; and that of the zoomorphic letter – composed almost exclusively of fishes and birds – which is a tradition going back to the time of the first Christians and examples of which Pliny the Younger claims to have found in the works of Roman scribes.

Over the centuries the parchment codex replaced the volume of papyrus, and the monastic centres for copying texts (the *scriptoria*) multiplied in Frankish Gaul. Expeditions were made to other lands, above all to Lombardy, and the travellers discovered records from the Orient as well as classical remains.

110

111

112

113

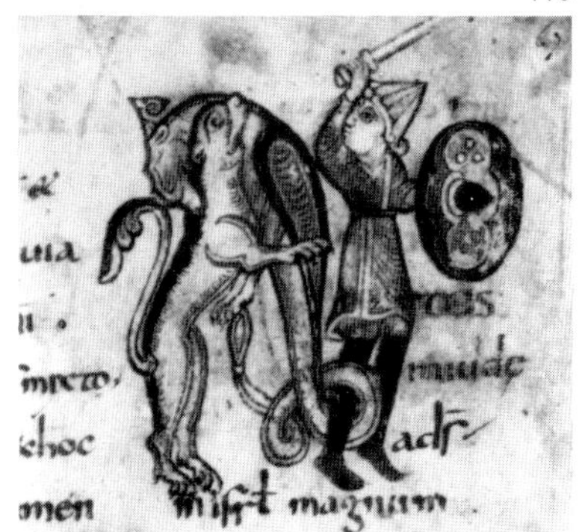
114

115

116

117

118

119

120

121

122

123

They brought back with them a new inspiration, derived from Byzantine and Sassanid ornamentation and Coptic art. Combined with Celtic and Germanic motifs, this way of decorating books gave rise to an original script, which would sometimes make use of the same themes which one can see in mural paintings of the time, and also in copper, ivory and enamel work.

While Merovingian illumination, which thus illustrated the Mediterranean tendency towards iconoclasm, left little room for the representation of the human form and generally made use of ruler and compass for the design of initials in the 67-68
shape of fishes, Carolingian decoration, which was more scholarly and more realistic, abounded in a new and rich flora and fauna.

The Gellone *Sacramentarium* (dating from between 755 80/107
and 787) is the most noteworthy example of a pre-Carolingian manuscript. It contains several hundred initials no longer designed only as birds and fish, but also as snakes, lions, boars, civet-cats, rodents, dogs, horses and lambs. The birds are very well represented, with cocks, ducks, peacocks, partridges, waders and vultures. The human figure also appears, sometimes associated with an animal, sometimes in the form of a knight or peasant. Various objects are also shown, and the most rare design in this prayer-book of 276 pages is a cross – the earliest known example in France – drawn as the initial T 107
(beginning the *Te igitur* of the Canon), and forming a crucifixion scene which is the first depiction of such a scene in French art. People and animals are sometimes accompanied by Biblical symbols, forming archetypes which can be found throughout medieval art and which show each of the evangelists with his own particular distinguishing feature: the eagle for John, the ox for Luke, the lion for Mark, the angel for Matthew.

Another extraordinarily valuable manuscript, dating from the beginning of the ninth century, is one usually called the Corbie 108/123
Psalter. Situated near Amiens, Corbie was one of the most famous *scriptoria*, with Tours, Beneventum and Cologne. The illuminator of this Carolingian manuscript has designed ornate initials which are a curious mixture of the classical tradition, of a specifically British ornamental style, and of designs reminiscent of Byzantine, Syrian and Sassanid art. Traditional borrowings are found side by side with mythological scenes drawn with great virtuosity, some of which, designating in symbols the text which they illustrate, have the quality of cryptograms. The whole fight of David and Goliath, for example, is shown in the one initial P: the unequal size of the 119
combatants, the giant's spear, the hand of God, the presence of the devil, the stone thrown from the sling and the same stone hitting Goliath's forehead. Elsewhere, the three who took part in the Presentation at the Temple form the strokes of the letter N, while other initials, such as Q and D display extraordinary 122 120 108
scenes of people carried off by horses, snakes or monsters.

NPR
CIPI
ER
VERBV

124

NITI
VM
EVAN
GELII

125

VO
NI
AM
QVIDE

126

IB
GE
R

127

128

129

130

131

132

133

134

135

136

137

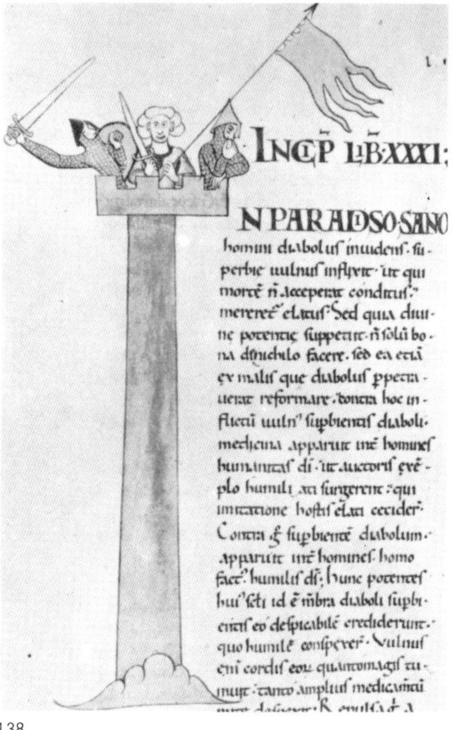

138

139

Besides giving unique information both about their period and for the study of 'animated letters' these two manuscripts have a value comparable to that of the famous Aratus manuscript in the British Museum.

Anglo-Saxon illumination at the end of the ninth century used zoomorphic decoration in the form of initials shaped as dragons, whose flexible and coiling bodies are ideal for the
143 contortions and curves needed by such compositions. However, the importance given to the vegetable world served for a time to exclude this type of animal representation. Intertwined foliage abounded, while stems, leaves and flowers grew ever thicker and gradually, as they were drawn in the round, became the three-dimensional designs of the following centuries. However, this luxurious vegetation was soon filled again with human forms, because French Romanesque illumination created its own style (which, owing to the increase in manuscripts and the opening of new copying

142

140

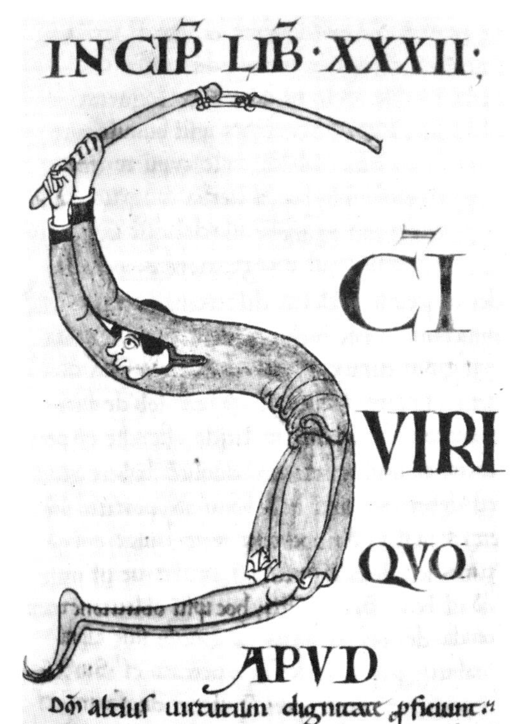

141

143

144

145

workshops rapidly spread to neighbouring countries) and this style re-introduced zoomorphic elements into manuscripts, the foliage interspersed with figures. Initials became more frequent – without ever repeating themelves in the same manuscripts – and grew in scale with the giant Bibles which the public could regard from afar during services. Drawing acquired a skill and authority rarely seen up till then, at the same time becoming more natural and realistic. Strange little creatures balance on the tips of leaves, run up the margins of manuscripts or even creep into the text, bounding towards the end of shorter lines. Whether they are the English 'babewyns' or the French 'caprices', these fantastic creatures have in common their morphological singularities: quadrupeds with human heads, two-headed birds, humans with paws, plants with beaks, reptiles with long ears, winged cattle and so on. These aberrations of nature are like the headless bodies or those 'with their mouths on their breasts' that Montaigne noted in the work of Pliny. They are also the precursors of Pantagruel's dreams (although these are really caricatures given the status of symbols), of certain visions seen by Jacques Callot, of Bosch's purgatory and of all the future 'temptations of St Anthony', as well as Grandville's 'transformations' and the maxi-monsters of our own day. They would not even be out of place in the realm of nonsense, in company with Edward Lear and Baron Münchhausen. In fact, the 'upside-down world' can be found in most European folklore, just as, at the time when the romance fables were being written, *Lügendichtungen* (lying verse) was fashionable in German-speaking lands.

146

147

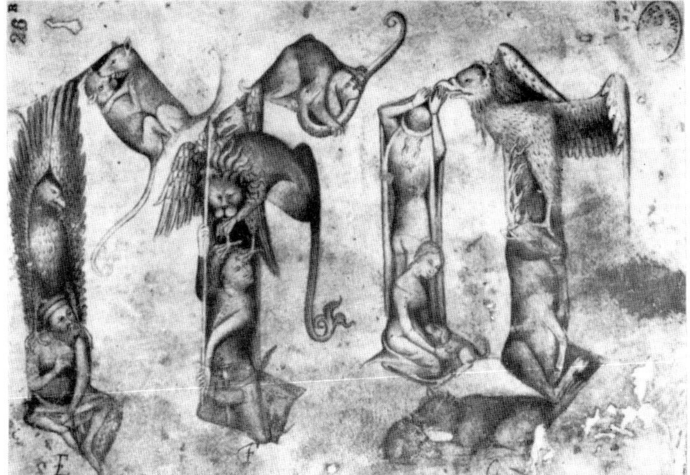

148/149

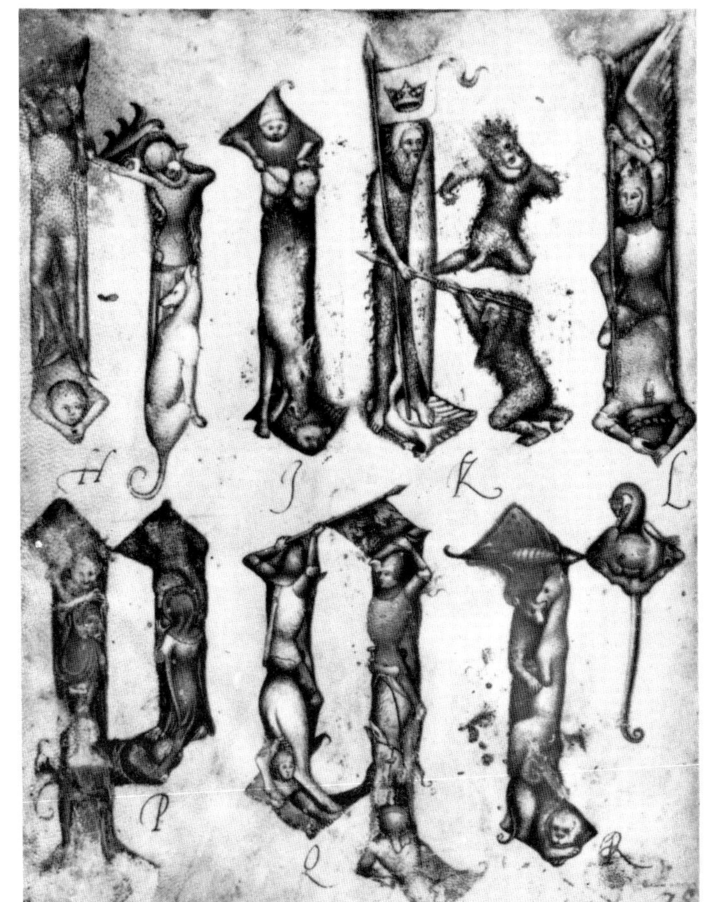

150

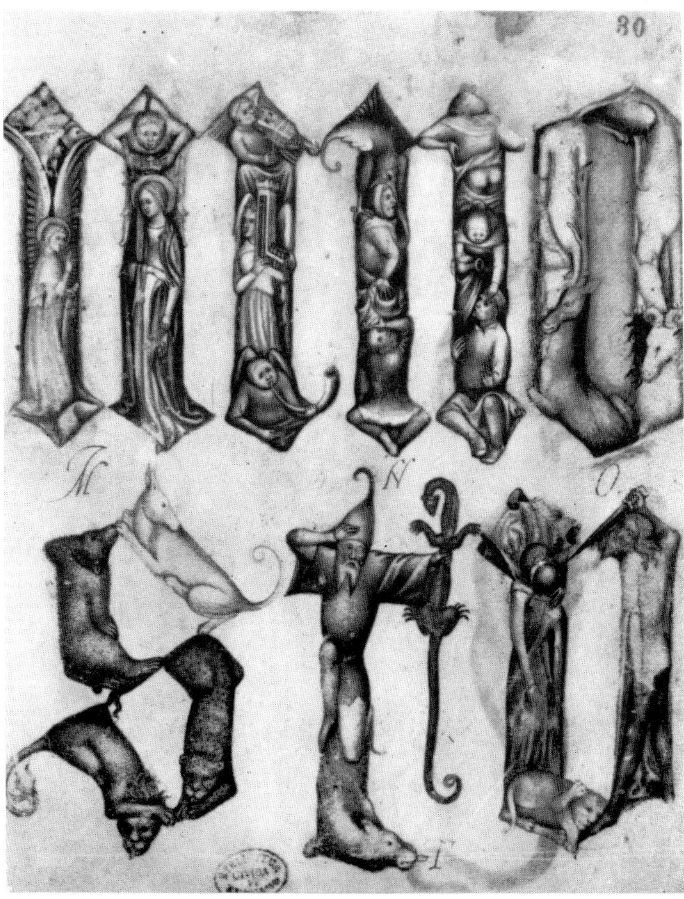

151

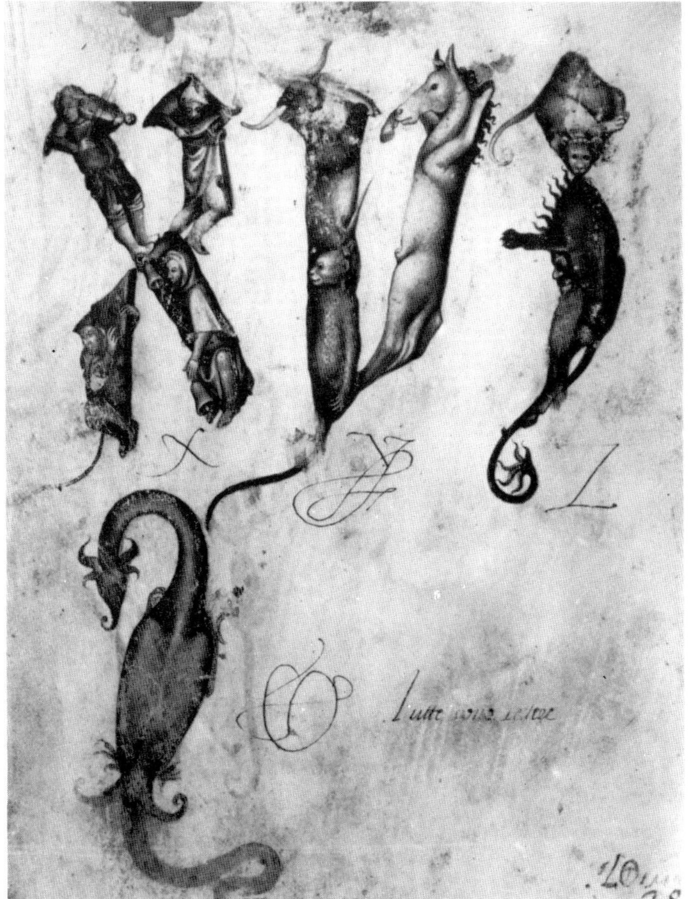

152

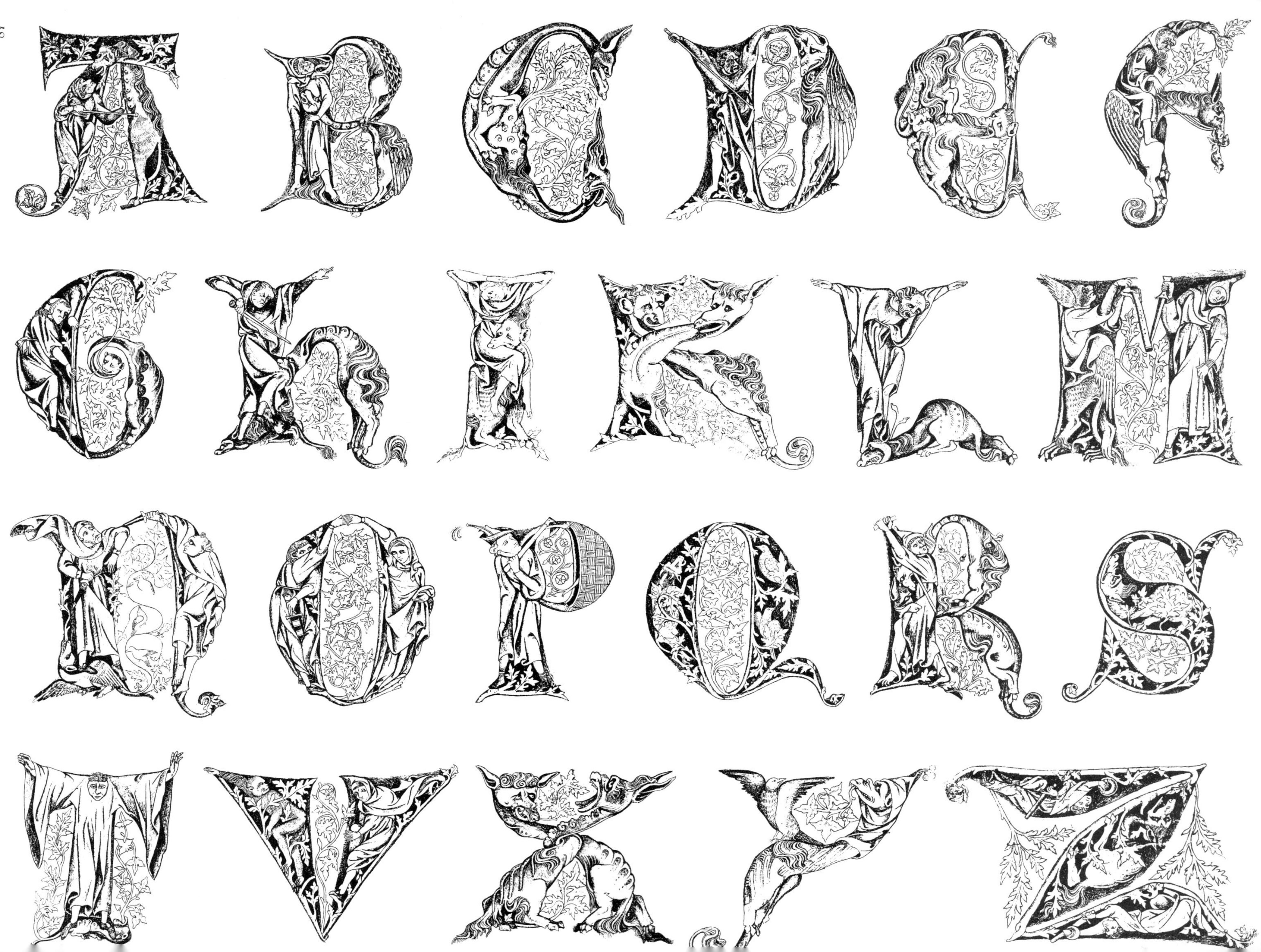

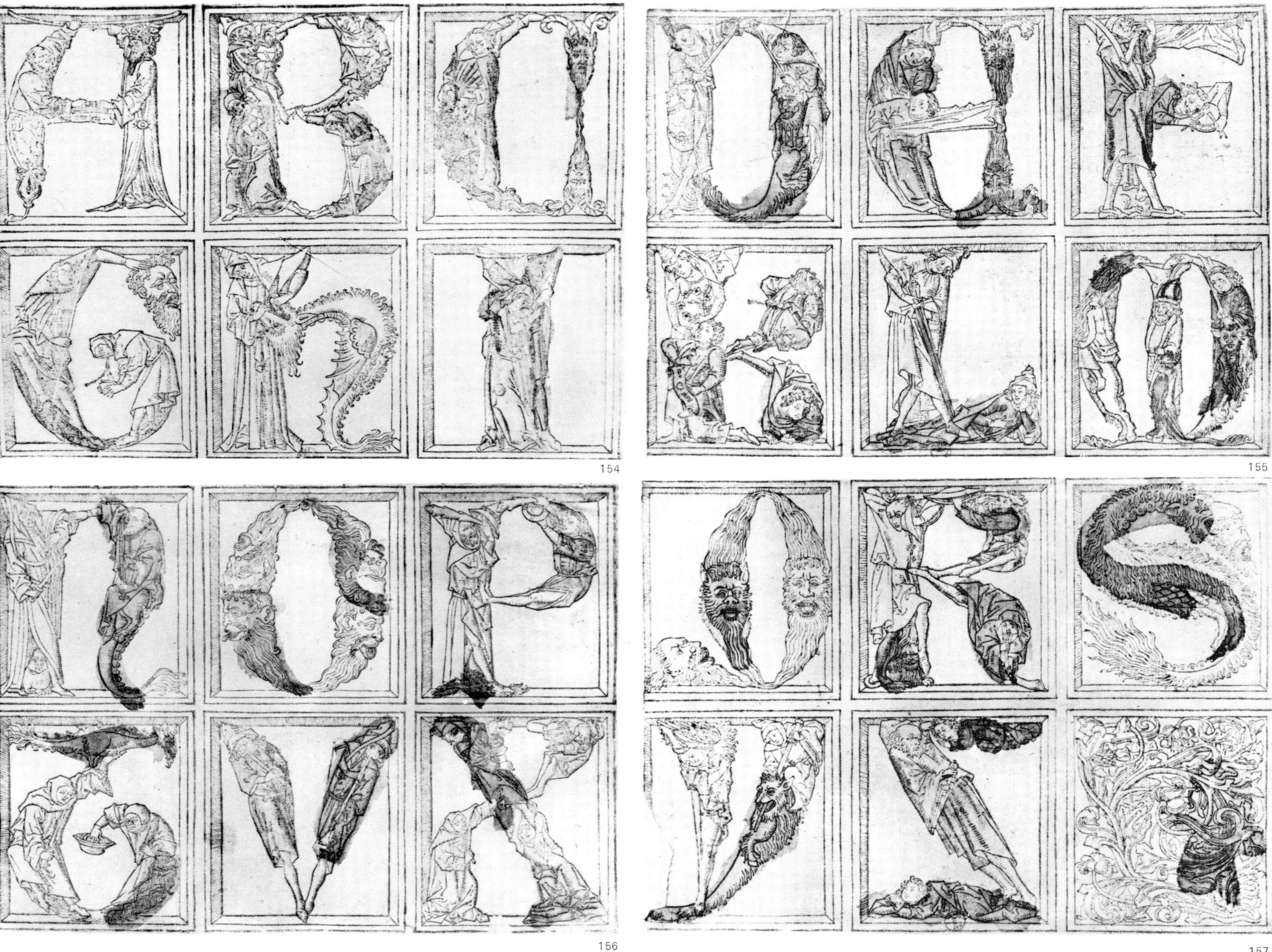

154

155

156

157

158

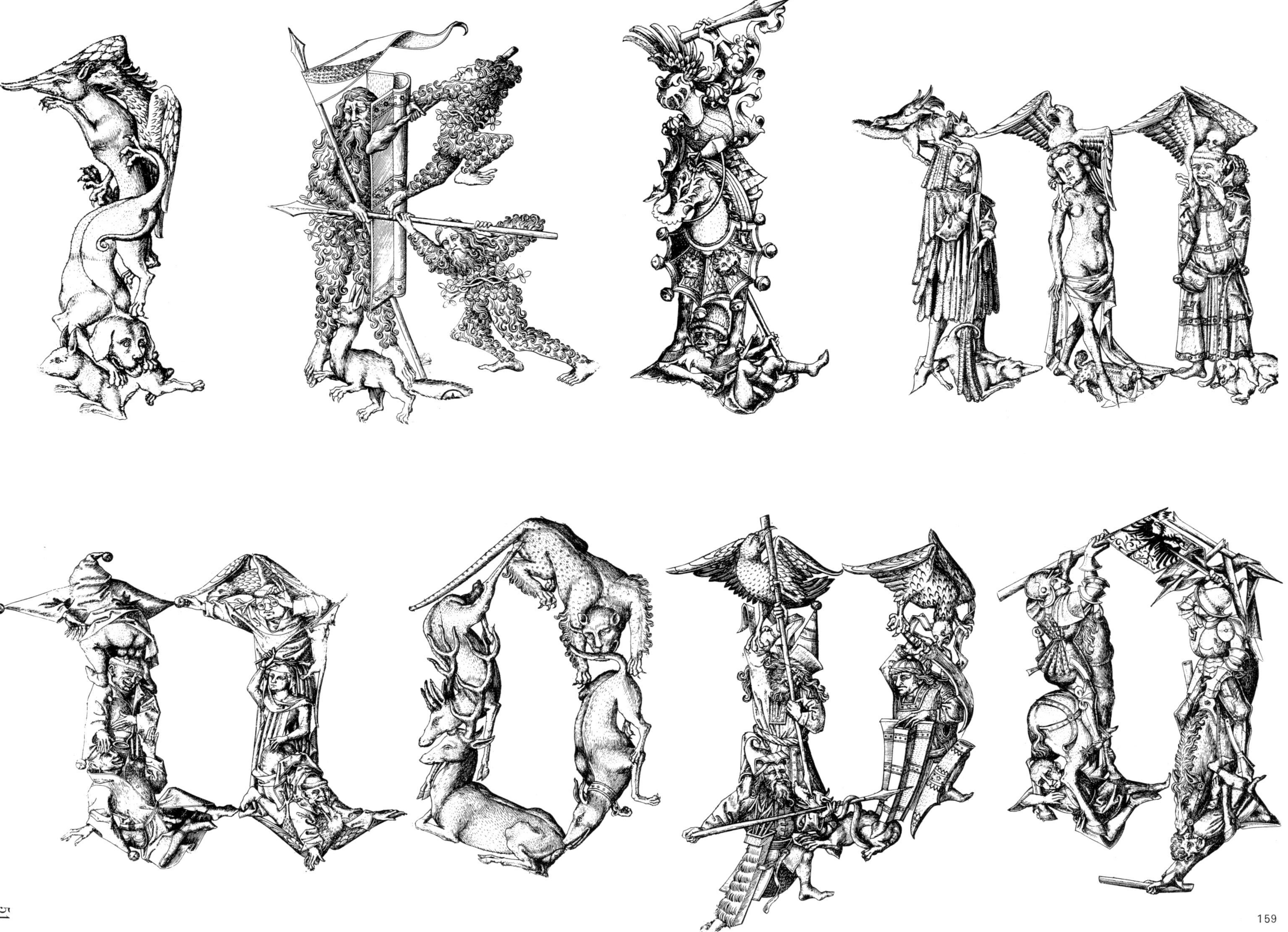

159

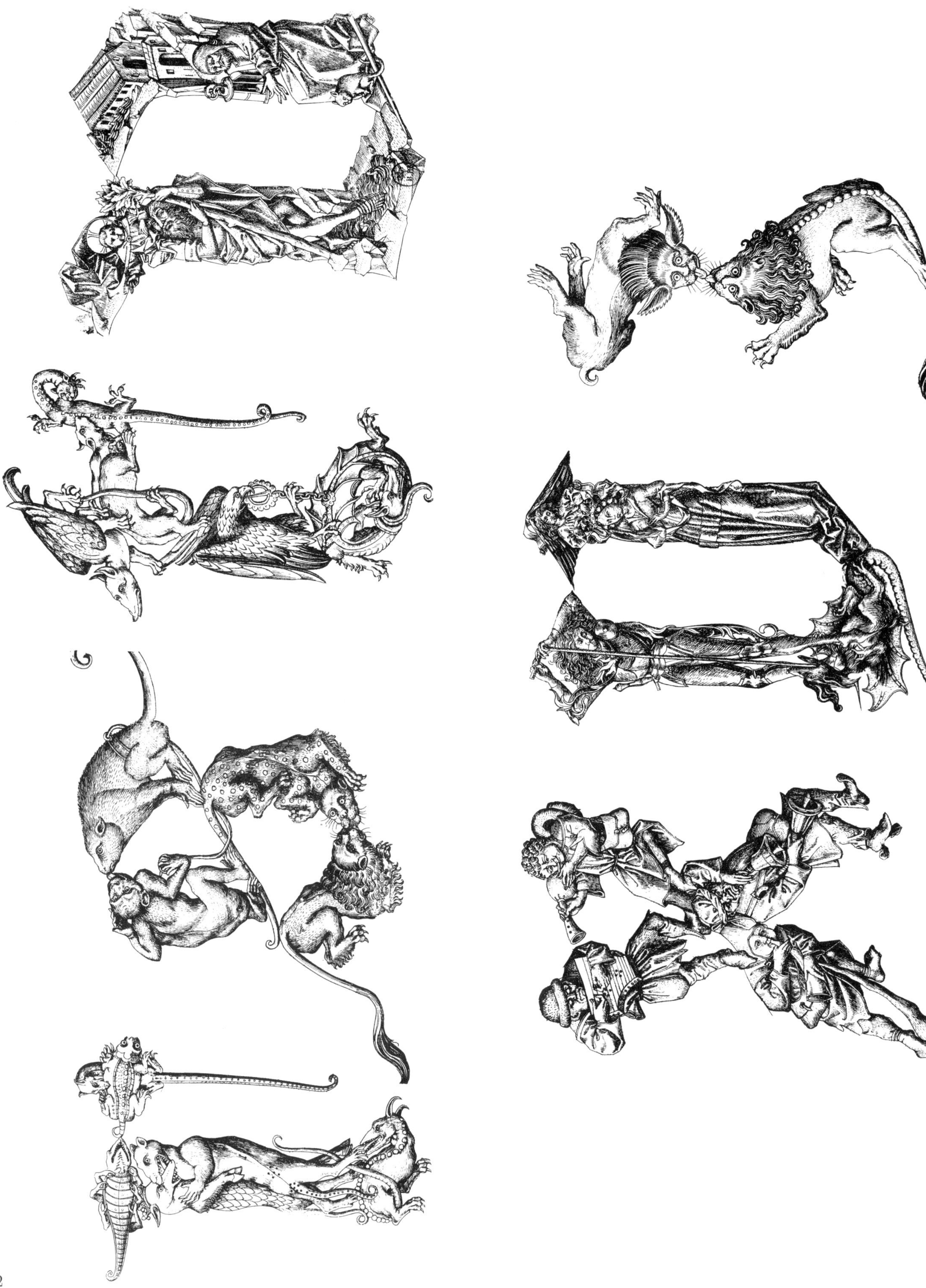

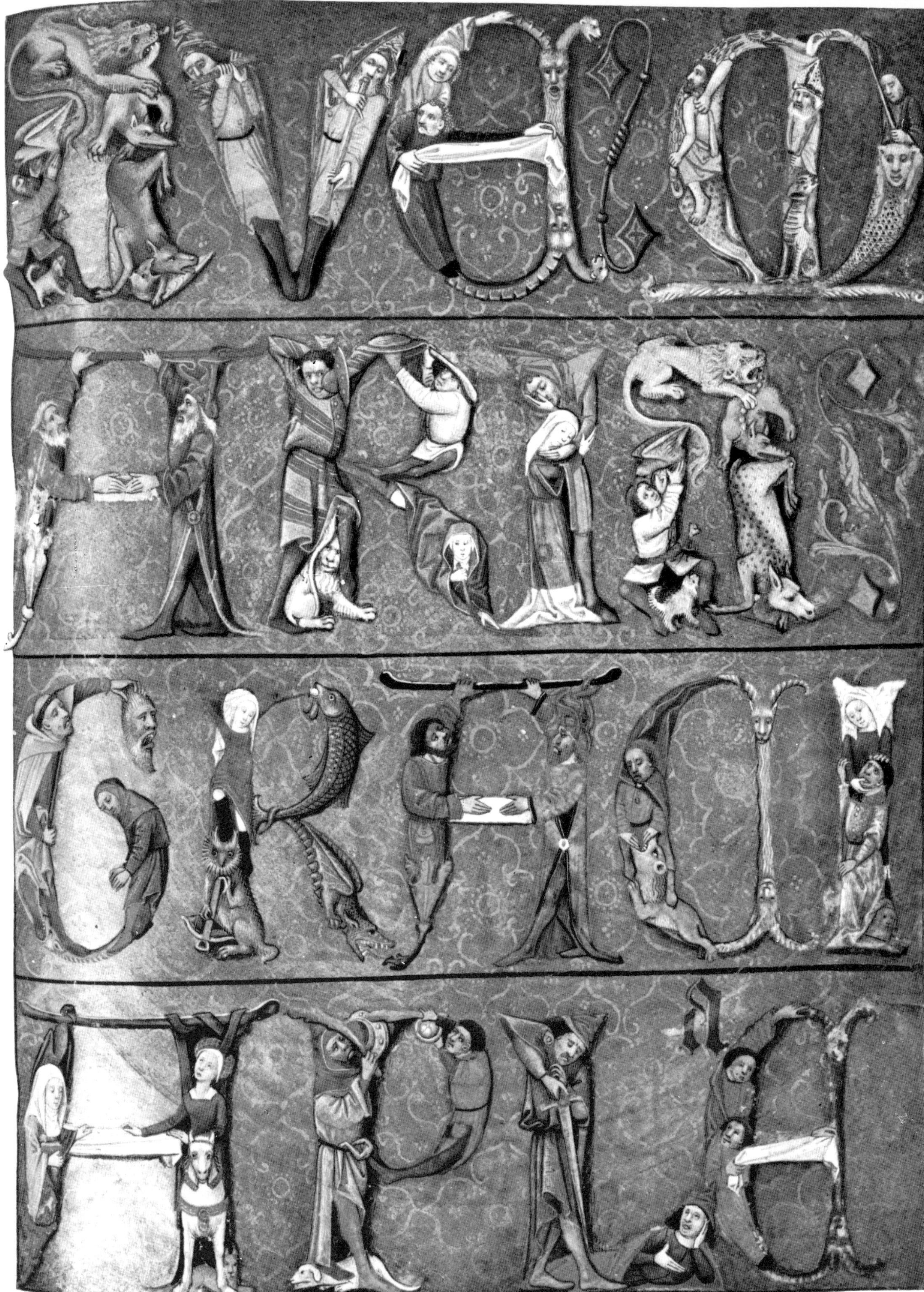

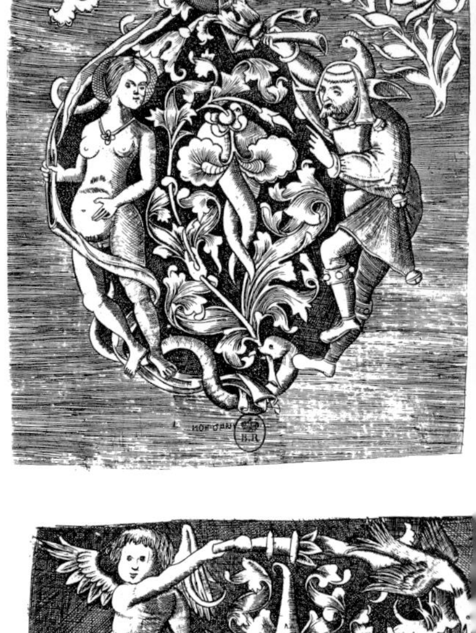

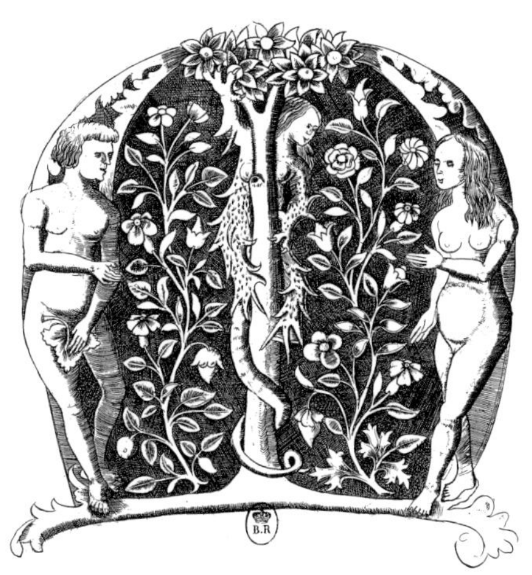

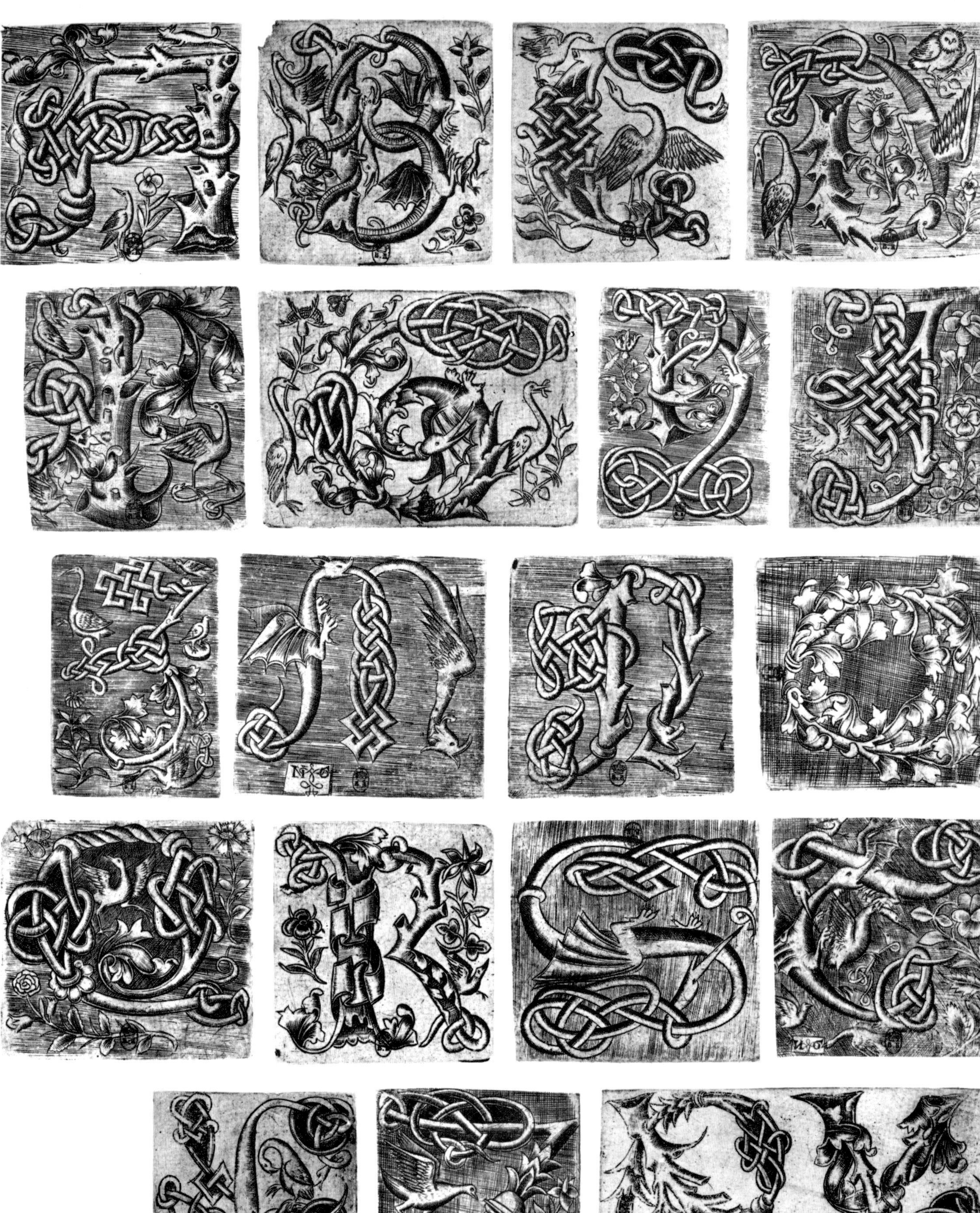

164-165

Both in marginal decoration and in initial letters, it is striking to note the absence of relationship between the text – usually of an edifying nature – and the image juxtaposed to it. The relation between the narrative and the visual image to which it gives rise, the phenomenon of osmosis which usually results from the word-image equation – which will be intrinsic to book illustration in future centuries – is virtually non-existent in the manuscripts of this period. A plastic unity is sought between illumination and writing, to the detriment of the most elementary symbolism. Either the painter and the scribe speak two different languages, or else, using tricks of style tacitly favoured at the time, they make use of antithesis the better to suggest by contrast the self-evident moral truth. Writers of fables, authors of apologia or parables, certain libertine raconteurs and most of the literary purveyors of Hell do likewise, with this difference, that they are only concerned to keep up appearances as a last resort. The same antithesis can be seen in Romanesque architecture: the vaults of churches are supported by diabolical creatures which grimace at the side of capitals. But whereas sculpture turns most readily to Biblical or mythological scenes, the 'gymnastic initials' (as Francis Wormald calls them) more often portray circus acrobatics. Wrestlers, jugglers and beasts fight in the body of a P or in the O's enclosure, while athletes use loops as apparatus or slip between the bars of a letter to perform acrobatic feats. The various manuscripts of St Gregory's *Moralia in Job* made in Cistercian abbeys during the first part of the twelfth century, show interestuing examples of anthropomorphic letters with a southern influence: one of these manuscripts dates from 1134, that is, a year after the death of Etienne Harding, abbot of Cîteaux, who imposed an insular style for twenty-five years. Certain initials, such as Q and S, which have a 140-141
Romanesque simplicity and resolutely modern treatment, show monks at work, with a hatchet or flail in their hand. After a while, however, the excesses caused by this competitiveness among illuminators led to reactions such as that of Saint Bernard of Clairvaux: *Litterae unius coloris fiant et non depictae* (letters should be executed in one colour only and should not portray figures). Whether this order was obeyed or not, during the Gothic period ornamental initials underwent a profound transformation. While evolving during the fourteenth century towards an ever greater realism, they were used marginally to the illustration of the great traditional themes, to depict scenes of everyday life – of the sort that could also be seen in frescoes, painting and stained-glass. It is from this period that what one could call the first 'strip cartoons' date, bristling with scroll-work. Henceforward the accent would be on descriptive illustration, while comic touches continued to crowd into margins, rather to the detriment of the initials themselves. In France, it was not until the fourteenth century that zoomorphic initials appeared again, in the *Book of Hours of Jeanne d'Evreux*. In

the interval, the 'animated' letter of the preceding centuries had been modified into the 'casket' letter: stripped of all animal or human shape, again geometrical in inspiration and with stark lines, without any narrative scenes in its actual outline. These casket letters contained their illustrations within themselves and did not superimpose themselves on drawings or mingle with them. This change in manuscripts illustrates well the same differences which separate Romanesque from Gothic architecture: in the former, all ornament is an organic part of the architectural function which it performs; in the latter, which is a more formal style, decoration is an end in itself, a purely aesthetic element. Thus the casket letter, and the ornate letters which assured its posterity (such as the beautiful *Alphabet of Death* drawn by the younger Holbein) fall outside the scope of the present study.

Nevertheless, even during the Gothic period, the tail-end of the Romanesque tradition continued to provide themes for illustrations in manuscripts and in the first books, and left its imprint on typographical design in those cases where letters were not reduced to their basic geometrical outlines. An example
148/152 of this is the 'Bergamo' alphabet, painted by Giovannino de' Grassi about 1390, which superimposes a Romanesque-type bestiary on to writing which is otherwise purely Gothic. The execution is all the more remarkable because the stiffness of the down-strokes, the oblique slants and sharp angles of this writing seem most unsuited, at first sight, to the representation of animals and people. All these qualities, however, adapt themselves subtly to the Gothic framework and perfectly match the geometric outline of letters such as those specified by Dürer in 1525 in his treatise on applied geometry called *Unterweysung der Messung mit dem Zirckel und Richtscheyt.* Although it is Italian in origin, this alphabet is clearly Germanic in inspiration, with its group of wild beasts and domestic animals, angels, old men and lovers, sacred and profane subjects. Moreover, the diversity of figures does not exclude a certain uniformity in their order: the letter K only shows people, the letters O and S animals, while M is always reserved for the Annunciation and V seems to have as its theme amorous rivalry in love.

153 The Berlin alphabet, drawn in pen and ink at the beginning of the fifteenth century, and contemporary with the above, shows once again the people and the dragons which filled the Romanesque letters of nearly three hundred years earlier... And those initials were themselves not fundamentally different from the ones decorating the Corbie Psalter or the grammars of
76-77 Servius and Asper, two centuries before that (although it is true that these latter were rather in advance of their time). How strange this centennial immobility seems to the twentieth century man, used to seeing the world change utterly in ten years!

166/172

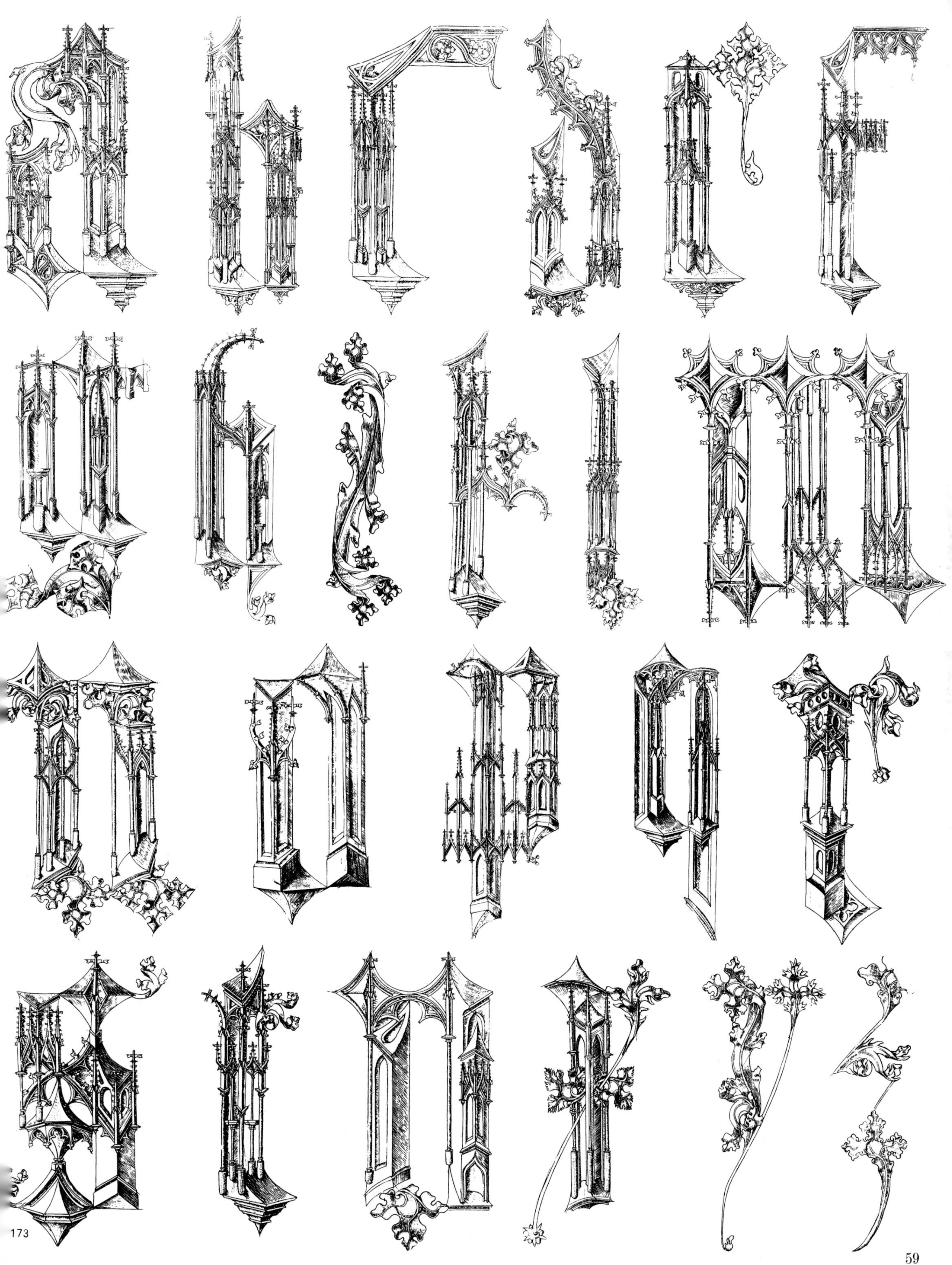

173

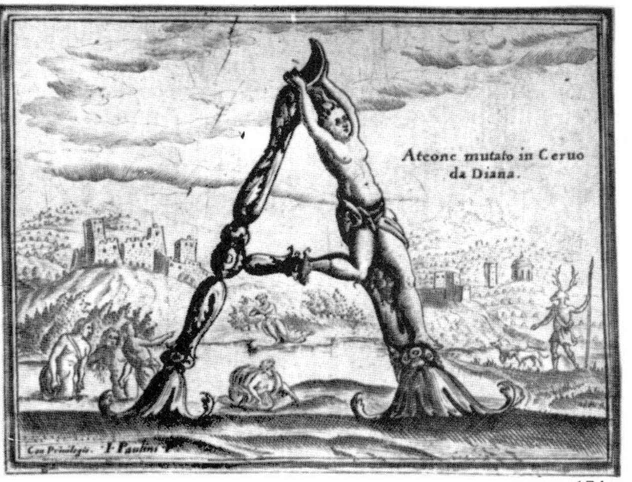

174

175

176

177

Fetonte guida il carro
del Sole.
Cum Priuil.

178

179

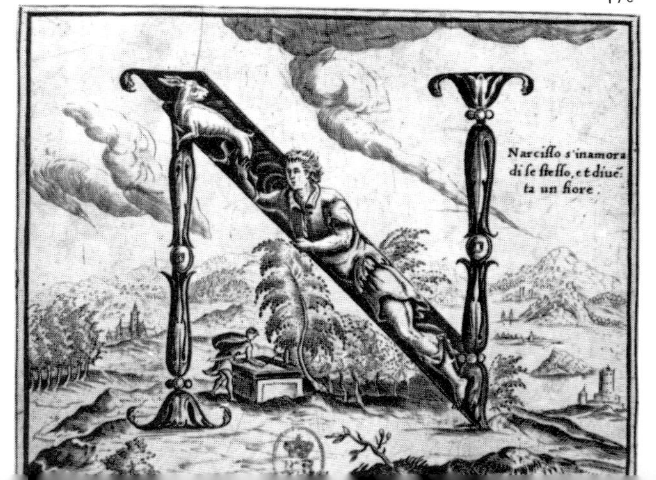

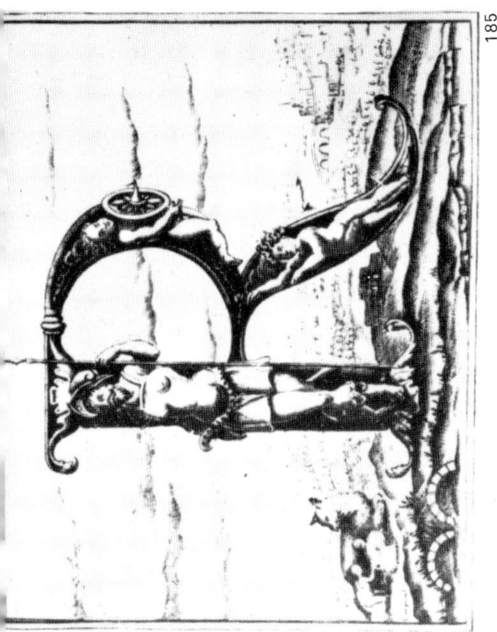

185

184

A hundred years later another famous alphabet very similar in style to that of Giovannino de' Grassi was designed, by a master who signs his work with the initials E.S. Certain letters, 158/160
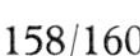
such as B, C, D, E, F and K have in both instances the same components arranged in an almost identical way: certain scenes show the same themes, a tournament for instance, for the letter Q, with the same details (a broken lance). However, in spite of these similarities the alphabet designed by E.S. has a very individual style, which is probably emphasized still further by the fact that it is engraved on copper and has a specifically Germanic character. It also shows the same skill in adapting Gothic script as does the Bergamo alphabet.

The historiated initials – seven in number – of the *Buch* 166/172
der Weisheit, published in Germany in 1482, make use of a Gothic imagery which successfully conceals the Romanesque origin of the letters, while the Basle wood-cut alphabet (later 154/157
engraved by the Master of the Banderoles) was still, in 1464, reviving Romanesque patterns. In France the Paris Book of Hours of Charles D'Angoulême (which, for the letters of the 161
Ave Maria, takes themes from the alphabet of the Master E.S., with those from the Basle and sometimes the Berlin alphabets) went right back, towards the end of the fifteenth century, to the Romanesque tradition. (The French contribution to these 'human alphabets' is however insignificant as compared to that of Germany, Italy or Holland.)

183

186

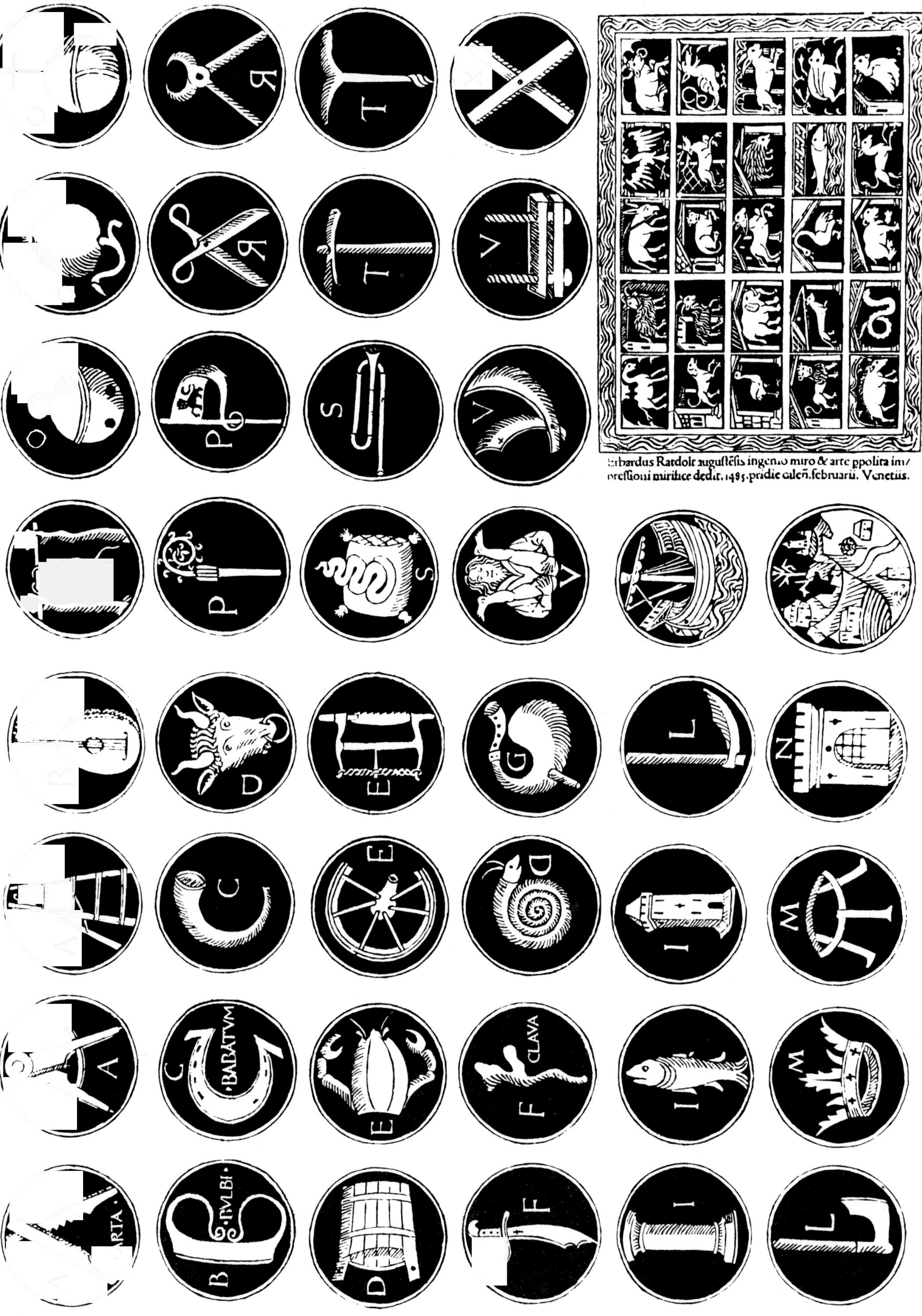
Erhardus Ratdolt augustẽsis ingenio miro & arte ppolita im/
pressioni mirifice dedit. 1485. pridie calẽ. februarii. Venetiis.

189

188

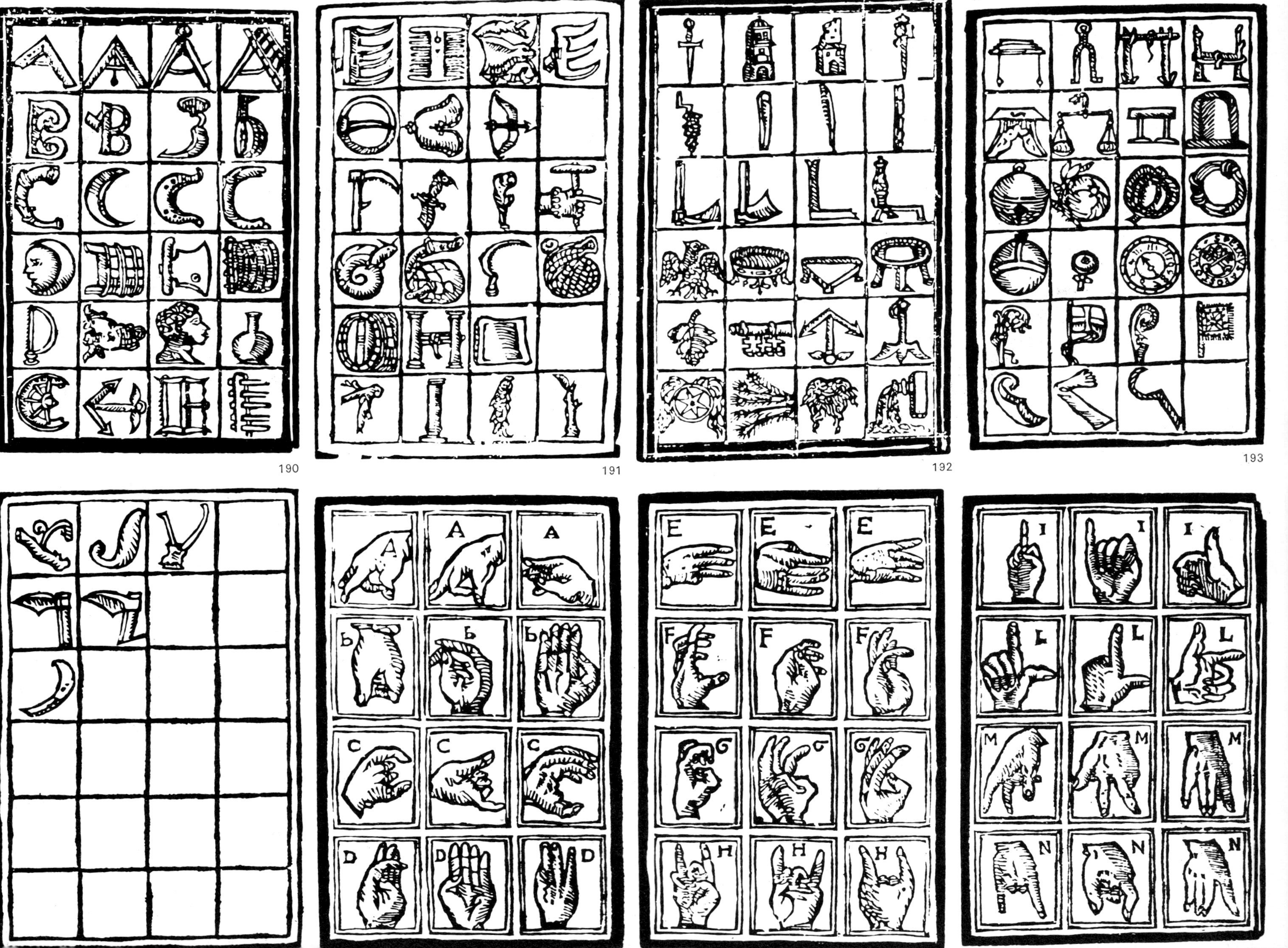

190

191

192

193

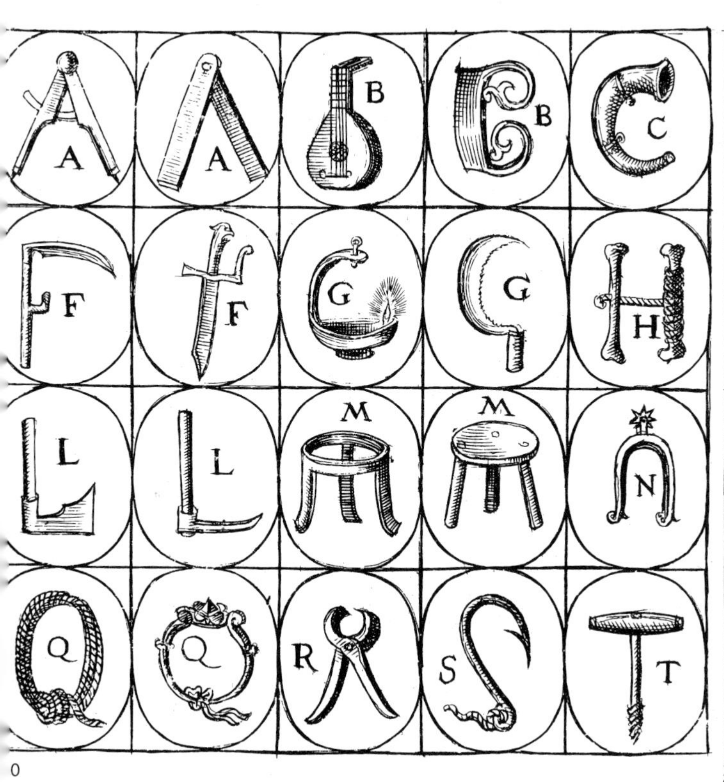

0

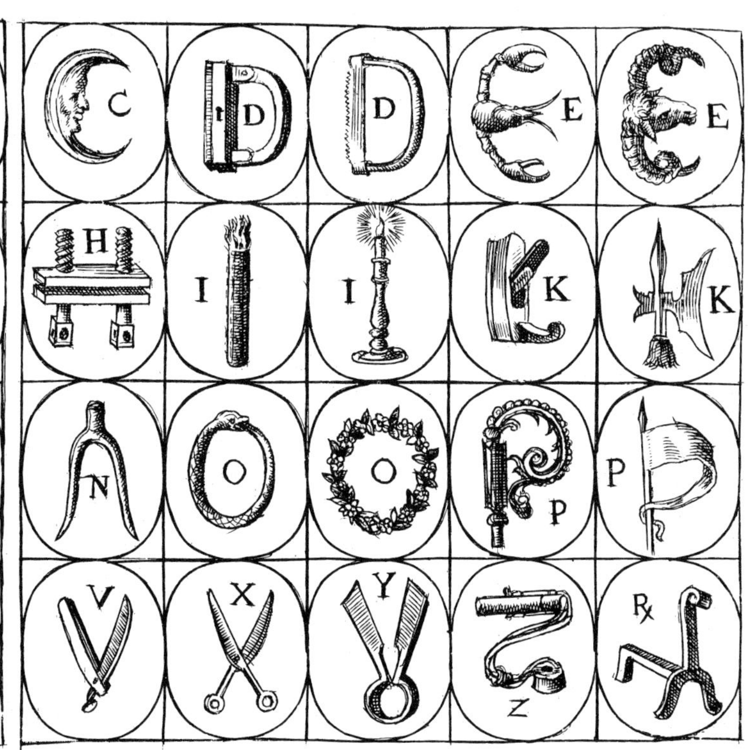

201

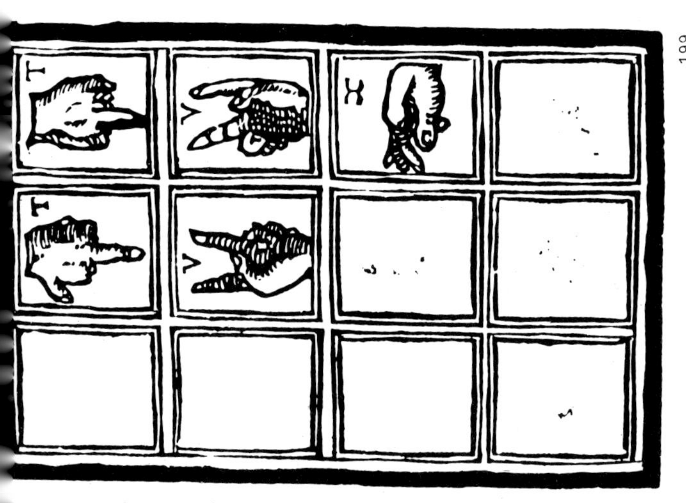

199

198

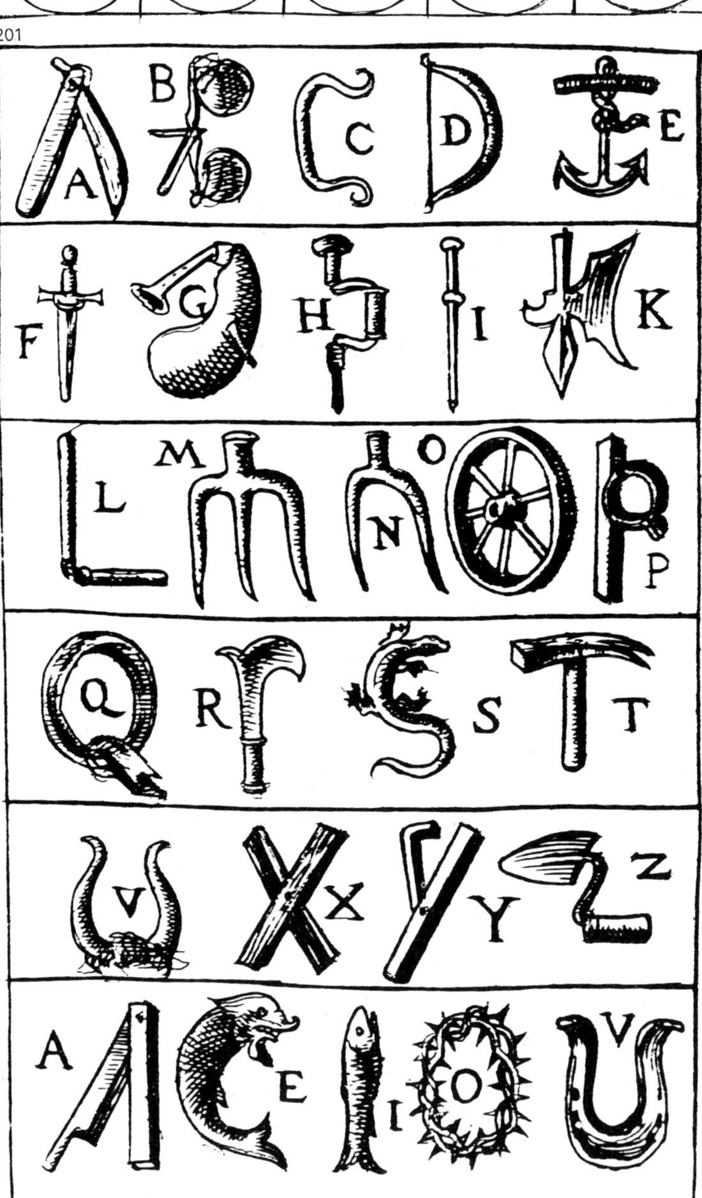

202

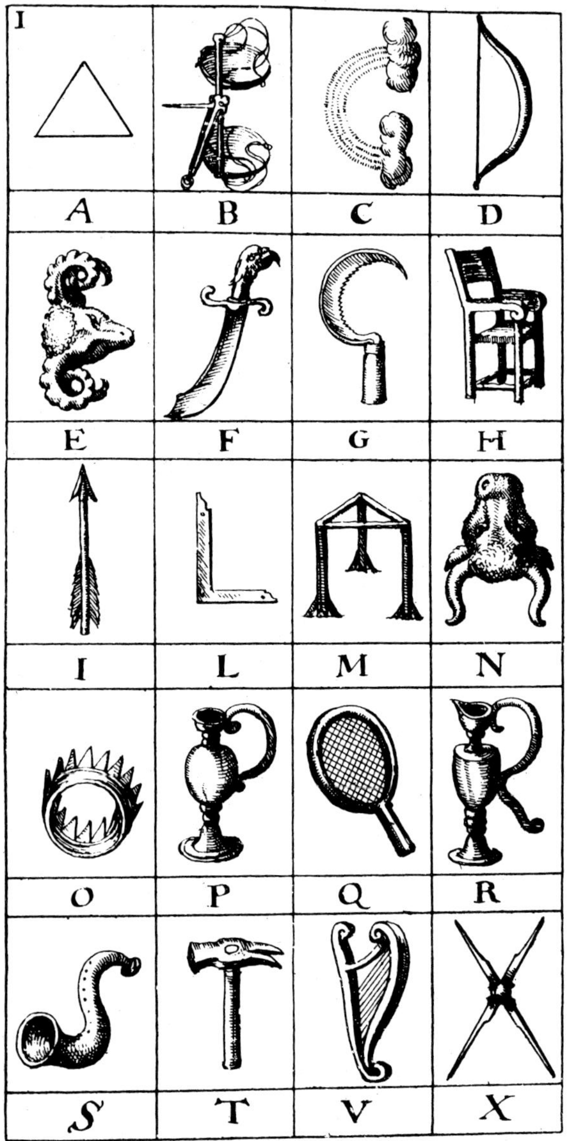

1			
A	B	C	D
E	F	G	H
I	L	M	N
O	P	Q	R
S	T	V	X

Ordo Characterum Arithmeticorum in hac arte.

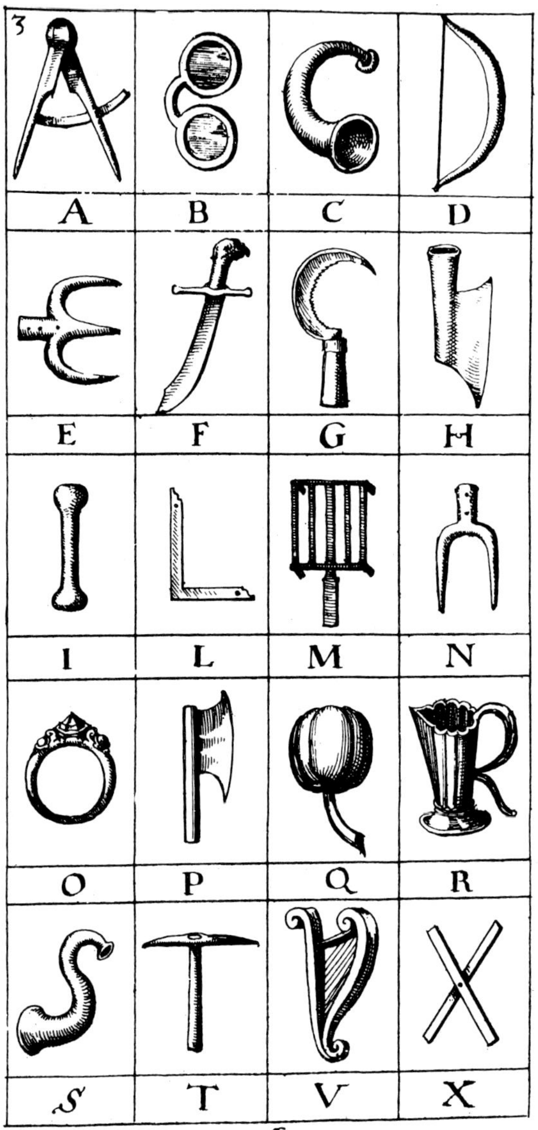

3			
A	B	C	D
E	F	G	H
I	L	M	N
O	P	Q	R
S	T	V	X

Characteres Arithmetici in hac arte.

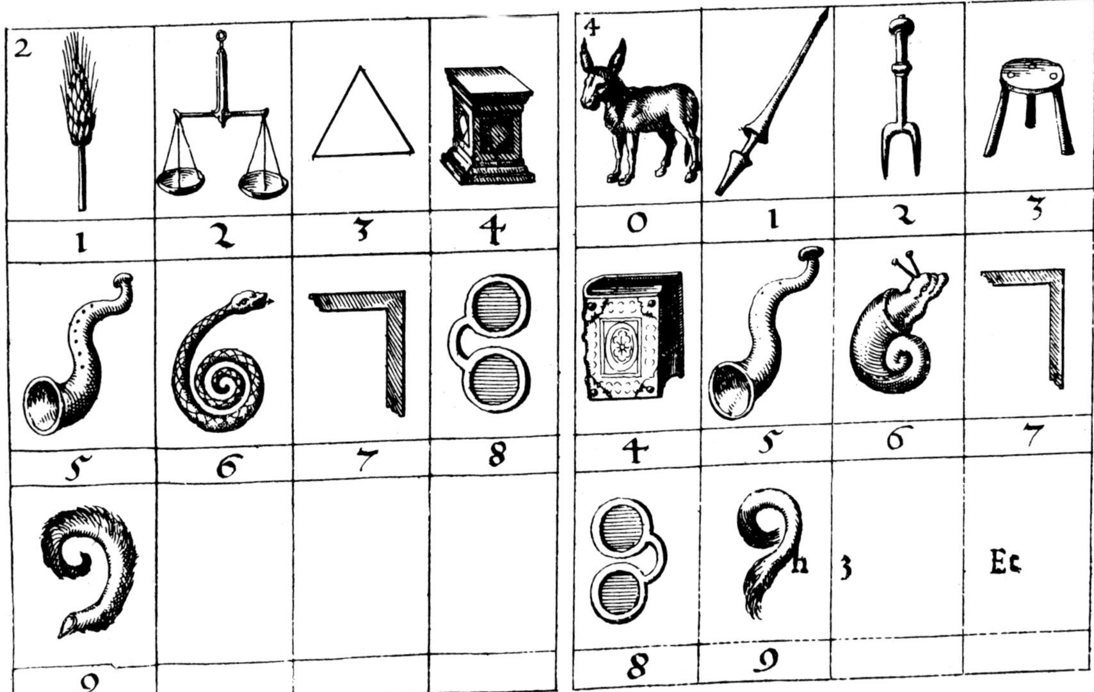

204

Several historical events, happening at roughly the same time, profoundly affected the Renaissance period: the discovery of the New World, the theory of gravity, the Reformation, the invention of printing and the flowering of Italy. Of these many events, some simultaneous, the last two were possibly the most important, because the discovery of America, for instance, had no immediate effect. On the other hand, owing to the inventions of Gutenberg, Schoeffer and Fust, nearly 9,000,000 copies of books were already in circulation by the end of the fifteenth century. And Italy produced the best printers in Europe, as well as helping other countries to progress along the 'rough and rugged paths of scholasticism' to 'the splendours of antiquity'. It was there too, in St Mark's Square, that the west discovered the east, in (still quoting from Michelet) 'the first salon on earth, salon of the human kind, where people of all lands have conversed, where Asia spoke to Europe in the voice of Marco Polo, where, in the dark ages before printing, humanity could peacefully communicate with itself, where the globe than had its brain, its *sensorium*, its first consciousness of itself'.

The Renaissance saw things brilliantly as in a mirror,
or as in a theatre. This can be clearly seen in its taste for
fantastic architecture (Dietterlin) and for *trompe-l'oeil* erected
on large, painted façades. It was in a century of words and noise
that Rabelais and Shakespeare wrote their work, and the study
of the Talmud and the Cabbala by men such as Pico della
Mirandola is perhaps not all that different from the creation
of alphabets *à lunettes*. Generally engraved on wood, they
constitute a new type of figurative art which is particularly
concerned with the representation of objects which sometimes
have a magic or esoteric significance. The alphabet of Jacobus
Publicius, published by Erhard Ratdolt in Venice in 1482, 188-189
dates from the same year as the German initials of the *Buch der*
Weisheit. That of Abraham de Balmes, reproduced by Geo- 187
ffroy Tory in his *Champ Fleury*, also comes from Venice (1523)
and its author, who called it 'writing from beyond the river' –
thus giving the impression of a Mesopotamian origin –
claimed to have found it in a very old book. There are two other
alphabets in this same genre, but they are later, since the
author of one was a contemporary of Descartes, the great
English cabbalist Robert Fludd, and the other Trithemius. We 203 200/202
can also add to this series of mnemotechnic alphabets that of
Cosmas Rossellius which is reminiscent of the sign-language of 190/199
the deaf and dumb, with its letters formed from fingers in
different positions.

ALFABETO IN SOGNO
ESEMPLARE PER DISEGNARE
DI
GIVSEPPE M.ª MITELLI
PITTORE BOLOGNESE
MDCLXXXIII
G.M. Mitelli I. e F.
Se del primo carattere il teuore
Brami sapere, ei staßi à bocca aperta,
Gridando à la uirtù si prenda Amore.

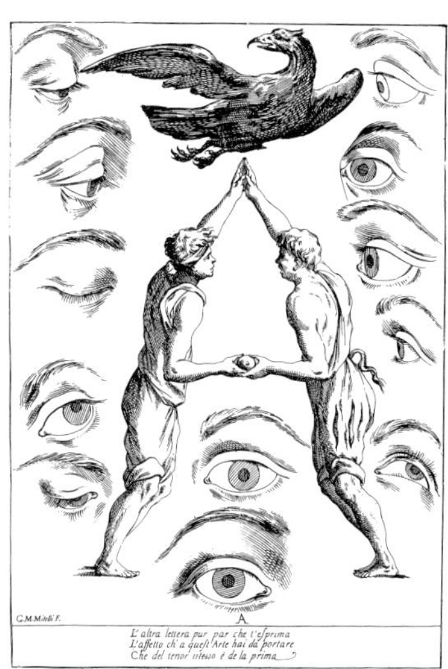
G.M. Mitelli F.
A
L'altra lettera pur par che t'esprima
L'affetto ch'a quest'Arte hai da portare
Che del tenor istesso è de la prima

G.M. Mitelli I. e F.
B
Quasi gonfiando il B le guancie sue,
Suona la tromba, e intuona a l'ignorante
Tu tu sarai, se non impari, un Bue

G.M. Mitelli I. e F.
C
Dal C spronarti à la Costanza io sento,
E però s'a lo studio utile è tanto,
Vna lettera sol uale per Cento

G.M. Mitelli I. e F.
H
Quello, à cui di saper nulla s'attacca,
Ben dir si pote, che non monta un Zero
Ben dir si pote, che non uale un Hacca.

G.M. Mitelli I. e F.
I
L'I sopra il tutto ad Imitar t'inuiti,
E d'arte, e di natura il più perfetto,
Ch'imitato sarai, se bene imiti.

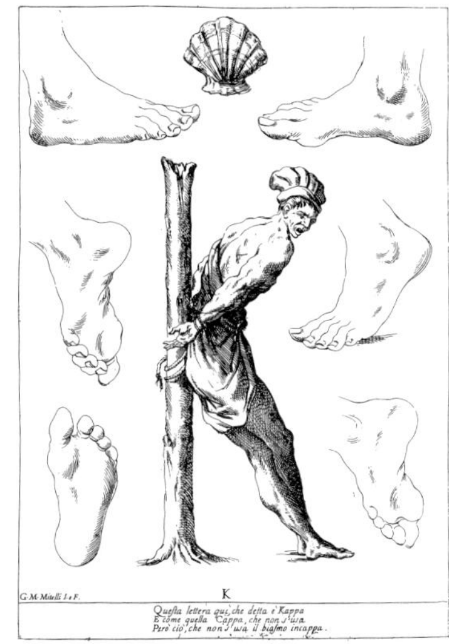
G.M. Mitelli I. e F.
K
Questa lettera qui, che detta è Kappa
È come quella Cappa, che non s'usa
Però ciò, che non s'usa il biasmo incappa.

G.M. Mitelli I. e F.
L
Tu, che dal tetro oblio fuggir presumi,

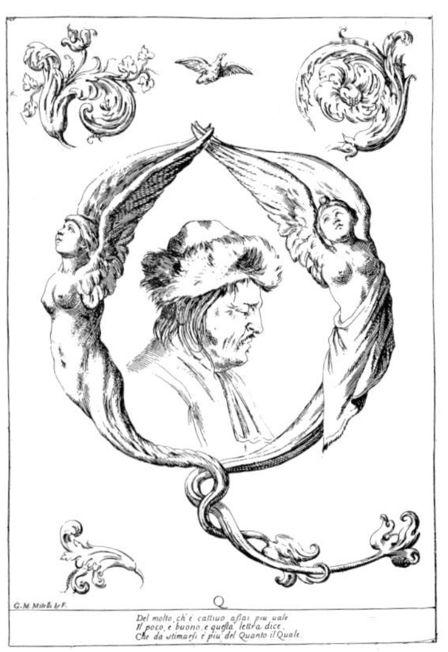
G.M. Mitelli I. e F.
Q
Del molto, ch'è cattiuo assai più uale
Il poco, e buono, e questa lettra dice,
Che da stimarsi è più del Quanto il Quale.

G.M. Mitelli I. e F.
R
Di quell'opra di in publico si pone,
Parlo Scolari à uoi, l'Autor ne deue,
Al parer di ciascun render Ragione.

G.M. Mitelli I. e F.
S
O miei cari Studenti io ui protesto,
Ch'osseruiate nel S la Simetria,
E ad aggiustarla adoperiate il Sesto.

G.M. Mitelli I. e F.
T
Se dipingi, o' dißegni il T. t'accenna,
Ch'hai da Temprar con regola i colori,
Ch'hai da Temprar con regola la penna.

D
Del D non può far il Pittor mai senza,
Se noi uogliam considerar, ch'ei dica,
Necessaria è al Pittor la Diligenza.

G.M. Mitelli I. e F.
E
Quei, ch'hà le uoglie à degna gloria intente,
D'esser uulgar Pittor pago non sia,
Ma l'E gl'imprima l'esser Eccellente.

G.M. Mitelli I. e F.
F
Vuol l'Effe dir Fatica, e senza alcuna
Difficoltà da lei nasce souente
Vn second'esse, e questo è la Fortuna

G.M. Mitelli I. e F.
G
Acquista à l'opre il G. senso simile,
Se conforme ti porti, ò male, ò bene,
Vn daratti del Goffo, un del Gentile

M
Tre gambe hà l'Emme, e sù trè gambe stà
La potenza de l'Huom, ch'à l'opre attende
Intelletto, Memoria, e Volontà.

G.M. Mitelli I. e F.
N
L'Enne amonisce ogni Pittor, che tale
Deue à gl'occhi mostrarn ogni pittura,
Quale à gl'occhi si mostra il Naturale.

O
E l'O per i Pittori un mal negotio,
Et è cagion, che mai non han denari,
Quando si danno à l'O, che uuol dir l'Otio.

G.M. Mitelli I. e F.
P
Dà la mente di uoi non sia disgiunto
Il P. che por ui deue in fantasia
Ch'il punto stà nel' osseruare il Punto.

V
L'V sopra tutto in mente hauer si dee,
Ch'à far non s'han, come le cialde à un modo,
Mà s'hanno à Variar gl'atti, e l'Idee.

G.M. Mitelli I. e F.
X
L'IX dal tuo cor già mai non si cancelli
Che uuol, ch'habbiam Xenocrate pudico
Per modello in copiar uiui modelli

Y
S'à ritrar mai n'andrai giouani Donne,
Auuerti à non imprimere à mariti,
In cima della fronte un Ypsilonne.

G.M. Mitelli I. e F.
Z
La Zetta insegna à te, che se dir bene
De l'opre altrui non poi, non dei dir male,
Ch'un ZOILO poco sano si mantiene.

In mid-Renaissance France, while treatises locking letters into a geometrical strait-jacket multiplied in number, Noël Garnier engraved, towards the middle of the sixteenth century, two
162/165 alphabets with figures full of nostalgia for the Romanesque style but using Italian *grotesques* descended from classical times. These engravings are sometimes stiff and clumsy, often fantastic, with modern touches. The alphabet of Julius Antonius Herculanus (1571), which is more supple but less exuberant has the same sources. And in Germany, this return to ancient Greek and Roman ideas is clearly seen in the 'human
208 alphabet' of Peter Flötner (about 1534), which no longer shows Biblical characters, devils, monsters or dragons, but Venuses and naked athletes. These artists showed the same skill in drawing the Latin alphabet as the Master E.S. had done, so that even the princes of the Golden Number would have found nothing in their work to criticise: and it is all the more remarkable because they achieved this feat without any extraneous material, if one discounts a semi-circular banderol for the letter Q and a child's figure added to the letter G. This exclusively anthropomorphic alphabet which seems to have directly influenced the Strasbourg lithographer Joseph-
212 Balthazard Silvestre, exactly three hundred years later, was valued in German-speaking countries particularly. Several
211 copies of it were made: one in Augsburg in 1560, others by Jobst Amman in 1567, by Theodor de Bry in 1596, by Sempronio Lancione in Venice in about 1615, then by William
210 Comley and Richard Daniel in London, in 1662 and 1664 respectively. Comley set out to 'initiate the young into the art of drawing and, at the same time, to teach them to write'. It was also an art teacher, Giuseppe Maria Mitelli, who
205-206 published a 'dream alphabet' at Bologna in 1683, the idea having come to him, he said, while he slept. Having shown him the letters of the alphabet in various fantastic forms, Morpheus bade him immortalize their fugitive shape by means of his art. The result, not in the least dream-like, was a human alphabet, of which the greatest merit is perhaps that it prefigures the countless examples of the romantic period.

The Age of Enlightenment was scornful of this type of expression, although in Germany it could still be seen in conjunction with calligrams, as will be shown later. A restrictive interpretation of decorative letters, combined with the use of metal type, served to prevent development in the typography of books during several centuries. 'Books are four centuries out of date' cried the painter Georges Mathieu in 1963 at Lurs-en-Provence in the course of a massive

207

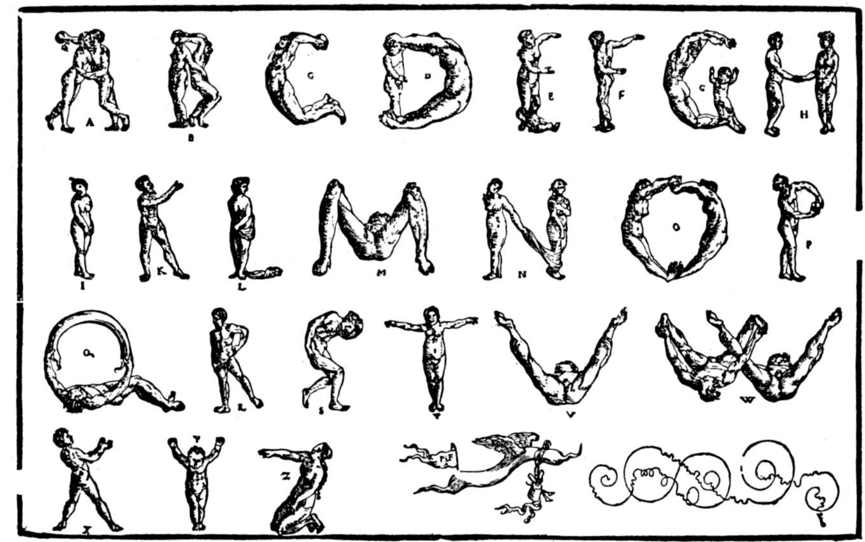

208

209

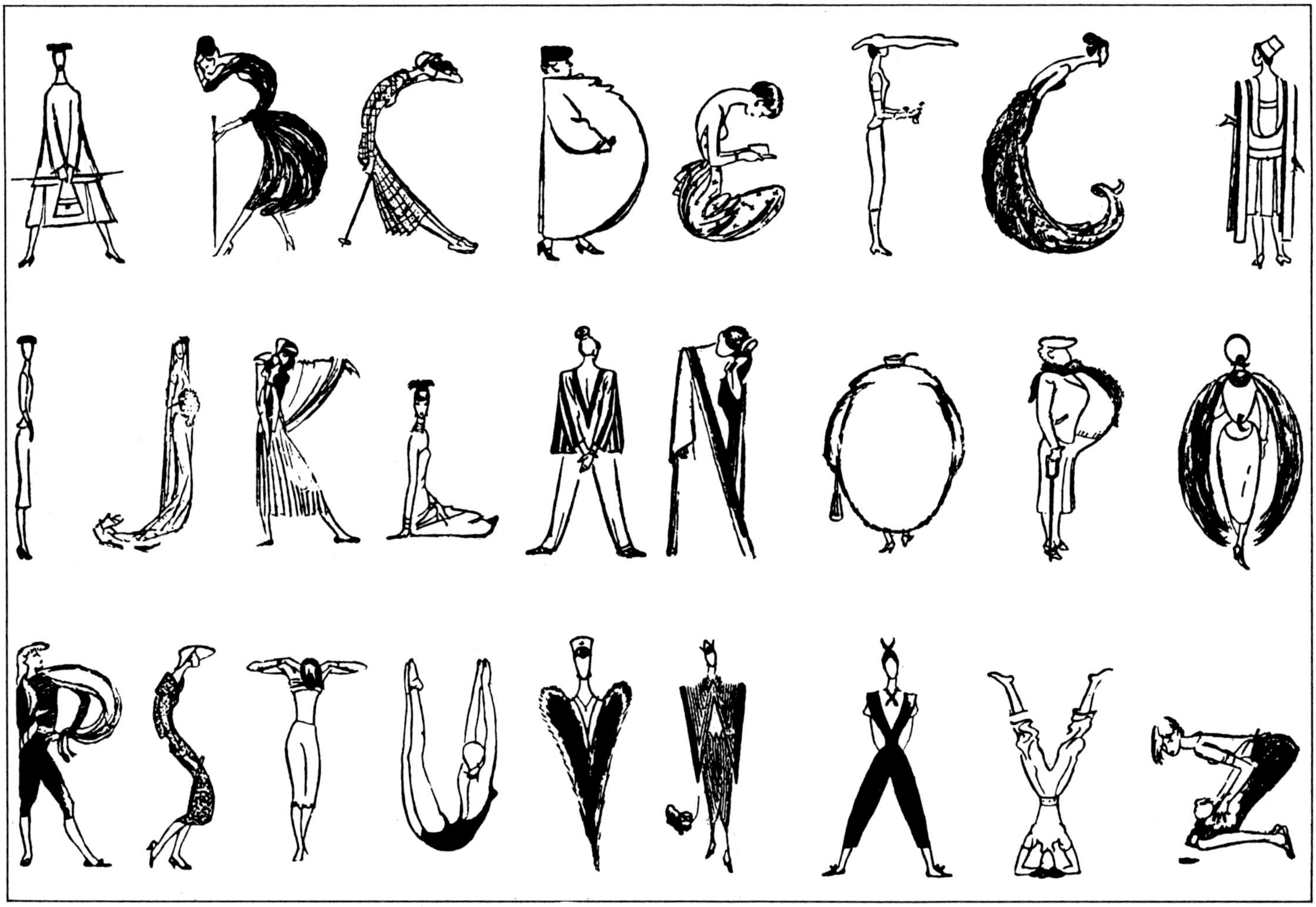

210

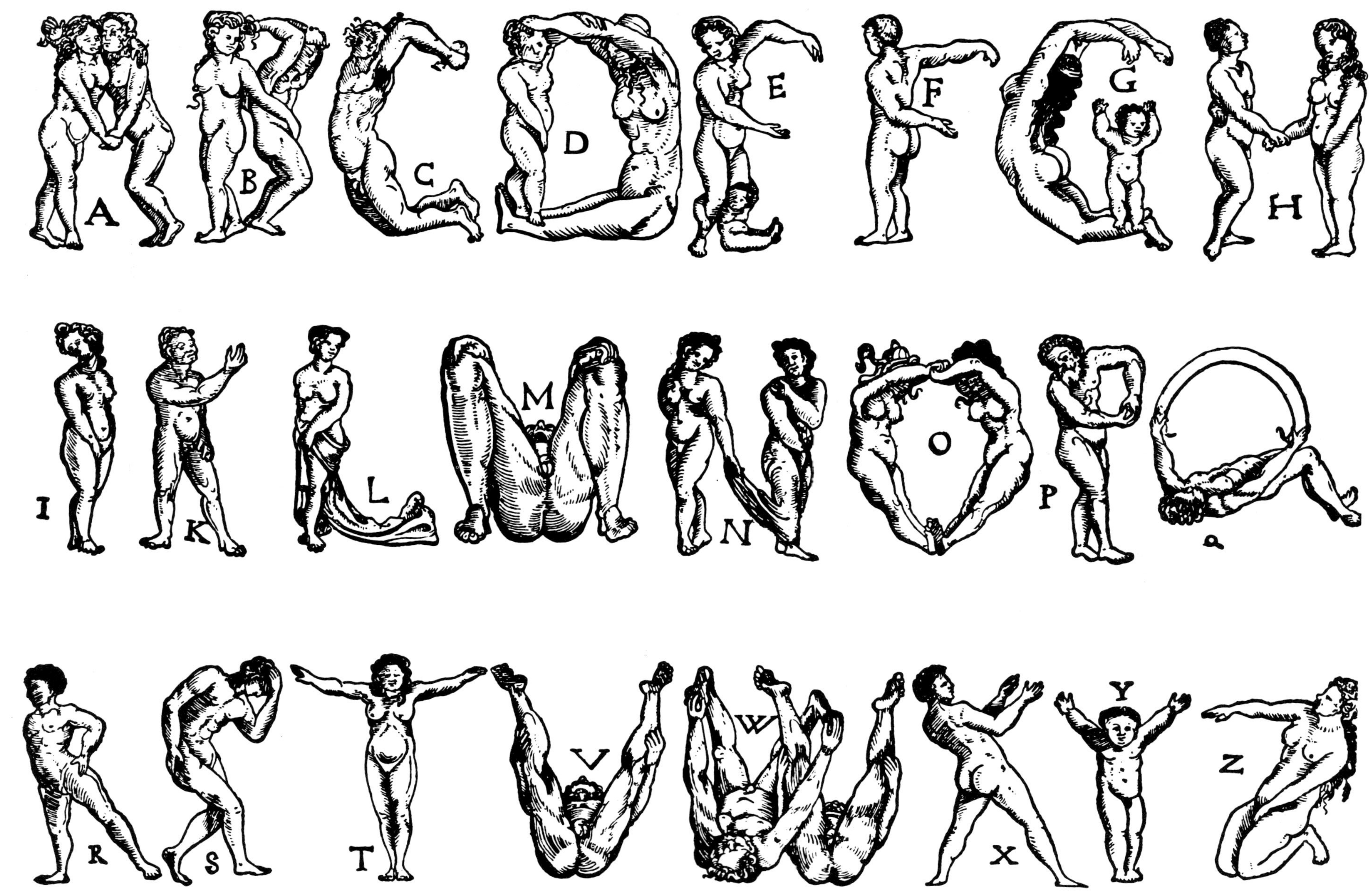
A B C D E F G H
I K L M N O P Q
R S T V W X Y Z

212

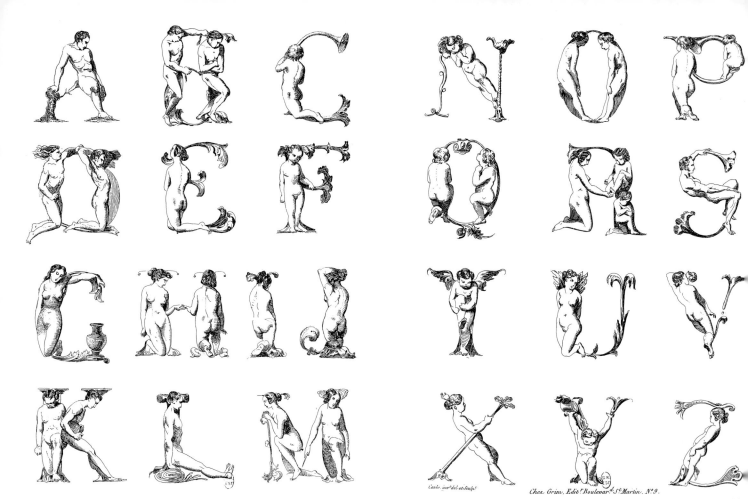

Caulo, inv.r del. et Sculp.t

Chez Grim, Edit.r Boulevard St Martin, No 9.

21

diatribe directed all in one breath against Charlemagne, Socratics, idealists, realists, rationalists, Descartes, bibliophiles, the Bauhaus movement, and, above all, the Renaissance, which caused 'the greatest sclerosis of the spirit until surrealism'. It was therefore not by chance that Mathieu, to whom André Malraux gave the title 'leading calligrapher of the west', spared from his whiplash of criticism the calligraphers who, during the seventeenth and eighteenth centuries, held to the tradition of figured letters, while gradually leading script derived from Bastard Chancery towards the full arabesque which the first lithographers would seize on.

I will only cite here for the sake of completeness the alphabets of Lucas Kilian (Augsburg, 1627), Mauro Poggi (Florence, *c.* 1750) and G. B. Betti (Florence, *c.* 1785), which show human figures to some extent, certainly, but in a secondary way, the accent being rather on ornamentation of an Italian or rococo type.

214

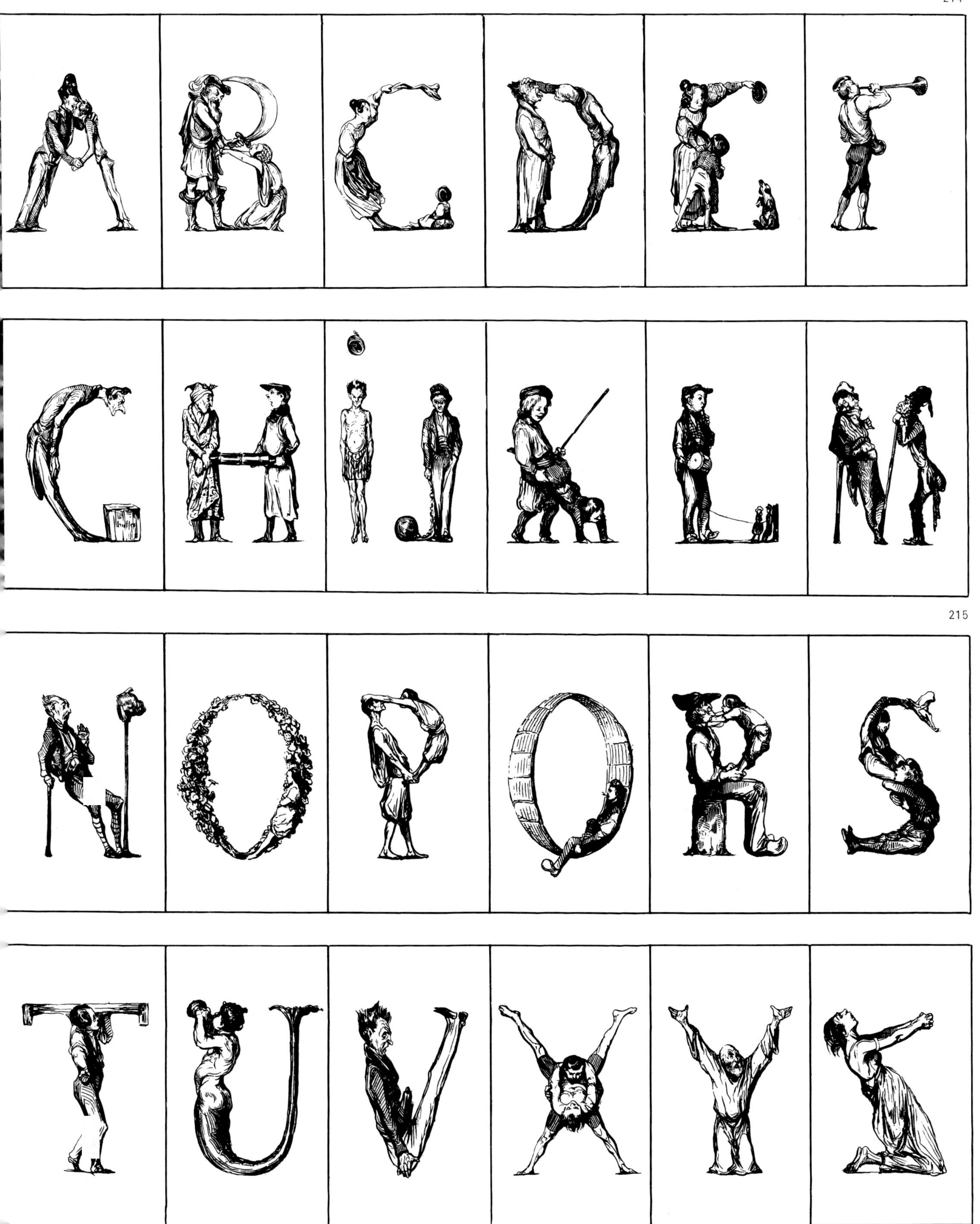

215

ALPHABET
A LA
JOCKO
Pour l'Amusement
DE
L'ENFANCE.

C. Cynocéphale.

D. Douc

E. Epagneul.

F. Finlandais.

G. Guenon
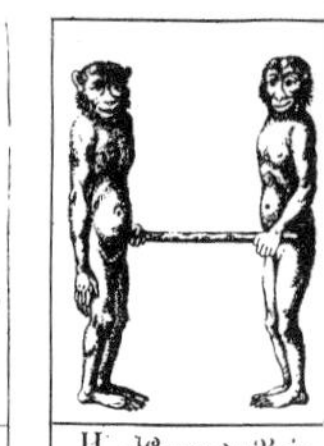
H. Homme des Bois
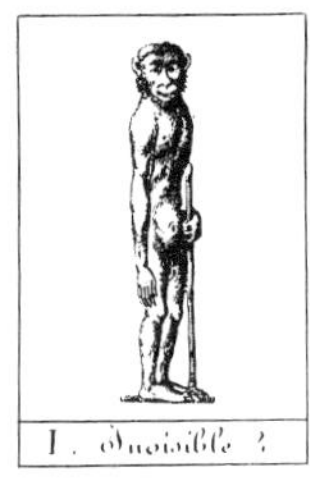

J. Jocko

M. Macaque.
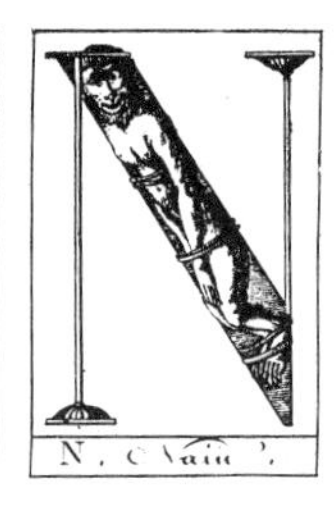
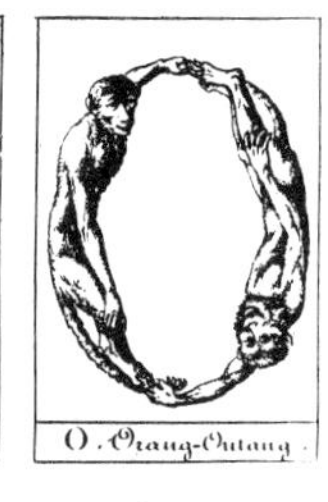
O. Orang-Outang.
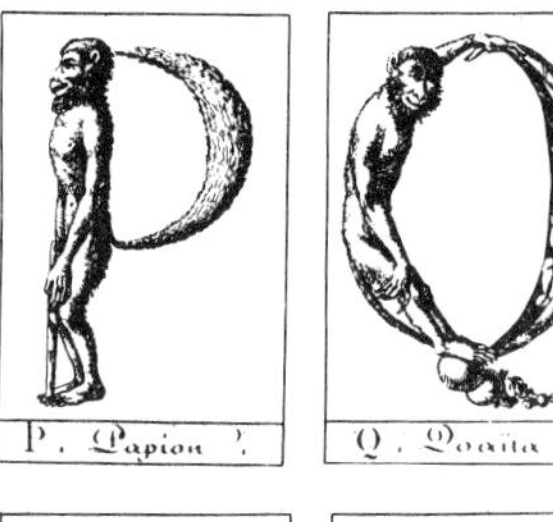
P. Papion

R. Raton

S. Sapajou

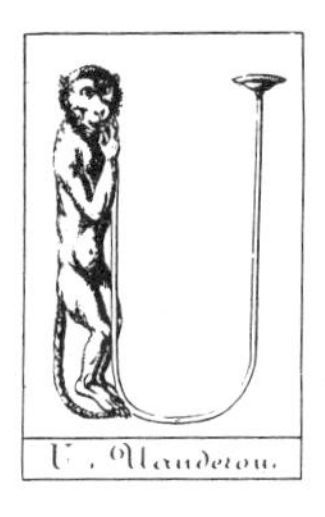
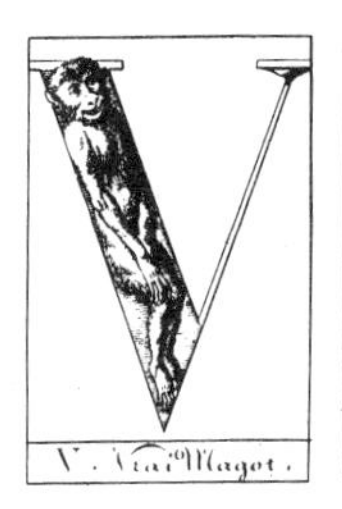

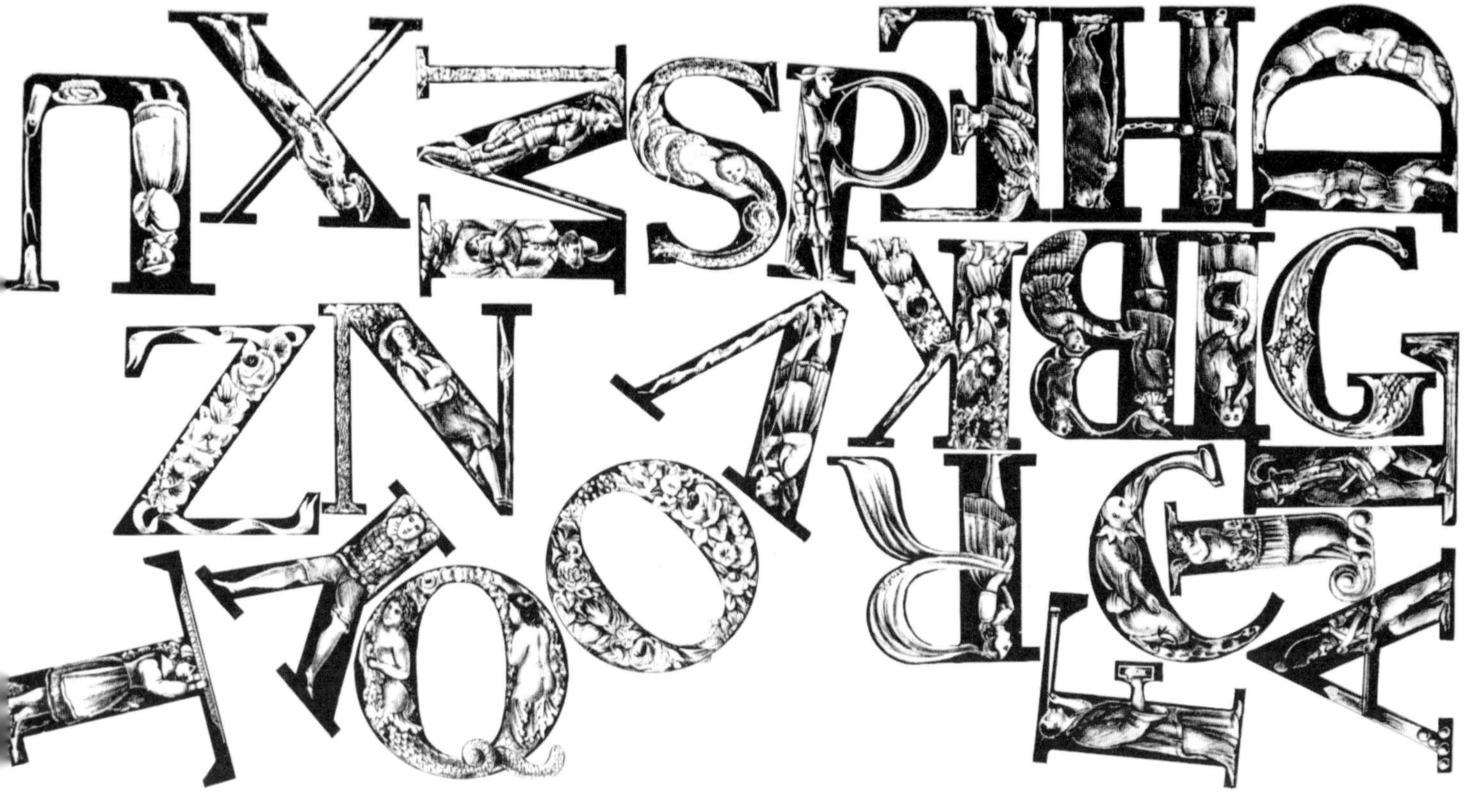

218

219

220

VRAI

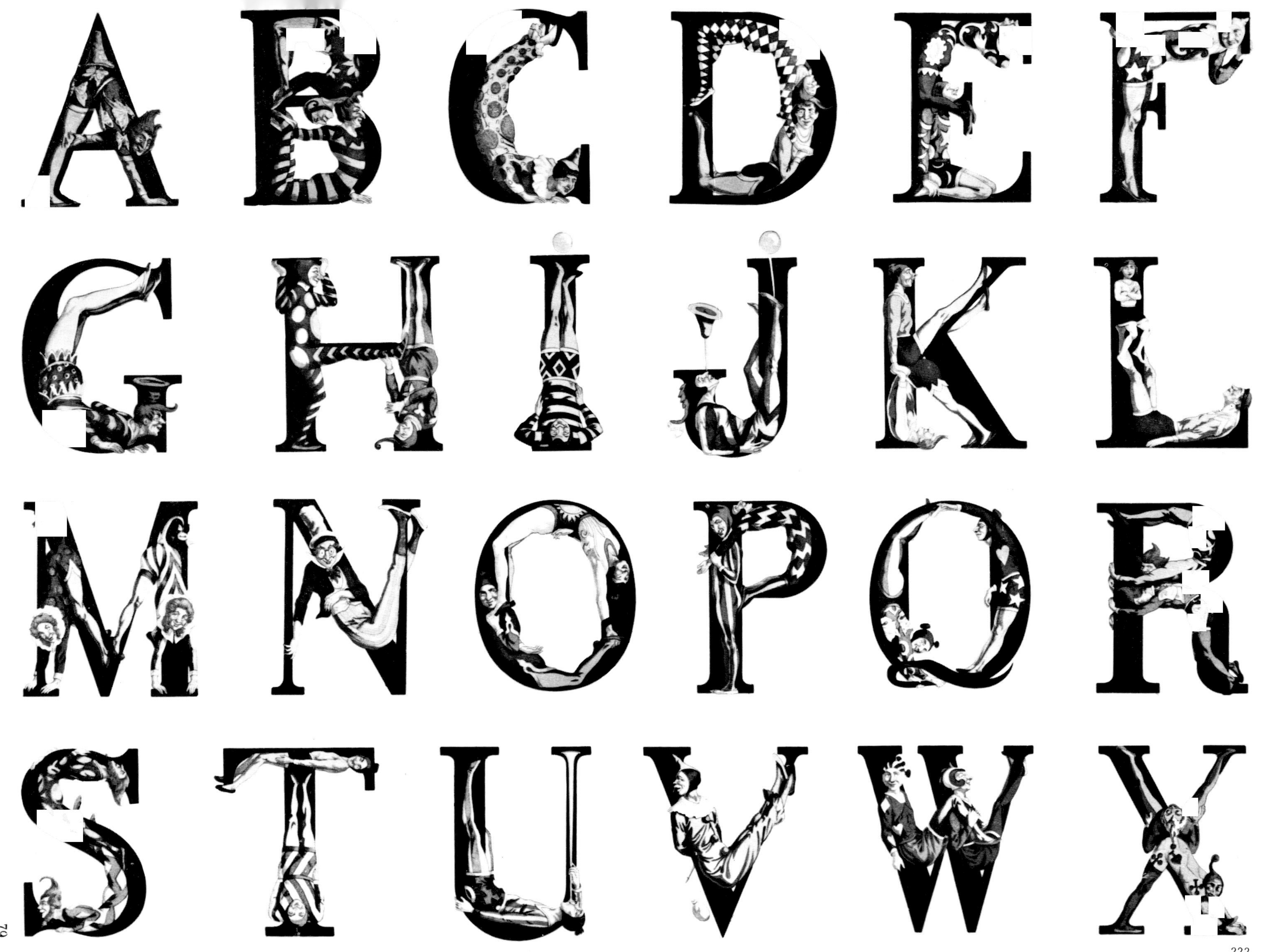

222

223

224

ALPHABET DIABOLIQUE.

Lith. d'É. Simon fils Editr à St

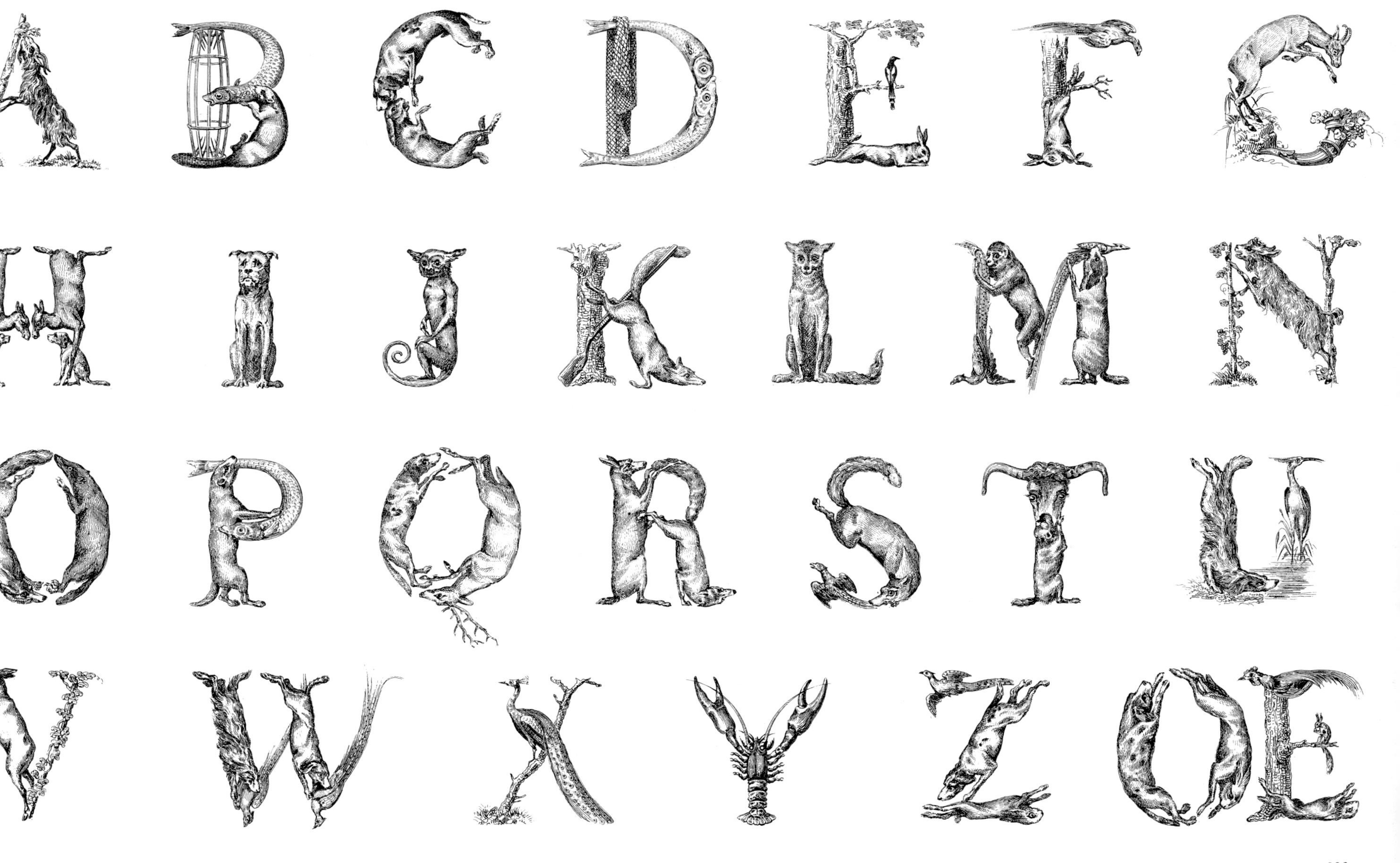

226

227

228

229

230

23

23

ABCDEFG

HIKLMNO

PQRSTVW

XYZÆJŒU

233

234

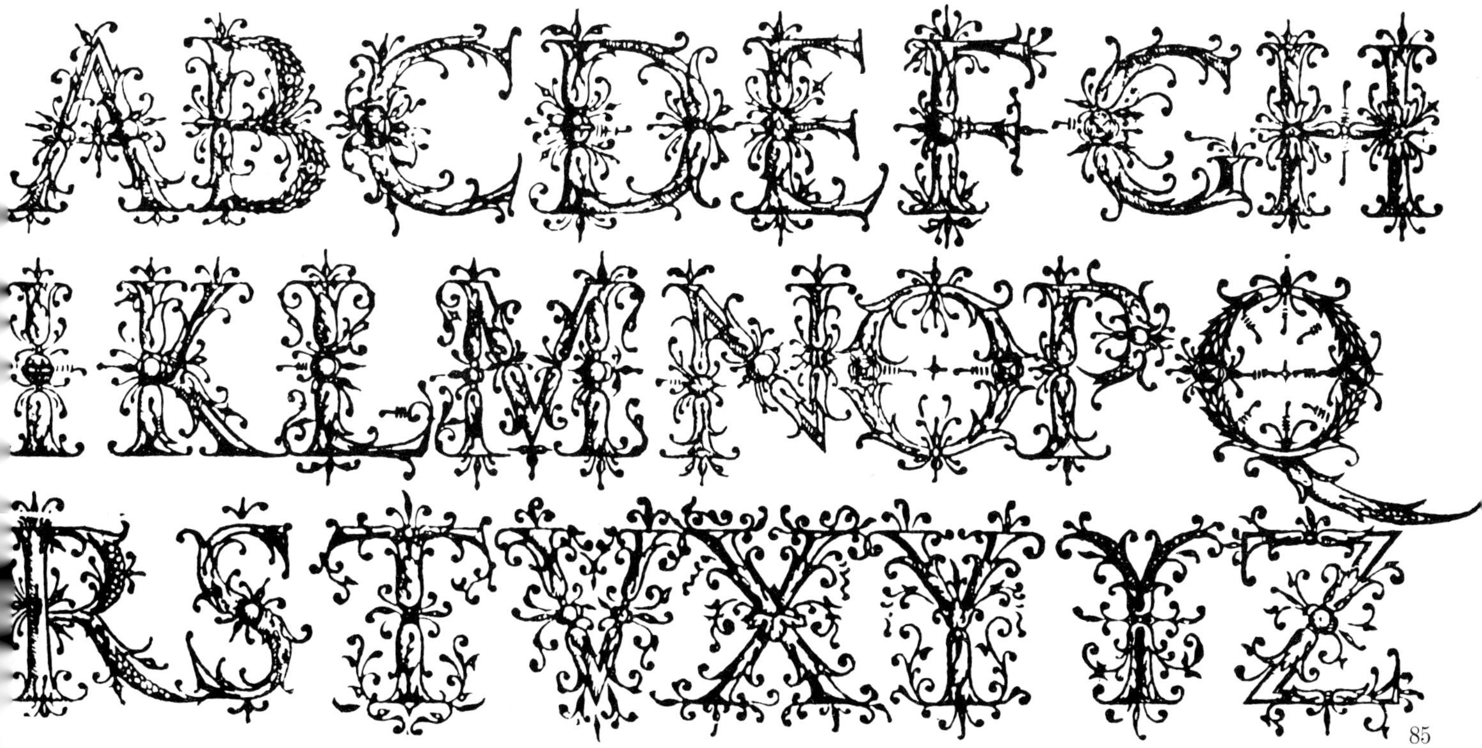

ABCDEFGH

IKLMNOPQ

RSTVXYYZ

FORESTIERE.

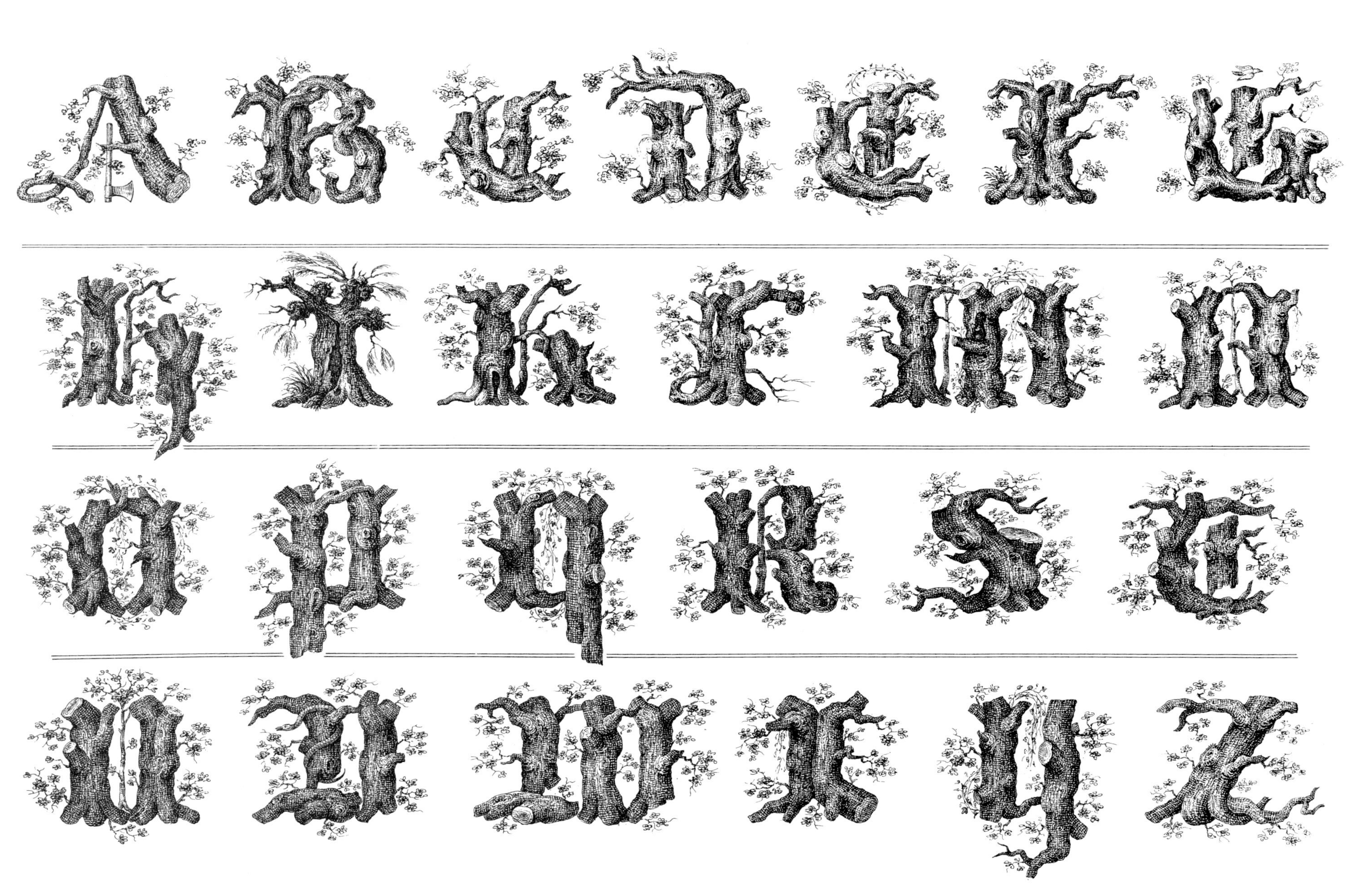

236

237

The invention of lithography, at the beginning of the last century, gave rise to a flowering of forms of a diversity and luxuriance rarely seen. Engravers vied with one another to design on stone exuberant, yet extraordinarily delicate scrollwork. Poets and musicians had made the Middle Ages fashionable; medieval cathedrals and castles were restored, or even entirely rebuilt; cabinet makers, printers, bookbinders designed Gothic chairs, pages and bindings, while scholars pored over books of black magic and incunabula. The element of fantasy reappeared, together with a craze for folklore, in German legends or English fairytales, and was preceded by
the devil himself. The devil would inspire whole alphabets 223/225
(corresponding perhaps to the ancient Dance of Death),
while trees, leaves and flowers also made up complete series. 231/237
There were even collections of letters which were dedicated 240/244
to Gothic or Renaissance architecture.

Victor Hugo, as always considering everything with a godlike eye, did not fail to take an interest in this aspect of typographical imagery which preoccupied his contemporaries so intensely. Travelling through the Alps in 1839, he jotted down his impressions en route and, starting from an amusing observation, went on to embrace the whole of creation in describing the twenty-six letters of the alphabet, in a piece of prose which is most relevant to this study:

'On leaving the lake of Geneva, the Rhône meets the long wall of the Jura Mountains which turn it back into Savoy and Lake Bourget. There it finds a way out and hurtles into France. In two bounds it is at Lyons.

In the distance on the rough green slopes of the Jura the dried, yellow beds of the torrential rivers drew Y's in every direction. Have you noticed how Y is a picturesque letter symbolical of endless things? A tree is a Y; the fork of two roads is a Y; the confluence of two rivers is a Y; the head of a donkey or bullock is a Y; a glass on its stem is a Y; a lily on its stalk is a Y; a supplicant raising his arms to the sky is a Y.

Moreover this observation can be extended to all the elements of writing. All the components of demotic language were made up of those from the hieratic language. A hieroglyph is the root of a letter. Letters were first of all signs, and all signs were pictorial images before that.

Human society, the world, the whole of man is in the alphabet. Masonry, astronomy, philosophy, and all the sciences find in it an invisible, but real point of departure; and that is as it should be. The alphabet is a source of all things.

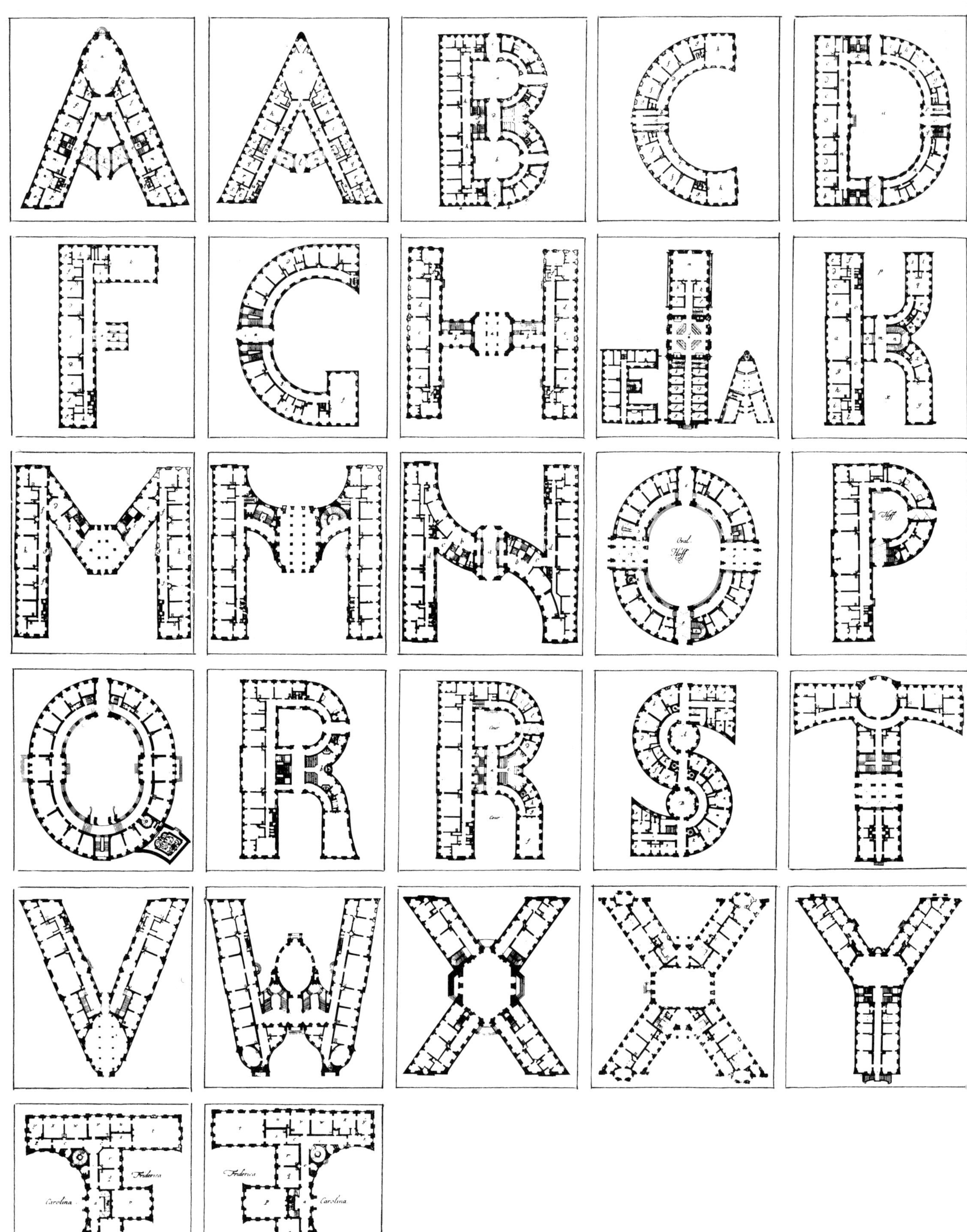
Oval.
Hoff
Hoff
Cour
Cour
Friderica
Carolina
Friderica
Carolina

23

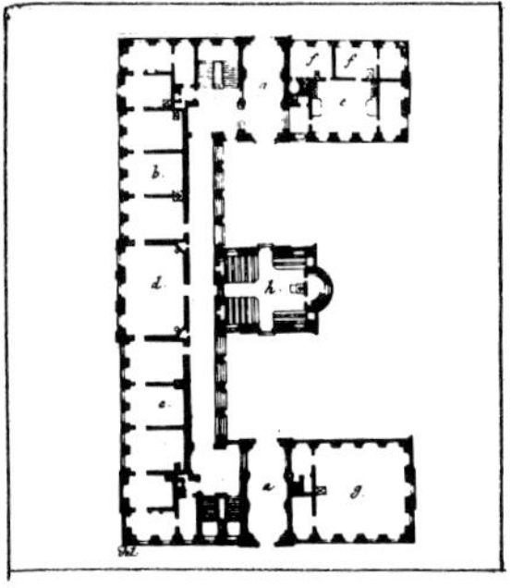

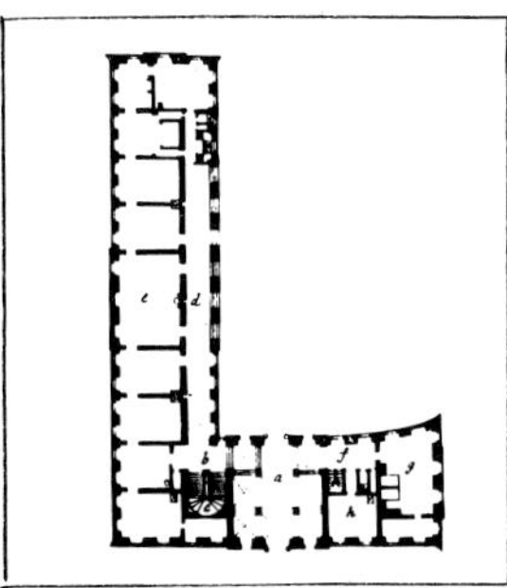

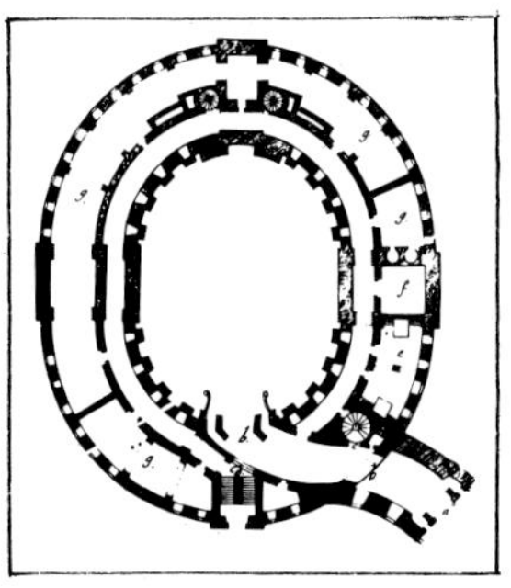

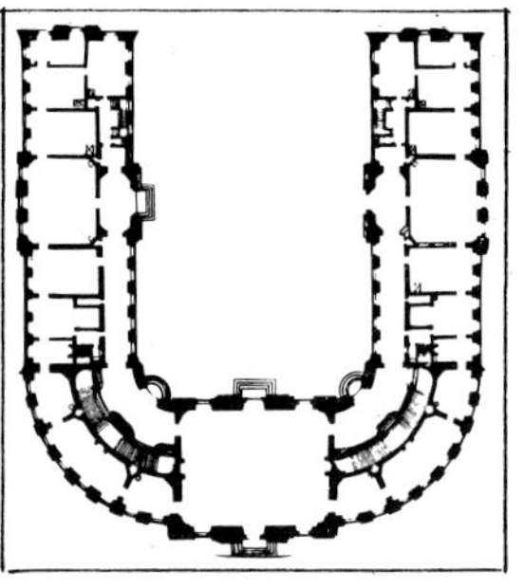

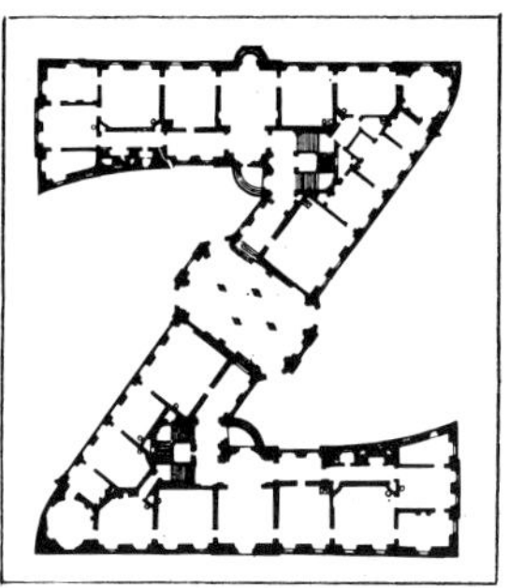

239

A is a roof, the gable with its cross-beam, an arc, *arx*; or it is the meeting of two friends who embrace and shake hands; D is a back; B is a D on a D, a back on a back, a hump; C is a crescent, or the moon; E is the foundation, the pillar, the corbel and the architrave, all of architecture in one letter; F is the crutch, fork, *furca*; G is a horn; H is the façade of a building with two towers; I is a war-machine hurling its missile; J is a ploughshare and horn of plenty; K is the angle of reflection equal to the angle of incidence, one of the keys to geometry; L is a leg and a foot; M is a mountain, or a camp, with tents side by side; N is a closed door with its diagonal bar; O is the sun; P is a porter with his burden; Q is the rump with its tail; R is rest, the porter leaning on his stick; S is a snake; T is a hammer; U is an urn; V is a vase (and therefore these two are often confusing); I have just said what Y is; X is crossed swords, a fight; who will win? no one knows; also, alchemists took X as the sign of destiny, algebrists use it as the sign of the unknown quantity; Z is lightning, and God.

Thus, first the house and its architecture, then the human body, its structure and its deformities; then justice, music, the church; war, harvest, geometry; mountains, the nomadic life, the life of the cloister; astronomy; work and rest; the horse and the snake; the hammer and urn, that can be joined and turned upside down to make a bell; trees, rivers, roads; finally destiny and God – all this is in the alphabet.'

And Hugo adds this conclusion, which could be, for initiates the keystone of this theory:

'Possibly, also, for some of those mysterious innovators of language who built the foundations of human memory and which human memory has forgotten, A, E, F, H, I, K, L, M, N, T, V, Y, X and Z were none other than the ribs of the framework of the temple'.

One cannot know for certain whether Hugo knew the lithographic work of Jean Midolle and Joseph-Balthazard Silvestre, which had been published from 1828 (a few years previously) onwards. These two artists were rivals in their art for several years, sometimes even working on identical themes, so that it is difficult to know which of them had the idea first. Their work – and that of Midolle is much the richer and more original of the two – follows two seemingly opposite courses: the creation of new-style letters, freed (already!) from the constrictions of lead, original in conception and colour and serving more and more the demands made by publicity and advertisements; and, on the other hand, a return to the subjects beloved of medieval illuminators (rather than to those favoured during the Renaissance), which was followed by the first systematic inventory of Merovingian and Carolingian figured initials.

240

241

242

ABCDEFGH
IJKLMNOPQ
RSTUVXYZ

243

244

Maniera bizzarra di esprimere le Figure Aritmetiche con Comiche positure
1
2
3
4
5
6
7
8
9
0

245

246

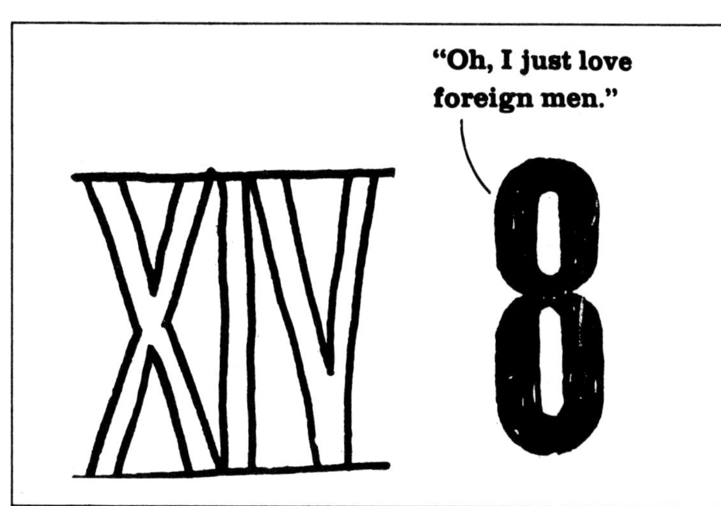
"Oh, I just love
foreign men."
XIV 8

247

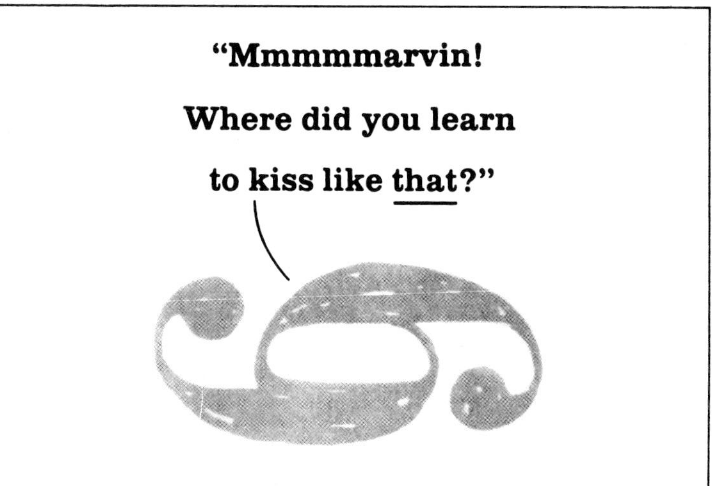
"Mmmmmarvin!
Where did you learn
to kiss like that?"

248

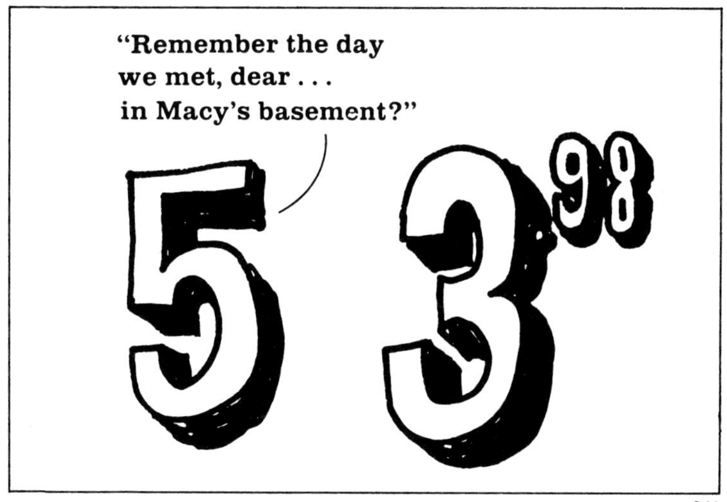
"Remember the day
we met, dear . . .
in Macy's basement?"
5 3 98

249

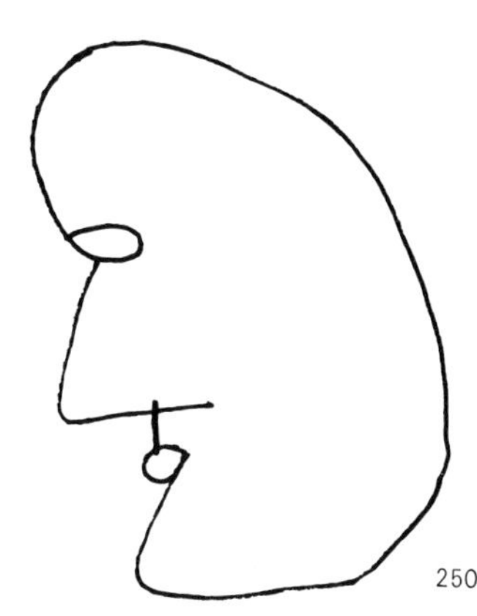

250

51

5555555666666

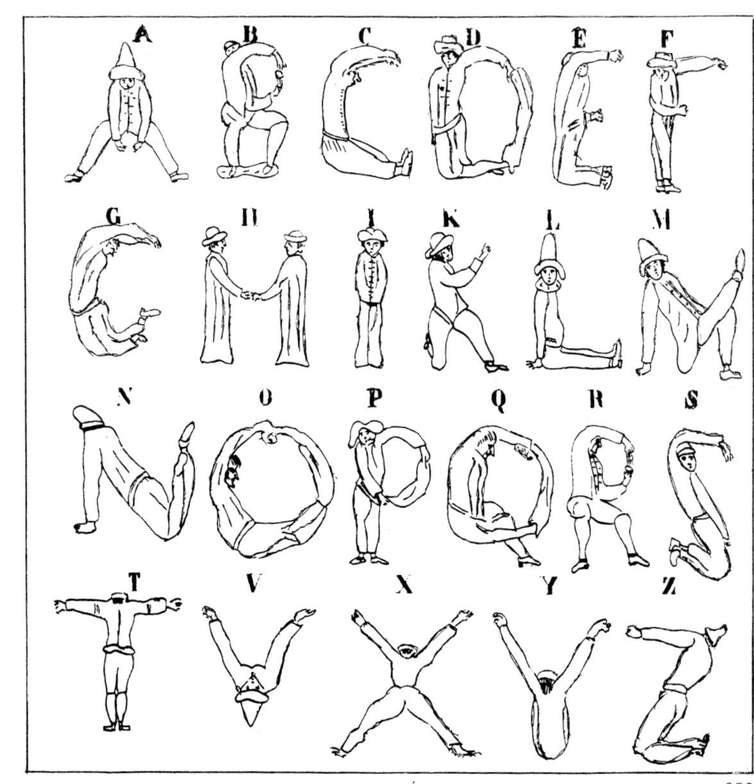

253

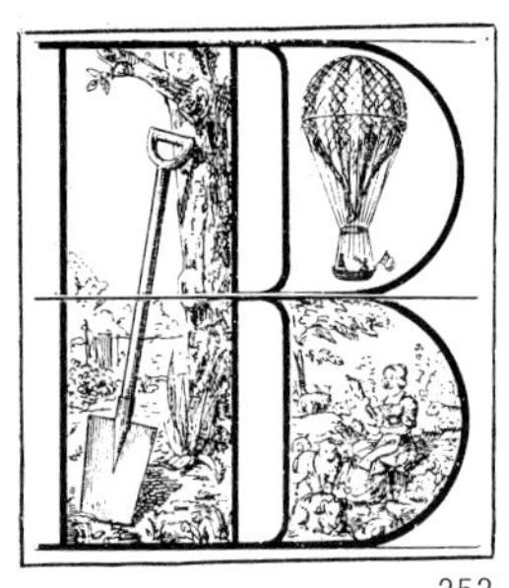

252

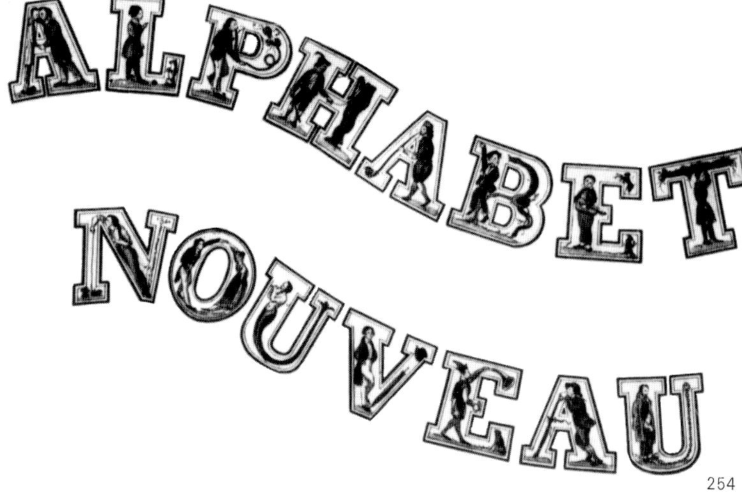

254

25

256

257

One must remember that these precious plates which
collectors today are eager to snatch up were not widely known
to the general public in their own day, but quite the contrary
is true of papers such as the *Charivari*, or other leaflets which,
from 1835 onwards published animated alphabets by such
famous artists as Daumier and Bertall, and which Victor 214-215 270/294
Hugo would doubtless have seen. Such a poet can hardly have
been ignorant, either, of the episode in the *Quart Livre* of
Rabelais, where, through the voice of Pantagruel he reminds
us that Aristotle held Homer's words to be 'in full spring,
flight, movement, and therefore animated'. Panurge, hearing
people speak in the air but seeing no one there, is suddenly
afraid, at which the ship's pilot, who is at that moment crossing an icy region, reassures him: the previous winter, a
great battle had taken place, in the course of which, 'the
cries of men and women froze in the air, and also the prayers
of the mass, the creaking of harness, the neighing of horses and
all the other noises of the combat. Now that the rigour of winter
is passed, and serene and temperate weather has returned,
they are melting again and can be heard'. Panurge – alluding

258

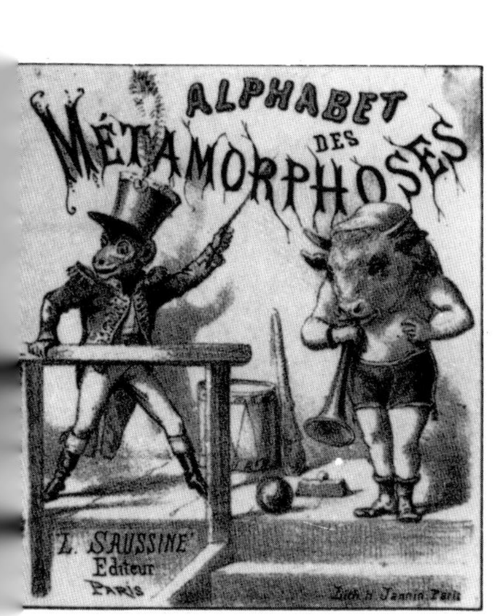

259

260

261

262

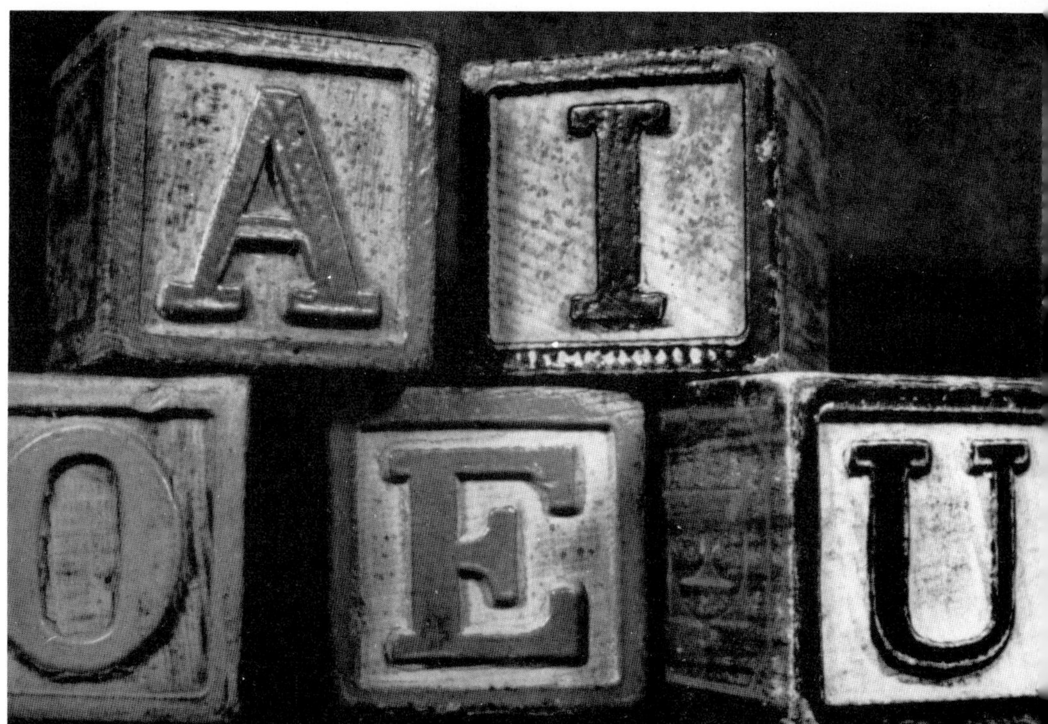

263

to *Exodus* – remembers having read that 'at the foot of the mountain when Moses received the law for the Israelites, the people could visibly see the voices which spoke' and demands to see one of these frozen words himself.

'Look, look, cried Pantagruel, here are some which have not yet melted. And he threw on the deck handfuls of frozen words, which looked like pearly drops of various colours. We saw red words, green and azure words, black and gold words . . . Then Pantagruel threw down three or four more handfuls, and we saw bitter words and bleeding words . . . horrific words and others very unpleasant to behold. And when they were all melted we heard hin, hin, hin, hin, hic, tic, toc, look, gabble, gabble, frr, frrr, frrrr, bou, bou, bou, bou, bou, bou, bou, hou, tic, trac, trr, trrr, trrrr, trrrrr, oh, oh, oh, oh, oh, ouououououah, gog, magog, and I don't know what other barbarous words.'

A noir, E blanc, I rouge, U vert, O bleu: voyelles
Je dirai quelque jour vos naissances latentes:
A, noir corset velu des mouches éclatantes
Qui bombinent autour des puanteurs cruelles

Golfes d'ombre; E, candeur des vapeurs et des tentes
Lances des glaciers fiers, rois blancs, frissons d'ombelles;
I, pourpres, sang craché, rire des lèvres belles
Dans la colère ou les ivresses pénitentes;

U, cycles, vibrements divins des mers virides,
Paix des pâtis semés d'animaux, paix des rides
Que l'alchimie imprime aux grands fronts studieux;

O, suprême Clairon plein des strideurs étranges,
Silences traversés des Mondes et des Anges:
— O l'Oméga, rayon violet de Ses Yeux! —

264

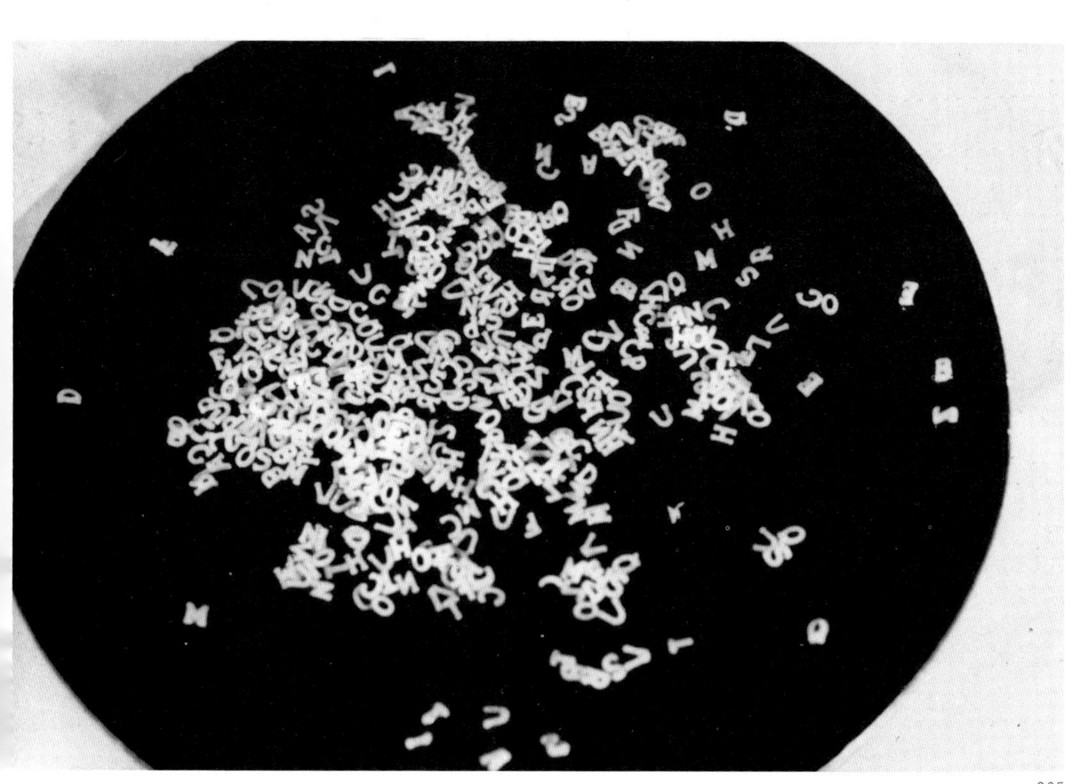

265

266

267

268

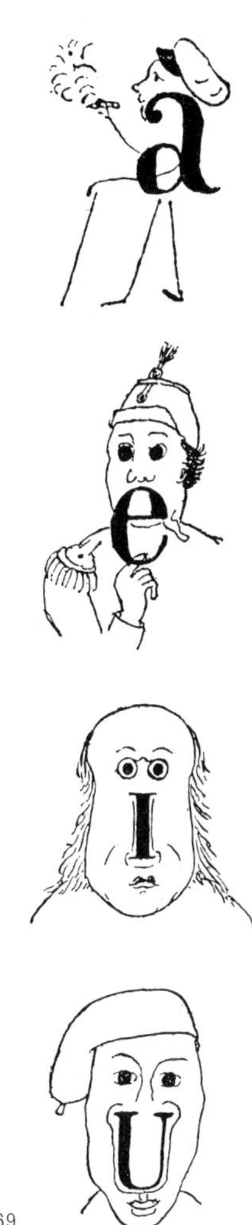

269

270

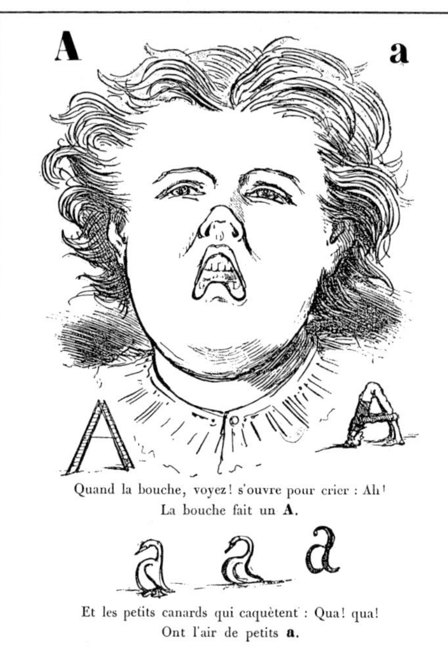

A a
Quand la bouche, voyez! s'ouvre pour crier : Ah!
La bouche fait un **A**.
Et les petits canards qui caquètent : Qua! qua!
Ont l'air de petits **a**.

271

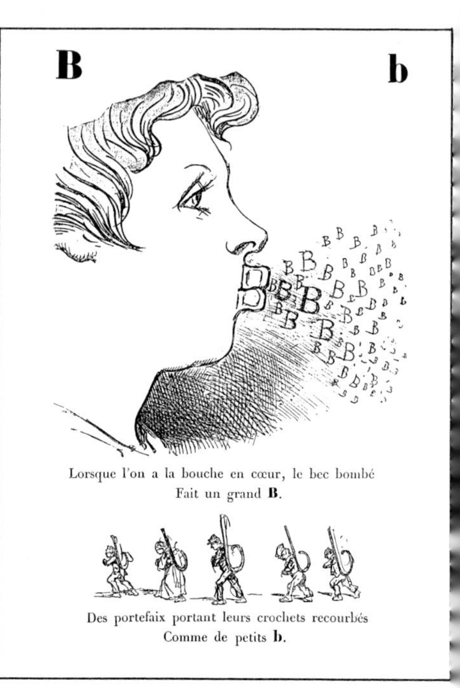

B b
Lorsque l'on a la bouche en cœur, le bec bombé
Fait un grand **B**.
Des portefaix portant leurs crochets recourbés
Comme de petits **b**.

272

295

296

297

302

303

304

C c
Petit Paul a brisé son cerceau mal lancé;
Mais il a les morceaux qui font juste deux C.
Un melon, trois flatteurs saluant l'argent, c'est
Autant de petits c.

273

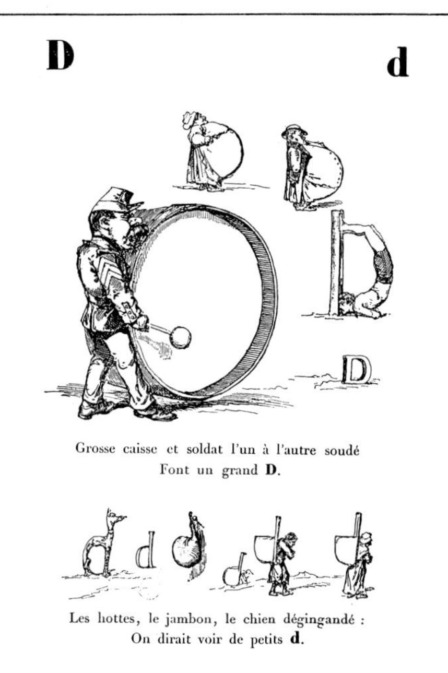

D d
Grosse caisse et soldat l'un à l'autre soudé
Font un grand D.
Les hottes, le jambon, le chien dégingandé :
On dirait voir de petits d.

274

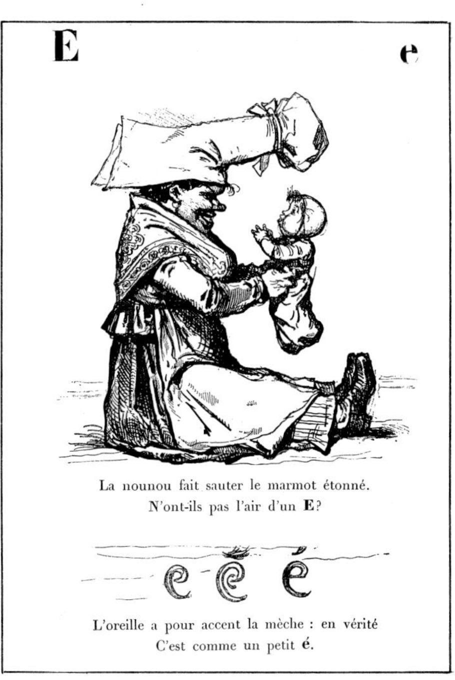

E e
La nounou fait sauter le marmot étonné.
N'ont-ils pas l'air d'un E?
L'oreille a pour accent la mèche : en vérité
C'est comme un petit é.

275

298

299

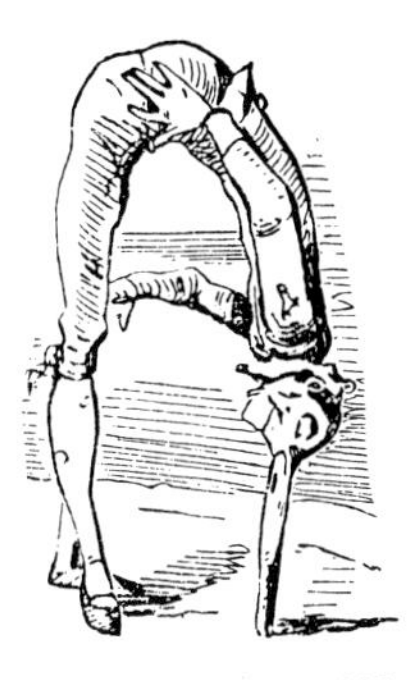

300

301

305

306

F f
A la main de Joseph, cette faux en relief,
Et l'homme qui salue au-dessous sont des F.
L'eustache de Joseph
A l'air d'un petit f.

276

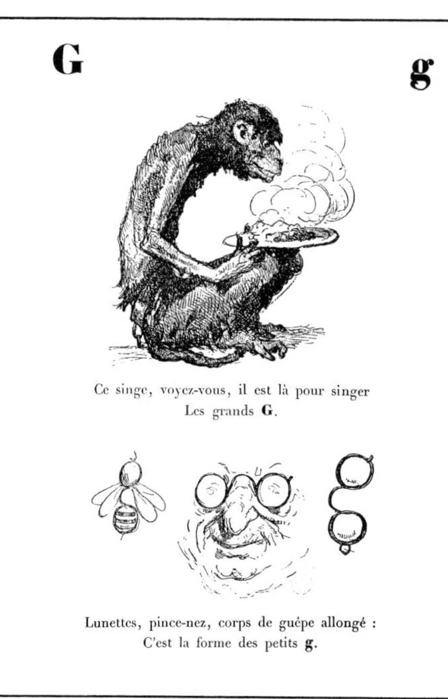

G g
Ce singe, voyez-vous, il est là pour singer
Les grands G.
Lunettes, pince-nez, corps de guêpe allongé :
C'est la forme des petits g.

277

H h
En se donnant la main on a, sans qu'on le sache,
La tournure qu'a le grand H.
La girafe, la chaise, et là, cette ganache,
Même la cathédrale, ont l'air de petits h.

278

307

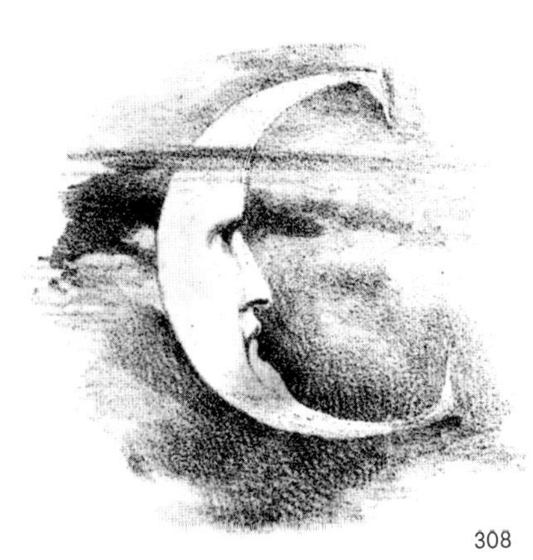

308

309

310

314

315

316

317

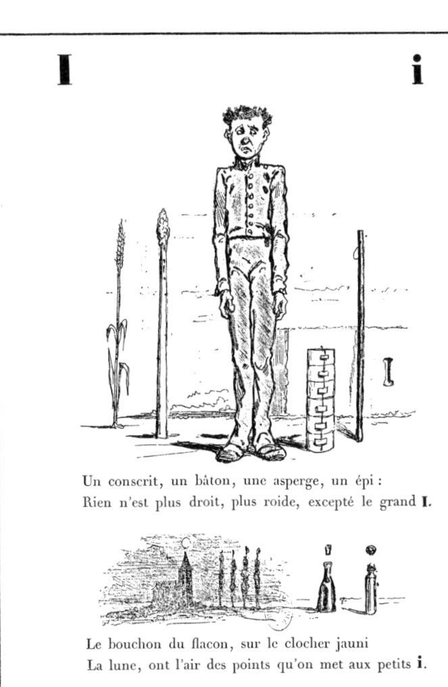

I i
Un conscrit, un bâton, une asperge, un épi :
Rien n'est plus droit, plus roide, excepté le grand I.
Le bouchon du flacon, sur le clocher jauni
La lune, ont l'air des points qu'on met aux petits i.

279

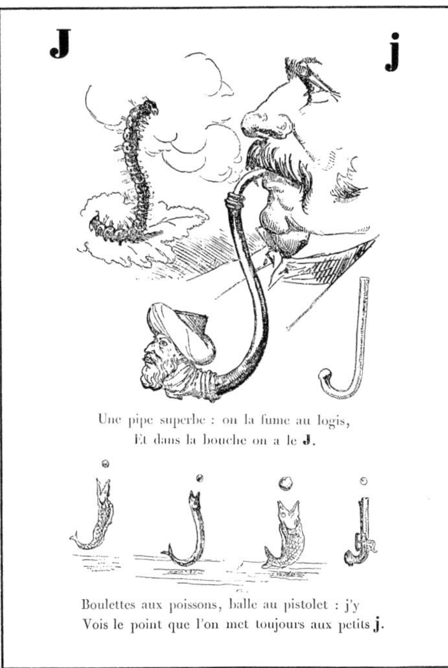

J j
Une pipe superbe : on la fume au logis,
Et dans la bouche on a le J.
Boulettes aux poissons, balle au pistolet : j'y
Vois le point que l'on met toujours aux petits j.

280

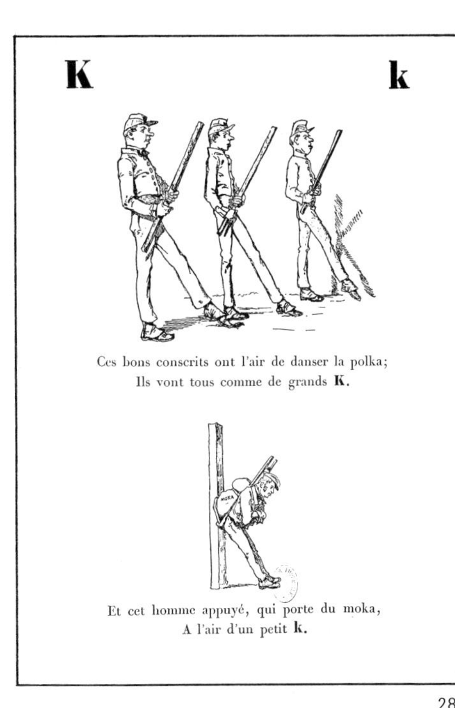

K k
Ces bons conscrits ont l'air de danser la polka;
Ils vont tous comme de grands K.
Et cet homme appuyé, qui porte du moka,
A l'air d'un petit k.

281

311

312

313

318

319

320

L l
L
Ah! je me suis coupé! mais qu'aperçois-je, ô ciel!
Homme, bras et rasoir, nous dessinons trois **L**.
Peuplier peu plié qui se tient solennel,
Tout comme un petit **l**.

282

M m
Chacune tient le drap par un bout et rit. Hem!
Qu'est-ce donc?... un grand **M**.
Ce banc de pierre, item
Ce chien : de petits **m**.

283

N n
N°1
Ce grand diable effrayé qui tient comme un lichen
A la terre, c'est un grand **N**.
Un pauvre homme à genoux : le plus simple examen
Fait reconnaître un petit **n**.

284

321

322

323

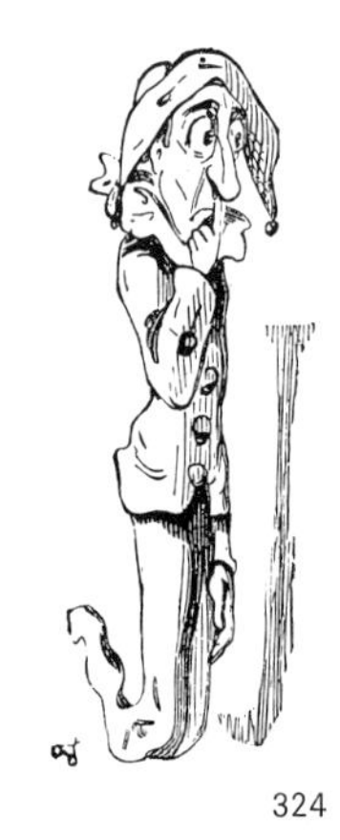

324

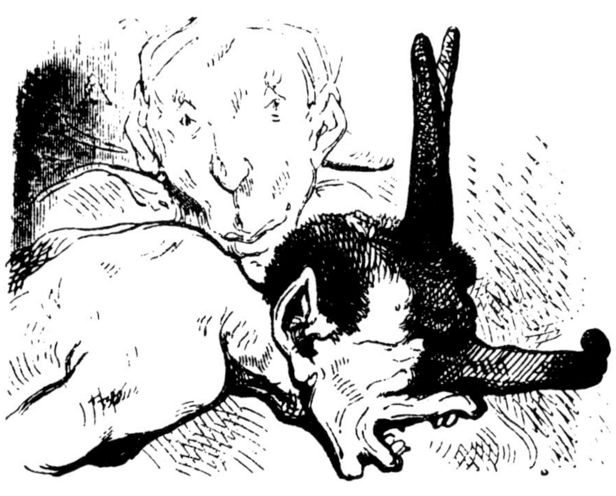

329

330

331

332

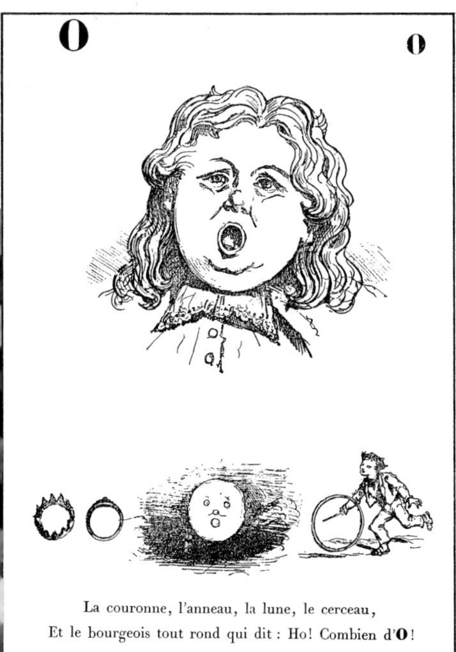

O o
La couronne, l'anneau, la lune, le cerceau,
Et le bourgeois tout rond qui dit : Ho! Combien d'O!

285

P p
Pauvre Polichinelle! Il est bien mal campé!
Dame Nature a fait en le créant un P
Et ce porteur de balle, et cet homme éclopé :
Petits p.

286

Q q
Un jour Polichinelle, ayant assez vécu,
Fait un nœud pour se pendre, et ce nœud est un Q.
Casquette d'épicier et besace : on a vu
Le petit q.

287

325

326

327

328

333

334

335

R **r**

Ces gamins se battant, d'un R n'ont-ils pas l'air?
Et la reine aussi, quel grand **R**!

Le pistolet, la femme et l'arrosoir en fer
Sont faits comme les petits **r**.

288

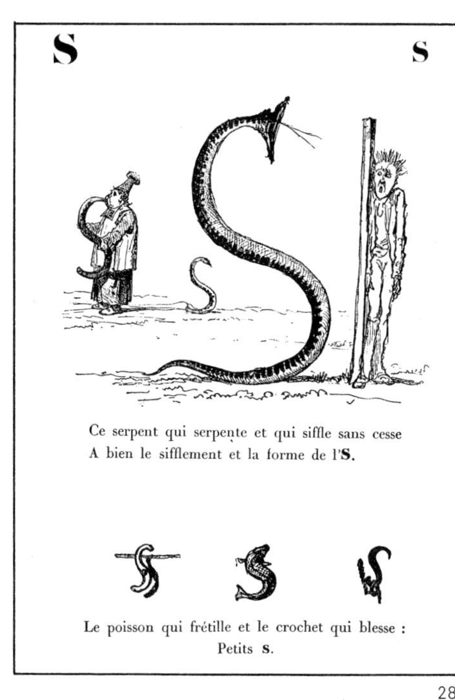

S **s**

Ce serpent qui serpente et qui siffle sans cesse
A bien le sifflement et la forme de l'**S**.

Le poisson qui frétille et le crochet qui blesse :
Petits **s**.

289

T **t**

Quand on voit ce marteau, l'on voit représenté
Le grand **T**.

L'enfant, le sabre turc avec l'ange à côté,
Sont tournés tous les trois comme de petits t.

290

336

337

338

33

343

344

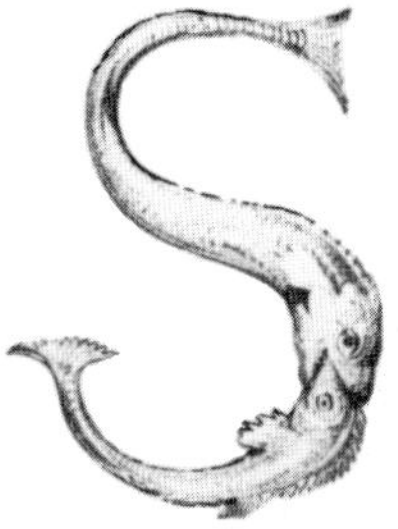

345

34

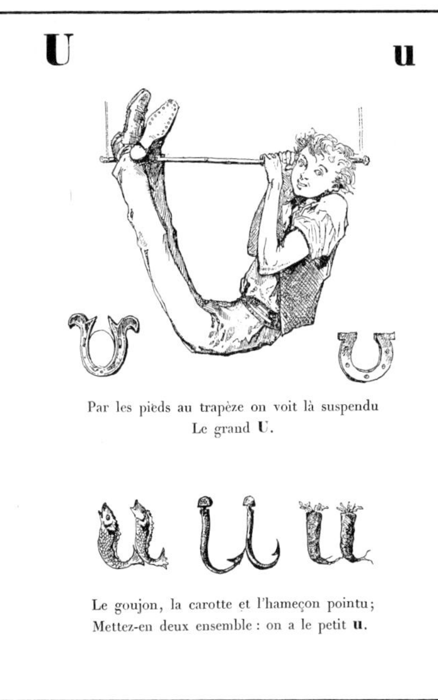
U u

Par les pieds au trapèze on voit là suspendu
Le grand **U**.

Le goujon, la carotte et l'hameçon pointu;
Mettez-en deux ensemble : on a le petit **u**.

291

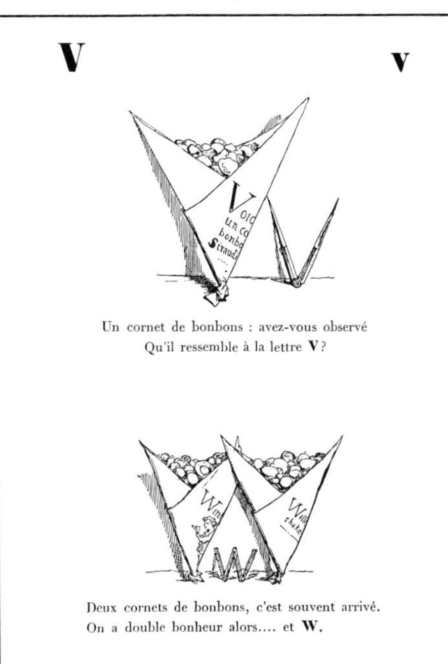
V v

Un cornet de bonbons : avez-vous observé
Qu'il ressemble à la lettre **V**?

Deux cornets de bonbons, c'est souvent arrivé.
On a double bonheur alors.... et **W**.

292

X x

Petit garçon faisant la roue, un vrai phénix :
Un **X**.

Y y

Tronc fourchu, bouc cornu, chandeliers à deux becs :
Grands et petits **Y**.

293

340

341

342

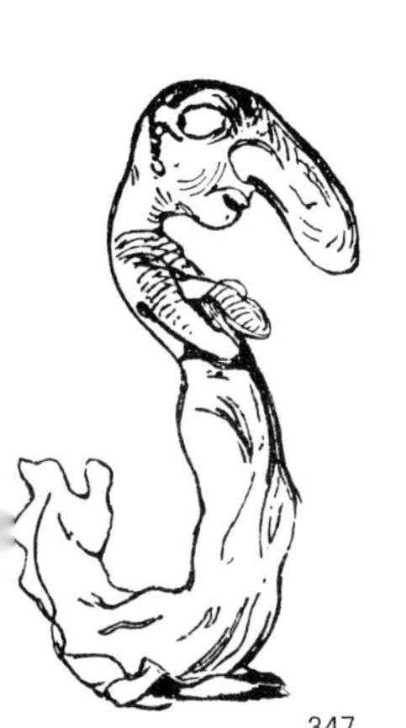
347

348

349

350

Z
Z
Z
Ces hommes à genoux, priant Dieu qu'il les aide,
Et l'éclair en zigzags, ressemblent à des **Z.**

294

LITTERATURE
ABC

351

352

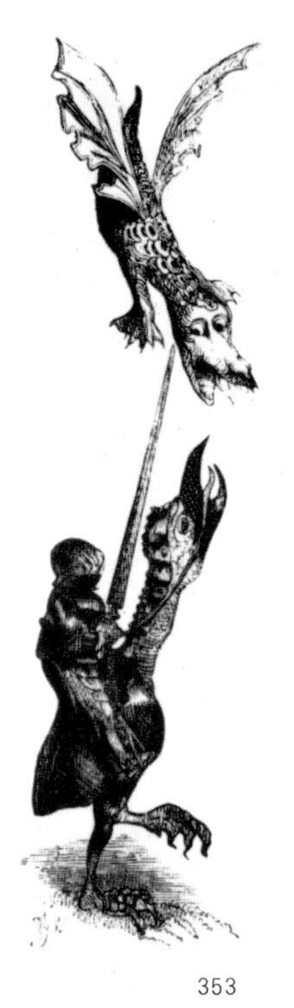

353

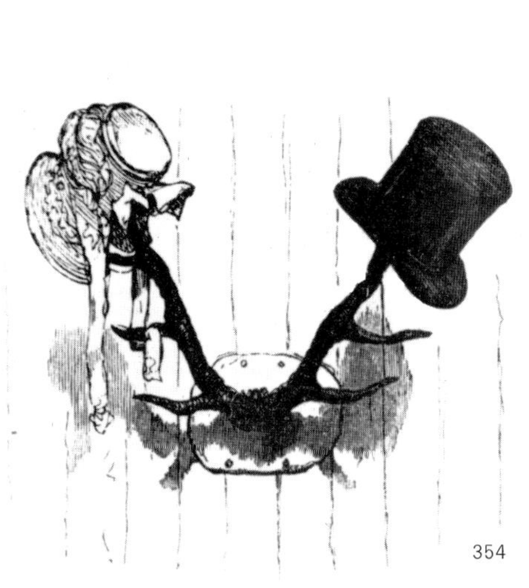

354

359

360

361

362

Theatre-Royal, Dunlop Street,

LESSEE MRS EDMUND GLOVER | GLASGOW | MANAGER MR CHARLES G. HOUGHTON.

Authorised to Perform the Pieces of the [illegible] Authors Society

TRIUMPHANT SUCCESS OF THE NEW PANTOMIME!

To give additional Effect to the GRAND FAIRY BALLET, the Celebrated Parisian Danseuse,

MDLLE. IDA IDALIE

HAS BEEN SPECIALLY ENGAGED.

The following Pantomimic Artistes are engaged, and will make their First Appearance in Glasgow:

Clown,	Mr CHARLES MORELLI.	Columbine,	Miss MARION INCH.
Pantaloon,	Mr GILBERT.	Harlequin,	Mr RICHARDE.

This Evening, FRIDAY, 22nd Dec., 1865,

The Performances will commence with the Comedietta entitled

BETSY BAKER!

Betsy Baker	Miss ERSKINE	Mr Crummy	Mr HENRY FLETCHER
Mrs Mouser	Miss WOOD	Mr Mouser, Mr PAULTON	Boy, Master SHAW

During the Evening the BAND will Perform—**OVERTURE**, **"Aladdin,"** **Foster**

After which a most Magnificently Magnuumptious Processional Production, Profusely Produced and Peculiarly Pretty, called

Or The SCAMP, The LAMP, and The LIGHT OF OTHER DAYS

RE-WRITTEN EXPRESSLY FOR THIS THEATRE BY H. J. BYRON, ESQ.

With its GORGEOUS SCENERY by **Mr WILLIAM GLOVER,**

Mr F. C. FISHER, Mr BRUNTON, and Assistants.
The Machinery by Mr WHITE The Magnificent Costumes by Mr GUY
The Ladies' Rich Dresses and Decorations designed by and produced under the Supervision of Mrs EDMUND GLOVER
The Splendid Presents, General Decorations, and Appointments by Mr MILES JONES.
The Ballet arranged by Mr RICHARDE The Harlequinade by Mr MORELLI
The Music composed for the occasion by Mr WM. FOSTER.
The Entire Pantomime arranged and produced by Mr HENRY EGERTON.
The whole being under the Superintendence of Mr C. G. HOUGHTON.

PREVIOUS TO THE OPENING WILL BE DISPLAYED,

A NEW ACT-DROP – Subject, "THE FLOWERY LAND,"

PAINTED BY MR WILLIAM GLOVER.

MORTALS

The Cham .... (a regal party in a regaler fix) .... Mr CARTER
The Vizier .... (his Prime Minister, an illustration of an (ex)chequered existence) .... Mr PAULTON
Pekoe .... (his son and heir, his father's hope and his own pride) .... Miss ERSKINE
Aladdin .... (a sad boy, also a bad boy, as well as a nice boy and a cool youth) .... Miss CRAVEN
Abanazar .... (a Magician and a Villain of the deepest possible *dye*, though he never says so) .... Mr KENDAL
Kasrac (his Familiar—more familiar than pleasant) Mr MURRAY A Mandarin Mr STEWART Another Mr KING
Another .... Mr FOREST Two others .... Mr COOKE and Mr KNOWLES
An Officer .... Mr DORICOURT Another Mr LEVER Two others .... Mr LOCKE and Mr GRAY
The Princess Badrouldbadour (a modern bard has said, "She was very fond of Dancing"—it will be seen how far this is fact) Miss GOLIER
Amrou } .... (her Handmaids) .... { Miss LAVIS
Zobeide } .... { Miss HODSON
The Widow Ching Mustapha (an old person, Aladdin's mother, remarkable for nothing but a lack of beauty and a lackadaisical manner) Mr LLOYD

IMMORTALS

The Genius of the Ring .... Miss WOOD The Genius of the Lamp .... Mr HOLLANDE
Orleck .... an indescribable, fiendish, and frightful ——) .... Mr DAMPIER

SLAVES OF THE RING

Pootyitipetsywetsy .... Madlle. IDA IDALIE
Nisypysy Miss MARION INCH Stuninlitleparti Miss CRADDOCH Nobbilitlesole Miss GOODWIN
Bonnigurls .... The Misses ACTON Dahlingpets .... Miss DEULIN and Miss MORRISON
Fifty or Sixty others .... By the CORPS DE BALLET
A Cat (Abanazar's cat) } .... (poor affairs who cannot stand [illegible]) .... } By THEMSELVES
An Owl (Abanazar's owl) }
THE MOB—Messrs Tag, Rag, Bob, Tale, &c. THE MARCH—Messrs Hose, Toes, Eelze, Nalze, &c.
THE MAIDENS—
"They were Numerous and Beautiful, both in Dress and *Ad* dress, but the Chronicler was so dazzled with their appearance that description is impossible."
SLAVES OF THE LAMP—By an entire ARMY of AUXILIARIES.

SCENE 1 (Fisher) **ABANAZAR'S STUDY.**
Incantation—Abomination—Absquatuation—How Abanazar longs for the Lamp, and how shortly he is to obtain it—The Plot!—The Plan!—How Orleck instructs Abanazar and conducts his own case—The Deed!—the Dis-Appearance—and departure of Abanazar in search of the Wonderful Lamp—
Song and Hornpipe, "Now, upon the Lamp I'll pop," Abanazar and others

SCENE 2 **HAND TEA ROOM IN THE EMPEROR'S PRECINCTS**
The Hop!—The Trip!—The Skip!—How Pekoe doesn't like concealment, *et cetera*—He tells his love—Proposition—Resolution—Songs and solicitations—How the Vizier assails the Emperor, and what a bad lot is knocked down—Duet, "Oh, my love, you like a lollipop," Pekoe and Emperor

SCENE 3 (Fisher) **A STREET IN PEKIN**
Abanazar arrives, and derives all before him—How he meets with the widow—The difference between guilt and innocence—The *long* lost brother—Promises—Precautions—Trio, "Kafoozleum," Abanazar, Aladdin, and Widow.

SCENE 4 (Glover) **THE BLASTED CEDAR**
How Abanazar invites Aladdin, and how it proves a cell—How Aladdin has mizzled, and how Abanazar is chizzled—Demons—Despair—Departure, and Magnificent Disruption of the Scene, which becomes

SCENE 5 (Glover) **CAVE OF THE WONDERFUL LAMP**
How Aladdin is locked in and falls out—How he obtains the Lamp—The Rub!—the Blubber!—and the Ring!—Appearance of the Genius—How the Fairy aids Aladdin and helps the two out—

GRAND BALLET

BY THE SLAVES OF THE RING (arranged by M. RICHARDE).
SOLOS by **Mdlle. IDA IDALIE** and Miss INCH, supported by the Corps de Ballet.

SCENE 6 **ALADDIN'S MODEST MANSION**
The Widow's joy—The Widow's boy—Return—Rapture—Rumbling—Appearance of Genius of the Lamp—Tumult!—Terror!—Tea!—How Aladdin falls in with adventure and in love at the same time—The Mystery—The Message—Duet, "Would I were a bird," Aladdin and Widow—How the Widow pops off and pledges Aladdin's faith to the Princess.

SCENE 7 **EXTERIOR OF THE BATH**
[illegible] Murder!—Mesmerism!—Magnificent Illusion.

SCENE 8 (Fisher) **VIEW OF THE CITY & PALACE OF THE EMPEROR**

GRAND PROCESSION

Of ONE HUNDRED & FIFTY Slaves of the Lamp

And PAS CHINOIS by Madlle. IDA IDALIE and the Corps De Ballet.

Aladdin's Nuptials—The Match—The Blow-up—How Aladdin makes eyes, and Pekoe doesn't seem to see it—How everything is generally satisfactory.

SCENE 9 **A STREET IN PEKIN**
How Abanazar plots and Pekoe plans, and how they mutually resolve to ruin Aladdin—Duet, "Jolly comes larking home," Abanazar & Pekoe.

SCENE 10 **EXTERIOR OF ALADDIN'S PALACE**
How Aladdin departs for the chase, and how the Princess adheres to him—How she gets into trouble, and is transported in the FLYING PALACE—How Aladdin hears of his loss, and the Emperor leers off his hose. **Scene 11** (Fisher)—**A WOOD**—How Aladdin thinks Abanazar carries his joke too far and the Palace with it—A Flight—A Fright with a following.

SCENE 12 (Glover) **THE EBONY PALACE**
Of the Wizard Abanazar in the Desert of Sahara—How the Princess is in his power, and what he makes of it—How everybody gets generally wrong, and how the Fairy sets it right, and how Abanazar gets tight—Appearance of Orleck—General danger dissipated by the Genius of the Ring—

GRAND TRANSFORMATION TO THE

ENCHANTED GROVE

And Perfumed Bowers!

(Glover)

During this Scene the Theatre will be Perfumed by Rimmel's Patent Vaporiser

Clown,	Mr CHARLES MORELLI	Harlequin,	M. RICHARDE
Pantaloon,	Mr GILBERT	Columbine,	Miss MARION INCH

SCENE 1.—Pawnbroker's, Barber's, and Photographer's.
POLKA - - - - - HARLEQUIN & COLUMBINE.
A camera and obscurer—Photographer, Mr Lenz Barber, Mr Rayser—Photographers, Messrs Pop and Whop Dandies, [illegible] and desperate persons, by a mutinous mob—"Won't go home till morning"—A row arising with a Little Swell—Clown's patent Shaving by Machinery—Frightful Murder—Awful Scrimmage

SCENE 2.—TOY BAZAAR and EXTERIOR OF BARRACKS.
ZINGARELLA - HARLEQUIN & COLUMBINE.
Soldiers, Messrs Erm and Lobster—Cobbler, Mr Last Toymaker, Mr Dgumpunjael.
CLOWN'S ADVENTURE WITH AN ELEPHANT
"In the middle of a German Band" A rise in red and a fall in Soldiers Clown in a quandary—The Backsliding Trombone Grand Review and Court Martial—Frightful Scene in the Gallowgate, the Military called out

SCENE 3.—CHANDLER'S and FISHMONGER'S.
GITANA - - - - HARLEQUIN & COLUMBINE.
A headless person and an armless policeman The sliding scale "What shall he have that killed the dear baby"—Spite Fright—A Fight Mysterious Disappearance. **A MISTY VIEW.** "But many a dark and cloudy morning brings forth a sunny day."

HOME of the GOOD FAIRIES.

"Then rest ye, merry gentlefolks, I send you all good cheer, A pocket full of money, and a cellar full of beer."

DOORS OPEN AT SEVEN—COMMENCE AT HALF-PAST SEVEN.

NOTICE—BOX OFFICE Open at the Theatre-Royal Dunlop-St. every day from 12 till 4 o'clock. Children in Arms not admitted—**SMOKING** in any part of the Theatre is strictly Prohibited—This Rule will be rigidly enforced. Places in the Boxes and Stalls cannot be retained after the end of the first Act. Tradesmen are respectfully cautioned not to supply Goods to the Theatre-Royal without an order signed by the Manager Mr Houghton.

Boxes 4s; Stalls 3s; Amphi. Stalls 2s; Pit 1s 6d; Amphitheatre 1s; Gal. 6d.

SECOND PRICE at 9 o'clock—Boxes 2s 6d. Stalls 2s. Amphitheatre Stalls 1s 6d. Pit 1s.—No Second Price to Amphitheatre or Gal.
CHILDREN UNDER TEN YEARS OF AGE SECOND PRICE.

Manager Mr CHARLES G. HOUGHTON | Principal Scenic Artist, Mr Wm. GLOVER

355

L'ARGENT???

356

357

358

363

364

365

DIABLE

Diablerles, corps 56.

MAGICIENS

366

370

371

372

3

378

379

380

3

367

368

369

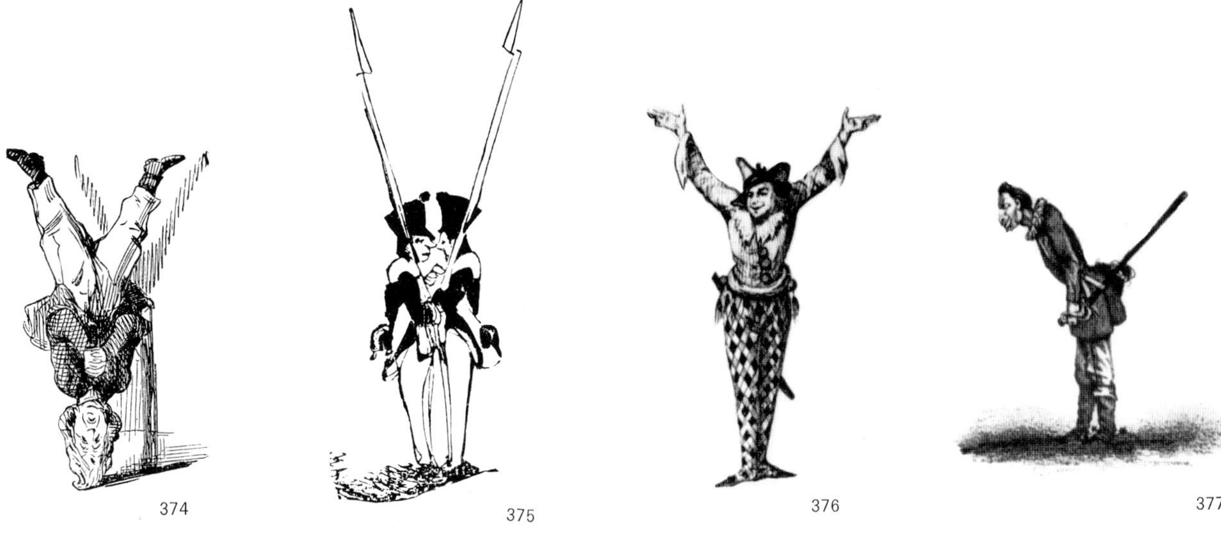

374 375 376 377

382

383-390

MUNCHHAUSEN

391

392-395

396

397

398

399

400

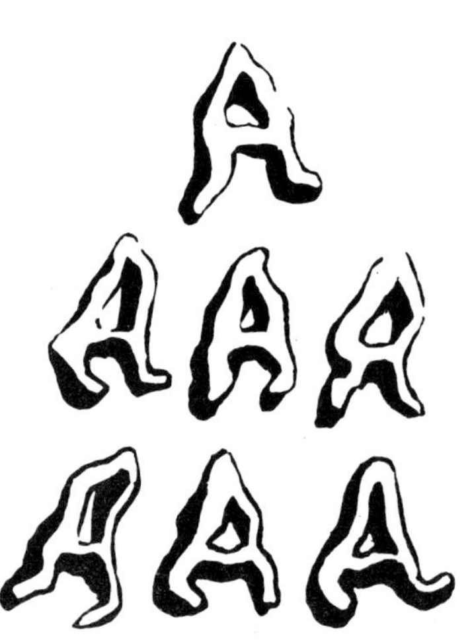

401

402

Whether it is a question of the visible words of Rabelais or the sonorous objects described by Pierre Schaeffer, the same process is used to enable the eye to see what can usually only be perceived by the ear. To demonstrate the interaction between the senses there is no need to call to mind the mysterious insight which guides a blind man among obstacles. One could even say that most of the images, metaphors, and even allegories, which are the ordinary figures of poetic expression, proceed from the same metamorphosis, without thereby masking any pathological disturbance of perception likely to lead to a perversion of the senses. For Aristotle 'a good metaphor implies the intuitive perception of the similarity between things which are dissimilar'; for Mallarmé, the entire universe is made up of analogies; an analogy, is even, for him, the only possible form of logic; then too, for Poe, 'there are exact analogies between the material world and the immaterial'. This phenomenon of transference by means of sympathetic identification, which the Germans call *Einfühlung*, possesses such strong powers of semantic suggestion that writers, from Rabelais to Joyce and Ezra Pound, from Balzac to Proust, from Baudelaire to Claudel, have not failed to make it part of their work. The whole Symbolist movement was influenced by the poetic revelation of *correspondences* with which *Les Fleurs du Mal* opens: 'Scents, colours and sounds correspond',

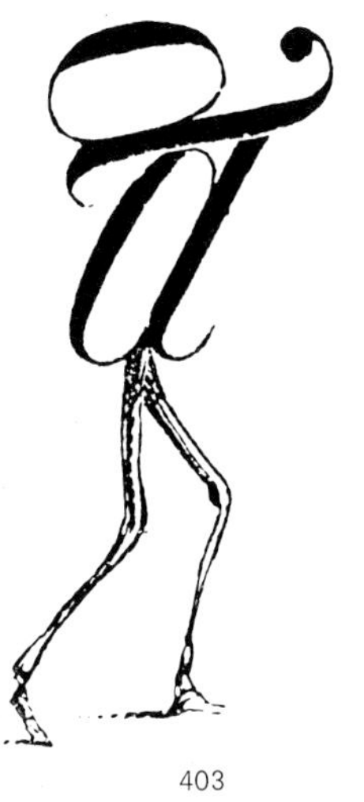

403

404

which Baudelaire, in the lines which followed, illustrated by an example: 'There are scents as fresh as children's flesh, sweet as the oboe, green as meadows' . . . As for Rimbaud, the attention
given by critics to the famous sonnet, 'Voyelles', from the end of 264
the last century onwards, is well known, as are the glosses, commentaries, interpretations, (mystical, erotic, cabbalistic and so on) which still accompany expositions of the poem, whose opening line 'A noir, E blanc, I rouge, U vert, O bleu: voyelles.' sums up all the preoccupations of the age with the phenomenon of 'coloured sounds'. Goethe – in an ambiguous way, it is true – had led the way with his *Harmony of Colours*. Court de Gébelin, with his *Natural history of words or précis of the origin of language and universal grammar* (1776) had given the question a seemingly scientific basis. For Balzac,

405

also (in *Louis Lambert*) ,sound, colour, scent and shape have the same origins'; while – in the *Club des Hachischins* – drunkenness made Gautier hear the sound of colours. It was Charles Gounod who told a pupil to play a 'lilac note' for him; Proust speaks of the orange tint of a syllable, of a redly glowing septet and a white sonata, while Eisenstein said that in *Potemkin* he wrote 'music for the eye', by means of the structure and montage of images.

However, no one went as far as Rimbaud managed to do in a single alexandrine line; the thirteen other lines of 'Voyelles' do no more than illustrate by example the initial proposition. Etiemble, with a real polemist's skill, has devoted forty years of his life and several massive works to 'demythifying' and 'demystifying' the poet, in particular on the subject of this sonnet, which was written in 1871. Carrying his investigations to vast lengths, collecting thousands of notes on the subject, he drew up 'tables of discordance' which showed clearly, it is true, that no one *sees* the colour of vowels in the same way. However, it is not really a case of whether, among 1076 persons interviewed, a majority of them affirm that A is black or E white, or whether Rimbaud's clarion call has any scientific basis (a question about which Rimbaud, according to Verlaine, 'did not give a damn'). This perception of vowels as each linked to a different colour is clearly a subjective concept and there is therefore no need to apply principles of common sense (which are so often *not* applied in other cases) to justify the conflicting evidence of different visual sensibilities. Besides, Etiemble, taking the matter seriously, plays a trump card in reminding us that vowels are not pronounced in the same way in every language; and that in French there are no fewer than twenty-one vowel sounds, whereas graphic notation does not go beyond six letters, of which two, I and Y, denote the same sound.

In composing this sonnet, which is strictly Parnassian in form, Rimbaud is only expressing a poet's idea – which does not mean that it is necessarily implausible or mere balderdash. Why, then, has this idea been so important a part of the poet's legacy? It is, I think, because 'Voyelles' latently and unconsciously reflects the wonderful world of childhood. Everyone remembers finding letters in his soup, and first discovering the alphabet. If intelligence can be defined as the ability to think in abstract terms, one can imagine a child's resistance to the mental feat required in comprehending the Latin alphabet. Which is why teachers have always tried to mitigate the rigours of this abstract idea; and why children, to be able to grasp the idea, have seized on any features which could be linked to the world around them. The demon of analogy thus comes into its own at an early stage: letters are learnt by sympathetic association and with the aid of colours, sounds, gestures and mime. Each letter will be identified with an object, an animal, a human being.

406

407

408

409

410 411 412 413 414 415 416 417 418

419

420

421

422

423

424

425

426

427

428

429

430

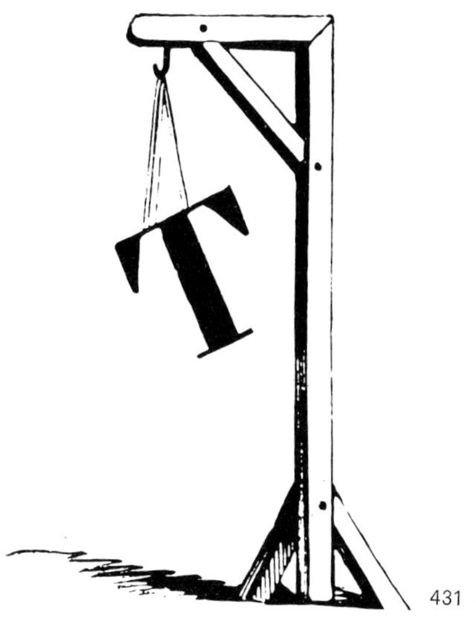
431

Audio-visual methods are thus merely extensions – of a more scientifically accurate and modern kind – of the method of teaching children to read current during the last century, which filled the pages of alphabet books of that time with processions of little personages who were, so to speak, ambassadors for the letters they accompanied.

It was not only these 'little childhood books' referred to by Rimbaud which contained the anthropomorphic figures so popular in England and France. Retail catalogues, German lithographic collections, caricatures, tracts, posters, popular books, wrappers, dioramas and press-out books, children's trinkets and keepsakes, trade signs and trade marks, naive and evocative advertising, all had them, and so did ballad and hymn sheets, almanacs, calendars, comic papers – and magazines such as the *Magasin Pittoresque* and *Punch*. There was also a fashion for picture-puzzles, and instructive pastimes (*joco seria*) were extremely popular, as for instance the countless children's games which were part game and part book and which have helped generations of children to 'learn while playing'.

432

N.Temperate
Torrid
S.Temperate
S.Frigid

A IS an Angel of blushing eighteen:
B is the Ball where the Angel was seen:
C is her Chaperon, who cheated at cards:
D is the Deuxtemps, with Frank of the Guards:
E is her Eye, killing slowly but surely:
F is the Fan, whence it peeped so demurely:
G is the Glove of superlative kid:
H is the Hand which it spitefully hid:
I is the Ice which the fair one demanded:
J is the Juvenile, that dainty who handed:
K is the Kerchief, a rare work of art:
L is the Lace which composed the chief part:
M is the old Maid who watched the chits dance:
N is the Nose she turned up at each glance:
O is the Olga (just then in its prime):
P is the Partner who wouldn't keep time:
Q's the Quadrille, put instead of the Lanciers:
R's the Remonstrances made by the dancers:
S is the Supper where all went in pairs:
T is the Twaddle they talked on the stairs:
U is the Uncle who "thought we'd be goin'":
V is the Voice which his niece replied "No" in:
W is the Waiter, who sat up till eight:
X is his Exit, not rigidly straight:
Y is a Yawning fit caused by the Ball:
Z stands for Zero, or nothing at all.

434

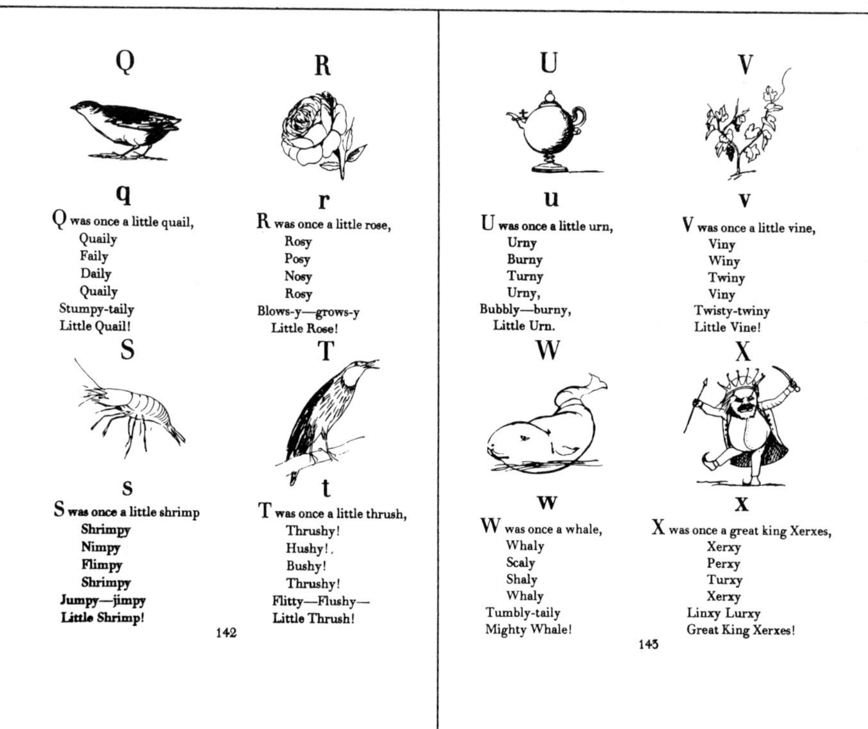
Q
q
Q was once a little quail,
Quaily
Faily
Daily
Quaily
Stumpy-taily
Little Quail!

R
r
R was once a little rose,
Rosy
Posy
Nosy
Rosy
Blows-y—grows-y
Little Rose!

S
s
S was once a little shrimp
Shrimpy
Nimpy
Flimpy
Shrimpy
Jumpy—jimpy
Little Shrimp!

T
t
T was once a little thrush,
Thrushy!
Hushy!
Bushy!
Thrushy!
Flitty—Flushy—
Little Thrush!

142

U
u
U was once a little urn,
Urny
Burny
Turny
Urny,
Bubbly—burny,
Little Urn.

V
v
V was once a little vine,
Viny
Winy
Twiny
Viny
Twisty-twiny
Little Vine!

W
w
W was once a whale,
Whaly
Scaly
Shaly
Whaly
Tumbly-taily
Mighty Whale!

X
x
X was once a great king Xerxes,
Xerxy
Perxy
Turxy
Xerxy
Linxy Lurxy
Great King Xerxes!

143

435

436

It was the fashion for alliteration and skilfully used spacing that led Mallarmé to write *Bibelot aboli d'inanité sonore* and which suggested fantastic etymologies, where imitative music played a leading part, for his *Mots Anglais*. 'Words make love', said André Breton, thinking perhaps of the 'vertiginous word equations' which fill the work of Jean-Pierre Brisset (whose analysis of words led him to the conclusion that man is descended from the frog), or the other makers of verbal magic such as Fargue, Leiris, Desnos, Michaux, and above all, Joyce. All of them, as was Rabelais before them, are the creators of new words and the makers of semantic portmanteaux. Most of them are fascinated by the similarities which abound between objects and the words which describe them. For Claudel 'words have a soul, and in the written word itself can be found more than a kind of conventional algebra. There is a rapport between the graphic sign and that which it represents . . . writing in the west has an intrinsic meaning just as much as does Chinese writing. And the meaning is all the more effective in that while Chinese characters are immobile, ours are mobile'. (A pertinent remark, if one remembers the writing in manuscripts, which is often leaning forwards, the italic letters inherited from the Aldine editions, and letters such as K or R, which one could call 'walking' letters). And Claudel goes on to describe that canto of Dante's *Inferno* in which he 'tells us that those whose punishment is hunger bear clearly on their brows the word *omo* ომო'.

437

439

ABECEDAIRE

440

438

THE SUNDAY FISHERMAN

A FISHERMAN, on angling bent,
One Sabbath morning left his tent.

The Tent, Λ

He took his can, and very quick
He dug his fish-worms with a pick.

The Pick, (— The Worms, ᔕ ᔕ

He thought he'd try for bass and smelt,
And fixed his fish-bag to his belt.

The Belt, ᑌ The Bag, ȣ

In case some fish of size he'd get,
He took along his landing-net.

The Landing-Net, ⁻ᑭ

As fishermen get very dry,
They always have a flask hard by.

The Flask, ⇧

As fishermen get hungry, too,
Of pretzels he procured a few.

The Pretzels, ჯ ჯ ჯ ჯ

Some lines he took along on spools
To teach them to the finny schools.

The Spools, ⊢⊣ ⊢⊣ ⊢⊣

He had some entertaining books
Of highly-tempered Limerick hooks.

The Hooks, J J J

And thus prepared, he got his boat,
And out upon the stream did float.

The Boat, ᗪ

Whene'er the wind began to fail
He used the paddle with the sail.

The Paddle, ⊂⊃

He stopped to fish, among the sedge,
A mile or so below the bridge.

The Bridge, ⊓⊓⊓⊓⊓⊓>

Some bites he straight began to get,
It was the gallinippers bit.

The Gallinippers, ⋈ ⋈ ⋈

One of his lines spun off the reel;
He landed in the boat an eel.

The Eel, ᔕ

Then quickly it began to rain,
But his umbrella was in vain.

The Umbrella, ⊤

Above his head the thunder crashed,
And all around the lightning flashed.

The Lightning, Z

The storm blew, and the boat upset;
The man went down into the wet.

The Upturned Boat ᗝ

And as he sank, his bubbles rose,
Smaller and smaller toward the close.

The Bubbles, O o o ∘

Oh, Sunday fishers, old and young,
You will get drowned, or you'll get hung!

The Gallows, ⊓

A. W. Bellaw.

441

442

443

444

Claudel's interest in what he calls 'western ideograms' seems to have been all the deeper because he was never to learn (he admits it himself) the different Chinese dialects, although he was French consul in the Far East for fifteen years. But before borrowing from Chinese signs, the images and word equations of which one finds traces in his work, he had read the book on ideograms by a Jesuit missionary in Shanghai, Father Wieger, 'on the transition to writing, and on that from image to sign, from the concrete object which they initially represented. For example, man is a pair of legs, a tree is a kind of man with roots and branches. The east is the sun which rises behind a tree, a child, a head, arms and body without legs . . .' Going on to look for a certain figurative representation in the Latin alphabet, Claudel quotes the English words 'pool' and 'moon', which 'make real little landscapes – and what is wilder looking than the word "fool"?' He describes the 'admirable and memorable letter Mm, which stands in the middle of our alphabet like a triumphal arch on its three pillars, or perhaps the letter makes an indented horizon. That of the Moon perhaps, and why not that of death (la Mort)?'

446

448

450

455

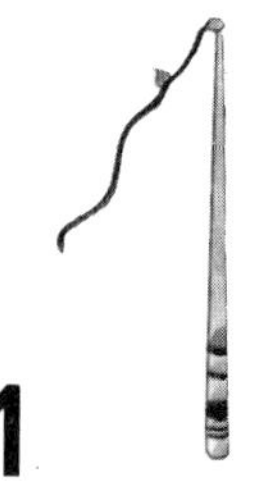

445

— 22 —

abcdefghijklmnopqrstuvxyz

Monsieur O raisonnable pensait que la vie sur l'île des Voyelles avait assez duré, ses habitants en connaissaient les recoins et les ressources et comme ils se ressemblaient à force de se rencontrer devant les mêmes choses ils auraient fini par se détester ou s'ennuyer. La société des Consonnes, plus nombreuses, leur ouvrait un champ de plus grandes activités. Madame A regrettait le passé qu'elle avait facilement régenté mais elle finit par accorder : "Si tu crois qu'il vaut

451

here they are set to
heir Alphabet. And
they had stared
t their books for a
while, *what* do you
happened? Why,
big letters came
to them on legs,
's and arms

447

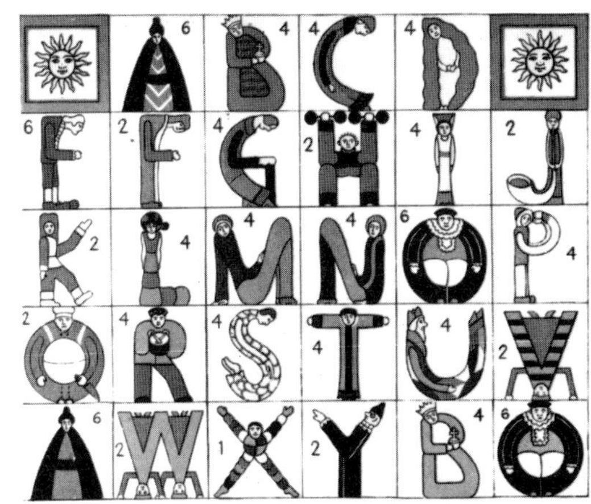

452

449

— 24 —

LE DÉFILÉ

Pour célébrer le mémorable événement qui changeait la face des choses, le lendemain, à l'unanimité, fut choisi comme fête nationale. Les boutiques mirent leurs volets, les écoles fermèrent leurs portes et si le soir on dansa sur les places et aux coins des rues, dans la matinée les Lettres, Voyelles et Consonnes réunies, défilèrent musique en tête à travers la Ville pavoisée dans un ordre depuis ce jour définitif et qu'il vous faut connaître :

A B C D E F G H I J K L M
N O P Q R S T U V W X Y Z

et sur leur passage tout le monde criait à pleins poumons : "Vive l'Alphabet !"

453

456

454

458

459

One can compare these symbols with the medieval archetypes we have discussed already, and with the symbolical names Samuel Beckett chooses, in our own time, for his characters. As Pierre Dommergues says, Molloy and Murphy begin with the same initial as 'man' in English or 'mort' in French, and if reversed to the opposite of this letter, W (Watt, Worm, Winnie) the M of 'myself' is united to the W of 'we'. Cleverly exploited coincidences, one could say, but which show once again the frequency of such coincidences, if they are such, in literature. It is only fair to add that Claudel did not intend that 'the reader should regard his work as anything other than amusement for a rainy day.' The poet continues: 'I know only too well the objections philologians could raise. Their arguments would be even more crushing as regards the symbolical value of written signs than that of phonetic signs. And yet, no proof would convince a poet that there is no rapport between the sound and the meaning of a word, for if there were none, he might as well give up his trade straight away. And is it really so absurd to believe that the alphabet is the epitome and image of all acts, all gestures, all attitudes, and in consequence, all feelings of humanity in the midst of the vast creation which surrounds us?' [One can see here the common ground between the views of Hugo and Claudel, and also what such a common denominator must signify.] 'Should one believe that between phonetic movement and written sign, between expression and that which is expressed, throughout linguistic history, the rapport is purely arbitrary? – or, on the other hand that all words are made up of an unconscious collaboration of eye and voice with the object, and that the hand draws while the mouth silently remembers? There are many indications that the latter case is true. For example, is not each vowel the portrait of the mouth which pronounces it? In the case of o this is self-evident, as it is also for u, which is made of two lips thrusting forwards; is it not just as clear in the case of a, which is an enlarged, modified o, underlined by a lateral line like a pointing finger, or e, which is an opening reduced to a half, the lower lip drawn back, or i which is the image of a parted mouth with the dot of the i between the teeth like the tip of the tongue?'

460/464

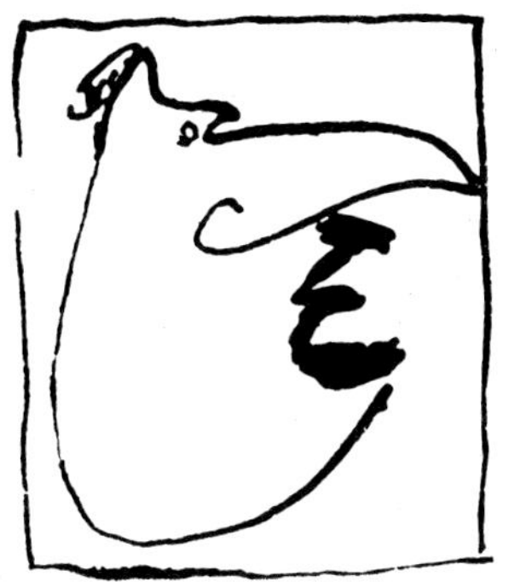

465

466

467

468

469

470

471

Roberts Pierre ist nuntod
schönd den frieden uns
O Gott
dieses wünsch ich der ganze welt
und dir handlung eingefürt

472

TO SMOKERS

473

74

475

476

If we look at a *Children's Almanac* for 1886, in the 'amusing
266/269 grammar lesson' there is a paragraph on vowels. 'Look at all these people, one who is in raptures (a), another who cries out (e), a third who laughs (i), a fourth who is trying to make his horse go (u), and finally one who is trying to stop his horse (o): they just open their mouths in a certain way and make a sound; neither teeth nor tongue are necessary: a, e, i, o, u, come forth of their own accord.' The author of this original teaching method then goes on to explain 'the form and movement of each consonant' and to show us in 'a great procession' these nineteen characters.

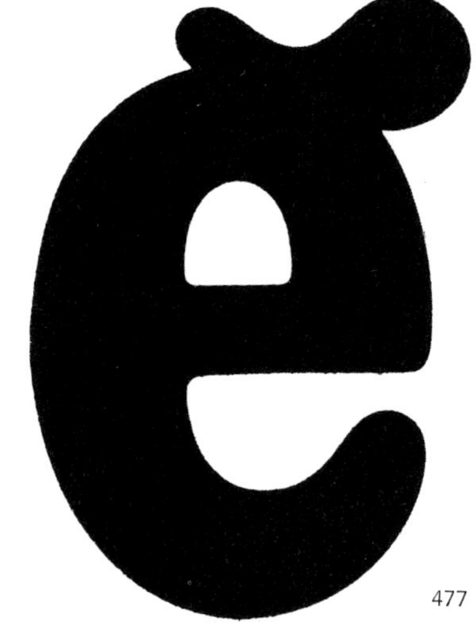

477

A disciple of Mallarmé, René Ghil, published in 1886 a *Traité du Verbe* which the poet honoured with a noteworthy foreword, which contains several famous phrases ('I say: a flower'), collected later under the title *Divagations (Ramblings)*. Saluting 'the accursed poet Arthur Rimbaud, inventor of the colour of vowels' and at the same time Paul Verlaine, 'master of nuances', René Ghil set out to integrate coloured *hearing* with his ambitious 'verbal orchestration'. He claimed that 'if a sound can be translated into colour, colour can be translated into sound, and so into the tone of an instrument'. For Ghil, harps are white, violins blue, the brass instruments red, flutes yellow, organs black, with their 'plangent' tones (a verbal inspiration of the kind which Lewis Carroll uses in 'Jabberwocky'. All the instruments of the orchestra can thus be linked to vowels and consonants (and even to what Ghil ingenuously calls 'diphtongues') by their individual tones and in accordance with the suggestive powers of 'vocal harmonies'.

A precursor of René Ghil, De Piis, who lived at the end of the eighteenth century, devoted a whole poem to 'imitative harmony'. Each letter has its own little prosodic and imitative

478

479

480

481

482

483

484

485

couplet: 'B, babbled by a weakly baby; R approaches rolling; M amuses itself in moaning and meets death meekly; N flees to the back of my nose with a nasal tune; with Xi, X gets excited in a trice.' An interesting detail is that F, which 'fans fire, flame and fumes' is rather reminiscent of Racine's line: Pour qui sont ces serpents qui sifflent sur nos têtes . . .' (For whom sound these serpents which hiss round our heads . . .)

Claudel found de Piis' verses 'remarkable' and was grateful to him for having laid stress on the consonants, which are essential elements of speech and give to a word its 'energy, shape, movement, while vowels represent the purely musical element'. In semantic writing where only consonants are noted and form the framework of the phrase, the absent vowels play a minor role. In Islamic writing, however, they are indicated by means of accents of a flowing shape, which explains the name for vowel in Arabic: *haraka*, movement.

Yet although the suppression of vowels is a part of certain psychological perception tests, and although their absence does not make a written text altogether incomprehensible, certain of them still play a very important role (just because of their frequency in any given language). In the sixteenth century, a bald Benedictine monk called Hucbald dedicated to his ancestor Charles the Bald a *Eulogy on Baldness (calvitie)*, in which each word begins with the letter c. In the following century, Johannes Placentius repeated this feat with the letter p, in *Pugna Porcorum.* In 1788, Gottlob Burmann composed thirty poems in which the letter r was absent, while Gregorio Leti delivered a whole speech without using this same letter. In France, in 1853, Jacques Arago published his *Journey Round the World Without the Letter A.* Such philological fantasies were considered childish by de Quincey, who compared them to a hopping race. Lope de Vega, however, did not consider himself above such exercises, as in five of his stories he omits one vowel in each.

Edgar Allan Poe, in *X-ing a Paragrab* gives a good example of the comic effects this kind of elision can create. In a town in the United States, the editors of two daily papers were waging a merciless war. One accused the other of abusing the vowel O, and of being incapable of writing a single work without it. Far from trying to prove the contrary, the editor in question was adamant that he would not change his style one iota and published as a counterblast a paragraph in which 'this beautiful vowel–the emblem of Eternity', is given pride of place: *'So ho, John! how now? Told you so, you know.'* etc. But when he came to set the text, the printer found to his horror that one of their rivals had traitorously stolen all the O's, both upper and lower case, so that there wasn't one in the whole works. As it is customary for a printer to set an X instead of a missing letter, the compositor set about the paragraph accordingly, and the following morning the readers of the paper found to their amazement an editorial column which began: *'Sx hx, Jxhn, hxw nxw? Txld yxu sx, yxu knxw. Dxn't crxw, anxther time, befxre yxu're xut xf the wxxds. Dxes yxur mxther knxw yxu're xut? Xh, nx, nx! – sx gx hxme at xnce, nxw, Jxhn, tx yxur xdixus xld wxxds . . . . .'*

Alfred Jarry was another designer of 'vowels' – creating
460/464 some for a 'Père Ubu' alphabet. With the collaboration of the painter Bonnard, he gave them the characteristics of his hero. A for hunger (Père Ubu's belly), E for his fierceness (his jaw), I for joy, O for admiration (the navel) and U for grief (Père Ubu's tears). Very reminiscent of the story of the Englishman who married 'for £ove'.

Nor is there any lack of authors who have assimilated letters to living creatures or to objects. In his *L'Enchanteur Pourrissant*, Apollinaire tells how: 'He who came to make a sacrifice desired to be killed instead of his victim. His belly was cut open. I saw there four Is, four Os four Ds'. And, while we are on the subject of vowels, need I add that the name of Jehovah – in the archaic spelling *IEOUA* – contains them all? 'I am Alpha and Omega . . . saith the Lord', writes St John – the beginning and the end. Then too, Egyptian magic, certain Gnostic texts, the Sefirots of the *Zohar*, Rosicrucian rites and those of Freemasonry, all make use, in different ways, of the incantatory power of letters – even sometimes attributing to them the ability to create life. One episode of the *Zohar*, for example, recounts how two thousand years before the world was created, when letters were still unknown, the Saint 'beheld them and rejoiced. When he wished to create the world, all the letters, but in inverse order, came and presented themselves to him.' The Saint assigned to each of them its definitive place in the alphabet, according to the symbolism of the words formed from the initial letter (Death, Untruth, Sin etc).

486

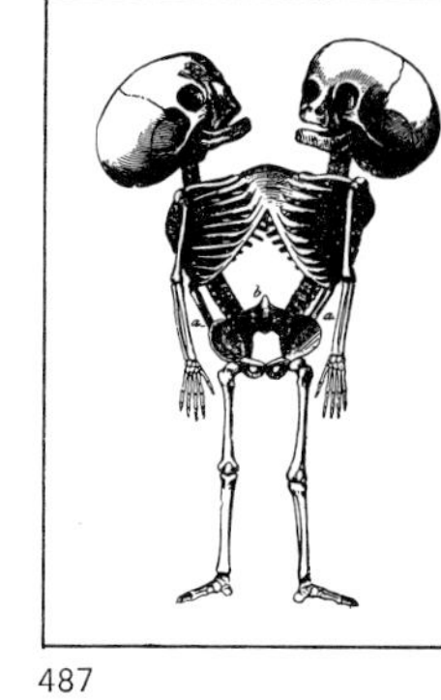

487

490

491

489

492

493

494

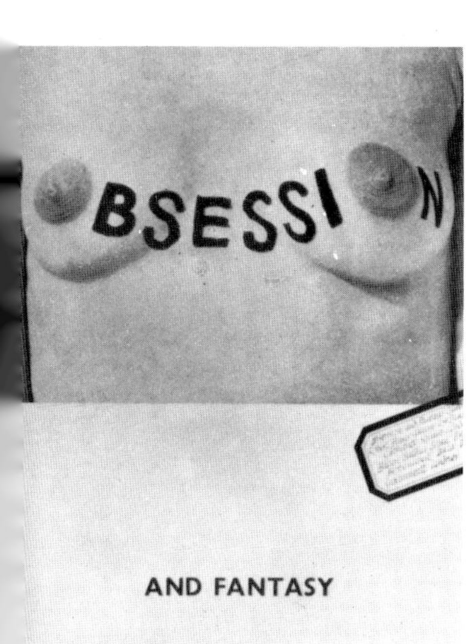

495

496

500

502

503

504

FROID

501

50

50

509

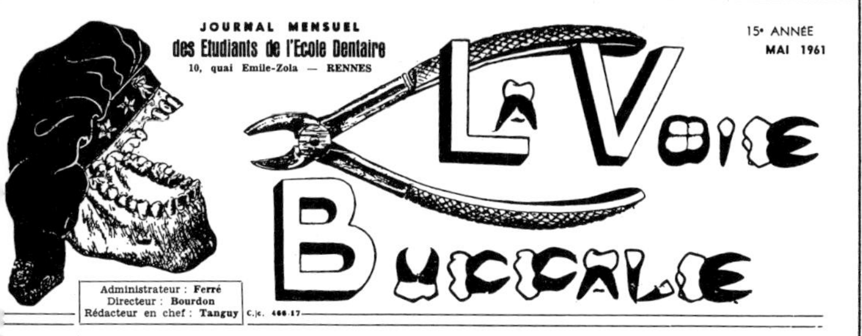

JOURNAL MENSUEL
des Etudiants de l'Ecole Dentaire
10, quai Emile-Zola — RENNES
15e ANNÉE
MAI 1961
LA VOIE
BUCCALE
Administrateur : Ferré
Directeur : Bourdon
Rédacteur en chef : Tanguy

497

Tél. 45

- *FUSILS :* vendus à la conformation du tireur et essayés sur pigeons d'argile SANS SUPPLÉMENT DE PRIX.
- *CARTOUCHES :* longue portée, haut rendement. Prix minimum, TARIF DEGRESSIF.
- *TIR AUX PIGEONS :* nouvelles installations « CHASSE ».

498

499

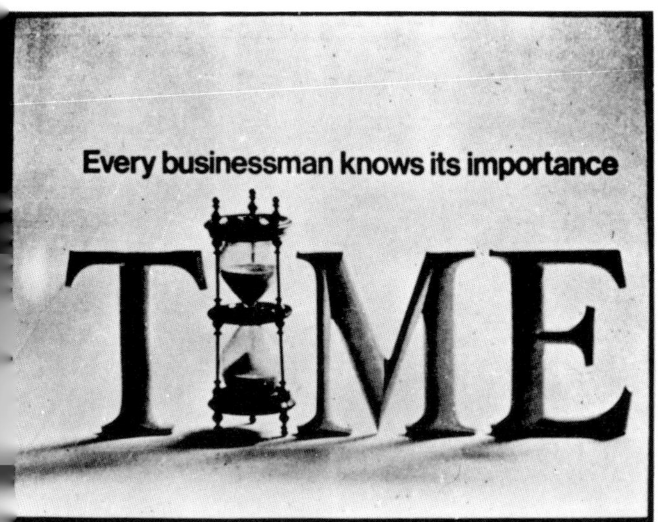

506

507

0

BONDISSEZ
Esso
EXTRA SUPERCARBURANT
sur la route des vacances
...avec un Tigre dans votre moteur!

511

512

513

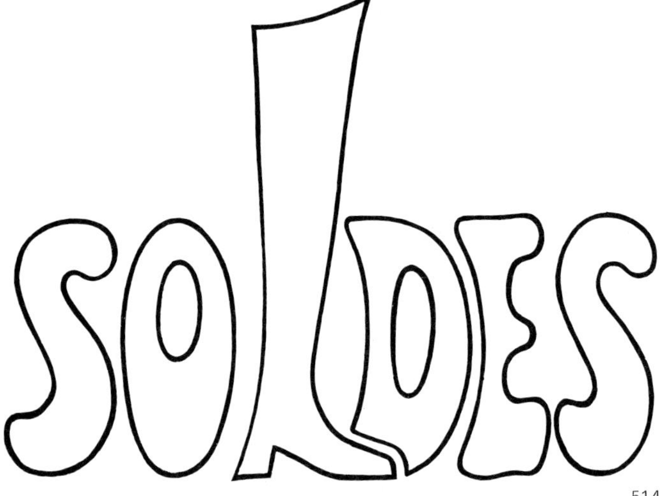

514

orientation professionnelle

515

516

bonheur conjugal

517

L'ENRAGÉ

518

TRIGANO

519

520

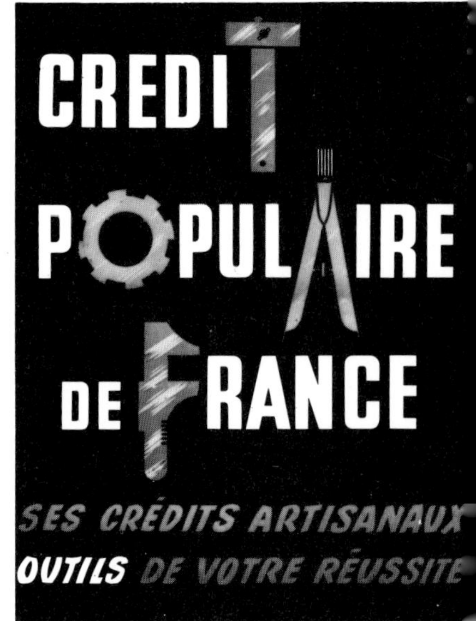

CREDIT
POPULAIRE
DE FRANCE
SES CRÉDITS ARTISANAUX
OUTILS DE VOTRE RÉUSSITE

521

CONFORT DOUX

OU CONFORT SOUPLE

OU CONFORT FERME

OU CONFORT TRES FERME

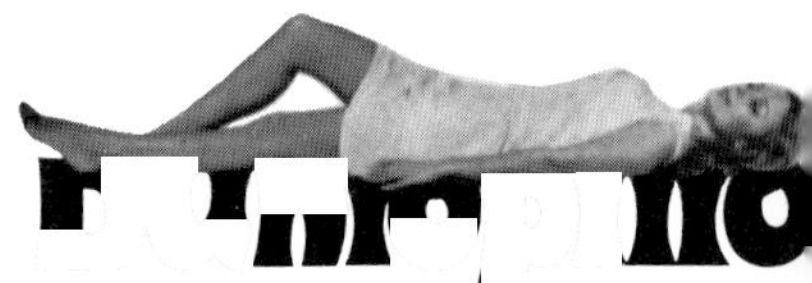

52

523

524

PARIS
UMMER TIMETABLE
19 MARCH - 28 OCTOBER, 1967

525

526

527

528

529

530

531

CIRAGE

532

offrez lui un Parapluie

533

534

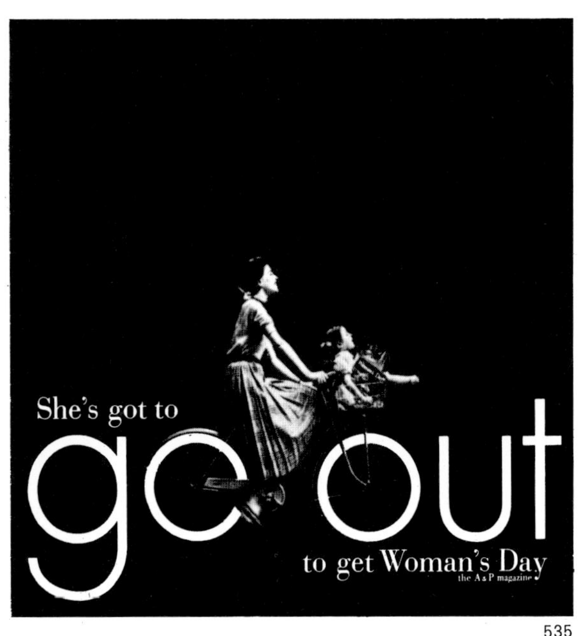

535

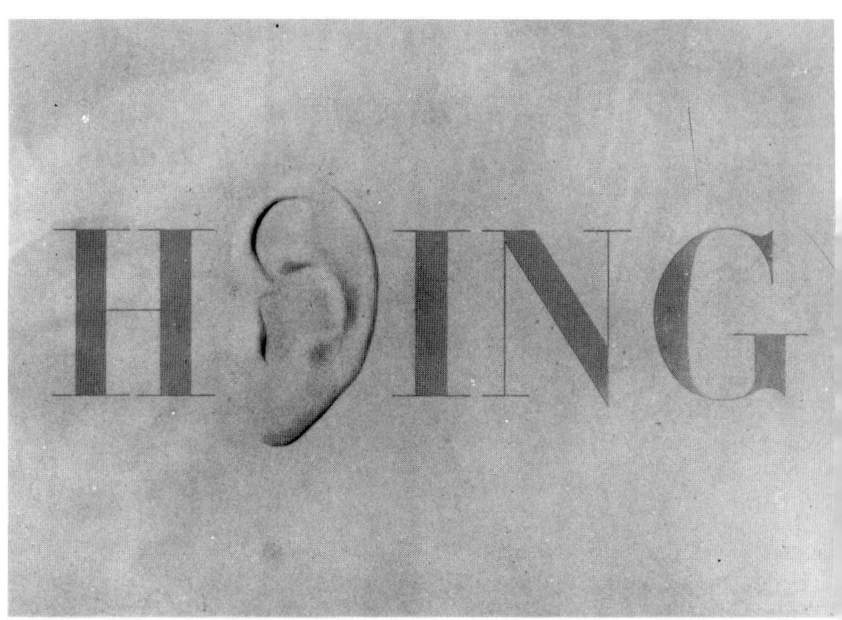

536

R SY

537

c eur

538

539

540

541

542

543

544

545

546

LES RUSSES ARRIVENT

547

CRICKET

548

SALE!

549

550

551

552

ΗΕΛΛΈΝΙΣΜΕΣ

A|N|A|L|Y|S|E L|O|G|I|Q|U|E

le côté subjectif

[illegible]

IÇNORANCE

ITALIANISMES

ANGLI CISMES

553

554

557

558

559

56

562

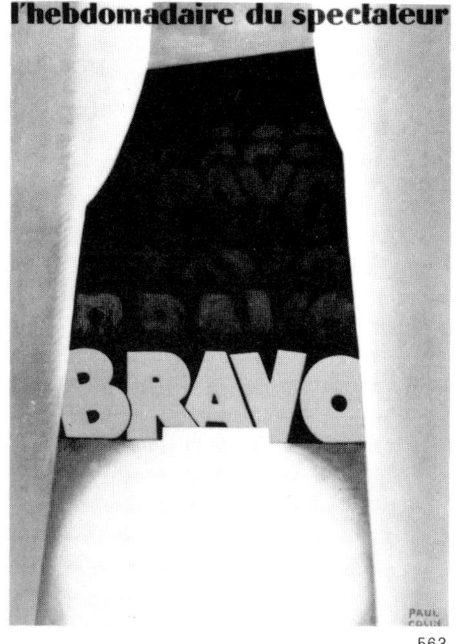

563

56

Psst! heu! AH! OH!
hum! ah! OUF! EH! tiens!
oh! PEUH! pouah! OUIE! ou!
AIE! eh! hein! heu! pfuitt!
TIENS! eh! peuh! oh! heu! BON!

555

556

561

565

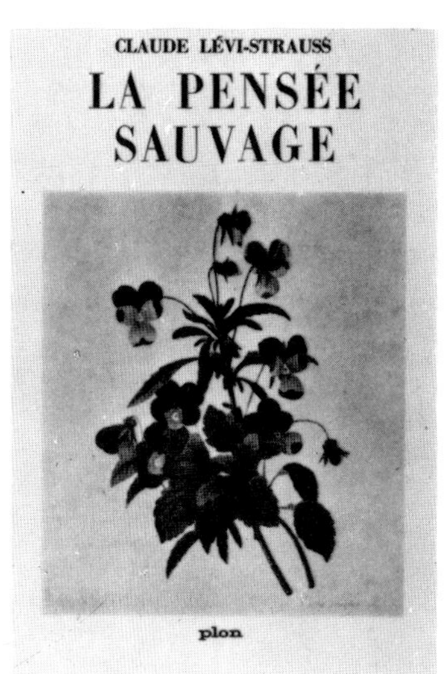

566

567

MOTHER & CHILD

568

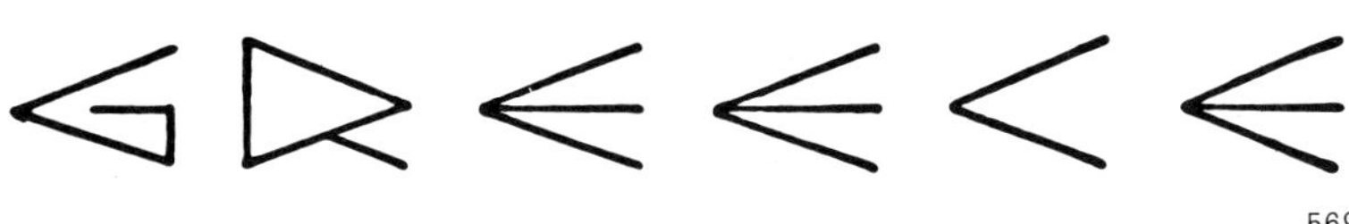

569

570

572

571

573

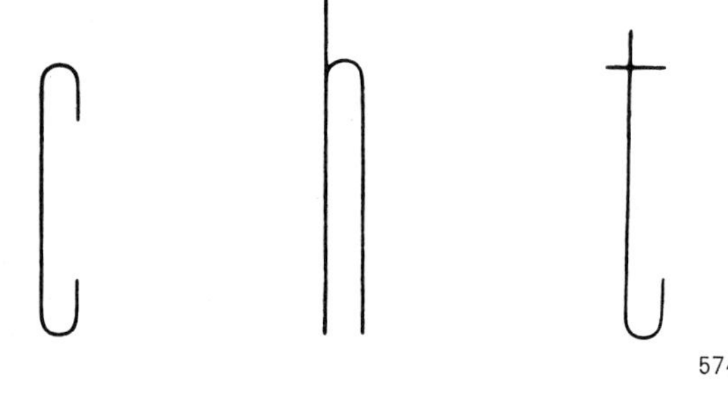

574

576

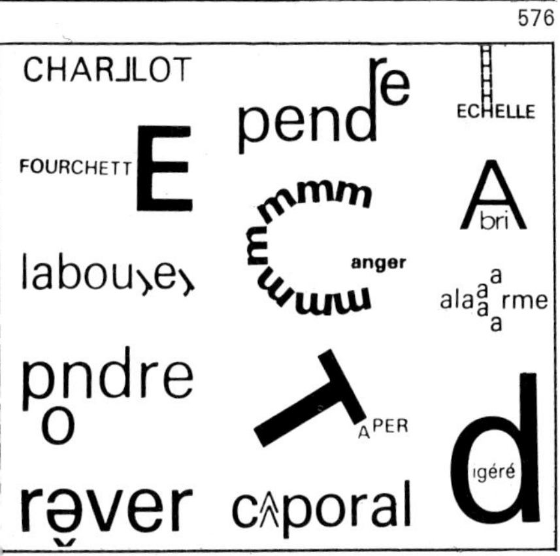

577

578

addding

subtrcting

multimultiplying

div id ing

579

ero
1ne
2wo
3hree
4our
5ive
6ix
7even
8ight
9ine
10en

580

In nursery rhymes also, one finds frequent examples of animated letters. Oliver Goldsmith, who made a collection of these rhymes in the eighteenth century, composed the following 'Learned Song':

Here's A, B and C,
D, E, F, and G,
H, I, K, L, M, N, O, P, Q,
R, S, T, and U,
W, X, Y, and Z.
And here's the child's dad,
Who is sagacious and discerning,
And knows this is the fount of learning.

To it he added the following note: 'This is the most learned ditty in the world: for indeed there is no song can be made without the aid of this, it being the gamut and groundwork of them all.'

Edward Lear, author of the *Book of Nonsense*, painter and
musician, and famous limerick writer, created some alphabets 435
in which each letter is identified with the first letter of an
animal's name. This tradition of 'nonsense verse' – which
one can trace back to Shakespeare and also to French poets of
the Middle Ages – and the taste for limericks (often risqué) are
both still very popular in Britain, and a whole class of children's
literature of the 'A is for Anything' type can be found. Cut-out 434 441/443
sheets, riddles in the form of rebuses, instructional toys,
chromolithography, which were all popular in England at the
end of the last century, made use of the same techniques and
created their own popular imagery, which was often based
on the work of Edward Lear and Lewis Carroll. The 'Bessy and
Bobby' alphabet is so full of these characteristics and also of 446/450
fantasy, that it seems to belong to the same unique world. The
two children, who live in a nursery in the Land of Happiness,
are trying to decipher the symbols in their alphabet book, when,
suddenly looking up, they see before them the letters A, B,

and C in person – that is to say, with a head, two arms and two legs – and accompanied by a Question Mark who introduces them to the other letters. They then take part in a great parade, which announces from sixty years away the passing of
451/454 *Once upon a Time*, and a similar scene celebrates the signature of a treaty between the vowels and the consonants, from which will spring a single people, the Letters. One expects to see the White Rabbit suddenly appear on a page, hurrying along out of breath, or some other character from *Alice*. True, in this picture book the letters have faces which resemble those of
457 rather monstrous beings, halfway between gnomes and fools or Jokers. But in Lewis Carroll's kingdom also, where smiles float in the air, it is the members of a pack of cards disguised as gardeners (and later changed into bushes) whom Alice meets painting white roses red. The contemporary film cartoon creates a world which is no less fabulous. Space, time, and weight are abolished. Carried along by the music, a picture is multiplied to create movement. Credit titles, publicity films and short animated strips – give us marvellous surrealist views of the world of objects and forms. But they also have in common the disadvantage of mechanizing invention and sometimes rendering the fantastic banal. Some of the pioneer animators with the help of a technique which was still feeling its way, displayed a no less surprising poetic audacity. Those shots of Felix the Cat for instance being surprised to find the window shut, and using the exclamation mark which indicated his surprise to lever open the window. Or in 1956, a masterpiece of this kind, which was made by the Canadian director Norman MacLaren – *Rythmetic*. In this world of numbers which gives a foretaste of the computer, one can see among other tricks of animation, the number 5 scratch its back with its transverse bar. At such moments MacLaren shows an imaginative flair which is akin to that of childhood (when, for example, a human profile is given to 6-4-2), and resembles Grandville, who dressed musical notes as dancers, Turkish
587/594 warriors, or sextons in the animated scores which are not so impossible to play as one might think, and which the readers of the *Magasin Pittoresque* asked for again and again.

581

These transferences of identity are made by means of an association of ideas or by a chance resemblance, the reason for which may sometimes remain hidden. Etymological origin, alliteration or assonance, phonetic or visual similarity, may all in one way or another, play a part, which, associated with reasoning by analogy, leads to a mutation of personality, the transition from one state to another (from concrete to abstract, or vice versa), typified by a mostly invariable outward relationship. The permutation thus works in the manner of a syllogism and pre-supposes (if this does not seem too absurd) the existence of the relationship.

58

584

585

583

586

VALSE.

Quatre cavaliers, en grande tenue de bal, invitent des dames pour la valse. — Les groupes s'élancent dans la salle. — Une dame tombe, au grand effroi de son valseur. — Les autres groupes passent en tournoyant. — La dame et son maladroit cavalier reprennent le pas de valse. — Plus loin, une banquette se brise sous le poids de trois personnes. — Une dame est légèrement blessée au genou; effroi et empressement du valseur. — Une mouche énorme (dièze), attirée par les lumières, s'est introduite dans la salle : une dame veut la chasser avec son mouchoir, et est près de se trouver mal; son cavalier cherche à la rassurer, et lui présente une chaise (bécarre). — La valse continue avec plus d'entraînement. — On s'assied : un cavalier essuie son front; une dame essoufflée s'appuie sur son coude. 587

MARCHE MILITAIRE ET ORIENTALE.

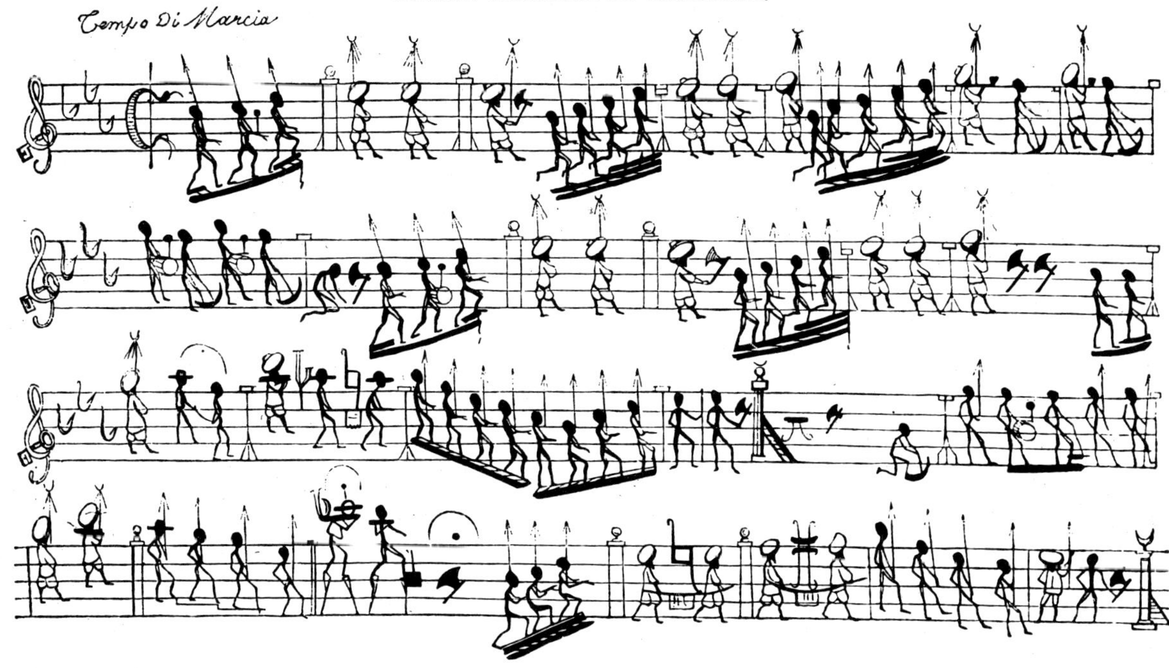

Marche de Turcs et de noirs. — Les Turcs s'avancent lentement et gravement, portant des étendards ou des haches (soupirs). — Les
negres montent ou descendent vivement les degrés, ceux-ci avec de grosses caisses et différents instruments de musique, ceux-là
avec des piques ou javelots. — On voit un prisonnier agenouillé; la hache se lève sur lui : un autre est conduit enchaîné. — On 588
porte sur des brancards du butin ou des présents (bémols, dièzes, bécarres).

MUSIQUE RELIGIEUSE.

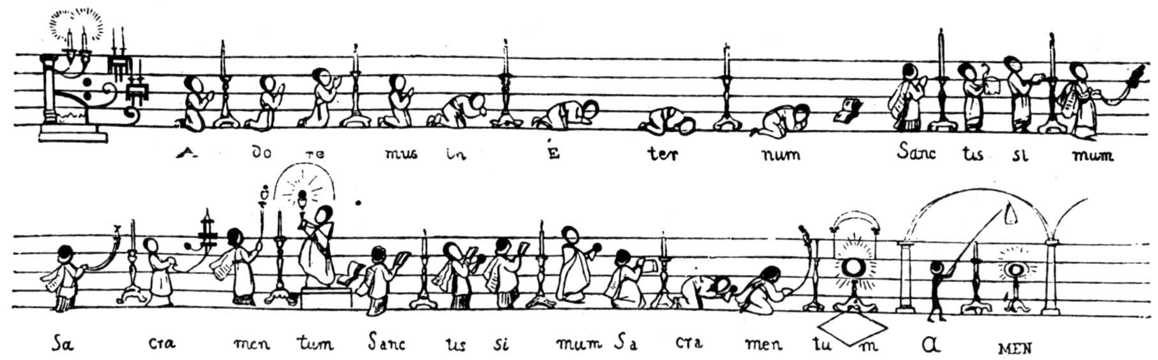

Les enfants de chœur s'agenouillent, se prosternent, chantent, encensent. — Le prêtre lève le calice (point d'orgue). — Autres
chants; autre adoration. — Le sacristain éteint les cierges. 589

BARCAROLLE.

Des pêcheurs (noirs) disent adieu à leurs femmes, à leurs sœurs; une femme confie son enfant à son mari. — Le temps est beau; les barques glissent mollement sous de vastes arches (signes pour lier les notes). — Mais le temps change: les nuages couvrent le ciel, la mer devient houleuse; les barques s'abaissent et s'élèvent avec les vagues; un homme tombe à l'eau... hélas! — Les ancres sont inutiles. — L'orage paraît se calmer. — Un pêcheur a sauvé l'enfant; il donne un coup de trompe (point d'orgue). — Mais le vent recommence à souffler avec violence. — Les pêcheurs se désespèrent, lèvent les bras vers le ciel. — La tempête redouble ses fureurs : une barque chavire; six pêcheurs sont engloutis; leurs corps flottent inanimés. — Des mouettes (soupirs) rasent la mer.
— Quelques barques, guidées par le phare, se hâtent de rentrer au port. — La mère éplorée attendait sur le rivage; elle reçoit 590
son enfant dans ses bras.

RONDE. TARENTELLE.

Ronde de noirs et de noires. — Equilibristes, grimaces, pantomime animée. — Redoubler de vitesse à chaque retour du refrain. — 591
Les dièzes sont figurés par des araignées ou tarentules.

GALOP DE MASQUES.

Une magicienne. — Pierrette avec une lanterne (dièze). — Mouvement précipité. — Danse furieuse. — Les masques se heurtent,
tombent, et roulent tous pêle-mêle sur la tête. 592

Marche héroïque. — Ce premier morceau est en mi majeur : quatre dièzes (carquois) à la clef (bannière). — C'est un presto ple de fougue. — L'action commence par une vive attaque. — Un chef entraîne ses soldats vers un pont. — Choc violent sur le por — Cliquetis; défense vigoureuse; un guerrier est percé de part en part. — Seconde attaque du pont. — Le grand chef harang ses soldats (point d'orgue). — A sa voix, les braves se précipitent sur leurs ennemis qui fuient éperdus, quelques uns jettent leu armes et invoquent le secours du ciel. — Un guerrier est blessé, comme Achille, au talon. — Le porte-étendard veut s'opposer la fuite de ses compagnons. — Derniers efforts pour reprendre le pont. Il est attaqué et défendu avec une fureur égale. — Un d chefs et son jeune fils sont tués et noyés au pied du fort, qui lance incessamment des obus (points d'orgue). — La victoire se chèrement achetée

593

Pastorale en ré majeur : deux doubles dièzes (corbeaux) à la clef (boa). — A trois temps. — La scène se passe dans une colo anglaise. — Une jeune fille veut quitter son hameau pour aller se mettre en service à la ville. *Un ministre cherche à la détourn de ce projet.* — Le voyage est long : il faut traverser une forêt pleine de dangers. Que va-t-elle chercher au loin? le bonheu il est au village aussi bien qu'à la ville. Elle se mariera; elle sera heureuse épouse, heureuse mère. Pour frapper son esp par un exemple, il lui montre *un jeune berger qui embrasse la main de sa fiancée, jeune bergère négresse.* — Mais la jeu fille ne tient compte des conseils du ministre; un matin elle part. Dans la forêt, *la fatigue, la fraîcheur, l'invitent à se r poser sous un sycomore. Des nègres marrons, avertis de son passage, s'approchent d'elle pour la voler. Elle est délivrée par nègre affranchi accompagné d'un chien.* Elle retourne au hameau, et, par reconnaissance, *elle donne sa main à embrasser son libérateur; une négresse porte plainte au ministre.* Dans la crainte d'une réprimande, la jeune fille s'éloigne de nouveau. Ce fois, pendant son sommeil, *les nègres marrons lui volent sa bourse* (bémol), sa seule fortune, et la maltraitent. *Ses cris attire son père et sa mère* qui étaient à sa recherche... son vieux père furieux (point d'orgue)!... sa vieille mère désolée qui suit de l à grand' peine et se désespère! Ils ramènent leur fille au village. La pauvre enfant n'a plus de dot. *Les jeunes gens la saluent goguenardant, et s'éloignent d'elle. Elle pleure amèrement sa faute. Ses compagnes elles-mêmes lui chantent des refrains ra leurs. Elle va implorer le pardon du ministre et la grâce du ciel.*

Nota. Entre le troisième et le quatrième arbre, les deux noirs-*noires* devraient être des croches. Les deux prétendus qui salu et raillent la jeune fille doivent être deux croches simples.

594

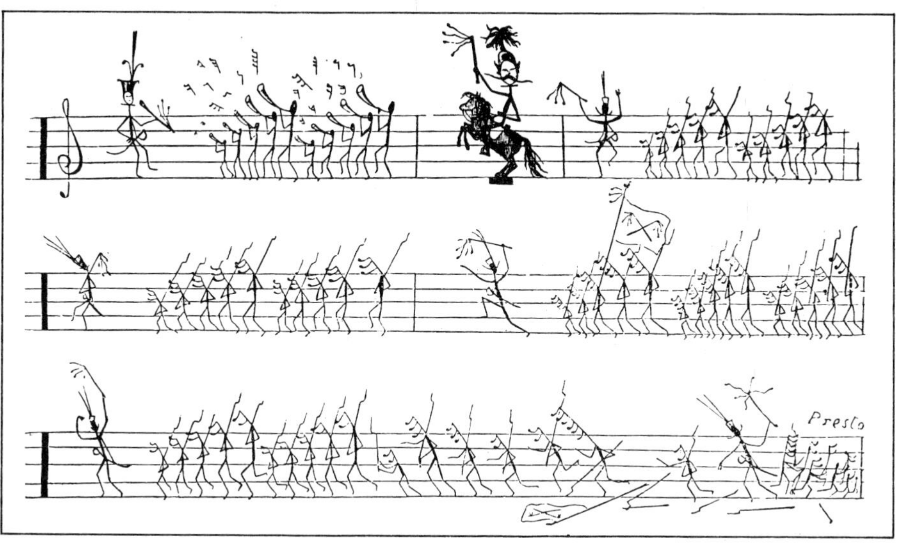

595

596

Fables, parables and myths all draw on these metamorphoses and these dynamic changes, but poetic incantation, in its choice of timbre and colour, returns to them again and again – as do maxims, aphorisms and proverbs. The art of music, made up of suggestion, in which sound patterns, rhythm, melody and harmony together form an infinite variety of combinations, abounds in metaphors; these are sometimes expressed in the title, as in numerous pieces which refer to the name of a composer – such as *Variations on the name Abbeg* by Schumann (a part of *Carnival* is called 'dancing letters'!), Liszt's *Minuet on the name of Haydn* and Ravel's *Berceuse on the name of Fauré*; or, in the realm of popular music, *The Bridge on the River Kwai* played by an orchestra of bamboos. After Bach, German notation, now common to the English-speaking world, used the letters of the alphabet, from which are also derived the clefs (soprano, bass, etc.), ornamented by the Gothic script of the letter G (sol) 𝄞 in the G clef 𝄞 and the letter C (do) in the C clef 𝄡 in plainsong.

597

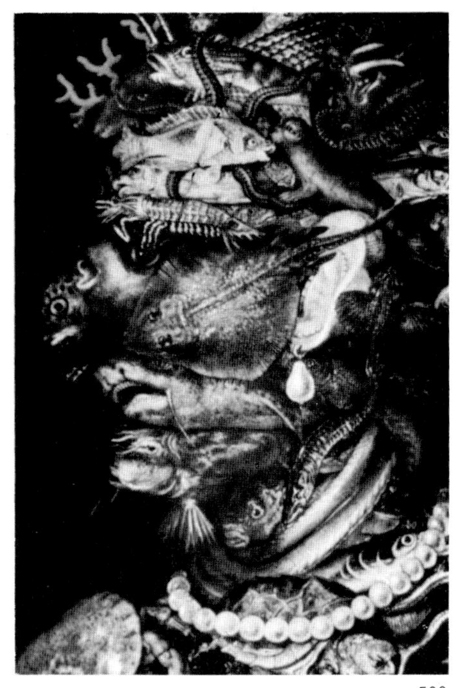

599

600

60

603

60

598

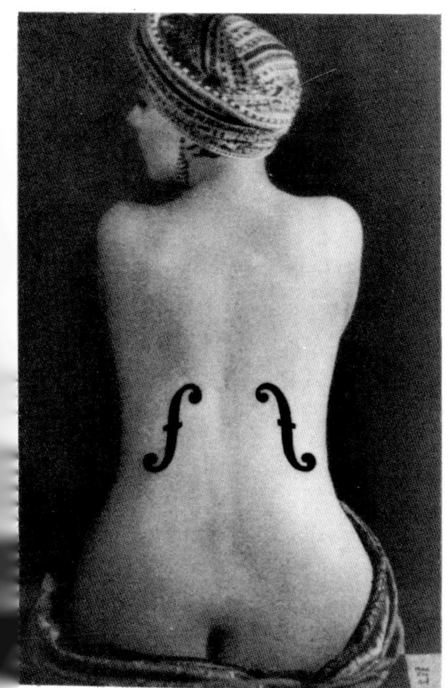

602

605

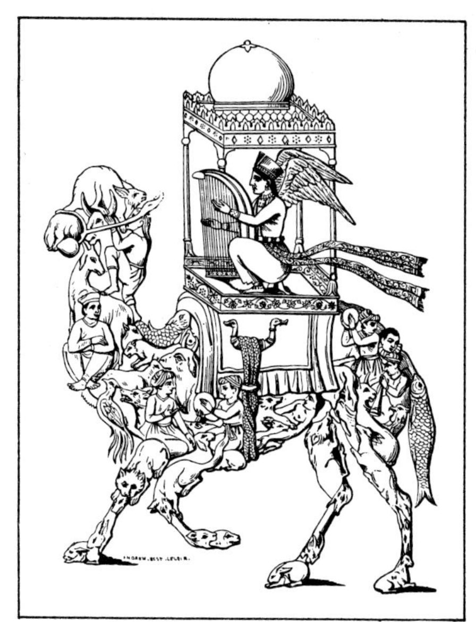

606

607

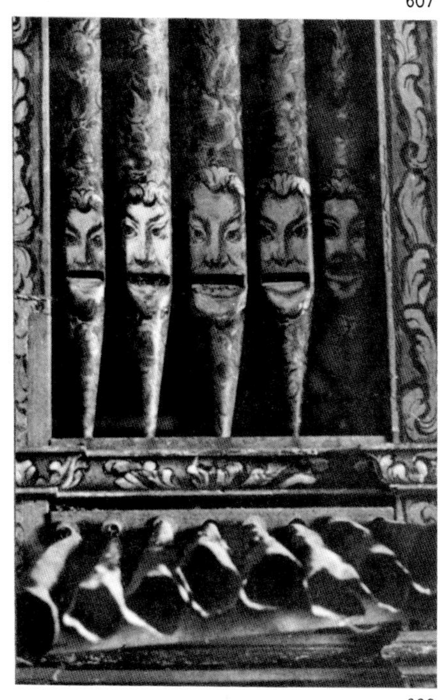

608

But it is naturally in the plastic arts that this shift of identity,
these suggested analogies, take their sharpest outlines. One
thinks for instance of the paintings of Bosch and Breughel in
which humans, animals and objects undergo incessant anato-
mical changes, or Jacques Callot's eye, perched on top of a
column of flesh and dominating the landscape (like the eyes for
heads in a theatre audience of Grandville's), or the portraits
599 by Arcimboldo made of fruit, vegetables, flowers or fish, shells,
shellfish – imaginative excesses which make some surrealist
inventions look feeble by contrast. In the sixteenth century
Flemish and Italian engravers designed allegories of trades
which, by their arrangement and superimposition of objects,
attributes and costume, identified at once the person represented. In the following century, Nicolas de Larmasin popularized
this fashion in France, showing the *Clothes of the Water-
Carrier, the Pastrycook, the Maker of Playing Cards*, and others.
Then it was the turn of monuments and architectural styles:
human faces and bodies could easily be shaped according to
603 the architectural whims of engravers as in figures *à la grecque*,
which followed the fashion for antiquity. In England, Cruick-
shank deliberately made his piles of objects in the shape of
people satirical, and there was everywhere a fashion for
604 peopled landscapes, in which rocks, foliage, ruins, valleys
besiege and confuse the eye and present glimpses of a profile,
a sleeping head, even several faces at once. The subjects of
these designs were usually sovereigns or politicians, being
destined either for their secret admirers or for a more satirical
purpose; the transformation of King Louis-Philippe's face
into a pear was used countless times in the French press, and
at the beginning of the same century Napoleon was trans-
600 formed into a ogre with an eagle on his head for the benefit

609

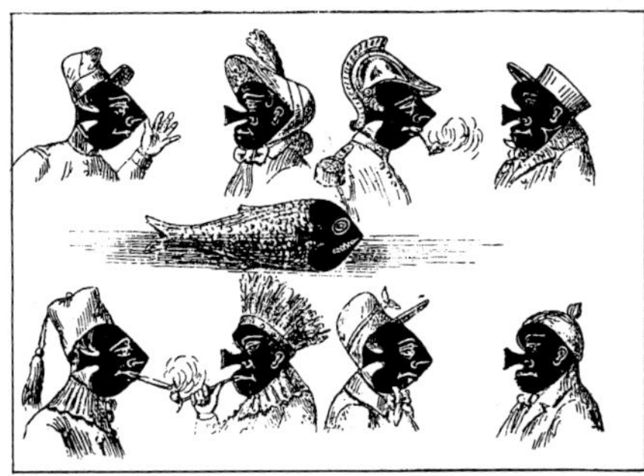
610

611

612

613

of the English public. It was in England too that Bunbury made a speciality of scenes made up of geometrical shapes, thus using the German pre-cubist ideas of a Bracelli. In German-speaking countries, representations of animals and objects
in the form of pieces of wood or foliage, which were popular 598
in the seventeenth century, seem to typify that calligraphic art which follows its own brilliantly inventive course on the borderline between typography and engraving, as for example in *New Examples of Writing of Universal Beauty*, published in France by Etienne de Blégny.

The most original work, however, remains that of Grandville. Endowed with imagination and a graphic fantasy raised lithography and wood-cuts to a new height which (although they were sorely tried by the growing demands of newspapers and the public), Grandville found, both in the world around him and in fiction, the right subjects to inspire
his enthusiasm. In his *Metamorphoses du jour*, because of 585
political censorship, he travestied as every kind of animal, politicians, magistrates, businessmen and shop keepers. He was thus carrying on the tradition of La Fontaine (whose work he illustrated) and Swift.

In *Les Fleurs Animées* he transformed most of the popular 581
flowers into romantic heroines; delicate, quivering peach blossom, mayflowers frightened by the gardener's secateurs, forget-me-nots and marigolds, all showing in the language of flowers a suitably feminine grace and modesty, a romantic pallor and melancholy. (Edmond Rostand, for his part, showed courtyard animals in *Chantecler*; a later symbolical work, *L'Oiseau Bleu*, Maeterlinck's fairytale, showed water, fire, bread, sugar and other objects which are all part of our daily happiness, and also vices and virtues, in the guise of
living people.) It is in *Un Autre Monde* that Grandville's 584
gifts can best be seen. The sub-title of the book, which has at least twenty descriptive nouns (transformations, visions, incarnations etc.) is in itself indicative of a splendid feast.

It may have been that fantasies from this other world haunted Grandville ceaselessly during his brief life, which ended in a mental home. The predecessor of Robida and Méliès, Grandville linked the earth to the other planets, sent brilliant rocket missiles skywards and propelled his hero into the air before celebrating his marriage to Publicity. He describes the metamorphoses of sleep, gives the recipee for a celestial salad, relates the battles of a pack of cards and analyses physiological appearances. Most of the objects in *Un Autre Monde* have a rudimentary life-form: sculptors' tools, brooms, musical instruments, lightning conductors executing a mechanical ballet from one end of the work to the other, punctuated with intermissions such as the 'steam concert' or 'melody for 200 trombones'. The mutations are sometimes made by means of an
601 intermediary state: from a sock turned stocking emerges a dancer with butterfly wings, who becomes a spool of thread, while an hour-glass is changed successively into a glass, a bottle, a washerwoman's beetle, and finally into lobster claws which applaud loudly.

It is only a short distance from Alice's Wonderland where one can see lobsters who dance a quadrille, squabbling figures
612 from a pack of cards, croquet parties with hedgehogs for balls, pink flamingoes for mallets and soldiers for hoops. In *Alice Through the Looking Glass* flowers speak, trees bark and words themselves have a specific personality.

'They've a temper some of them', said Humpty Dumpty – 'particularly verbs, they're the proudest – adjectives you can do anything with, but not verbs – however, *I* can manage the whole lot!' And the Duchess said to Alice: 'Take care of the sense, and the sounds will take care of themselves'. And when
613 Alice introduced herself to Humpty Dumpty, and he said, 'It's a stupid name enough . . . What does it mean?' Alice asked doubtfully, 'Must a name mean something?' 'Of course it must', Humpty Dumpty said with a short laugh: '*My* name means the shape I am . . .'

614

615

III Figured verse and calligrams

616

For thousands of years the history of writing has illustrated man's attempt to give words a fixed form, to *paint* then. Whether writing is ideogrammatic or syllabic, whether preference is given to the image or to the sound (depending on the place, the period, the type of society and the degree of culture or technology involved), the two processes can never be identified as long as we are entitled to accept them in different ways. Even when those miraculous coincidences between phonetics and graphic representation do occur within a language, this could never be transposed into another language: we have ample evidence of this in attempts at translating plays on words, puns, spoonerisms, alliteration, assonance (not to mention rhymes and rhythms), limericks and riddles.

The ancient world saw the business of transcribing words by means of writing merely as a convenient way of setting down permanently the sounds belonging to a language. But very soon writing inherited the magical quality of the Word of God; and also very soon man began to identify himself quite naturally with writing, because it offers evidence of the writer's personality: 'May these characters traced by me proclaim what I am,' cried a medieval monk as he put the finishing touches to his task. Later on the invention of printing and, later still, the compilation of dictionaries, helped to congeal writing, to depersonalize the written word and to fossilize spelling, whereas pronunciation – which already varied from one area to another – continued to evolve.

Pictography, which probably represented man's earliest way of expressing himself, focuses attention on the image, but is not as a rule successful in translating abstract concepts. The ideogrammatic writing of the Chinese links the phonetic

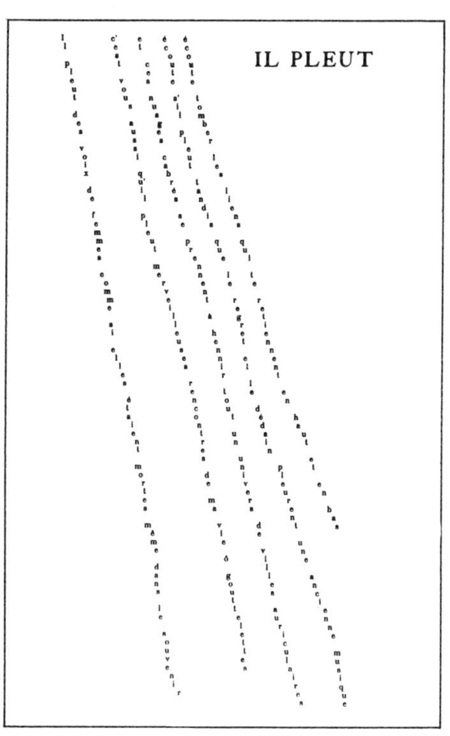
IL PLEUT

617

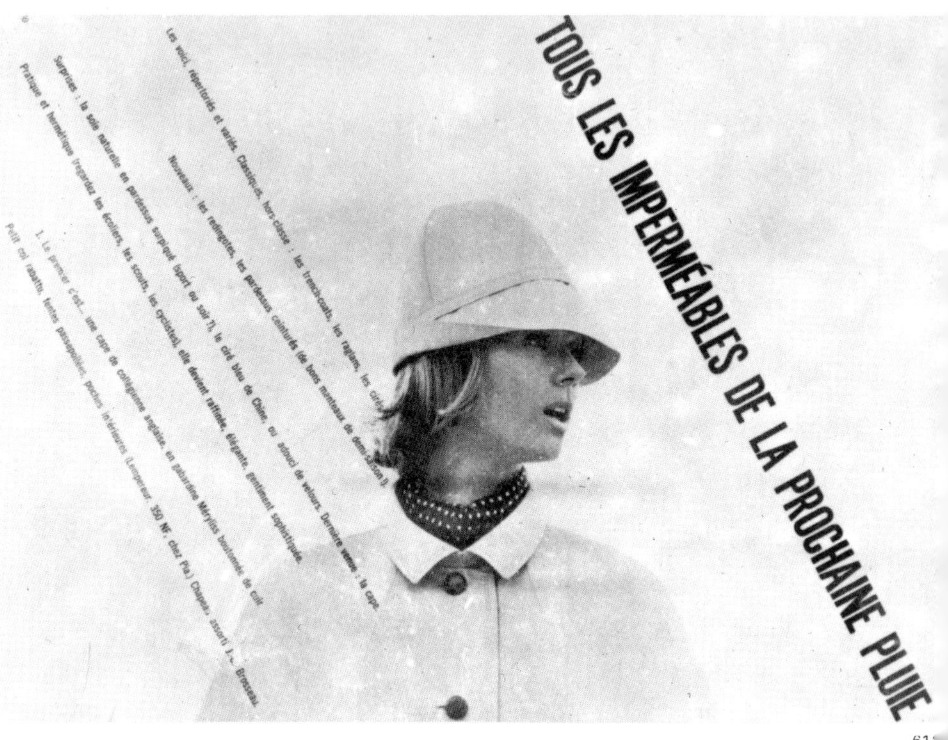
TOUS LES IMPERMÉABLES DE LA PROCHAINE PLUIE

61

sign (indicating sound) with the meaning (represented by an ideographic sign). But this dual character merely serves to underline the divorce between writing and reading; what is more, because of the general wear and tear suffered by words and the introduction of keys – which allow various different meanings to be attributed to a single sign – Chinese ideograms became extremely complicated and relied mainly on the reader's memory, since he had to be familiar with a large number of signs. This type of writing is undoubtedly pictographic in origin, but virtually no traces of pictograms have survived in the outline of the signs. Two other scripts, the Sumeric and the hieroglyphic, also borrowed from pictography before becoming ideogrammatic. They also took far longer to decipher than any other language.

Compared with these ornamental scripts, the Latin alphabet, with its smaller number of sound-symbols – or phonograms – is totally rigid. So the art of calligraphy, which is used to vary writing to such an extent that its basic forms are exaggerated, was compelled to develop, precisely because of the progress made in printing and the increasing spread of printed books. In a way calligrams reconcile decorative script and typography (this is true of contemporary examples in any case).

Guillaume Apollinaire was the first person to use the French word '*calligrammes*', selecting it as the title for a

O Bouteille
Plaine toute
De misteres,
D'vne aureille
Iet'escoute
No differes,
Et le mot proferes,
Auquel pend mon cœur.
En la tant diuine liqueur,
Baccus qui fut d'Inde vainqueur,
Tient toute verité enclose.
Vint ant duin loin de toy est forclose
Toute mensonge, & toute tromperie.
En ioye soit l'Airo de Noach close,
Lequel de toy nous fist la temperie.
Somme le beau mot, ie t'en prie,
Qui me doit oster de misere.
Ainsi ne se perde vne goutte.
De toy, soit blanche ou soit vermeille.
O Bouteille
Plaine toute
De mysteres,
D'vne aureille
Ie t'escoute
Ne differes.

619

— Une interview ? Avec plaisir... Je me présente : Dominique Blaseix, starlette, 15 mois, 10 dents, 11 kilos. Parisienne. Joues bien rondes et yeux bleus. Ce que j'aime le mieux ? Jouer avec les enfants à la crèche de la rue Lamarck ou maman me dépose tous les matins avant d'aller à son travail. J'aime le soleil qui joue entre mes doigts et les poupées qui dorment dans mes bras. J'aime aussi manger. Mon plat préféré ? Le biberon, bien sûr. On me le prépare avec l'eau Charrier, une eau spéciale pour les bébés. On n'a pas besoin de la faire bouillir, cette eau, pour préparer le biberon. Elle est pure, légère, pas gazeuse et pas salée du tout. Elle ne contient presque pas de sels minéraux. C'est une eau de montagne : elle coule à 900 mètres d'altitude, dans un endroit qui a un très joli nom : les monts de la Madeleine, commune : la Prugne. Le village s'appelle Charrier. Vous dites que c'est un nom de personne ? Je le sais bien, puisque c'est le bon vieux Charrier qui a donné son nom au village. Comment ? Vous ne connaissez pas l'histoire ? Maman me l'a racontée, c'est un vrai conte de fées, avec plein de miracles : Il y a longtemps, bien longtemps, plus de deux siecles, vivait un brave paysan nommé Charrier. Au milieu de ses terres chantait une source. Les voisins venaient dire bonjour à Charrier et ils buvaient son eau vive puis repartaient contents, si contents qu'ils en parlaient à d'autres paysans qui venaient à leur tour boire l'eau de la « Bouna Font ». C'est comme cela qu'ils appelaient la bonne fontaine. Et depuis lors, ceux qui avaient bu de cette eau se portaient bien. Le brave paysan eut beaucoup d'enfants, qui eurent d'autres enfants, et bientôt il y eut un véritable village qui s'appela Charrier. Un jour, une grande société qui s'installait dans le village se mit à la recherche d'une bonne eau pour ses ouvriers : c'est la Bouna Font qu'elle préféra. C'était en 1928. Depuis tous les ouvriers étaient vigoureux et tout le monde se mit à répéter :

POURQUOI J'AIME CHARRIER

« Mais alors, cette eau merveilleuse de la Bouna Font ce n'était pas uniquement une légende... » Deux ans plus tard, un ingénieur, plus très jeune et malade (il avait de l'urémie et des rhumatismes), vint visiter l'usine. Comme les autres, il but l'eau de la Bouna Font. Au bout de deux jours, il se sentait mieux. Retournant à Paris, il emporta une centaine de bouteilles de cette eau. Cet ingénieur avait des amis médecins, dont l'un était membre de l'Académie de médecine. Les médecins ne croient pas aux miracles, et ils ne croient pas non plus aux légendes. Le professeur fit analyser cette eau et dit à l'ingénieur : « Votre eau, c'est une perle. Il faut l'exploiter comme eau minérale naturelle. » Ce qui veut dire : « Il faut en donner à tout le monde pour que tout le monde se sente mieux, même les bébés. » L'histoire de la Bouna Font faisait déjà le tour de la France et tout le monde demandait de l'eau de Charrier. Alors les hôpitaux se mirent à faire des essais et les docteurs déclaraient que c'était une eau merveilleuse et qu'il fallait en faire profiter ceux qui vivaient loin du village. En 1933, une autorisation d'exploiter était accordée pour la Source dite « La Bonne Fontaine Charrier » ou « Bouna Font ». C'est la Société Perrier qui s'est chargée de mettre cette eau dans des bouteilles que l'on peut maintenant acheter n'importe où. Elles sont remplies et bouchées automatiquement. Aucun méchant microbe ne peut s'y glisser. Vous connaissez la Société Perrier ? C'est elle qui fournit à maman l'eau de Contrexéville et à papa l'eau Perrier. Moi, je n'ai pas droit à une eau qui pique : je bois l'eau Charrier. Mais je l'aime tant ! Et je ne suis pas la seule, puisque l'année dernière on n'a retiré en tout que 150.000 bouteilles de cette eau et que maintenant les machines modernes sortent chaque jour 100.000 bouteilles qui partent aussitôt en camion vers tous les malades, les cardiaques et les rhumatisants, et vers tous les beaux bébés.

620

Here
hang my bangs
o'er eyes that dream,
And nose and rose-
bud lips for cream.
And here's my
chin with dim-
ples in.
This is my
neck with-
out a speck,
which doth these snowy shoulders
deck ; and here is — see, oh,
double T-O-N, which girls all
wear, like me; and here's a
heart, from cupid's dart, safe-
shielded by this corset's art.
This is my waist too tightly
laced on which
a bustle big
is placed.
This is my
dress. Its cost,
I guess, did my
poor papa much dis-
tress, because he sighed
when mamma tried it on,
and scolded so I cried;
but mamma said I soon would
wed and buy pa's clothes for him
instead. It's trimmed with lace
just in this place, 'neath which two
ankles show, with grace, in silken hose
to catch the beaus who think they're lovely,
I suppose. These are
my feet in slippers
neat, and now if we
should chance to meet we'll flirt
a little on the street. How sweet.

621

UNE
RAVIS
SANTE
IDIOTE
UN
film de
EDOUARD
MOLINARO
UNE
RAVIS
SANTE
IDIOTE
EDOUARD MOLINARO
GEORGES ANDRE TABET
GEORGES ANDRE TABET
GREGOIRE
ASLAN
DENISE
PROVENCE
HANS VERNER
JACQUES MONOD
ROBERT MURZEAU
JEAN-MARC TENNBERG
ANDRE LUGUET

622

collection of his work published in 1918, and after hesitating between 'lyrical ideograms' and 'an album of lyrical ideograms'. Earlier on he had thought of grouping five calligrammatic poems together under the title *anch'io son' pittore*, thus adopting Correggio's exclamation of: 'I too am a painter!' as he stood before one of Raphael's paintings. Apollinaire's preoccupations and intentions are clearly revealed in this choice, and it also illustrates the good fortune of one word; it might be compared to the happy fate of the word 'surrealism', which made its first appearance in the preface to his *Mamelles de Tirésias*.

'Calligram' means a combination of script, design, thought; it represents the shortest route which can be taken for expressing a thought in material terms, and for forcing the eye to accept a global view of the written word. So it is not surprising that this highly special projection of language has proved tempting for poets and also, in our own day, for people whose business is advertising: as far as the poet is concerned, calligrams are capable of fusing a visual image and a script, and give a tangible quality to the metaphor; the advertiser sees it as offering a slogan, which is made up of words, a concrete presence and an immediate significance, so that its power is reinforced to a remarkable degree. A page about mackin-
toshes in a women's magazine, riddled with sophisticated 618
advice, is fairly closely linked in its inspiration to Apollinaire's
famous poem which shows rain falling drop by drop, letter by 617

620 letter. Or an advertisement singing the praises of a mineral water evokes the *épilénie* or vintage song sung by Panurge
619 and is reminiscent of the '*dive bouteille*', representing both its counter-form and its antithesis. Or a poster made up
622 of words moulded to form a woman's body reproduces an
621 English calligram composed in the nineteenth century and called 'a type of beauty'. Nowadays electronic composition ought to offer new horizons both to the poet's inspiration and to the businessman's imagination, by allowing the letter to be liberated completely.

Before Apollinaire calligrams were known as 'figured verses' or sometimes as 'rhopalic verses' (from the Greek *rhopalon* = mace). They were called this because of the way they were arranged and the way they increased and then diminished, which meant that the overall composition conjured up the image of a mace. For the same reason, they were occasionally classified as 'pyramid verses'. Up to Apollinaire's time, figured verse constituted a minor poetic genre; it was restricted to entertainment and philological riddles and was often looked down on as mere typographic whimsy, or at the most as a childish game which was deemed unworthy of great authors.

The first figured verses appeared in Ancient Greece, but they do not seem to go back any further than the fourth century BC. Simmias of Rhodes, who lived during the reign of Ptolemy I, founder of the Lagid dynasty and Satrap of Egypt, is the author of some verses generally considered to be fairly mediocre, which include a number of epigrams. He left three small pieces of figured verse, 'Wings', 'Egg' and 'Axe', which form part of *The Crown of Meleager* and are counted by various authors as the first known examples of figured verse.

623 Each of the 'Wings' consists of six feathers pictorially represented by six choriambic verses which become gradually shorter the nearer they get to the centre. The author makes the winged god, Cupid, speak through them – not the vulgar deity who was born of Venus but (as a compiler was to write later) 'that ancient Cupid sung of by the old Cosmogonies, the principal creator and a contemporary of fate'.

624 The 'Egg' composition is rather more erudite and its meaning remained obscure until an ancient scholiast discovered that the reader was intended to travel from the first verse to the last, then from the second to the second-to-last, from the third to the antepenultimate verse, and so on until he comes to the middle lines. The poem tells of a Dorian nightingale's egg which is dedicated to the reader, and it ends with the following words, which give an idea of the patient labour expended on it by the author: '. . . with a tread as rapid as a young fawn's, the god beats out the rhythm of this poem with its complicated
625 and sonorous metres.' As for his 'Axe', the same code applies; this time the poem represents an inscription on an axe which

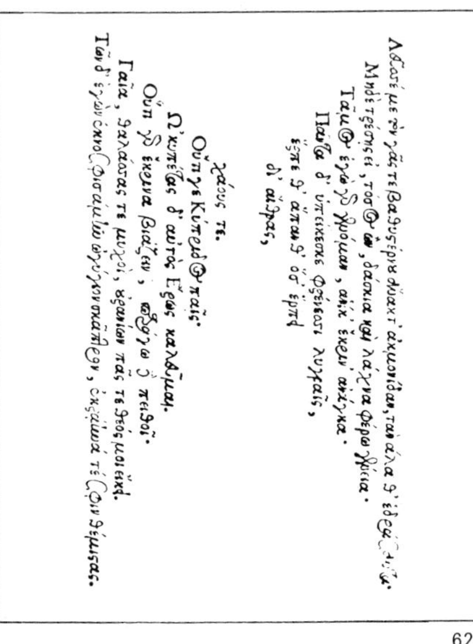

623

1 Κωτίλας 3
2 ματέρος τὶ τόδ' 5
3 ὤιον νέον· πρόφρων 6
4 θυμῷ δέξο δὴ ἁγνᾶς. 7
5 τὸ μὲν θεῶν ἐριβόας 8
6 Ἑρμᾶς ἀείκιζε κάρυξ, ὄνωσε δ' ὄρ- 11
7 σας ἐκ μέτρου μονοβάμονος μέταν 11
8 πάρεθεν αὔξει, θοῶς δ' ὕπερθεν ὠ- 12
9 κὺ λέχριον φέρων νεῦμα ποδῶν, πίασκε 13
10 θοαῖσιν αἰόλαις κῶλ'. ἀλλὰ σου ὀροιπιδῶν 14
11 ἐλάφων τεκέεσσι, πάλαι κραιπνοῖσιν ὑπὲρ ἄ- 15
12 κρων ἰθμία ποσὶ λόφων κατ' ῥύθμιον ἴχνος 16
13 πθ' ὥας, καὶ τὰν ὁμοθύμων ἀμφίπαλτον αἶψ' αὖδ' ἂν 16
14 θὴς ἐν κόλποις δεξαμένα πυκνότητα. τοῦ δ' ὠκυβοᾶ 17
15 κοὰν (μεθέπων τόδ' ἄφαρ) ὅγ' ἐκ λασίων ὀπισθ[illegible] ἀ- 18
16 ν ὀρέων ἔσσυτ' ἀνάγκαις τῇ δὴ δαίμων κλυταῖσι, θοαῖσι 18
17 ποσσὶ πονέων, πολύπλοκα μέτρε μέζα μολπαῖσι, ῥίμφα 18
18 [illegible] ἐκλιπὼν ὄρεις δῖνα, ματρὸς πλαγκτὸν χαιομῶνας 19
19 βαλίας ἑλεῖν τέκος. λάχαι δ' οἴων, πολυβότων ἀν' ὀρέων 20
20 νομὸν ἔβαν, τανυσφύρων τ' ἄντρα νυμφῶν. τοὶ ἀβρατὶ 16
21 ματρὸς φίλας πόθῳ ῥόων αἶψα μεθ' ἱμερόεντα 16
22 μαζὸν, ἴχνει θείων τὰν παναίολον Πιερίδων 15
23 μονόδουπον αὐδὰν, ἀριθμὸν εἰς ἄκρον δέκα 14
24 ἰχνίων κόσμον νέμων ῥυθμόν, φίλος 12
25 λεπτοεργὸν ὑπὸ φίλας ἑλὼν πτέ- 11
26 ρυγι μαζός. Λίγα μὲν 8
27 κ' αὐτιμάτος ἀδὶ 7
28 ἀγναῖ ἀηδόνος, ὠ- 8
29 ρύων δὲ ἄγριος. 5

624

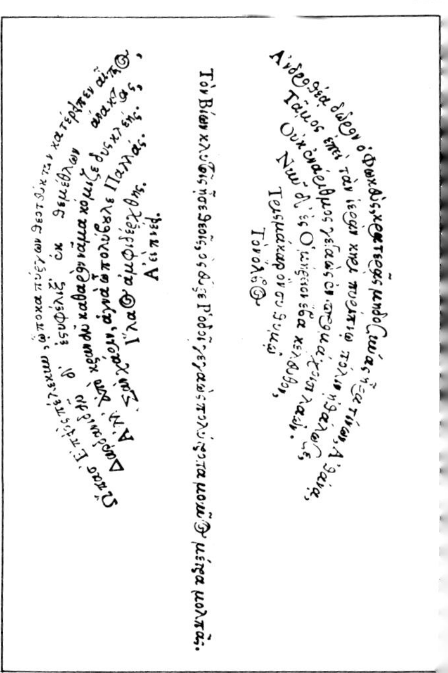

625

Εἰμάρσενός με στήτας
πόσις, μέροψ, δίσαβος
Τεῦξ', ὁ σποδεύνας, ἶνις ἐμπούσας, μόρος
Τεύκροιο βούτα καὶ κυνὸς τεκνώματος,
Χρύσας δ' αἴτας· ἆμος ἔψανδρα.
τὸν γυιόχαλκον οὖρον ἔρραισεν.
ὃν ὡ πάτωρ δίσευνος
μόρησε μητρόρριπτος.
ἐμὸν δὲ τεῦγμ' ἀθρήσας
Θεοκρίτοιο κτάντας,
Τριεσπέροιο καύτας,
ἄϊξεν αἰν' ἰύξας·
χάλεψε γάρ νιν ἰῷ
σύργαστρος ἐκδὺς γῆρας.
τὸν δ' ἐλλινεῦντ' ἐν ἀμφικλύστῳ
Πανός τε ματρὸς εὐνέτας, φὼρ
δίζωος, ἶνίς τ' ἀνδροβρῶτος ἰλιουραίσας
ἠρ' ἀρδίων ἐς Τευκρίδ' ἄγαγον τρίπορθον.

626

Ὀλός οὐ με λιβρὸς ἱρῶν
λιβάδεσσιν, οἷα κάλχη,
Ὑπὸ φοινίησι τέγγει·
Μαύλιες δ' ὕπερθε πέτρης Ναξίας θοούμεναι
Παμάτων φίδοντο Πανός· οὐ στροβίλῳ λιγνὺι
Ἴξος εὐώδης μελαίνει τρεχνέων με Νυσίων.
Ες γὰρ βωμὸν ὁρῆς με, μήτε γ' αὐροῦ
Πλίνθοις, μήτ' Ἀλύβης παγέντα βώλοις·
Οὐδ' ὃν Κυνθογενὴς ἔτευξε φύτλη
Λαβὼν τὰ μηκάδων κέρα,
Λισσαῖσιν ἀμφὶ δειράσιν
Ὅσσαι νέμονται Κυνθίας,
Ἰσόρροπος πέλοιτό μοι.
Σὺν οὐρανοῦ γὰρ ἐκγόνοις
Εἰνάς μ' ἔτευξε γηγενής·
Τάων δ' ἀείζωον τέχνην
Ἔνευσε πάλμυς ἀφθίτων.
Σὺ δ' ὦ πιὼν κρήνηθεν, ἣν
Ἶνις κόλαψε Γοργόνος,
Θύοις τ' ἐπισπένδοις τέ μοι
Ὑμηττιάδων πολὺ λαροτέρην
Σπονδὴν ἄδην ἴθι δὴ θαρσέων
Ες ἐμὴν τεῦξιν· καθαρὸς γὰρ ἐγὼ
Ἰὸν ἱέντων τεράων, οἷα κέκευθ' ἐκεῖνος
Ἀμφὶ Νέαις Θρηικίαις, ὃν σχεδόθεν Μυρίνης
Σοί, Τριπάτωρ, πορφυρέῳ φὼρ ἀνέθηκε κριῷ.

627

ΣΥΡΙΓΞ.

Σύριγξ οὔνομ' ἔχεις, ἀλλὰ δὲ σε μέγα θεῖν,
Οὐδενὸς εὐνάτειρα, μακροπτολέμοιο δὲ ματρός,
Μαίας ἀντιπέτροιο θοὸν τέκες ἰθυντῆρα,
Οὐχὶ Κεράσταν, ὅν ποτε θρέψατο ταυροπάτωρ.
Ἀλλ' ἀπέλειπες οὗ αἶθε πάρος φρένα τέρμα σάκεος,
Οὗ νόμ' ὅλον δίζων, ὃς τᾶς μέροπος πόθον
Κούρας γηρυόνας αἶθε τᾶς ἀνεμώδεος.
Ὃς μοίσᾳ λιγὺ πᾶξεν ἰοστεφάνῳ
Ἕλκος ἄγαλμα πόθοιο πυρισμαράγου,
Ὃς σβέσεν ἀνορέαν ἰσαυδέα
Παπποφόνου, Τυρίας τε ἀφείλετο,
Ὧι τόδε τυφλοφόρων ἐρατὸν
Πᾶμα Πάρις θέτο Σιμιχίδας
Ψυχάν. ὦ βροτοβάμων,
Στήσας οἶστρε Σάγας,
Κλωποπάτωρ, ἀπάτωρ,
Λαρνακόγυιε, χαίροις,
Ἁδὺ μελίσδοις
Ἐλλοπι κούρᾳ
Καλλιόπα
Νηλεύστῳ.

628

ORGANON

Post Martios labores,
Et Caesarum parantes
Virtutibus per orbem
Tot laureas virentes,
Et Principis tropaea;
Felicibus triumphis
Exsultat omnis aetas,
Vrbesque flore grato,
Et frondibus decoris,
Totis virent plateis.
Hinc ordo veste clara
Cum purpuris honorum
Fausto precantur ore,
Feruntque dona laeti.
Iam Roma culmen orbis
Dat munera et coronas
Auro ferens coruscas
Victorias triumphis,
Votaque iam theatris
Redduntur et choreis.
Me sors iniqua laetis
Sollemnibus remotum
Vix haec sonare suit
Tot vota fonte Phoebi
Versuque compta solo
Augusta rite saeclis.

AVGVSTO VICTORE IVVAT RATA REDDERE VOTA

O si diuiso metiri limite Clio
Vna lege sui, vno manantia fonte
Aonio, versus heroi iure manente
Ausuro donet metri felicia texta,
Augeri longo patiens exordia fine,
Exiguo cursu, paruo crescentia motu,
Vltima postremo donec fastigia tota
Ascensus iugi cumulato limite cludat,
Vno bis spatio versus elementa prioris
Dinumerans, cogens aequari lege retenta
Parua nimis longis, et visu dissona multum
Tempore sub parili, metri rationibus isdem,
Dimidium numero Musis tamen aequiparantem:
Haec erit in varios species aptissima cantus,
Perque modos gradibus surget fecunda sonoris
Aere cauo et tereti, calamis crescentibus aucta.
Quis bene suppositis quadratis ordine plectris
Artificis manus in numeros clauditque aperitque
Spiramenta, probans placitis bene consona rithmis,
Sub quibus vnda latens properantibus incita ventis,
Quos vicibus crebris iuuenum labor haud sibi discors
Hinc atque hinc animaeque agitant, augetque reluctans
Compositum ad numeros, propriumque ad carmina praestat,
Quodque queat minimum ad motum intremefacta frequenter
Plectra adaperta sequi, aut placidos bene claudere cantus,
Iamque metro et rithmis praestringere quicquid vbique est.

629

Vides vt Ara stem dicata Pythio
Fabre polita vatis arte Musica
Sic pulchra sacratissima gens Phoebo decens
His apta templis quis litant vatum chori
Tot compta sertis et Camenae floribus
Heliconiis locanda lucis carminum
Non caute dura me poliuit artifex
Excisa non sum rupe montis albidi
Luna e nitente nec pari de vertice
Non caesa duro nec coacta spiculo
Artare primos eminentes angulos
Et mox secundos propagare latius
Eosque caute singulos subducere
Gradu minuto per recuruas lineas
Normata vbique sic deinde regula
Vt ora quadrae sit rigente limite
Vel inde ad imum fusa rursum linea
Tendatur arte latior per ordinem
Me metra pangunt de Camenarum modis
Mutato nunquam numero duntaxat pedum
Quae docta seruat dum praeceptis regula
Elementa crescunt et decrescunt carminum
His Phoebe supplex dans metrorum imagines
Templis chorisque laetus intersit sacris.

630

Praecelsae quercus frondenti in vertice pendens
Testor templa loci Faunos celebrare frequentes
Disparibus compacta modis totidemque cicutis

Dulcisono Panum oblectans modulamine siluas
NaiadumDryadumque choros arcanaqueBacchi

Orgia et heuuantes Satyros per musica Tempe
Me Pan ad thiasos docuit modulamine cantus

Et variata sonis vinxit consortia primus
Attis almus amans tua maxima cura Cybele

E roseo terit ore deus molliqueе labello
Accenditque tuos Idaeos mater amores

In me felices animauit carmina musas
Me iudex formae alta gestauit in Ida

Me laeti sociam voti vicina marito
Eoo lucis canit inuitata sub ortu.

631

Epeus, the man who invented the Trojan Horse, is consecrating to Minerva.

We know relatively little about Dosiadas of Crete. In *Lexiphanus or the Fine-Speaker*, Lucian of Samosata mentions him alongside Lycophron, who was the author of an eccentric poem consisting mainly of words invented by himself, and declares that he dislikes poets whose work requires a glossary. Dosiadas composed two 'altars' made up of uneven lines,
627 one of which forms an acrostic and is dedicated to the muses.
626 His 'Altar of Jason' is consecrated to the King of Iolchos in Thessaly, who organized the famous expedition of the Argonauts, and conjures up a picture of the terrifying incidents in the hero's life; various different interpretations of it seem to have been offered by authors such as Salmatius, Scaliger and a grammarian called Manuel Holobolus, who was a contemporary of Michael Palaeologus. There was also a seventeenth-century Italian scholar called Fortunio Liceti who actually devoted three whole volumes to the figured poems of Simmias of Rhodes and Dosiadas. These erudite studies were published between 1630 and 1640 (and thus *after* various Renaissance works had popularized Greek calligrams), and in them Liceti offers different variants on their poems, sometimes involving modifications to the structure and to the number of lines; he adds some new material of his own, reconstructs altars, eggs and axes in Latin verse and refers to some earlier scholia.

The bucolic poet Theocritus fell into line with the taste of
628 his age by composing a 'syrinx' or pipe of Pan made up of decreasing lines which convey an image of Pan's ancient flute and celebrate Echo, 'the mysterious maiden with the languishing and beautiful voice'. Another 'syrinx' is attributed to Callimachus, but meanwhile this particular poetic *genre* seems to have fallen out of favour.

A work published last century called *La Papesse Jeanne* ('Pope Joan'), written by the Greek writer Roïdis (and translated by Alfred Jarry) evokes 'the Bacchic songs of the Gallic poets in the shape of a bottle or a barrel'. The Latin authors do not seem to have been much tempted by figured verse, with the exception of the poet and statesman Publius Optianus Porphyrius, who lived at the beginning of the fourth century under the reign of Constantine the Great. The Emperor first exiled Porphyrius, then later recalled him to thank him for having sent a collection of his work consisting of about twenty poems, some acrostic, some forming a square. These compositions are forerunners of the work of Hrabanus Maurus and are made up of lines which cross each other perpendicularly or diagonally to form the letter V or the letter Y, or diamond shapes, or again a series of branches linked to a central stem. Apart from these
630 *cancellatiflexus*, Porphyrius also composed an 'altar' and a
631 'syrinx' (which are almost identical with the designs brought into favour by the Greeks a few centuries earlier) and also an

Item de signaculo sanctæ Crucis.

632

AVGVSTIDVNENSIS OPVS TIBI SOLVO SYAGRI.

633

DE SANCTA CRVCE.

634

SVLASASALVS
LASATASAL
SATRTAS
TRERT
RECER
ECICE
CIHIC
M IHIHI M
VI HIMIH CV
IGV IMXMI MEÇ
GVFERIHIMXVXMDOMINIME
VFERIHIMXVRVXDOMINIM
FERIHIMXVRCRVXDOMINI
VFERIHIMXVRVXDOMINIM
GVFERIHIEXVXEDOMINIME
IGV SEXES MEC
VI TSEST CV
M QTSTQ M
VQTQV
AVQVA
MAVAM
SMAMS
ESMSE
MESEM
PMEMP
EPMPE
AREPERA
ODARERADO
ORODARADORO

635

OTTO VALENS CAESAR NOSTRO TV CEDE COTVRNO
Te felix atavis quoT coelo ſydera lucenT
Te dominum ſibi Saxo Tulit, et roma notaviT
Orbis et ipſe capit, SolO contentus alumnO

Virtutum titulis et Vir cognoſceris actV
Ac domitor patriae pAcis ſectator in aulA
Lumen ubique micans iubar Lucendo velut SoL
Ergo Dei ſOlita reddEntur ſanCta benignE
Nec deeriT virtus omNis, qua grAtia culmeN
Scandit eT occultiS — — vEnia cauſiS

Certe nos Omnes tibi Caeſar ne Scius et nunC
Auſtraſios quae terra mAnet cereAlis opimA
Et foecunda ſecu pollEt ſatis ubeRe glebaE
Summis cara viriS ac ſaevis plena coloniS
A patris imperio non Abſit iſmaelithA
Rexit cum ſolers et Regnans induperatoR

Nunc auguſte tuum poNam venerabile nomeN
OTTO VALENS CAESAR NOSTRO TV CEDE COTVRNO
Solus enim regnans obSens, o caeſaris haereS
Totus avo ſimilis, ſi Te nova vita reſignaT
Rex fuit ille potens Romanae legis amatoR
Omne decus patriae ſoliO prognatus avitO

Tempora pacis erant, Tali dum iure vigereT
Vir tantus quem ſic dVxi deſcribere verſV

Cur ergo nAtale tuum, Cur contrAhis et nunC
Exulis in Bellis defErs pia deBita pompaE
Dum vates Bonus opto Dari miraBilis iſtuD
Expandes Opus, ipſe mEum tractAbilis indE

Caeſar ut invictis ſCuto munituS et ex hoC
Omnibus utilior, mirO datus ante triumphO
Terribilis clemens tuTo diadema riſiT
Vultus avi patriſque tVi praeclarus amictV
Rurſus uterque fuit diRo ſub tempore VictoR
Nunc unum vivens digNum cum patre vocameN
OTTO VALENS CAESAR NOSTRO TV CEDE COTVRNO

636

'organ'. This organ is a design of his own and is a relatively faithful reproduction of a water organ; it is made up of three separate sections: the key-board, consisting of twenty-four lines which equal those in the lower section; another twenty-six lines, each with one more letter than the preceding line, sketch in the top section consisting of the organ-pipes; the pipes are supported in the centre by a single horizontal hexameter.

The square acrostic devised by Porphyrius was taken up again by a Latin poet of the Merovingian period called Venance Fortunatus. He was a wandering poet who came from Ravenna and crossed the Alps and Swabia, attracting the attention of the various courts by his charm and his culture; he was always ready to repay any patronage offered to him by writing a poem; (when he was cured of blindness, thanks to the intercession of St Martin, he dedicated to the Saint a poem of thanks made up of more than two thousand hexameters). He won the favour of St Radegonde, whom he met in Poitiers before he became Bishop of the town in 597. He sent a tetragon during that period to Syagrius, Bishop of Autun, which dealt with the
sin of Adam, the fall of man and redemption. It consists of 633
thirty-three lines of thirty-three letters each – a reference to Christ's age – and forms five acrostics.

After Fortunatus, in the eighth century, the English scholar Alcuin who was chosen by Charlemagne to reorganize education in the Frankish empire, and the Spanish Visigoth Theodolfus, who had become the Bishop of Orleans, both composed poems which can be read in various directions, with a different meaning each time. In the following century, the genre also attracted Milon de Saint-Amand, who sent a long poem in
imitation of Virgil to Charles the Bald, as well as Hincmar, 636
Archbishop of Rheims, and Abbon, Abbot of Fleury.

All the same, none of these was to go as far as Hrabanus Maurus, the German Benedictine monk who was born in 784, and first became Abbot of Fulda and then Archbishop of Mainz. He had been a pupil of Alcuin's at Tours and is the author of the hymn *Veni creator,* which would at any rate have been enough to ensure the fame of this man who was known to
his contemporaries as 'the light of Germany'. But posterity 637/668
also has his collection *De laudibus sanctae crucis*, the whole of which is dedicated to the glory of the Holy Cross. It consists of no fewer than thirty figured poems arranged into acrostics, all of them picked out in red (as Fortunatus' tetragon was); this use of colour adds a new plastic element and at the same time makes the letters, words or groups of words stand out, along with some geometric figures and human figures. We can also see a portrait of Louis the Pious (son of Charlemagne) armed with his pilgrim's staff surmounted by a cross, Greek and Latin characters which sometimes form syllables, and sometimes, according to the way the red letters are grouped, build up oblique lines, squares, circles, crosses, pyramidal forms,

637

638

corollas, cherubim and seraphim, the symbols of the four Evangelists, and, of course, Christ on the Cross.

There are various different manuscripts of this collection in existence, some of which are illuminated in purple and silver, which adds a brilliant decorative touch to the mysterious appearance of the text. And we really must mention here the allusion which André Malraux once made to 'Charlemagne's purple gospel-book, which no-one ever saw, not even the Emperor, until the period when Otto removed it from his body for the oath taken by the leaders of the Holy Empire.'

These figured poems, which Tabourot des Accords was to refer to in his *Bigarrures* as 'curiously monstrous subtleties', were intended by the author to allow any reader who knew how to decipher their occult message to 'have access to the love of the cross' and to reveal to him not only the secret relationships which are set up between numbers, the months, the elements, etc., but also divine grace. So the purpose of these figurative compositions is somewhat ambiguous, in that they are superimposed onto a 'background' of text and place the reader on two different planes, the earthly and the supernatural.

If we were compelled at all costs to search for archetypes for Apollinaire's calligrams, we might well find them as much in Hrabanus Maurus' invocations as in earlier Greek poems. Indeed – at any rate in the typographical transcriptions of his work which were set at the beginning of the seventeenth century – the letters are skilfully arranged within a grid, which means that they are isolated for the first time, thus prefiguring, though involuntarily, Apollinaire's method of breaking up a word.

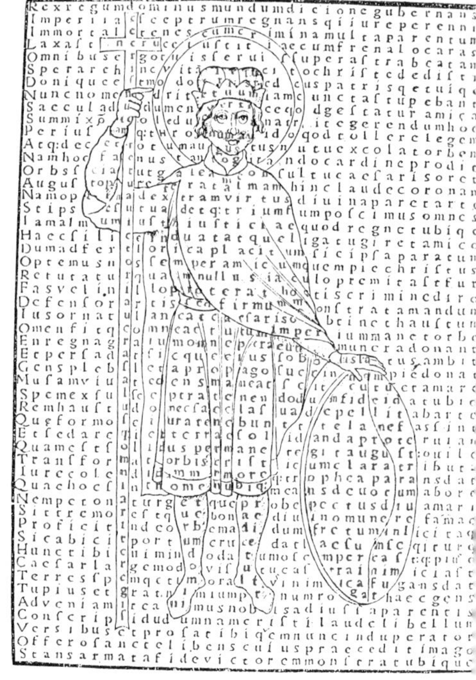

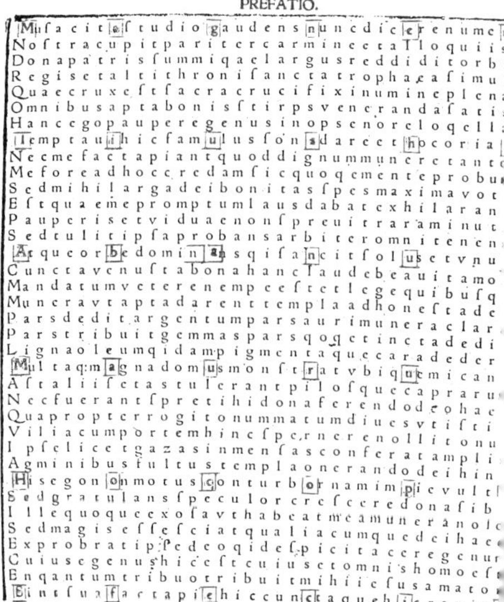

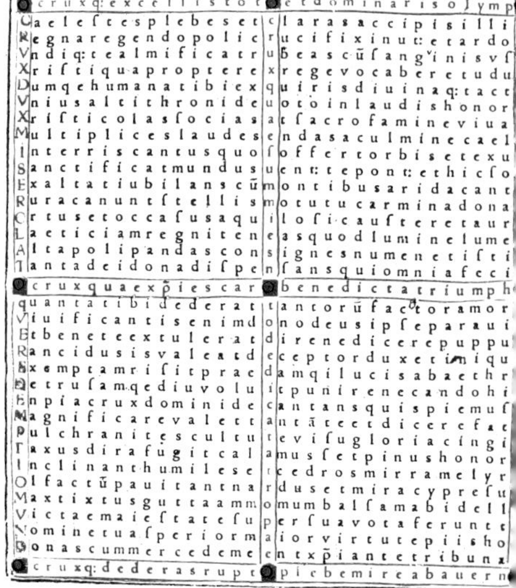

II. figura. De Crucis figura que intra tetragonum est scripta, et omnia se comprehendere manifestat

639/641

64

Prima figura. De imagine Christi in modum Crucis brachia sua expandentis. & de nominibus eius ad diuinam seu ad humanam naturam pertinentibus.

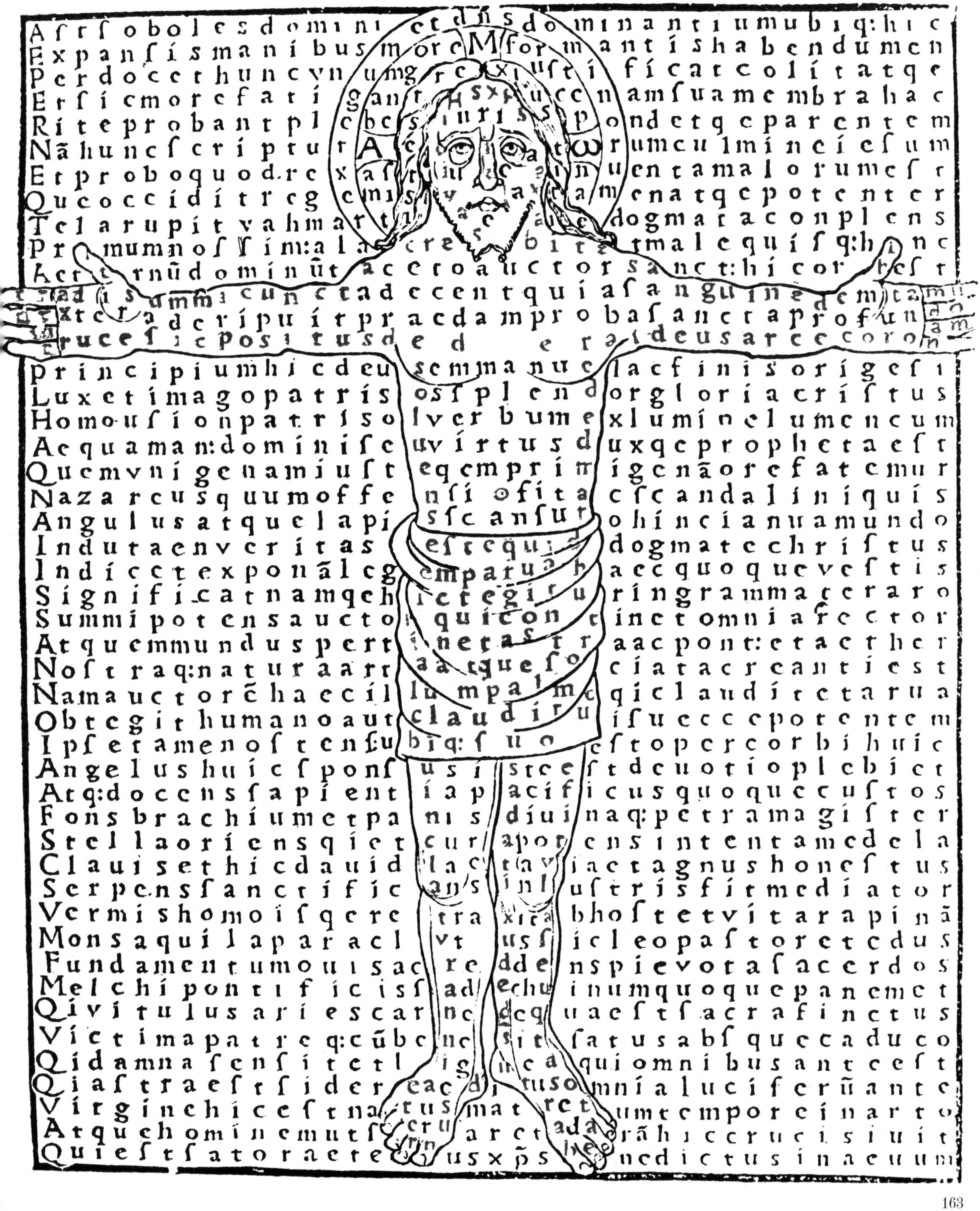

Afrsobolesdominietdn̄sdominantiumubiq:hic
ExpansismanibusmoreMformantishabendumen
Perdocethuncvnumgrexiustificatcolitatqe
ErsicmorefatiganťHsxpuccnamsuamembrahac
Riteprobantplebesiurisspondetqeparentem
NāhuncscripturAeoniatωrumculmineiesum
Etproboquodrexasirincinuentamalorumesr
Quecoccidítregemnisyaxtamenatqepotenter
Telarupitvahmartiecaedogmataconplens
Primumnossimalasacrebitetmalequisq:hinc
Aeternũdominũtaceroauctorsanct:hicortest
tradissummicunctadecentquiasanguinedemtamu
dextraderipuitpraedamprobasancraprofundo
cruceficpositusdederatdeusarcecorona
principiumhicdeusemmanuelacfinisorigesi
Luxetimagopatrisossplendorgloriacristus
Homousionpatrisolverbumexluminelumencum
Aequaman:dominiseuvirtusduxqepropheta est
Quemvnigenamiusteqemprimigenãorefatemur
Nazareusquumoffensiofitacscandaliniquis
Angulusatquelapisscansuruohinciamuamundo
Indutaenveritasestequitdogmatechristus
Indicetexponãlegempatuaĥaecquoquevestis
Significatnamqehicregiturringrammaceraro
Summipotensauctorquiconcinetomniarector
Atquemmunduspertineraetraacpont:etaether
Nostraq:naturaarraatquesociatacreantiest
Namauctorẽhaecillumpalmeqiclaudiretarua
Obtegithumanoautclaudirutisueccepotentem
Ipsetamenostensubiq:suoestopercorbihuic
Angelushuicsponsusisteestdeuotioplebiet
Atq:docenssapientiapacificusquoquecustos
Fonsbrachiumetpanisdiuinaq:petramagister
Stellaoriensqietcurapotensintentamedela
Clauisethicdauidlactaviaetagnushonestus
Serpenssanctrificansinlustrisfitmediator
Vermishomoisqeretraxitabhostetvitarapinā
Monsaquilaparaclvtussicleopastoretedus
Fundamentumouisacreddenspievotasacerdos
Melchipontificissadechuinumquoquepanemet
Qivitulusariescarnedequaestsacrafinctus
Victimapatreq:cũbenesitsatusabsquecaduco
Qidamnasensitetligneaquiomnibusantecest
Qiastraestsidereacdituomnialuciferũante
Virginehicestnatusmaterettumtemporeinarto
Atquehominemutscruarcetadrãhiccrucisiuit
Quiestsatoraeternusxp̃sbenedictusinaeuum

Ocherubinseraphind c caelonomenie susiam
Exaltateignisnamhi n cvesterfaminelucet
Cuwdiuinaecrucisver a estlaushaecviavita
Fruct:luciscrist:ve r usqietfociaestlaus
Vicittriumphatuncre x nuncq:ecsultatvbiqe
qiestsedspincar:or a fiantcelebrandohic
Ocelestraconstramu l tahaclaudesupernum
Vumesupernarumaea m aulunamconclamatam
Sacratamatquedecus a raefirmantq:voto
Eduntqaesitvirtusa c bonaquaetribuitrex
Consultuhaecristus r ecumconbussitiniqa
Enpassuscunctosqef u gauitcalsepotentes
Etdistrictarupitex c usiclausteracelydri
Etveteresanctusters i tdeditipsabenignus
Qissterebadamson s regnasabaorhinarce
Quaeorapprobantvirt: e tnumenhuicibiferre
Auxiliaitenebrisi n carcereiwssabeatum
Incrucefactoremcon f ixuminstipiteregem

Enchronushicregish a ecconciliatiomundi

Vexillumframeasors b elliinsignedecorum
Proterithochostesar m aconfringitiniqua
Subleuatatquesuosv i rtutispraemiadonat
Namhincecsuligniss c itoquetestalaterent
Stantchelubinhaecq: a raeassistuntarcaeq:
Hichaecelasparadant s ignoritiseratisora
Sanctaaralapiuntun a quoqesacraopefiunt
Vectathriumphumq:co n at:ferculacondunt
Laetaqedistensisdu c unthaecfacabeando
Enalisenfimtradun t almaaltaquepandunt
Pennisosquesuumser a finutiapropetempus
Quocarnalisseatluxu f dicantvitiaquehinc
Tensaacbrachiasalu a ntishicofficiodant
Hisq:trahiatq:vehice l soq:iudiciipsehinc
Tumdispcnfansintut u mlegetipsaprobando
Quaeiamnonanteauc t vetcarapprobauitubiq:
Decrucenonitubant i ustorumnuntiavatum
Decrucenonfalluntis s torumsignanimantum

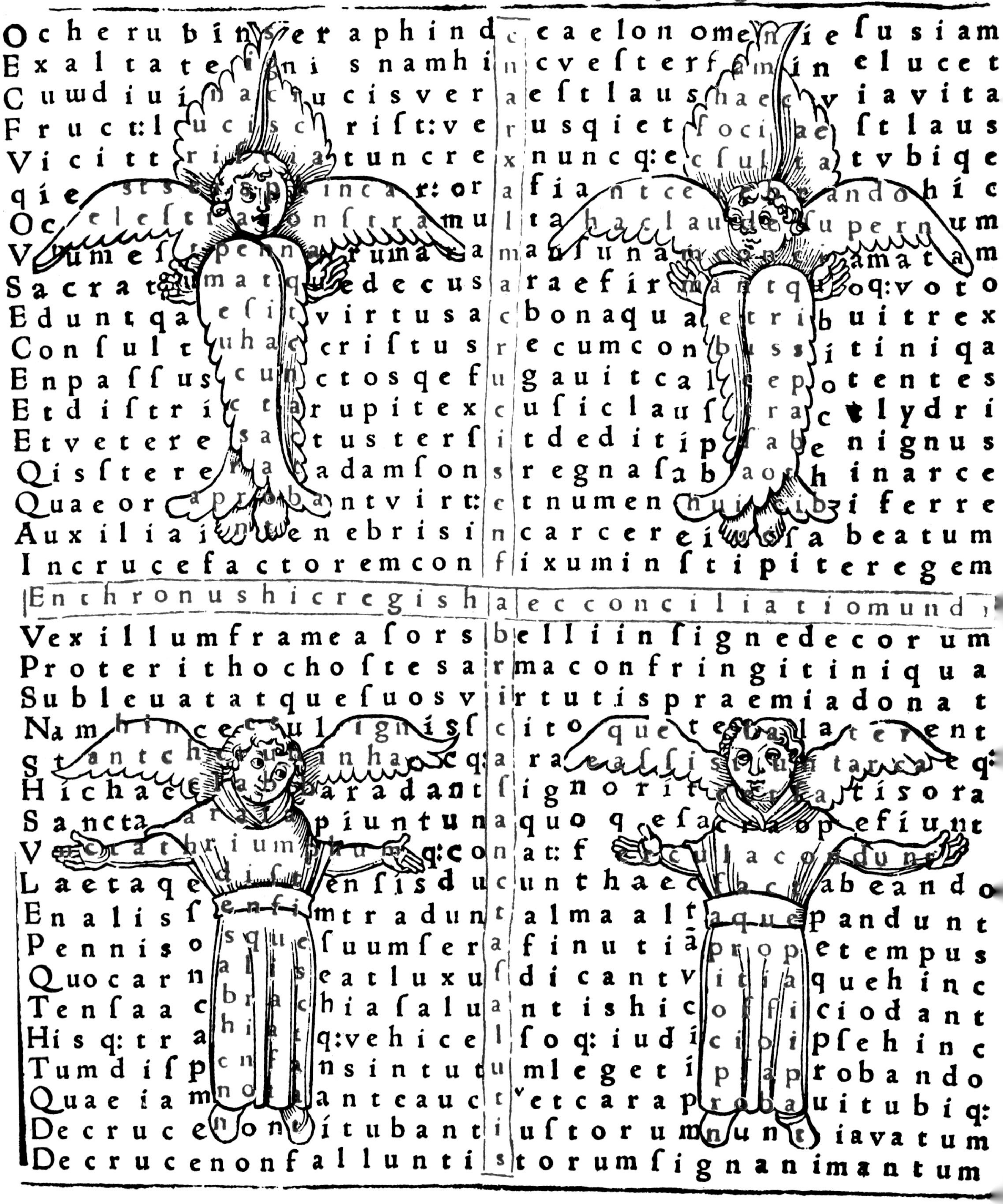

III. figura. De nouē ordibus angelorū, et de noībus eorū in Crucis figura dispositis.

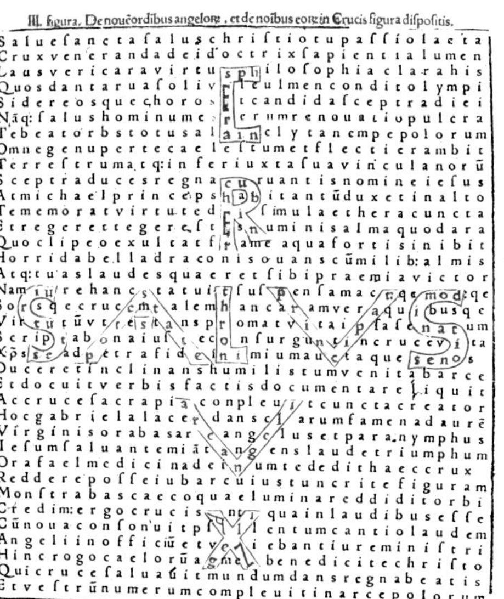

VII figura. De .iiii. elementis. de .iiii. vicissitudinibus temporum. decp .iiii. plagis mūdi. et de .iiii. quadrantibus naturalis diei. quomodo omnia in Cruce ordinentur, et in ipsa sanctificentur.

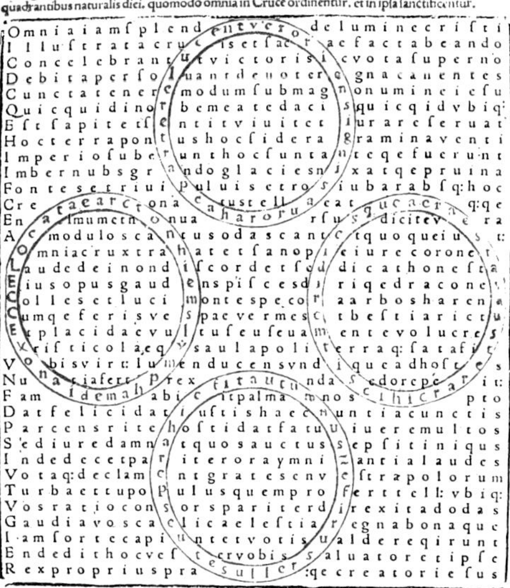

X. Figura. De numero Septuagenario et sacramentis eius : quomodo Cruci conueniant.

V. figura. De quattuor figuris tetragonicis circa Crucem positis. et spiritali ędificio domus dei.

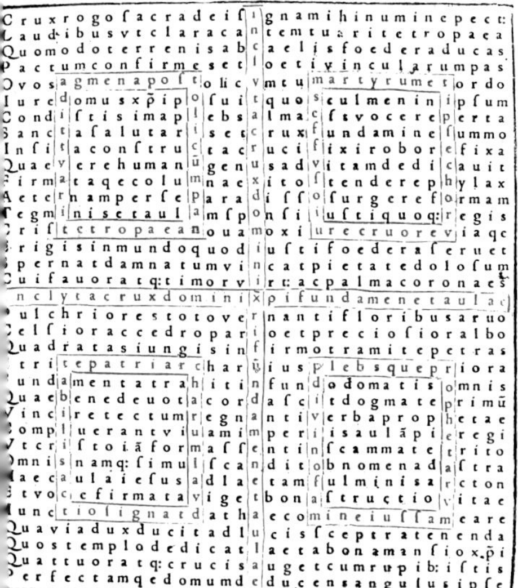

VIII figura De mensibus duodecim. de duodecim signis. atcp duodecim ventis. et de apostolorū predicatione. decp cęteris mysteriis duodenarij numeri. quę in Cruce ostenduntur.

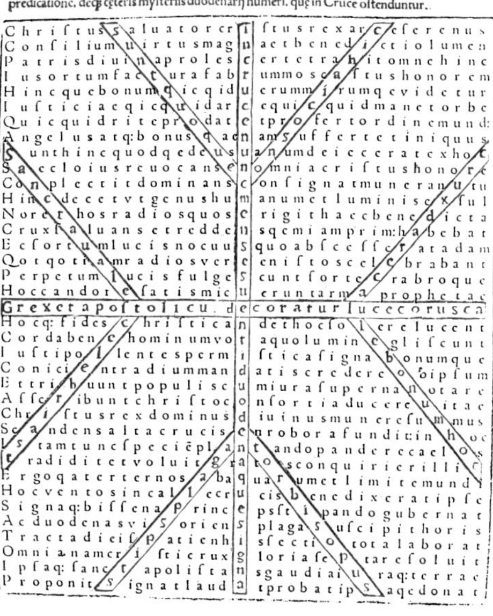

XI figura. De quincp libris Mosaicis. quomodo per Crucem innouentur. exponitur.

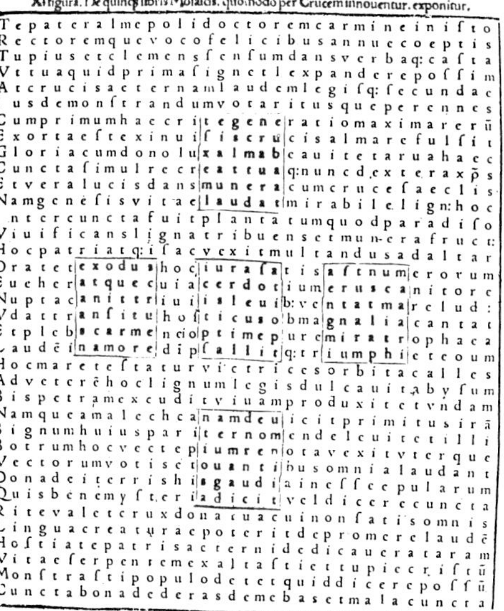

VI. figura. De quattuor virtutibus principalibus quomodo ad Crucem pertineant. et quod omnium virtutum fructus per ipsam nobis collati sunt.

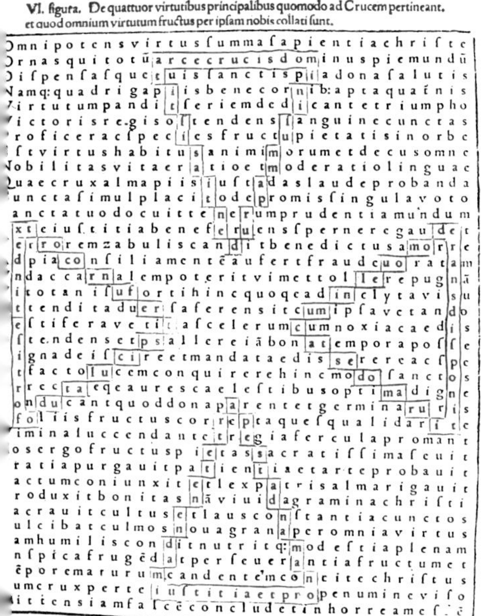

IX figura. De diebus anni in quattuor hexagonis et monade comprehensis. et de bisextili incremento. quomodo in specie sanctę Crucis adornentur et consecrentur.

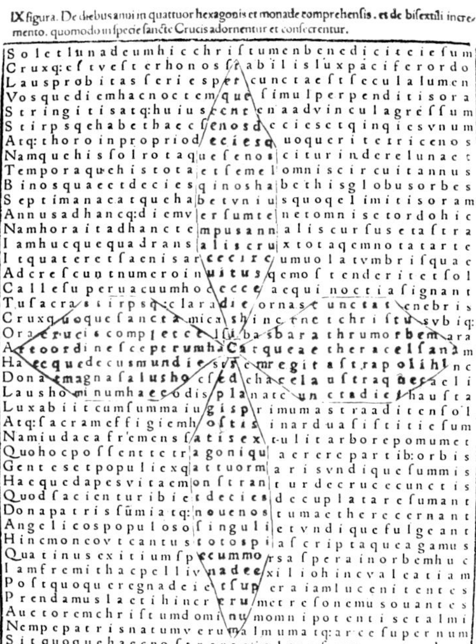

XII figura. De nomine Adam prothoplasti. quomodo secundum Adam significet. et eius passionem demonstret.

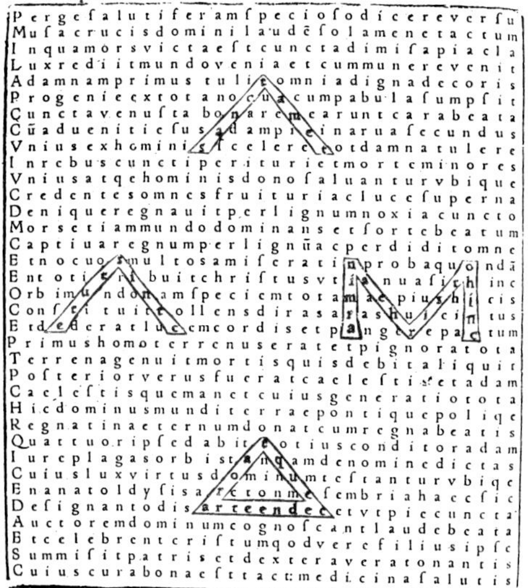

XIII Figura. De diebus concepcionis Christi in vtero virginis: quattuor Crucibus demōstratis, hoc est, cc.lxxvi: et eiusdem numeri significatione.

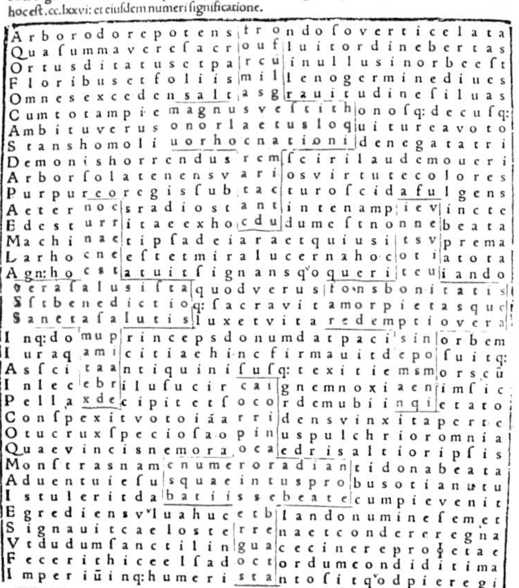

XIIII Figura. De annis ab exordio mundi vsq; in annū passionis Christi, in notis grecarū litterarū secundum formam sanctę Crucis dispositis, simul cum sacramento quod in hoc reuelatur.

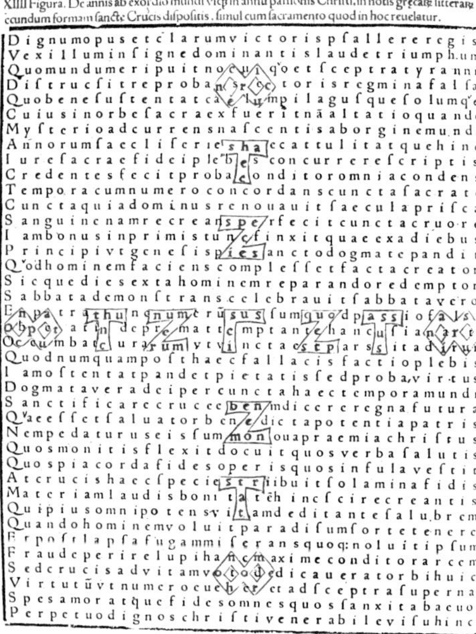

XV. figura. De quattuor euangelistis et agno, in Crucis specie constitutis.

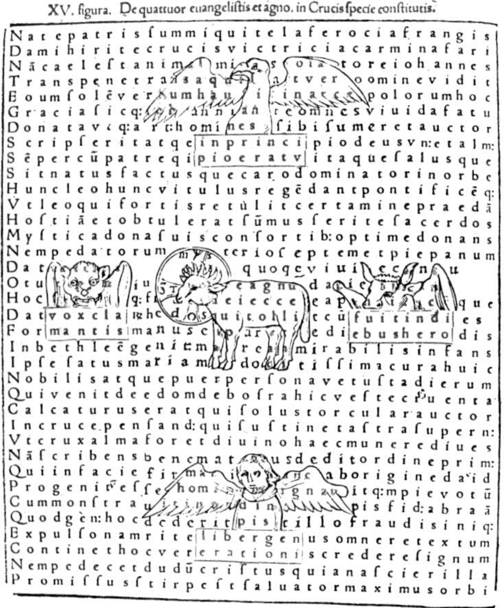

XVI Figura. De Septem donis spiritussancti, que propheta Esaias enumerat.

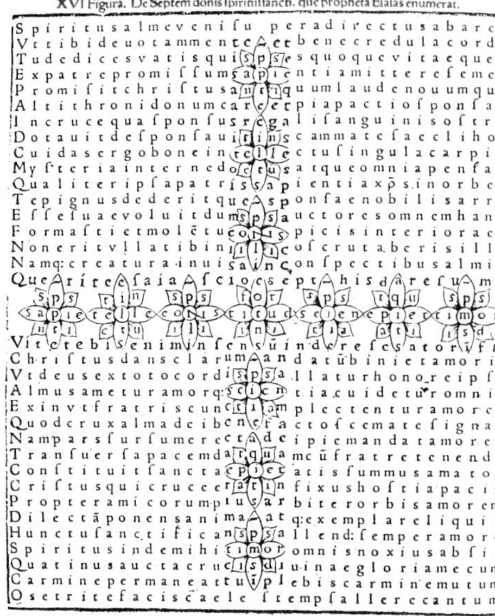

XVII Figura De Octo beatitudinibus euangelicis.

Sanctabeatapotensvitaclausgloriachristi
Cruxvenerandadeituprosperatunctiosaecli
Dignabonaatquepiaxpoafficerasquiamembra
Stipitesuspensafflictossubcarcerisvmbra
Deriperaspopulosregnuminsublimerepostum
Quisdederasquoniamspeciatiolongapolorum
Redditaiurepiisbeatolimetstemmatedignos
Nambonaquaeinterrampiusarbiterorefereno
Seminadisparsitsacramultiplicauitamauit
Quaequesedensmontisorauitinarcemagister
Discipulistribuenspactumpiafoederaiuris
Incipiebatenimalmificouncordinesanctis
Virtutūhistitulisdominuspiapanderedicta
Vtbenedictapatrisprolishocdogmatesignet
Cruxquiatotabonaconplectitetoptimaperse
Datdocetalmaannectitamantibusatquebeata
Sicfelixdiuinamardoretromenspremecordam
qvicesfacetiustitiamhostepioalgidaserua
Flentesquicupidosnamhisursumomenadeumq:
quisconsulaeternaaesitmiseratiocernent
Dolatioidq:refectiopastiolargaacetinarce
Nonaltoactioconpetitorerepensquesupernū
Opsestnuncvalethicatqhocsatisintertuacum
Longeabsunthumiliuesolequodpronusadorat
Cumverbumhaudsolummitessedinordinemores
Omnitenensposcitsemperhoctemporequeomni
Ergobeatorumesthabitareinlucevolentumet
Octenohocnumerovtsuperarduadonareqirant
Hocq:resurgentesregnumquiasiccrucevadent
Cruxviascalarotapatriaduxportatriumphus
Vitabeatahominummeritorumetmaximamerces
Binaquaterpositaenregnipiaformulapandit
Sanctabonosbenedonapoiumscandendomereri
Cunctipotensqedeidominushocomnipotentis
Spiritusipsemodisvultpaciscanderesedem
Septenosq:gradussuperisrexeratatrisquo
Altapolihincpiepossebenignospanderetire
Quoscomitaturamorratioluxlausbonavirtus
Gloriastemmathronusqisadditurarcepolorū

XVIII. Figura. De Mysterio Quadragenarij numeri.

Pandesalutaremdominovincentetriumphum
Linguafiguramanuslabiumvoxsyllabasensq:
Magnacrucisdominiquemgloriaposcitvbiq:
Sideracelsasuperetquopertingitabyssus
Luxvbipuramanetquotetrasilentianoctis
Perpetuaelatitantvbinoxq:diesq:vicissim
Succeduntceduntq:sibiquotemporecunctus
Labiturorbisvbivariabilisindit:ordoest
Quattuoristovincirevixsufficitasthaec
Paginadignacrucipraeconiatramitedenas
Hasquequadragenassanctodecallemonades
Arteligaresimulplenasquoquelucēserena
Mysticaqasvirtusornatconsecrathonorat
Temporisinstantisnumerushicritefigurā
Gestatquototachristosubprincipesancta
Aeclesiarabidopiefertcontrariatelahac
Opponenshostibellatrixconsciaprestans
Virtutumetpucnisvitiasibiilauseacuncta
Cumfideiscutodomathaecrituhaltaq:verbo
Loricāligatetbeneiustitiacinctuitalmam
Atq:salutarisgaleamhancinverticegestat
Ipsacrucisclarāfaciuntinsigniafrontem
Frontisetaduersaefunduntformosadecorē
Incrucesaluatorsacuumnamvicerathostem
Eiusethocnumerosuadesertoalmatrahebat
Exdapibuscunctisiciuniasobriachristus
Strinxeraterípuitqertodefaucesuperbi
Raptorishominemquemcastrimargiatraxit
Infacinusdiruminmitemsimulattulitiram
Huicphilargirialevisetcenodoxiatrusit
Quemaregnodominusaeternaredemtioiesus
Sedpressithostempraedamsaluauitabipso
Dapsilisatqehumilismitisetsobriusipse
Cuiuspugnasaluscuiusvictoriasanctaest
Cuiusinarcethronusaspect:ininfimacuius
Cruxouatorbishonorcruxesterectiomundi
Cruxmihicarmeneritcristivictoriaclara

XIX figura. De quinquagenario numero et sacramento in eo manifesto.

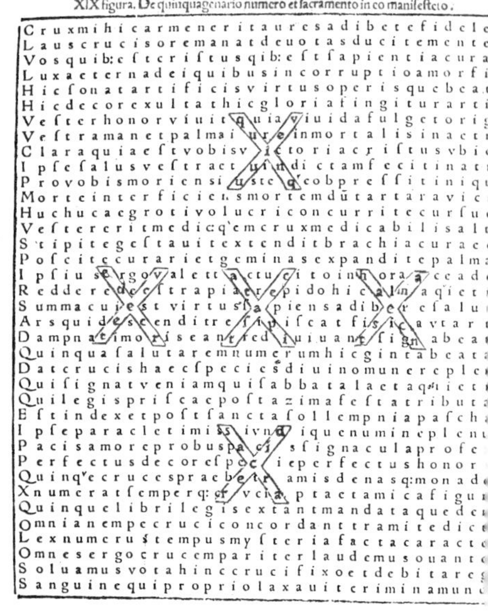

XX figura. De numero centenario et vicenario, et mystica eius significatione.

XXI figura. De septuagenario numero & binario cum eius significationibus.

Lexquoqueveradeivincendaestfortebea
Eccecrucisstrictisquasoluiturorbesabi
Duciturad vitamportumcapitatquequiet
Aruigenaeprimilapsumpostnaufragusip
Namquiapervetitummorsvicitnoxialign
Etgenushumanumseralteabsumpferatom
Faucibusamortisperlignumtolleretvth
Iurecrucisplacuitreparantiponerepal
Direquodqueatroxmadiodglutiueratal
Euomeretsiccoluerctqehincdebitepoen
Inuasitrapuitdominatumquodmaletruxf
Idvoluitsignaremodisindogmatescript
Testamentorumdeusauctoropuscrucisip
Praedixitdocuitsesetcomplessesatet
Magnipotenscruxhincideosetotacorde
Excipereinlucemmonstratdatalledica
Ritefarosiustisfecunctaperaeratetig
Gentesacpopulosadcelsaetprouocatat
Exempeosnotatetnocitisoratvalaerefle
Nonparuumfacerehincetregniducitadal
Hostefitexpulsovictrixnecfallitinar
Sedsolumgenerisdominansmiraculafit
Omniaregnalibipropterfuadominatistr
Deuotaetplacidamansuetaquietaredemp
Quodhabetenlinguasorbisetiuraloquel
Hocnumerosignataditumuenientibusatc
Tramitishocpanditsaluatordificitorb
Namocticsvtnouiesvariecosdicitorbe
Hincquenouempierellquiasinlucebeat
Spirituumdaturoctauatsupplerecreat
Vellitritedihocetclauderefaeculafi
Omnianamqorbisfleracfonsumpsitinip
Flammiuomocrucisardorepaciendocrea
Sedtamenexcarnispartesdiuinarelux
Naturainscriptoforiumproduxitetort
Legemnempesuauemercisordinecitamat
Iureleuemsuauemeticandendimuneredit

653/6

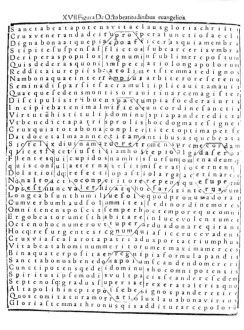

XXIII figura. De monogrammate, in quo Christi nomen comprehensum est.

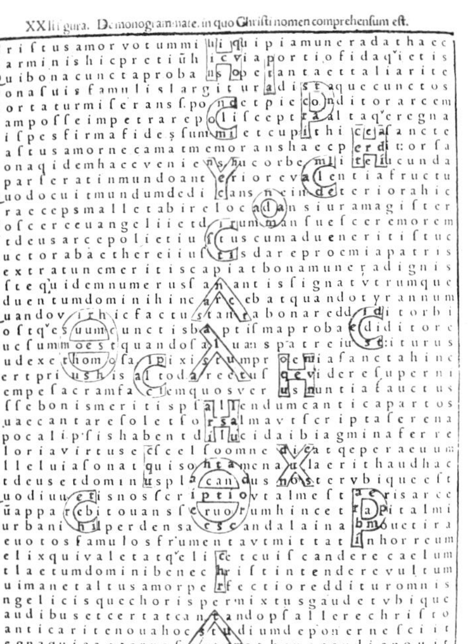

XXV figura. De Alleluia et Amen, in Crucis forma ordinatis:

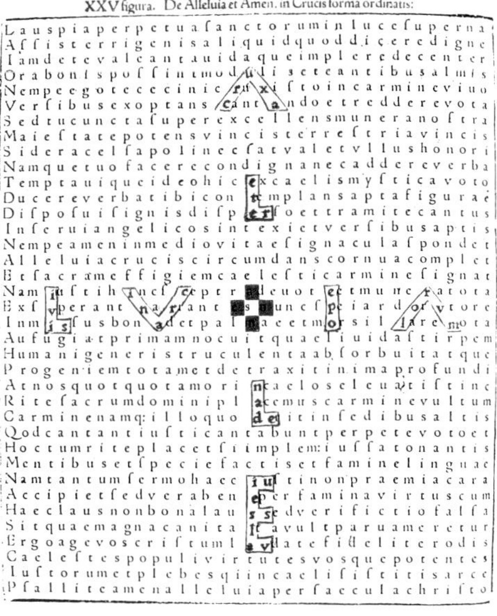

XXVIII. figura. De adoratione Crucis ab opifice:

Omnipotensvirtusmaiestasaltasabaoth
Excelsusdominusvirtutumsummecreator
Formatormundihominumtuvereredemptor
Tumealausvirt:tugloriacunctasalusque
Turextudoctortuesrectorcaremagister
Tupastorpascensprotectorverusouilis
Portiotuqemeasanctesaluatoretauctor
Duxvialuxvitamercesbonaianuaregnies
Voxsensusverbumvirtutumlaetapropago
Adtedirexietcumulansnuncdirigoverba
Mensmeateloquiturmentisintentiotota
Quicquidlinguamanusoratetbuccabeate
Corhumileetvitaiustasacratavoluntas
Omniasetelaudantetcantantcristeserene
Namq:egotedominumpronusetlaetusadoro
Atqecrucidemisetuachincdicosalutans
Spemoroteramusaramarasumaretorehinc
Hocmeusestardorclarushocignisamoris
Hocmeamensposcitprimumhocfamenetora
Hocsitisestanimimandendimagnacupido
Vtmetupiesuscipiasbonecristeperaram
Oblatumfamulumqodvictimasimtuaiesus
Hostiaqodtuasimmemetcrucifixiototum
Iamtuaconsumatetpassiomitigetaestum
Carnalemvitiaconfringatdeprimetiram
Refrenetlinguampietatisverbareponat
Mentempacificetvitamdeducathonestam
Namquetuusquandototofulgesceteolympo
Igneusaduentustorrebitetardoriniqos
Tempestasstridetcornuiammugitetorbe
Anteapparebitquandoecrucisaeresignum
Tumrogomeeripiatflammisvltricib:ipsa
Atqepoetamagnipropriumdefendatabira
Cuicanoiurecanamhymnusversibusore
Cordemanusemperdo[illegible]morabilecantu
Quoddederatvitaem[illegible]menterinara
Qandoipsaiesuscle[illegible]oaberuitimo
Infernireqiemnunc[illegible]arcepolorum
Damihihocposcosperoc[illegible]omniacredo
Quaepromisistihocten[illegible]catefideqe
Quodveraxfacisordineiudi[illegible]mniavero
Inuncadsuperosincaelisritetriumphas
Olausalmacrucissempersinefinevaleto

662/668

XIIII figura. De numero vicenario et quaternario, deque eius sacramento.

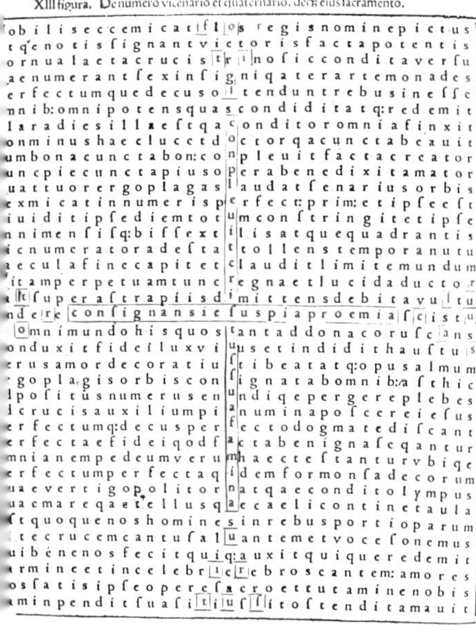

XXVI figura. De prophetarum sententiis, quae ad passionem Christi, et ad nostram redemptionem pertinet.

Ergoprophetarumbenetecruxfamenhonorat
Praedicatacsacrotuncsonattuafactafutura
Inspiratasacrotuncplebsqodprotulitore
Spiritusetsanctusillismandaueratintus
Omniacumcristumreparareloquunturetinte
Confixumdominumconcedereregnabenignis
Dauidpersosasillhicpalmasquepedesque
Dixeracatqecibofeltradietpoculoacetum
Dequetuolignoregemafferitomnibusipsum
Huicpuerohumerisesteimperiũoratesayas
Corpuspercussummanumextensumorebeato
Consputamfaciemperpendensfunusetastum
Atq:leuatamadedispersoscurrereisrahel
Hieremiasagnumdecribitceuholocaustum
Adtractumsinevocepiumlignoquecibandum
Hiezechielcernitviputaugrammatesignum
Erueteplebematq:crucisducentisadinstar
Sicutadcastasalusvirtusesvisaprophetis
Esplacitasuperiscruxhuicesnauitamundo
Namdanielcristumdixithicplebeabiniqua
Multandumetfinemdehincnoxiatenere
Oseesaluandumpopulummortisquoquemorte
Praedicatatqeiohelillapraedixerathora
Ettolemetstellaslucemnonfunderetterris
Hocidemetinfaustafestapraedixeratamos
Abdiasinsidiasionassquoquefuneratfinxit
Michadeimontemnaumuntiatultioquidsit
Cornuasanctacrucisabbacupraedicatore
Sofoniasquediemdudumdominiauditamaram
Aggeushinceqepolosdixitterramquemouegri
Zachariasiesumrenotatperfordidavestes
Plagasinmanibusfixasplangereq:uemultos
Malachiascernitsummumdominareperorbem
Ardentiquerogomundumetsudareministros
Haectuafactaprobiendicebantoreprioresj
Cruxalmavateshaecedidicitauctorinhisque
Tupiaconplerashaecomniapassiochristi

XXIIII figura. De numero centenario, quadragenario, et quaternario, eiusque significatione.

tnuncvoscantatenouumbenedicitecristo
lebscantumdilectadeosanctissimusordo
sallitenonaliisvosmetimitabilecarmen
nmortaledecuscaelestehocantetribunal
ntequatersaenossenioresquattuoratque
iuersaeformaeanteanimaliaiuresuperna
imitiaechristoinmaculatonuminisagno
:qedeoveroimmaculataeetfortishonores
stisvosemptaeqecohortessang'inisostro
eloexterrigeniscantatisritetropacum
tharismodulansastvultumlaudeserena't
:stramanussacravocib:atriarepletvbiqe
:uvocestonithrufusisclamoribusaetram
mqametmultarumvallesvoxrepletaq'arum
nguaqevestradolisignaranecnouitiniqa
tethronumdominisCitisseddiceredigne
udescarminaetaratisbenehicveparati
rsignaquaenonspernitvestergremiorex
hocnullusdiffVditduXnisolusetauctor
derisofaminnecqihocmodosplendidadonat
neracantatehincilliprobusordopiique
rgineoinhabitumaResqoq:feminalactans
fansatq:anuspariteriuuenesqesenesque
nonpollutestisnexuumq'uammulierumhic
apropteriamitisvbiinstisproemiadonat
nipotenspergitiesusquovirginisagnus
pratisdepascitouatqemritesequentes
deracelsasuperopascuapascitisagriet
nciamvestracapitvirtutumpraemiavita
restolamqamvirginisenresattulitvnam
mpealiaminfineagnuscumcorporereddet
sciteposeocrucisvosmetpersignabeata
opulitirmaeplebsagminaturbacohortes
isuperastralocumsedesq:tenetisinarce
odnobisvestralausrexetconferatagnus
aemialaetadeuscumsanctislucesuperna
direvtliceatvestrumpersaeculacantum

XXVII figura. De Apostolorum dictis ex eadem re in nouo testamento.

Necminusergotuacustoditiuracaracter
Ritenouitestamentetpiamunerapandit
Quaedeusaltushomodiuinosdetulitorbi
Pertecruxsacravotovenerandafrequenti
Promisumconplensetveraxdogmatavatum
Sedominumetestanslegisveterisq:nouaeq:
Quigeminummundopateverbosecitabysum
Noshilaratactusartansvotoanteriores
Quisolabaturveraxbonusomnibusaequus
Vndeqeapostolicusiustaperfaminafida
Almatropaeatuasermocruxlaudatvbique
Princepsorbesonatreximopectorepetrus
Taliterenlaudesfatupiusoptimedicens
Estfratreschristopovobisstitipepass:
Exemplumtradensclarumvestigiaqodvos
Eiuspergatisciuissacravulnerasanant
Hinccredoaccipiatorantisfaminaiesus
Sidonisuseietihonosartemibitterodis
Ipsequiamitisnonsordentmuneraraecci
Astiacobushincnoshortaturfaminepuro
Exemplumponenschristumdefinelaborum
Hincq:monetscribensalt:duxoreiohannes
Castusamormaneatetsobriavotaserenet
Iesusvtestpassusdevotepropteramorem
Sicnosmentepiasociopatiamuramorehic
Iesumpertypicumpieverumpsallitiesum
Iudasductoremeptesumfidisetiniquis
Pauxillumhaudpaulusorauitemetinore
Cruxsacracumdixitseiamnesceireloq:iam
Tesineneclaudemsciredar:faucib:vllam
Incaelisterrismagnumpertartaranomen
Tepropterchristispondetsatritevalere
Sicetapostolicilaudatconcorditerordo
Vatibusantiqisconiungisicunctarapina
Passiosanctapieisupersaeculacristi

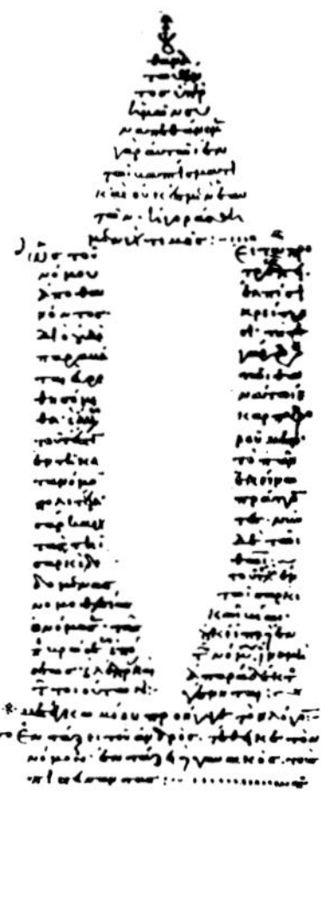

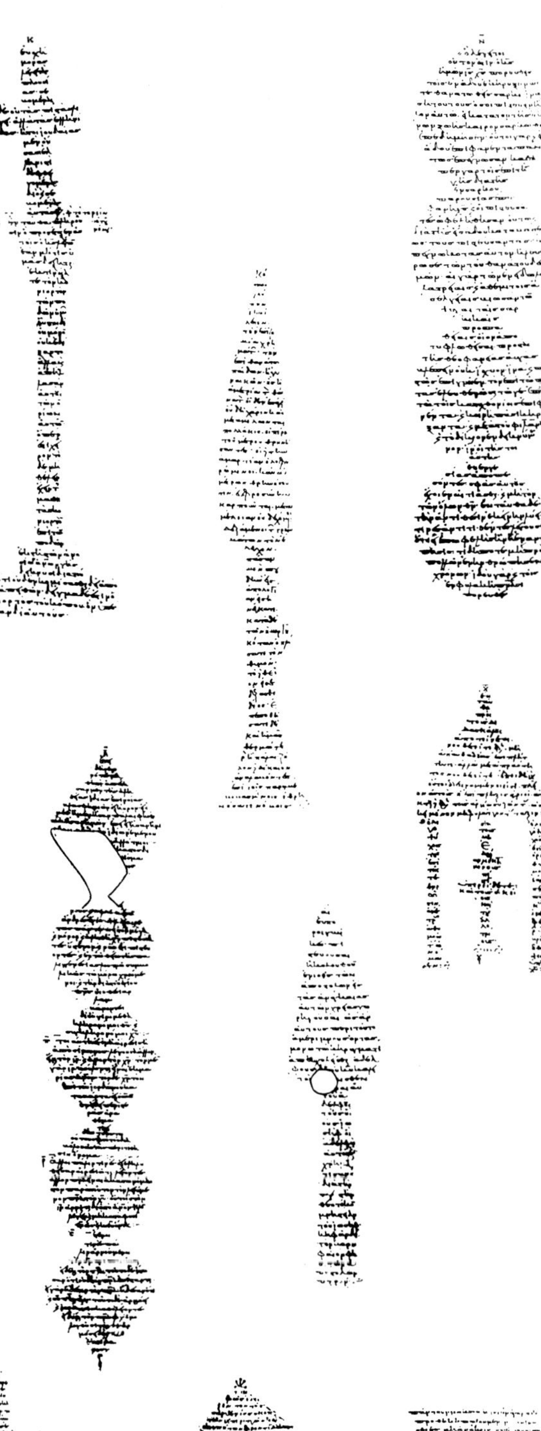

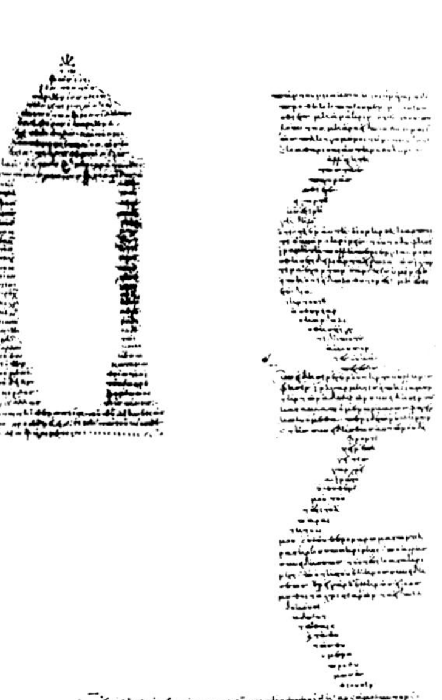

669/680

68

68

6

Namque & iam eridanum cernes in parte locatum
Caeli funestum magnis cum uiribus amnem
Quem lacrimis mestae phaethontis sepe sorores
Sparserunt letum merenti uoce canentes
Hunc orionis sublaeua cernere planta
Serpentem poteris procera que uincla uidebis
Quae retinent pisces caudarum parte locati
Flumine mixta retro adpistricis terga reuerti
Haec una stella nectuntur quam iacit ex se
Pistricis spinae ualida cum lucere fulgens
Ex inde exiguae tenui cum lumine multae
Inter pistricem fusae sparsae que uidentur
Atque gubernaclum stellae quas contegit omnis
Formidans acrem morsu lepus his neque nomen
Nec formam ueteres certam statuisse uidentur
Nam quis sideribus claris natura poliuit
Et uario pinxit distinguens lumine formas
Has ille astrorum custos ratione notauit
Signaque signauit caelestia nomine uero
Has autem quae sunt paruo cum lumine uel quae
Consimiles specie stellas parilique nitore
Non potuit nobis nota clarare figura

But it is perfectly possible that Apollinaire, who was very well read, also knew of a collection of figured poems which are forerunners of his own calligrams even more than Hrabanus Maurus' were, and were brought to light in 1836 by William Young Ottley. It is a Carolingian version (now in the British Museum) of a poem by the Greek author Aratus, who came from
681/701 Asia Minor. It bears the title 'Phenomena' and is an 'astronomical' manuscript listing the various heavenly bodies, their respective positions, their degree of brilliance, their relationship with the twelve signs of the zodiac, etc. It was translated by Cicero in his youth; then Hugo Grotius completed this unfinished version by adding some lines of his own; and finally the Saxon artist Julius Hyginus added some strange forms full of *capitalis rustica*, generally drawing them in red lead or brown, but also using bluish tones and various different shades of grey. The twenty-five plates which make up the manuscript depict a succession of figures comprising characters from fables, birds, fish and various objects, among which we come across Perseus, a hydra, a dolphin, a swan, an eagle, a ship, the planets, a lyre, the sign for *delta*, etc. Apart from an altar which is a fairly obviously plagiarism of Dosiadas' poetical exercises, most of these figures display great originality: for the first time the texts are set round illustrations of living creatures or inanimate objects. The latter stand out from a sort of seed-bed of letters, rather like the bits of newspaper in collages by Braque or Picasso. And no doubt today the designers of the tiniest advertisement who make use of the banal photographic process which involves superimposing a text over an image have no idea that they are borrowing from illuminations a thousand years old.

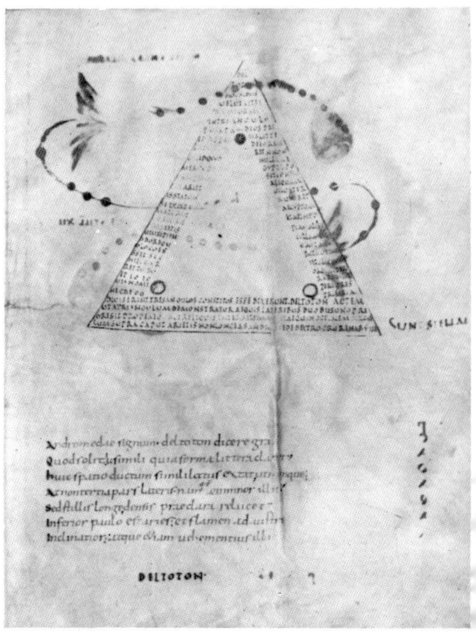

685

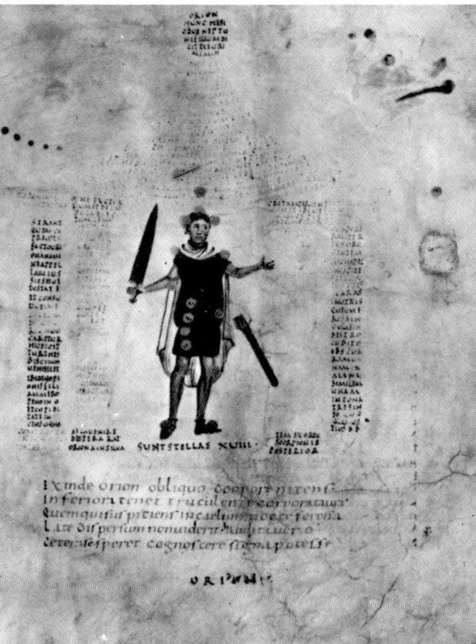

68

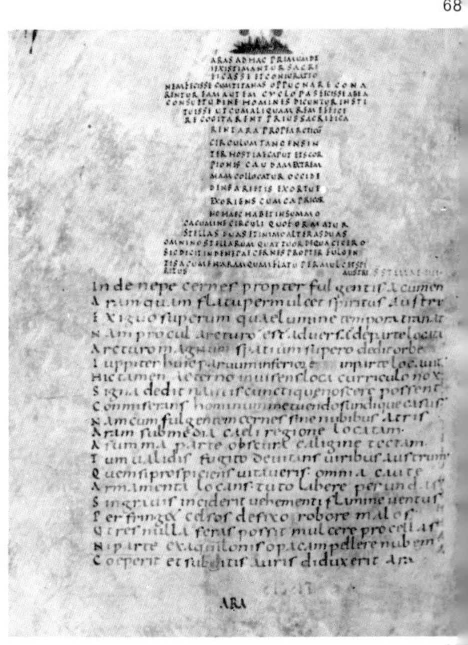

6

However much imagination and ingenuity these artists and poets display, it must be admitted that the Latin alphabet does not lend itself particularly well to this type of figured work, because of its baldness and the rigid geometry governing its design. Not only do the letters seem to want to resist any distortions of this type by means of their own inertia, but at the same time the organic character of the words, the horizontal structure which is imposed on the reader and the linear arrangement of the text are all obstacles in the way of decoration.

On the other hand, the various forms of Arabic script have a number of qualities which are so naturally decorative that any text, however small, for which they act as a vehicle, implants the outlines, rhythms and colour of an image in the reader's mind from the outset. The etymology of the word 'arabesque' ('decorative motif in the Arab style') is instructive enough in itself. Their religion forbids the Arabs to depict the human form or, in a general way, anything alive, but although they have observed this rule strictly when decorating buildings intended for worship, elsewhere they have not been able to resist the

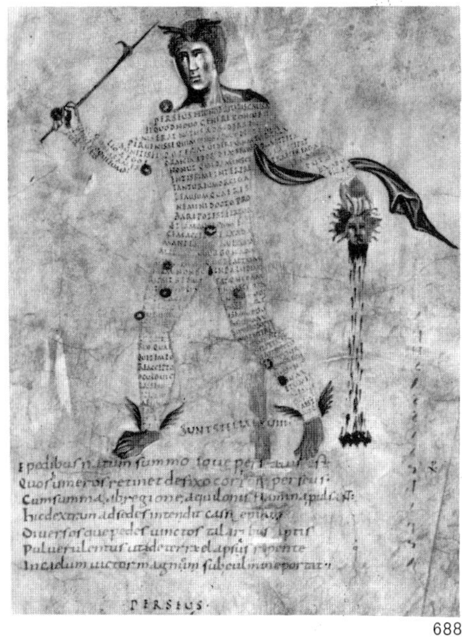

688

691

694

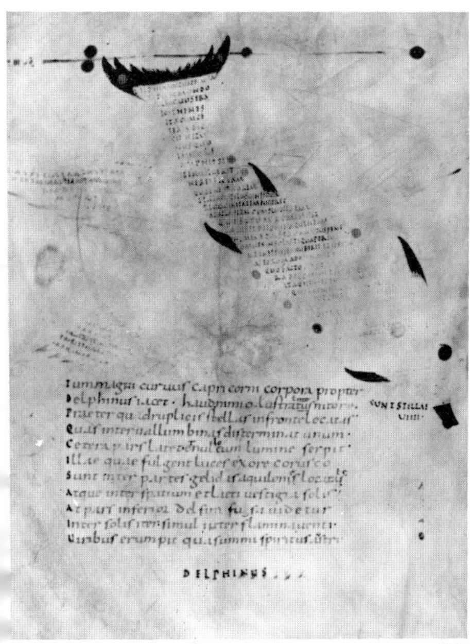

689

692

695

690

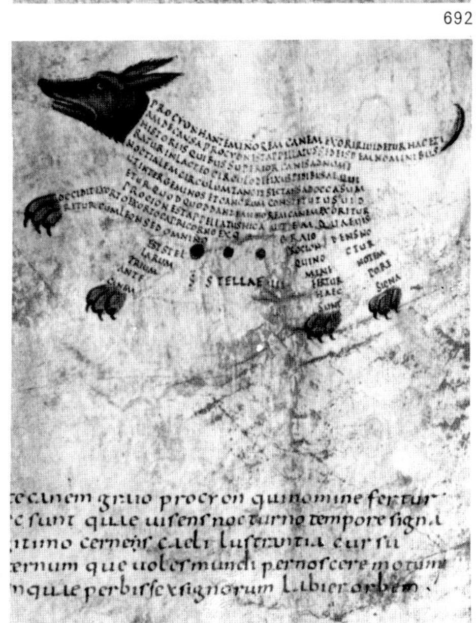

693

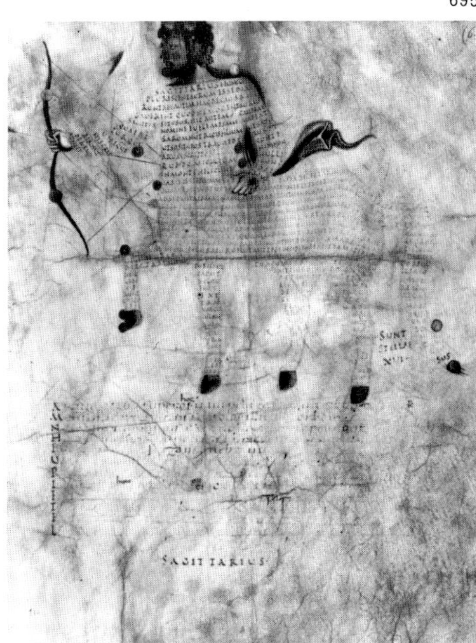

696

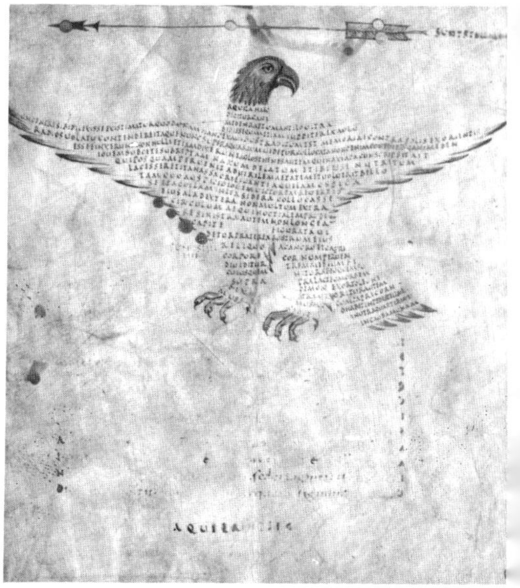

697

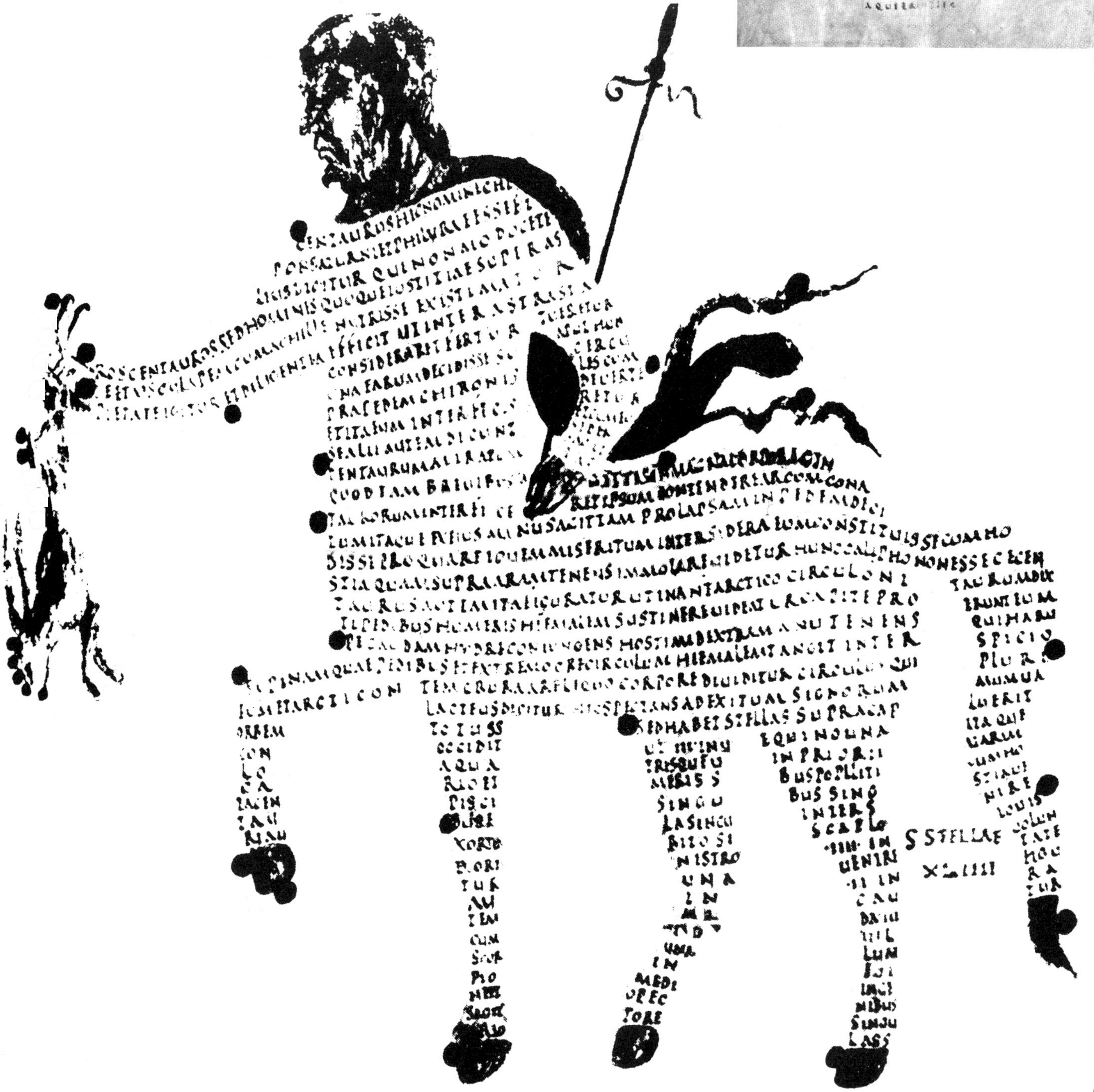

69

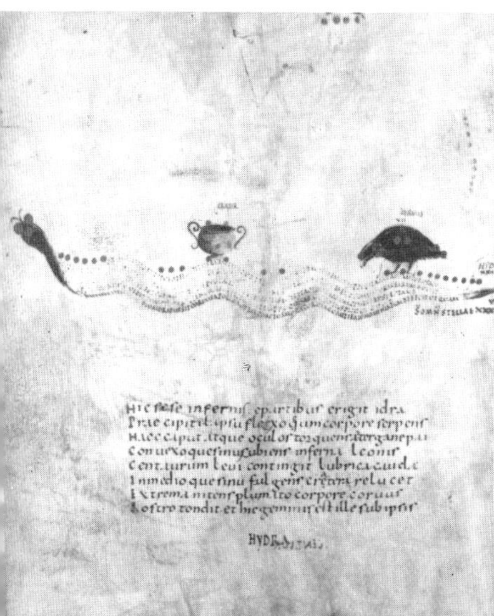

699

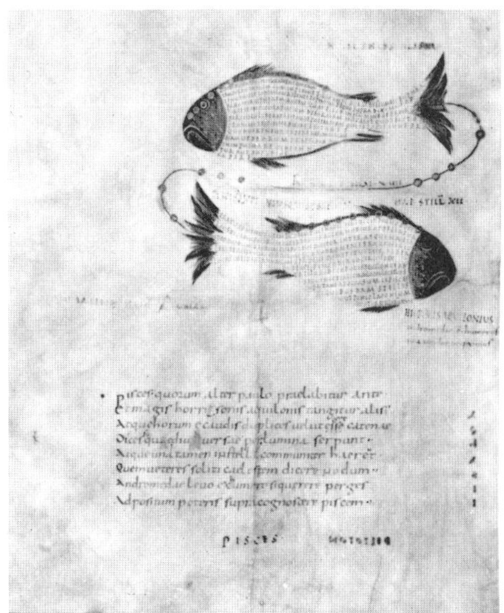

700

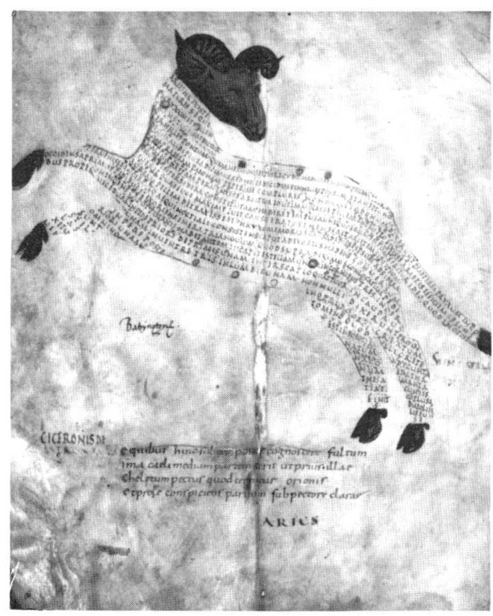

701

universal tendency to fashion objects in the image of man and to depict nature as alive and full of life. All the same, they have always taken care to leave a note of ambiguity by giving the human form a vague or incomplete outline, as in the case of
the horseman in figure 703, whom some Orientalists see as an 703
image of the prophet Mohammed on his mare El-Borak; others see him as the Caliph Ali, who claimed that 'beautiful handwriting is one of the keys to riches'. The image of the sparrow- 702
hawk and the lion are achieved with the help of letters or words 704
which are sometimes, it is true, moved slightly out of position to fit the requirements of the image. In the same way, an inscription in Cufic characters reproducing the Moslem creed, 707
'There is no God but God, and Mohammed is God's prophet', is repeated symmetrically, no doubt so that not a single one of the domes and seven minarets surmounting the temple of Mecca needs to be omitted. The same type of requirement made another calligrapher resort to mirror-writing for his face which brings together the names of Allah, Mohammed, and Hassan.

Scripts in the Far East offer a number of examples similar to this which, as the experts would put it, 'achieve a perfect equation between matter and manner'. In this monosyllabic language, in which every sign represents a word, a syllable of a phoneme, the art of calligraphy rapidly merged with the arts of painting and poetry. According to the *Chouo Wen Kiai Tseu*, Ts'ang Kié 'drew the shapes of objects or beings so as to begin to invent characters', thus establishing the visual reference which is that of the ideogram. As Charles Nodier wrote in *A Letter Concerning the Invention of the Alphabet*: 'The ignorance of travellers and historians has greatly exaggerated the difficulties involved in such a study by raising the number of signs in Chinese writing to more than ninety thousand, without pausing to think that in fact there were a mere four or five hundred positive signs, all the rest being modifications of these. For instance, one sign in Chinese writing which is virtually hieroglyphic, for it is very graphic, signifies a stream. You simply use it twice for a small river, multiply it indefinitely to turn it into a vast river and draw a jerky and broken outline for a torrent'.

The Chinese scholar Abel Remusat meanwhile assures us that there is a Chinese description of the Flood in which the shape, outline and arrangement of the ideograms suggest falling rain.

We know that ideograms are not necessarily restricted to representing objects, that certain types of ideogram denote action, quantity or movement, while others combine a generic meaning with a phonetic element, and yet others call on analogy or alternatively are combined as groups of ideas. Their dominant common feature is the symbol, and their role is to impose an image on the mind without the intervention of sound. We can give three examples to illustrate this dual mis-
708 sion: a poster by the Japanese artist Yamashiro which was chosen
by an international jury as the best piece of graphic work sub-
709 mitted to them; the highly suggestive sign for 'death' as
drawn by Hakuin in the eighteenth century; and finally,
710 though this is a curiosity of a rather anecdotal type, an 'Ox'
combines an ideogram and a calligram in a single image and takes us back to the attempts made by western artists to incorporate pictorial notation into writing.

702

703

Apart from the banderoles or phylacteries used in Gothic illumination, which sometimes spread out in all directions round the human figures (and which may be seen as the first pictorial representation of the Word), it does not seem as if the art of expressing oneself through calligrams had much appeal for western artists for several centuries. Even the Renaissance, although it gave rise to various anthropomorphic alphabets in Italy, Germany and France, did not produce a single calligram. Curiously enough, figured poems did not reappear until the early years of the Enlightenment.

704

A man called Jacques Cellier spent four whole years of his
life, beginning in 1583, filling 217 large leaves of a book called
711/732 *A Study of Several Peculiarities*, by 'Sieur François Merlin,
comptroller-general of the household of the late Madame Marie-Elisabeth, only daughter of Charles IX'. This collection of pen-and-ink drawings includes writing-patterns and architectural models, musical and astronomical instruments and specimens for alphabets in several different languages; it ends with a series of twenty-two extremely successful calligrams. Pastoral scenes, houses, churches and citadels alternate with vases of flowers, a carvel, a horseman, a stork and some wrestlers. Some of the motifs are purely ornamental and borrow elements from the arabesque motif and from mosaics, whereas others, such as the hunting-scene, have a note of realism and display a

705

706

707

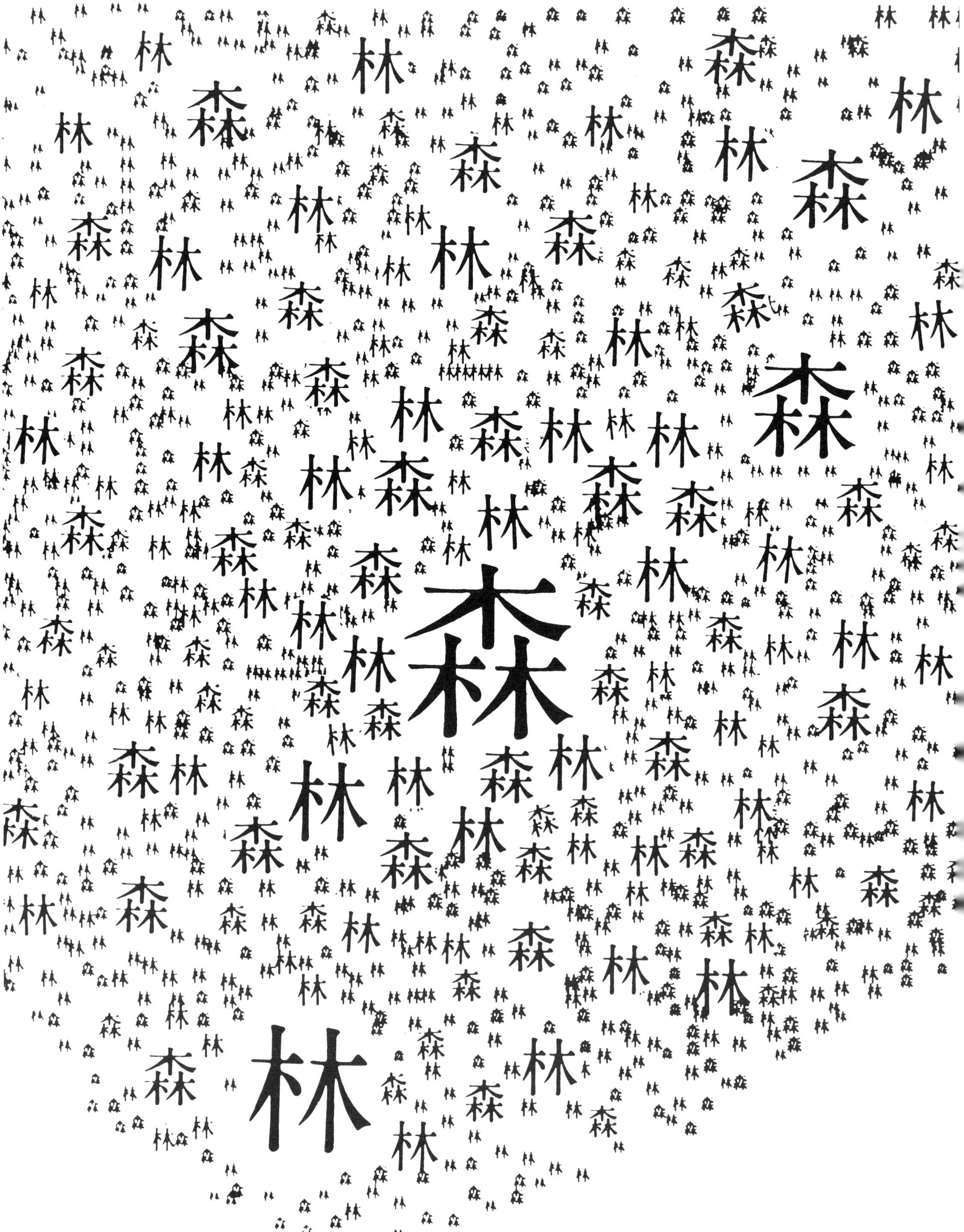

709

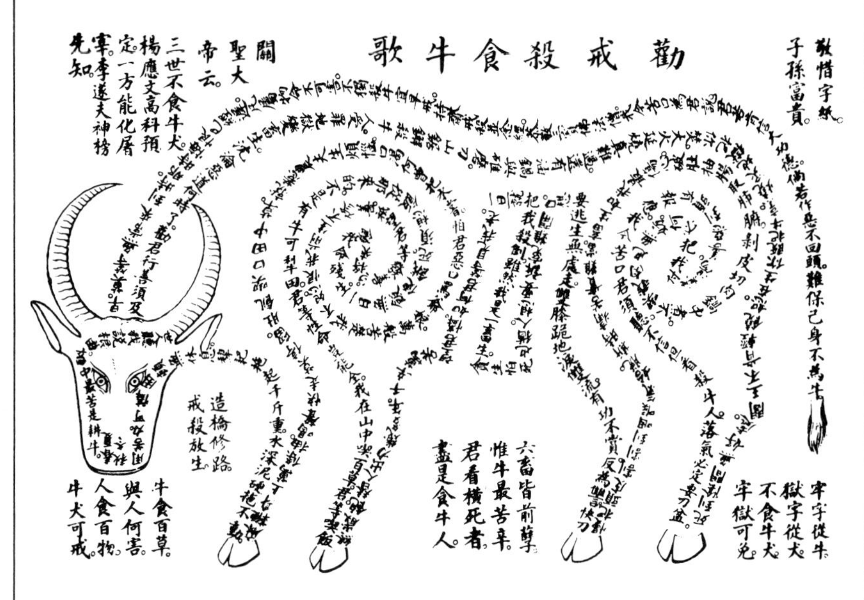

710

concern for absolute precision which is quite astonishing if we imagine the difficulties involved in this type of illustration.

In the field of typography, this period produced a fair number of rhopalic verses. In 1592 a small volume of Greek and Latin verse by the pupils at the Collège de Dôle was published; their ages ranged from twelve to eighteen and their work was dedicated to Monsieur de Vergy, the Governor of
the province. It includes a Latin pipe of Pan which is a new 734
version of Theocritus or Porphyrius, and a labyrinth; concentric circles; two triangles, one Greek, the other Latin; a 744 745 746
pons asinorum by Claude Gillabod d'Arbois, who also contri- 750
buted a Latin rhombus, a square, and a Greek rhombus and 748-749
parallelogram; a hexagon in Latin; two altars, one in Greek 747 735
and one in Latin, both of which were clearly inspired by 736
Dosiadas' altars; nine eggs; two axes; two pairs of wings and 737-738
two pairs of spectacles, one in Greek and one in Latin in each 742-743
case.

A few years later, a poet from Rouen called Jean Grisel
dedicated his poetry to Henri IV; here we can see a 'battleaxe 753
in the old style', 'wings of love worn by virtuous women'; 752
'Easter eggs for the French', as well as three madrigals ('or 751
double prosopopeii of the *fleur-de-lys*') spread out over fold-out pages, with the design of the royal emblem brought out by the use of capitals; and also some 'figured acrostics' which are reniniscent of Hrabanus Maurus' 'grids'.

Shortly after this, Robert Angot de l'Eperonnière published his *Chef-d'oeuvre Poétique* (Poetic Masterpiece), which bore the sub-title 'The first part of the concert of the French muses' – the wording alone is enough to conjure up the music of
François Couperin. Apart from some twin bottles and Easter 792
eggs which are far from original, this collection includes three 761
figured poems, 'The laurel bough', 'The cross' and most of all 754 760
'The lute' which owe nothing to classical models from the 755
ancient world.

711

712

713

714

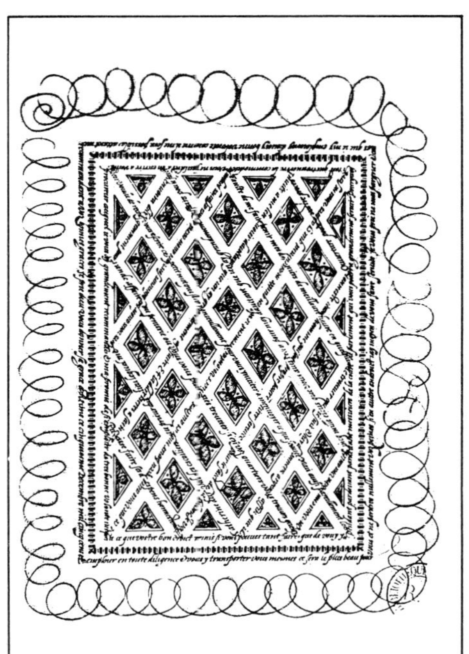

19

720

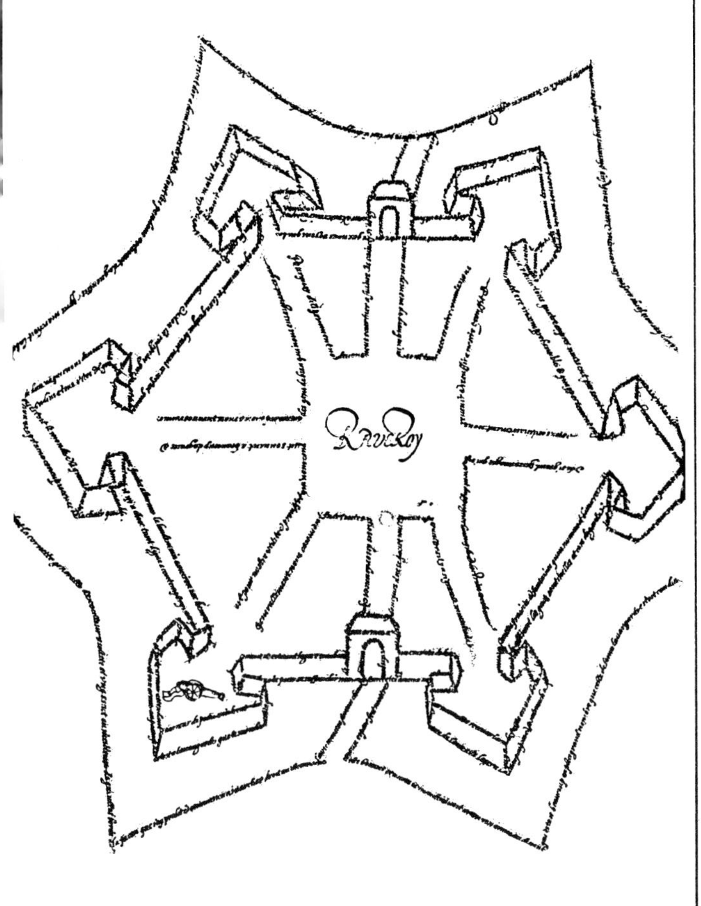

21

722

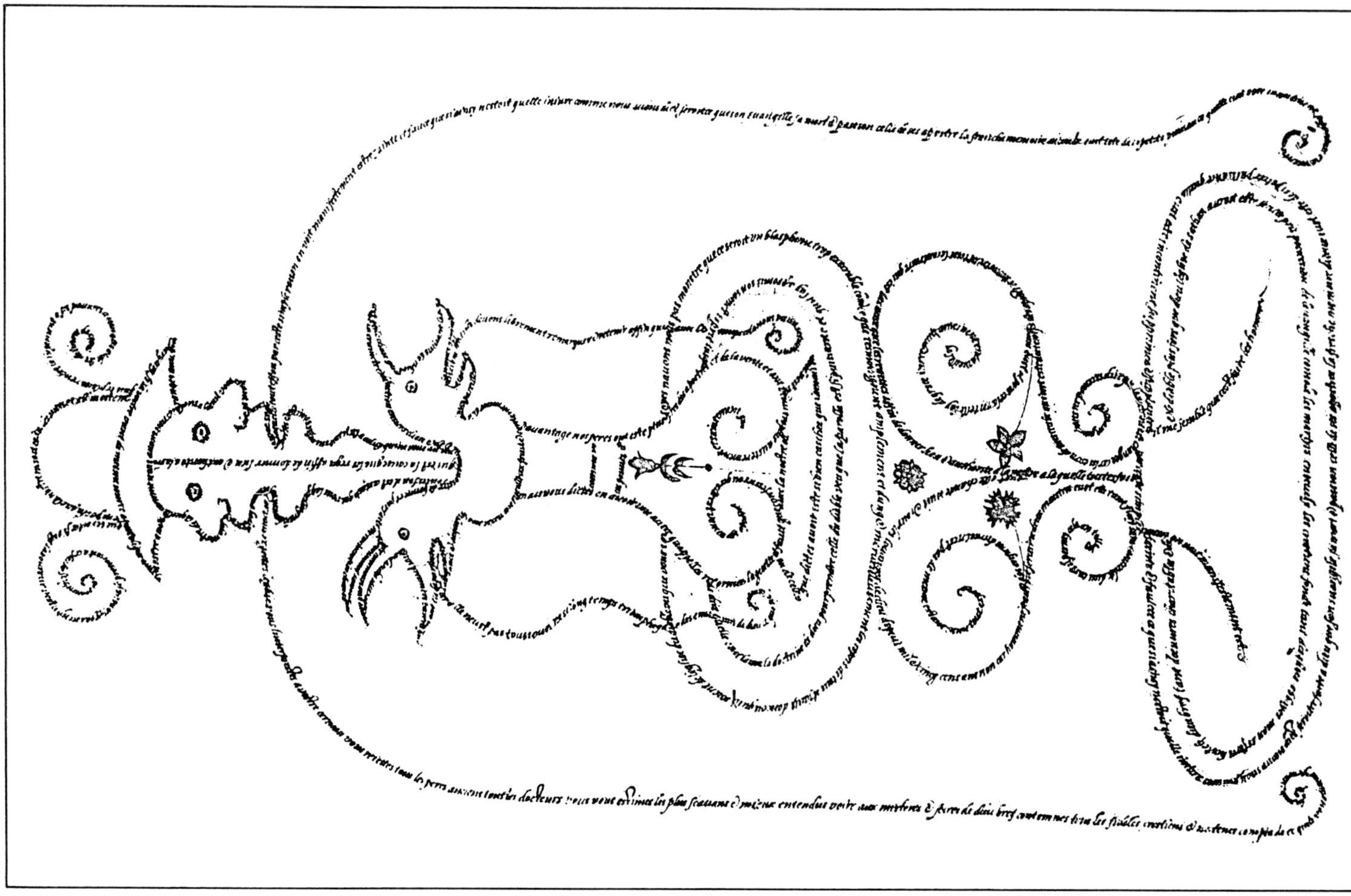

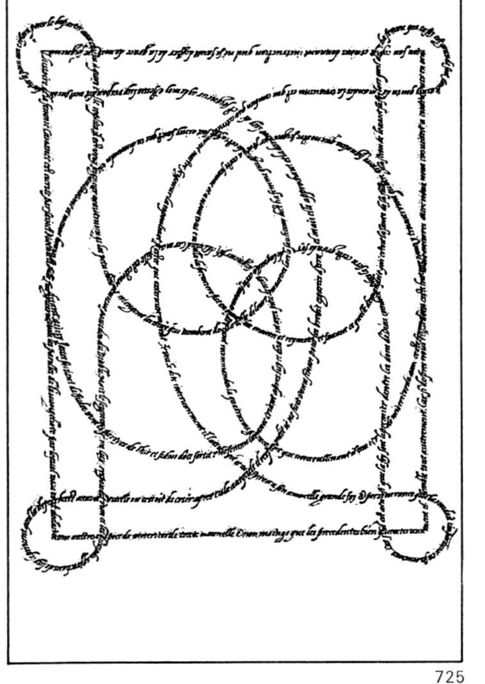

725

726

727

728

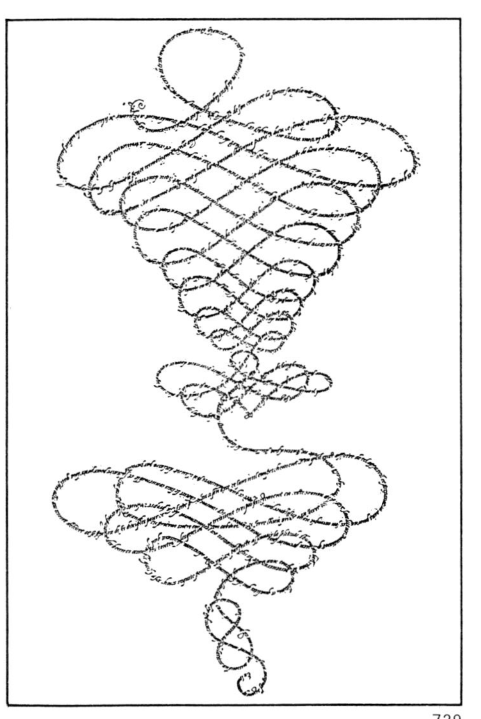

729

730

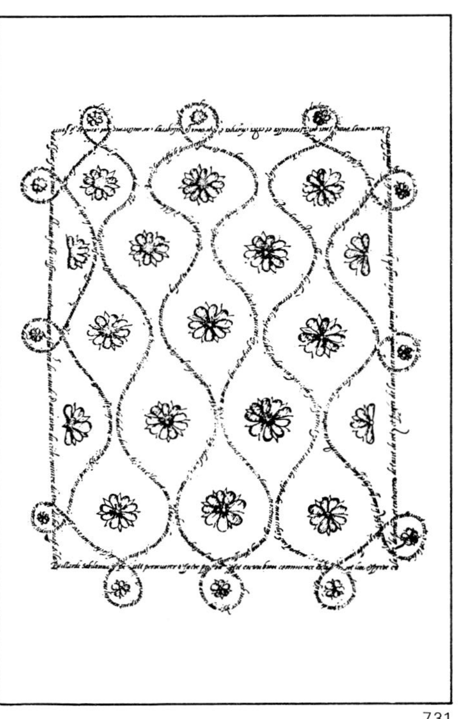

731

732

In England, *The Arte of English Poesie*, of which George Puttenham is alleged to be the author, took stock from 1589 onwards of the shapes most frequently used by poets for their
765 rhopalic verse; there were squares, rectangles, triangles, diamonds, some elongated, some not, also broken circles, etc. The book gives detailed instructions about how to compose such poems, and refers to various strange customs practised at the Chinese and Tartar courts, where the princes would communicate by means of figured poems. Thus when the great emperor Can, whose name comes from his successes in war and his wide conquests, falls in love with the Lady Kermesine, a dialogue ensues which involves drawing two diamonds made up of letters decorated with amethysts, rubies, emeralds, topaz and gold; later on Ribuska, of Persia, converses with the Lady Selamour, and their conversation forms two triangles joined together at the tips. And then again we come across two more pieces of verse in the shape of columns, with shaft, pedestal and capital; plus two pyramid-shaped poems, and another one which mingles God, the world and the Queen within a single allegorical circle.

When the seventeenth-century English poet Samuel Butler comments on the work of his compatriot Edward Benlowes, he describes the temples and pyramids which can be found in it and declares that he has surpassed all his predecessors in the genre by giving the words the exact timbre and resonance of the sounds made by the objects they evoke, examples of this being a grill and a frying-pan.

SYLVÆ,
QVAS VARIO
CARMINVM GENERE PRIMANI SCHOLASTICI
COLLEGII DOLANI SOCIETATIS IESV,
IN PVBLICA TOTIVS CIVITATIS GRAtulatione, lætitiaque ex tempore obtulerunt.
NOBILISSIMO,
INVICTISSIMOQVE
D. DOMINO DE VERGY, COMITI CHAMPLITENSI, ETC. ÆT. COMItatus Burgundiæ Gubernatori desideratissimo.

DOLÆ,
Typis ANT. DOMINICI.
CIƆ. IƆ. XCII.

OVA MAIORA, ET MINORA.
Inuentum præclarum Simmiæ Rhodij.

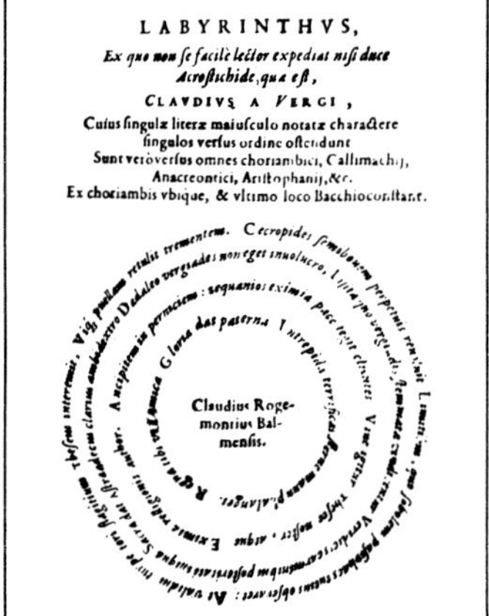

LABYRINTHVS,
Ex quo non se facilè lector expediat nisi duce Acrostichide, qua est,
CLAVDIVS A VERGI,
Cuius singulæ literæ maiusculo notatæ charactere singulos versus ordine ostendunt
Sunt verò versus omnes choriambici, Callimachij, Anacreontici, Aristophanij, &c.
Ex choriambis vbique, & vltimo loco Bacchio constant.

Claudius Rogemontius Balmensis.

744

ΤΡΙΓΩΝΟΝ.
Id est, Triangulum versu iambico, qui ab vna syllaba ad plures semp[er] crescit.

Amandus Pratanus ...

745

ISOSCELES.
Versu iambico, qui ab vna syllaba deinceps semper crescit.

Syrinx πολυκαλαμ⊛.

Ingeniosissimum inuentum Theocriti.

Euterpe calamos modulantibus vrgeo ventis.
Huc Patarae meæ flatus immitte cicutæ
Auree tibicen, Cyrrhæq́; habitator Apollo:
Pulmones leuibus mihi ludere flatibus, &
Da sæuire mihi modulamine multiplici,
Quo satus Amphion magno Ioue dicitur
Thebis Heptapylis validissima mœnia
Cõstruxisse; mei vt ducis indomitum
Robur, & acta canã, Hectoreosq́; toros,
Cuius hyperboreos adyt sinus,
Leucothoëq́; rubrã vaga gloria.
Vndiq; fac resonare polos
Delie, spirituumq́; potens,
Parnaßique bifrontis
Cantu non solito
Cornua læta tubæ,
Cui' vterq; portus
Spiret Achilles
Inuictos, &
VERGIADAS
Ductores.

734

ΘΕΟΚΡΙ΄ΤΟΥ ΒΩΜΟΣ.

Ου βούλομαί σοι ῥέζειν
Ἐν τουτέῳ τῷ βωμῷ
Θυάδει, τειχεσιπλήτης Ἄρης
Δικαίων κύριε χρυσόμορφε,
Καὶ αἰγάδας τὰς ὀρεσκῴους,
Καλλιτριχόντε ἄρνα τῶν μήλων
Και ὀρθοκέροτα βῶν
Ιφθίμων κάρηνα μὴ
Θύω τῷ ἐμῷ Διὶ
Βροντάιῳ, βαρυκτύπῳ
Καὶ κλειτῷ τὰ θύματα
Αρχῆς. ἀλλὰ πάντα με
Ού μὴ ὄντα ἀξιόνυν
Ὅς αἰὲν τὸν αἰνήσω,
Μετ' εὐτυχοῦς πᾶν τὸ μὸν σόλου
Εὐφραδέισι ξυμπράκτορας,
Οὓς ἀργυρότοξ⊛ Ἀπόλλων,
Καὶ αἱ μοῦσαι φίλαι φιλεῦνται.

Ant. Tabetus Dolanus.

735

ARA THEOCRITI.

Nonne paras Calliope bidentis
Innocuæ frangere guttur ense
Sanguineo; nonne paras sacrificũm mucrone
Hinnuleos, atque boues, & teretes iuuencos
Obijcere? an inficies fors pecudum cruore
Fana deũm forsan, & aræ veteres vapores
Sanguineis excipient fauillis,
Numina quo syderei tonantis
Sequamio concilies Achilli?
Imperij Romæ caput capacis
Quà viget ex Hesperio cubili
Vectus equis ad mare sol eoum,
Polluerit sanguine tẽpla diuũm,
Capreolos Barbara gens & ipsa,
Colla virum perfidiosis superis sacrarit:
At mea, clarissime dux, ara tibi cruore
Non tepido fœda fluet læta tibi sed instar
Metra dei sacrificat; fers caput auctum honore
Ad superos, fama canit te patriæ parentem.

Philippus Merceretus Dolanus.

736

738

739

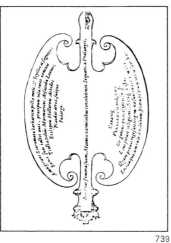

ΤΑ ΠΤΕΡΑ

740

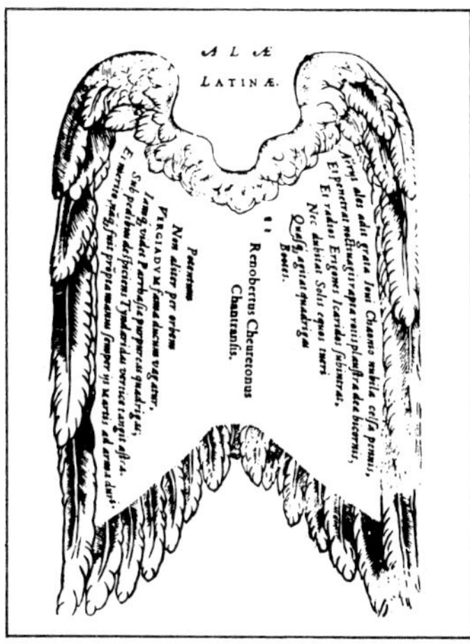

741

Ad lectorem non propitium. ὄμματα.
Versu choriambico Aristophanio, &c. maiusculæ ordine
Alphabetico carminum ordinem denotant.

742

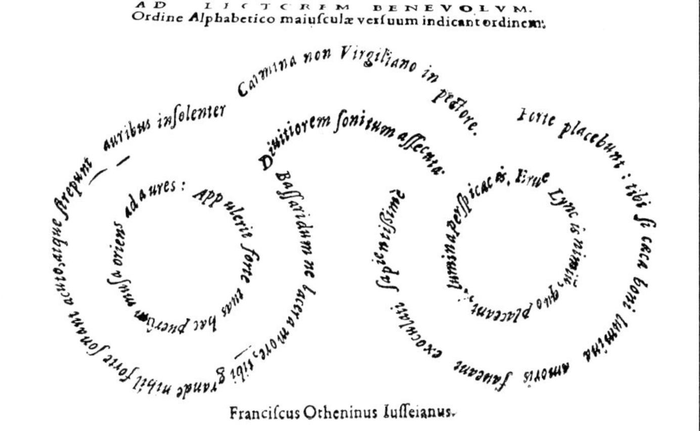

AD LECTOREM BENEVOLVM.
Ordine Alphabetico maiusculæ versuum indicant ordinem.

Franciscus Otheninus Iusseianus.

743

HEXAGONVM.
Versu iambico.

Hîc Hexagonum ne putes
Frustra nigro colore pictum:
Nam sex habere te dotes patet:
Virtute vincis æqua Scipiones,
Priscos lacertis bellicosis Hectoras,
Agamemnonasq; hoc toto in orbe fortiores
Bello decoros principes, Heroas inclytos
Mauorte; quamuis laude binas Herculis columnas,
Nilum vagosq; Tethyos vastos sinus petant.
Ne se locuples conferat tibi Darius,
Xerxesq́; nummis: ne suas iactent opes,
Et fulminantes militum cateruas.
Humanitate præstas Cæsari.
Te Nestoremq́; prædicamus,
Aequiq́; seruantissimum.

Franciscus Cornutus, Religiosus Benedictinus,
Carolanus. Anno ætat. 18.

747

Parallelogrammum Anacreonticum.

ἰδίου τὸ σχῆμα τοῦτο,
Δείκνυσιν, ὀυεργέτε,
Ἥρωα ἐμμεναί σε,
Καὶ ὁμμεναι θεοῖσιν
Ἐν τῷ βραχεῖ ἀριθμόν.
Ὡς πάντοθ' οὐκ ὅμοιον
Μὴ σχῆμά ἐστιν. οὕτω
Σὺ μηδὲ θνητὸς ἀνήρ,
Ἠ μὴν μάκαρς ὑπάρχεις.
Ἀλλ' ἡμίανθ⊛ος ἥρως,
Καὶ ἡμίθε⊛ ὁ ἀρχός.

ῥομβοειδὲς ἐνδεκασυλλαβόν, ἢ φαλεύκιον.

Claudius Gillabodus maior.

748

Τετράγωνον Ἀναπαιστικόν.

Καρτερόχειρ, τυχόν, ὄρχαμε λέξεις·
Ἐνθάδε τί σὺ γράφεις τετράγωνον·
Εἰς ἰσόπλευρα ἔχει, τόδε σχῆμα,
Μηδὲ τὰ μείζονα, μηδὲ ἐλάττω
Τέτταρα: ὧδ' ἀρεταί, πανάρεις,
Τέτταρες οὐδὲ ἐλάττονες, οὐδὲ
Μείζονες αἱ ἕτεραι ἑτεράων,
Ἀλλὰ ἴσως συνάγουσι κατ' ἡμᾶς
Σοὶ δύναμις, δίκη τε σεμνή,
Καὶ σύνεσις, μεγαλοφροσύνη τε
Φιὺ τετραγώνου τῆς ἀρετῆς πιάων.

Claudius Gillabodus maior.

Rhombus.

749

[illegible] Anacreonticum, & Iambicum, quod quo ordine legi debeat docet Acrostichis, quæ hæc verba constituit.
CLAVDIVS A VERGI VIR NOBILIS
Claudius Gillabodus maior Arbosianus.

Choros agens reperta
Lætatur hac figura,
Atq; ense colla tauris
Votiua trũcat: amplũ
Dicat superobecatũba
Ioui, dusque magnis.
Vouet suaue carmen Suauis Heliconiounda
Apollineaque dignum
Virtute quitribunal
Existimabat animas
Rutilum repetere cœli
Gemmatum, & reuerti
In multiplex cadauer.

VERGÆ regum fulgido
Illustrium orte sanguine
Rerúmque portus vnice:
Nobis medullæ pruriunt;
Omnes reperto te duce
Bis, ter, quatérque gratiam
Ingentem habent Celtæ Deo,
Lætique se totos ei,
Ipsique tibi, domos suas,
Suósque iuuenes deuouent.

750

LES
OEVFS DE PASQVES

François
Doux-courtois
Et du monde
Race plus ronde,
Fidelle nation,
Par vne immitation
Ces œufs sõt vos œufs de Pasques:
Ils ne sont pas de ces oiseaux
Qui pour vn font cent coquedaques:
Pourtant vous les trouuerrez beaux,
Si vous aimez la douce gentillesse
Et d'Ipocrene, & du flot de Permesse.
En ces lieux ie les ay trouuez,
Contentez-vous donc de ma peine,
Et qu'ils soyent par vous approuuez.
Qui pres ceste fontaine,
Et beau fleuue n'ira
De tels n'en aura
Car personne
n'en donne.

De l'homme vnicorne
monstré à Paris.

AVX FRANCOIS.

Ces œufs
Qui sont deux
Sans escalle
Comme vne oualle,
Ont bien plus de bon-heur
De la diuine faueur
Que les deux de la Sparthaine
Mere de Pollux & Castor,
Et de Clytemnestre, & d'Helene,
Ils sont bien plus diuins encor:
L'vn d'eux tenoit de Iupiter en signe,
L'autre mortel de la mere estoit digne:
Et ces deux sont du tout diuins,
Tirans leur chaleur de la Muse
Dessus ces verds bords cristalins
Où l'esprit bon s'amuse.
Receuez-les François
Chantans d'vne voix
De Parnasse
leur race.

A vne belle Dame.

Phœbus au ciel monstre ses feux,
Vous esclairez parmi le monde:

751

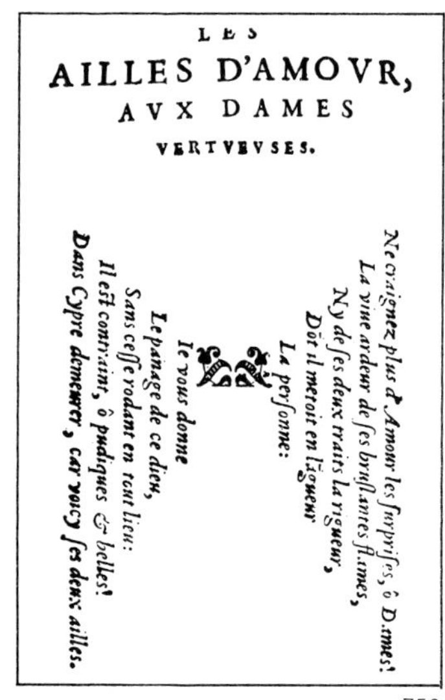

752

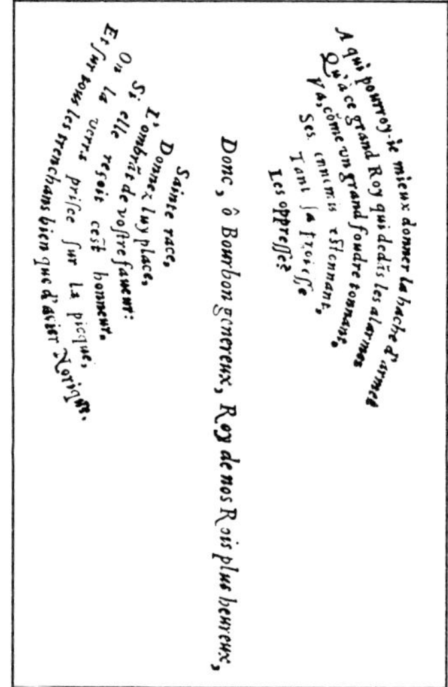

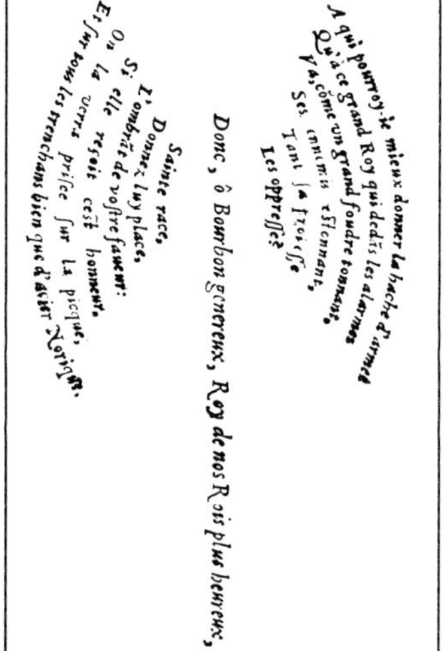

753

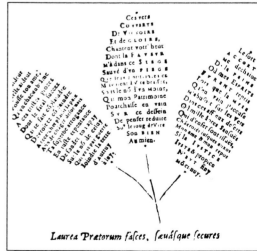

Laurea Prætorum fasces, sæuâsque secures

754

Compared with this example of imitative harmony, George
766 Herbert's verse exercises in *The Temple* (1633) – an altar
767 and a pair of wings – seem pretty feeble, although one commentator thought he could see in the shape of the lines in 'Easter wings', which first grow longer and then shorter, a visual interpretation of the lark's song, which is associated with the allegory of the Fall of Man and his resurrection in Christ. Other equally traditional shapes can be seen in Anomo's
768 'Altar' and in the pyramid-shaped dedication to Josuah Sylvester's translation of du Bartas's *La Semaine ou la creation du monde* ('The Week, or the Creation of the World'). Meanwhile the cross which the English clergyman Robert Herrick composed for his *Hesperides* (1648) was originally very similar to the one designed by Angot de l'Eperonnière; it has undergone a series of new editions, in the course of which it has inspired a very wide variety of typographic versions, right
764 down to William Morris, who added colour vignettes in the lines of his texts in 1895.

It is entertaining to find out to what extent the worship of Bacchus has inspired people composing figured poems over the centuries. After Rabelais's *'dive bouteille'*, which was
784 accompanied by a glass – though not as well known and rather vague in outline – Aldus Manutius (who, it is said, invented the Italic script for his correspondence with Laura,

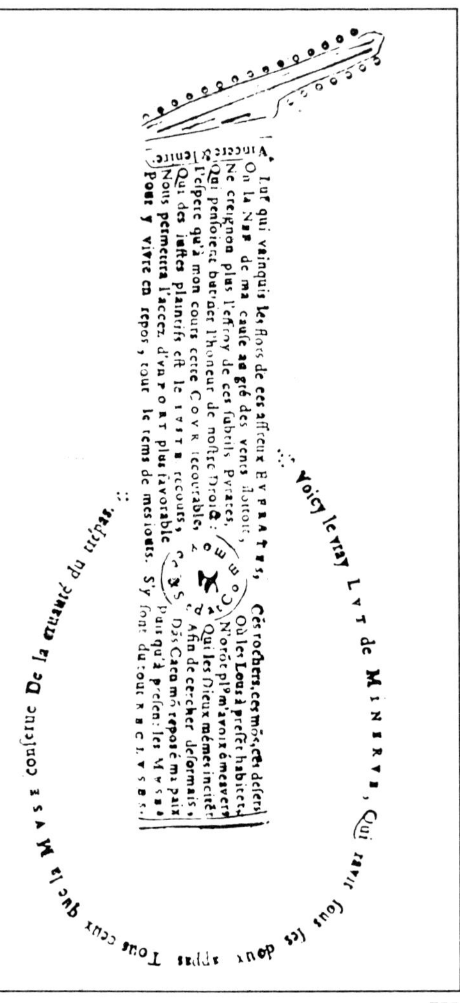

Voicy le vray LVT de MINERVE, Qui ravit sous ses doux appas Tous ceux que la MVSE conserue De la cruauté du trépas.

755

A
HKOS

756

DNO
N.
P.P.
Animarum
Sũmo Pastori
Militãtis Ecclesię
Soli Capiti Visibili
DEI VICARIO
Orthodoxorũ Monarchæ
Inferni Cælique Clauigero
Tergemini Orbis Arbitro
VRBANO OCTAVO
Almo Disciplinarum Propagatori
Sacerdotio Principatu Doctrina
Heroicis etiam æratibus Trismegisto
Augustissimo veri Principis Exemplari
NESTOREOS ANNOS 757

IHC
Hic re-
quiescũt
cineres ea
rum, quæ
in sæculo, mortuę sęculo, Tibi vni
CHRISTE vixerunt. Tu hos
iube, quæsumus, Terra ne compri-
mat. il-
las, cum
dies bea-
tæ retri-
butionis
aduenerit,
pius & miseri-
cors ad dexte-
ram tuam colloca 758

gne en vng autre
estage. Les Anci
ens pour la plus-
grande partie,
ne faisoient leurs montees que en droicte ligne couchee, comme
on peult encores veoir en beaucoup de lieux, & comme iay conside-
re en Romme, & par Italie, semblablemẽt en Languedoc, & beaucoup dautres lieux. Si on veult entre noz lettres significatiõ daultre
sorte de montee &
degrez, qui sõt de
grez a viz, esquelz
on va tornant au
tour du cẽtre & no
yau de la dicte viz
Le I, & le O, & le
S, en dõnerõt sin
guliere apparen-
ce a cause de le I,
qui est en ligne per
pẽdiculaire & droi
cte, qui represen-
tera le noyau de
la viz, & le O. la
rondeur, & le S. la montee
et la tortuosite des marches. la
quelle chose porra estre moult bien cõ-
sideree, & entẽdue facillemẽt par la figure qui sensuyt. 759

O sacrée Croix
Du Roi des Rois
Mis au supplice
Pour notre vice;
Croix, ie te veux
Sacrer mes vœux
Et l'asseurance
De ma créance,
Puis que la foy
Que ie te doy,
Ne se console
Qu'en ta parole.

Si pour patir
Comme vn martir
Dix mile peines
Que i'ay souffertes
Dans les excez
De mes procez,
Digñ no' couronne
De ta couronne
Desbié heureux
Il espere aux Cieux
Trouver la gloire
De ma victoire.

† IHS

Que i'ay receus
Dans ma pensée
Vers toi dressée
Fay qu'à iamais
Ie vive en paix,
Loin du vulgaire
Pour te complaire
Lors q̃ ma voix
Parmy les bois,
Bruit tes louanges
Dignes des Anges.

Puis qu'il te plut
Pour mon salut
Pẽdre à cét arbre
O cueur de marbre
Qui n'est touché
De son peché,
Puis que tõ crime
L'a fait victime
Sur les AVTELS
Des Iuifs cruels,
Qu'ee PILATE,
Comm' vn Pyrate
T'expose à tort,
Sur vne mort,
La plus severe
Que le Caluaire
Trouva iamais,
Pour les forfaits.
Vierge infinie,
Du Ciel benie,
Qui de ma voix,
Fai que la Croix
Soit le REFVGE,
Qui vers mõ Iuge
Et mon Sauveur,
Guide mõ cueur.

760

LES OEVFS DE PASQVES,

A mon Mœcene.

Ce couple d'œufs
Qui restent veufs,
Et de poule & d'assistence,
Ne seroient de cette essence,
Si notre MVSE par hazard
Ne les eust trouvez à l'écart,
Pour les fomentant sous son aîle
Les fomer d'essence immortelle
Et dessur tout Divin AVIEL,
Consacrer leur estre immortel,
Afin qu'vne dixiéme MVSE,
D'vn tel germe ne fût excluse,
Ainsi que Pollux & Castor,
Qui d'vn œuf prindrẽt leur essor
Pour briller sur les Nacelles
Parmy les ondes crueles,
Cõme toi qui fus mõ Tyfis
Au milieu des flos boufis
Qui mon Nauire
Vouloiẽt de-
struire.

Ces œufs sacrez,
A tes yeux consacrez
Suivent l'antique mode
Du jour de Quasimode,
Puis que tes merites divers,
Qui donnent la vie à mes Vers,
Font qu'en leur rondeur ie figure
Le roc de ta Foy ronde & pure,
Comme ils témoignent la rondeur,
Et de mon ame & de mon cœur,
Qui n'a rien de plus favorable,
Que ton merite incomparable,
A qui les plus beaux Esprits
Sacrent leurs doctes écrits;
Ainsi mon cher MECENE,
Le puissãt fils d'Alcmene
Dont tu portes le Nõ,
Cõseruoit le renom
De la belle gloire
Des Filles de
memoire.

Perbellè hoc cecidit, Paschali Sole, rotundo,
Ova rotundus ego sacro rotunda tibi.
Si malè sunt torno tornata hæc ovula nostro,
Quid facerem? torni fata tulêre mei.

SONET.

761

SIMON BOVQVET
ciuis Parisiensis, populi suffragio no-
minatus, & ab omnibus vrbis ordinibus designa-
tus, Regiæque Maiestatis autoritate confirmatus, ad
rerum vrbanarum administrationem & Æditiam pote-
statem gerendam anno Domini milless. quingentess. septuage-
simo CAROLO Nono inuictissimo regnante. Eo ipso anno cum
Rex ciuilium bellorum tumultibus toto regno compositis, & fœli-
cissimo suo matrimonio cum serenissima Principe ELISABETA Ma-
ximiliani Augusti filia perfecto, ingressum sibi parari in eandem vrbem
Parisiensem iussisset, & Præfecto vrbis, quatuórq; Ædilibus curationem e-
ius appratus ritè commisisset, distributione facta suarum cuique partium,
dictus BOVQVET prouinciam triumphalium arcuum, statuarum, ta-
bularum pictarum, inscriptionum, & omnium quæ ad ornamentum tanti
spectaculi erant necessaria sortitus est. In quibus ille obeundis operam dedit vt omnia (sicuti veteri consuetudine in huiusmodi apparatibus rece-
ptum est) temporum conditioni responderent: iisque à Maiestate Re-
gia probatis, & in lucem emitti iussis, idem ea collecta atque digesta in
commentarium redegit ad perpetuam rei memoriam. In quibus omnibus disponendis, & explicandis siquid erroris obrepserit, aut si
stylus impolitior visus fuerit, norit candidus Lector, hoc esse ipsius velut præludium, in quo nihil operæ ei ponere
vacauerit, nisi raptim & horis succisiuis propter
maximas & assiduas occupationes, qui-
bus per id omne tẽpus publicè
priuatimque deti-
nebatur.

GRÆCI,
& Latini ver-
sus præter eos qui
ex antiquis sunt excerpti,
sunt AVRATI Poëtæ Regij:
vero Gallici qui R. literâ subnotan-
tur, RONSARDI: quibus B. litera sup-
ponitur, dicto BOVQVET ascribendi.

762

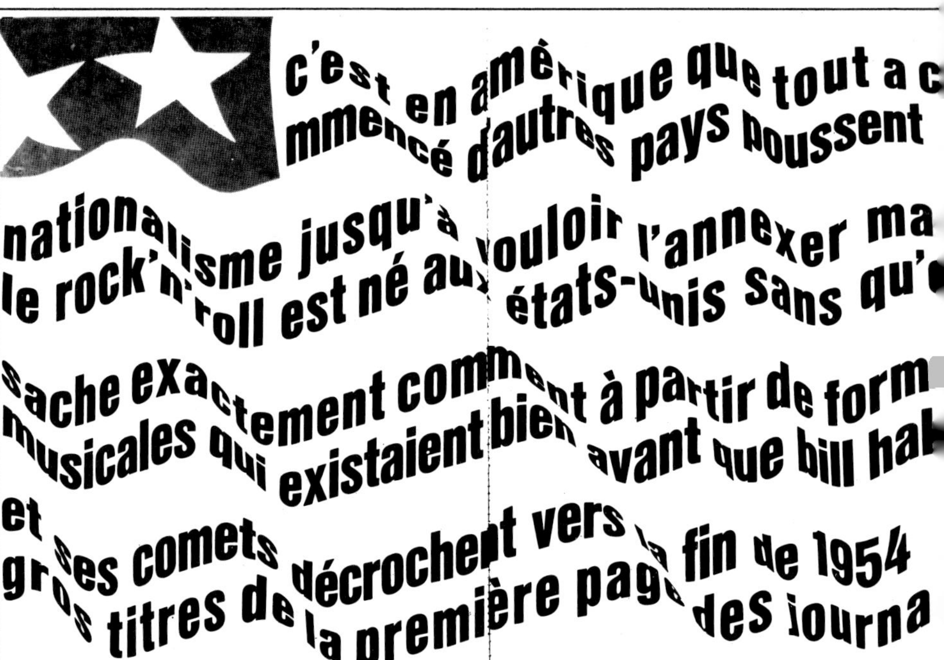
c'est en amérique que tout a c
mmencé d'autres pays poussent
nationalisme jusqu'à vouloir l'annexer ma
le rock'n'roll est né aux états-unis sans qu'
sache exactement comment à partir de form
musicales qui existaient bien avant que bill hal
et ses comets décrochent vers la fin de 1954
gros titres de la première page des journa

866

En 1956 l'Angleterre vit à l'heure du Skiffle. Tout avait commencé quelques temps auparavant avec l'orchestre "Trad" de Chris Barber qui tenait régulièrement le sommet du Hit-Parade – le Melody Maker et le New Musical Express, revues de jazz, existaient déjà depuis plusieurs années – grâce aux classiques du jazz Nouvelle-Orléans : *"Sweet Georgia Brown"*, *"Bourbon Street"*... Or parmi les musiciens de Chris Barber, se trouvait un joueur de banjo dont les goûts personnels étaient plus proches du Folk et du Country & Western que du Traditionnel. Lonnie Donnegan, car c'est de lui qu'il s'agit, était originaire de Glasgow; à l'âge de 17 ans, il avait appris à jouer de la guitare et du banjo. Il s'était engagé ensuite dans l'armée et avait vécu deux ans à Vienne où il s'était mis à chanter pour des copains de chambrée. A son retour dans la capitale, Chris Barber l'avait engagé dans son orchestre. C'est précisément en 1956 que Lonnie décida de former son propre groupe. Presque immédiatement, ce fut le succès avec *"Rock Island Line"* qui était, au départ, une des plages d'un 33 tours de Chris Barber. Couplé avec *"John Henry"*, ce morceau se vendit à plus d'un million d'exemplaires des deux côtés de l'Atlantique. Le Skiffle était né, et Lonnie en était devenu le roi. Au fait, qu'entendait-on exactement par Skiffle? Essentiellement un "compromis du folk-blues, de la chanson cow-boy, le tout accompagné de certains relents de New Orleans". Le créateur de ce genre musical insistait surtout sur l'origine noire et le blues; *"John Henry"* est un vieux worksong du Texas. Et Lonnie Donnegan de rappeler le personnage légendaire de Lonnie Johnson, son guitariste de blues favori. Le phénomène Skiffle vit aussitôt des milliers de groupes se former : il suffisait d'une guitare, d'un banjo, d'une caisse en bois, d'une de ces fameuses contrebasses fabriquées avec des boîtes de thé, un manche à balai et un peu de ficelle, pour se lancer dans la grande aventure. Partout en Angleterre, jusque dans les villages les plus reculés, les jeunes s'entraînaient dans le style nasal et aigu de Lonnie Donnegan. De nos jours le Skiffle a gardé bon nombre de fans; dans notre pays, Hughes Aufray lui doit sa réussite... Mais à quoi ressemble la jeunesse anglaise de cette époque? C'est loin d'être la folie. Seule une minorité fait vraiment parler d'elle et en général de manière assez péjorative : les Teddy Boys. Teddy, Ted, Edouard, ils ont reçu cette appellation en raison des habits édouardiens qu'ils affectionnent tout spécialement : vestes ..., longues redingotes, pantalons étroits et sans revers (une vraie révolution!); issus de la classe ouvrière, ils n'hésitent pas à investir 20 guinées (environ 300 F) dans un costume, somme considérable alors! Leur coiffure diffère aussi de celle de l'anglais moyen; celui-ci arbore la "short back and sides" qui tient plus de la tonte militaire que d'une véritable coupe de cheveux; les Teddy Boys sont coiffés à la Tony Curtis, cheveux mi-longs, rejetés en arrière, et pattes. Hollywood est passé par là. Dernière caractéristique vestimentaire, les Winkle Pickers, d'immenses souliers aux extrémités très pointues. Le Teddy Boy est un violent. Il vit en bande et sur une moto. Il passe ses nuits dans les "all-night cafés". Son passe-temps favori "the coin in the juke-box", la pièce dans le juke-box. Après avoir glissé quelques pennies et sélectionné un disque, il lui faut bondir sur sa moto, effectuer un parcours déterminé puis revenir à plein gaz vers son point de départ avant que le disque ne soit terminé. Le parcours devient de plus en plus long et de plus en plus dangereux; le premier à échouer est désigné comme le "chicken", le dégonflé de la bande. Autre amusement du même type : le jeu consiste à aligner une dizaine de motos à un carrefour et à démarrer en trombe lorsque le feu s'allume au rouge. Là aussi, celui qui hésite à la dernière seconde devient le "chicken". De 1954 à 1958, les Teddy Boys instaurèrent un climat d'insécurité qui atteint son paroxysme lors des émeutes raciales de Notting Hill Gate, auxquelles ils participèrent activement. Néanmoins ce ferment de révolte allait s'avérer propice à l'implantation du rock'n roll en Angleterre. Il fallait des fans pionniers : ce furent les Teddy Boys. Le premier événement majeur dans l'épopée du rock anglais, l'étincelle qui déclenche la folie générale, ce fut la sortie du film "Rock around the clock" et la première tournée de Bill Haley. Le Daily Mirror organisa un service de cars et fréta un train spécial pour emmener ses fans voir à Southampton le timide Américain et son groupe, les Comets. En dépit d'un succès triomphal, les critiques restèrent partagés quant à ses possibilités musicales. C'est que, quelque mois auparavant, un chanteur bien de chez eux avait fait dresser l'oreille aux Anglais : Tommy Steele leur semblait nettement supérieur au créateur de *"See you later, alligator"* et de *"Razzle Dazzle"*. Fin 1956, Tommy Steele faisait ses premières apparitions en public en Grande-Bretagne. Un Hit, *"Rock with the caveman"* et Tommy était passé des soirées à cinq shillings dans les sous-sols de Soho aux cachets les plus élevés de tout le pays. Peter Jones, journaliste au Record Mirror, nous raconte l'un des premiers shows de Tommy Steele : "A gauche du public, un jeune garçon, Dennis Price, est debout au piano. Debout, notez-bien : l'influence de Little Richard se fait sentir dans le jeu de scène. Il porte une chemise blanche, un pull noir et des jeans noirs. Près de lui, le saxo-ténor Alan Stuart, le contrebassiste Allan Weighell et le batteur Léo Pollini. Dans la salle, une foule de bras se tendent, des programmes déchirés volent dans tous les coins, des filles s'évanouissent, le cri de guerre "Tommy, Tommy, Tommy" retentit. Tommy entre alors en scène; les hurlements montent en un crescendo continu. Il chante *"Giddy up a ding dong"*. Ses cheveux se balancent à droite et à gauche. Ses jambes semblent être en caoutchouc; ses membres ne restent pas un instant immobiles. Il chante *"Dont be cruel"*, *"Rock with the caveman"*, *"Singing the blues"*. Il tient une guitare en bandoulière, un fusil vers la partie la plus bruyante de l'auditoire. Tommy présente ses morceaux avec un fort accen... il explique à la salle qu'il ne réalise pas très bien lui-même ce qui lui arrive. Le show se termine en ...

Comme tous les jeunes Anglais de cette époque, Tommy aimait fréquenter Soho, le quartier pittoresque ... étrangers, des boîtes de strip-tease et des cinémas, du show-business en général. Il existait à l'ép... Old Compton Street, un coffee-bar appelé *"The Two I's"* dirigé par deux ex-catcheurs australiens, Paul ... Ray Hunter. Le commerce marchait mal, mais lorsque les deux propriétaires se décidèrent à livrer leur so... "guitaristes itinérants", tout alla beaucoup mieux. Par la même occasion, les Two I's entraient dans la ... la Pop-Music anglo-saxonne. Depuis quelques temps y jouait un groupe de Skiffle, les Vipers, ensemble déjà ... grâce à un morceau : *"Pick a bale of cotton"*. C'est là qu'un jour Tommy descendit, sa guitare sou... et que le plus naturellement du monde, il fit le bœuf avec les Vipers. Les choses en restèrent là, ma... trois mois plus tard, Tommy se retrouva en présence du groupe, un homme vint le contacter après le... John Kennedy, ex-photographe de presse à Fleet Street, lui proposa ses bons offices en tant que ... Tommy, qui n'avait rien à perdre, accepta. Et Kennedy allait s'avérer être "the right man, in the hig... En 1957, Tommy Steele s'imposa comme le seul chanteur de rock anglais capable d'atteindre le numéro ... coup. *"Singing the blues"* fut un Hit massif que les seules vedettes britanniques à réussir dans ... étaient des chanteurs à voix, comme Frankie Vaughan ou Jimmy Young. Le reste des charts était ... Elvis Presley, Bill Haley, Little Richard, l'Alan Freed Big Band et une multitude de rockers américains. John Kennedy s'associa à Larry Parnes et la carrière de Tommy prit un nouvel essor. "The Tom... Story" fut le premier film ayant pour vedette un chanteur de rock'n'roll britannique. Terminé en mars ... ne fut pas une production très inspirée; néanmoins, elle remplit à bloc tous les cinémas. C'est à ce ... qu'il faut noter la première grande émission "pop" à la télévision, le "Six Five Special" de J... Jack, un producteur et animateur de talent, adorait la Beat-Music; beaucoup de vedettes d'alors ... leur réussite. Son show hebdomadaire était très varié; il présentait à la fois des chanteurs de ... chanteurs noirs de Rhythm & Blues, des groupes de Skiffle et de jazz New Orleans. Le "Six Five Speci... événement attendu dans la fébrilité par des millions de teenagers, et leur rêve à tous était d'... autorisation de la BBC pour danser devant les caméras pendant l'enregistrement de l'émission. Quant ... elle avait beaucoup évolué; les Teddy Boys avaient abandonné leurs oripeaux édouardiens pour se barde... la manière des rockers venus des Etats-Unis : Gene Vincent, Vince Taylor. Ils portaient désormais des ... en cuir constellées de badges métalliques à l'exemple de Marlo Brando dans "L'Equipé... L'apparition des chaînes qu'ils portaient autour de la ceinture ou du cou est typique de cette époque. D'ailleurs, par assimilation aux forçats américains, ... surnommés les "chain gangs". Cependant on peut encore difficilement as... partie de la jeunesse aux Rockers, avec un R majuscule, parce que la notion n'interviendra que beaucoup plus tard, vers 1961-1962, à une époque où, le... du rock étant retombés dans l'oubli, une minorité qui aura gardé les vêt... goûts et les attitudes sociales de 1957 viendra prendre la défense ... noms tels Eddie Cochran, Buddy Holly, Carl Perkins et Bill Haley. Face ... ex-Teddy Boys, on trouve pêle-mêle deux types de teenagers : les Trads amateu... Orleans et de Skiffle; ils sont habillés d'une manière assez bohème, blue-jeans délavés, chemises flottantes et cheveux bouclés; les Mods, sophistiqués, dont les prédilections vont au ja... Ceux-ci fréquentent plus particulièrement le Flamingo dans Wardour Street et les Two I's devenus de... clubs "in" d'où sortent les idoles. A l'heure du lunch dans Old Compton Street, vous étiez ... rencontrer des jeunes musiciens, la guitare sur le dos, qui entraient dans la boîte où Tommy Stee... ses débuts, avec l'espoir secret que le même conte de fées se reproduirait pour eux. Pour revenir ... un problème majeur se posait alors : Lonnie Donnegan et Tommy Steele venaient de ... récompenses de l'Industrie du disque, décernées chaque année aux meilleures ventes nationale... Compagnies voulaient savoir maintenant qui allait faire le prochain gros boom. Depuis quelques mois, ... venus étaient de simples étoiles filantes; un 45 tours ou deux, puis ils retombaient dans l'oubli. ... tout le monde attendait. Et une fois de plus ce fut Larry Parnes qui trouva la solution. Depuis so... avec John Kennedy, Larry avait monté une écurie assez incroyable de "pop singers". Il prospectait un... à Londres et ailleurs, prenait de jeunes chanteurs en main et créait une image autour d'eux. Il i... tout à ce qu'ils aient un nom qui frappe... Marty Wilde, Georgie Fame, Duffy Power, Vince Eager, Bi... Marty Wilde fit une entrée très remarquée dans la profession avec *"Endless Sleep"*, resté depuis un classique du ... Marty se spécialisa surtout dans les chansons tristes et dans les ballades; beau garçon, ses passages à la

867

COURRIER
DU COEUR

868

IMPERIA

869

La circulation
est dense malgré
l'heure matinale. L'air
n'est pas encore trop surchauffé.
Les lourds tapis aux points noués, les
populaires moquettes, les confortables descentes
de lit, les rapides carpettes se croisent dans
des chuchotements laineux. Seuls, quelques clochards
circulent sans façon sur de minables
nattes effilochées qui claquent au vent .

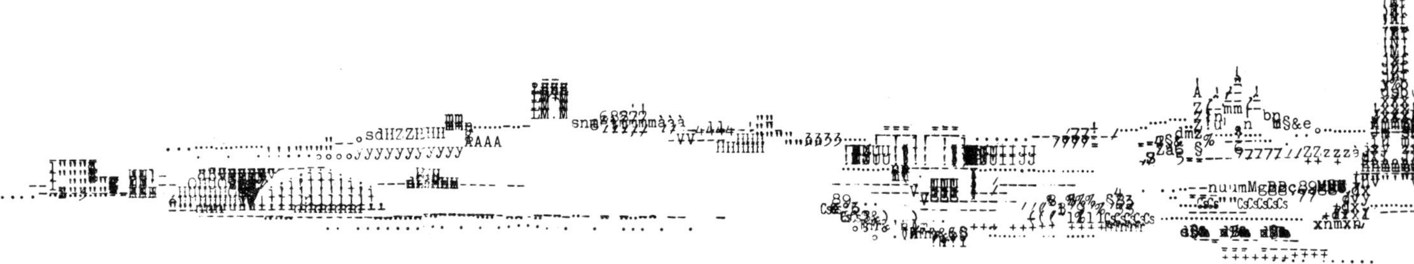

870

871

872

873

874

A play on words involving 'a long and a sad tale' and 'a long
tail' led to the tale shaped like a mouse's tail which appears in 903
Alice in Wonderland and is probably one of the most famous and
popular figured poems in England. In Lewis Carroll's original
manuscript, the mouse's tale was identical in design but seemed 904
to fit in better with the narrative because it depended on the
mouse's hatred for dogs and cats. The tail may have originated with Alfred Lord Tennyson, who told Carroll of a dream he had had, in which he imagined that he had written a long poem about fairies, beginning with extremely long lines and then tapering down to lines of no more than two syllables each.

In this connection we might also refer to a famous poem
by Victor Hugo called 'Les Djinns' which appeared in his 897
Orientales (1829). It consists of 120 lines divided up into octets, each of which has a different metre; the poet has used an arrangement of rhopalic lines which grow first longer and then shorter for his description of the djins as they emerge from the depths of the night, fly past in a tumultuous roar of noise and then fade away into the distance. If we take the trouble to place the stanzas end to end – which is never done on the printed page – the poem takes on the shape of an elongated diamond and thus has a doubly descriptive quality, for as well as the *image* traced by the lines of the poem we have a superimposed *sound* which starts up, grows, is amplified, dies down and then fades away altogether. The choice of rhymes, some whispering, some shatteringly loud, and the skilful use of alliteration and assonance strengthen the sound image contained in the poem.

On parle
d'interdire
es vieux tacots
usables venus
ut droit de Perse en
ontrebande...

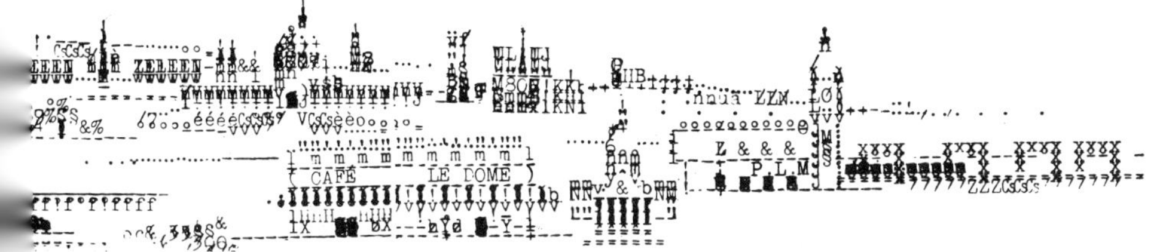

« Croyés que c'eſt la fureur poëticque
Du bon Bachus: ce bon vin ecliticque
Ainsi ses sens et le fait canticqueur :
Car, sans mespris[1],
A ses espritz
Du tout espris
Par sa liqueur,
De cris en ris,
De ris en pris,
En ce pourpris,
Faict son gent cueur
Rhétoricqueur,
Roy et vaincqueur
De noz soubriz;
Et, veu qu'il eſt de cerveau phanaticque,
Ce ne seroit acte de topicqueur
Penser moucquer un si noble trinqueur.

784

ſipunculo perilquale emanaua laqua della fontana per artificio perpetua in la ſubiecta concha.
Nel Patore dunque di queſto uaſo promineua uno pretioſiſſimo mō ticulo, mirabilmente congeſto di innumere gemme globoſe preſſamente una ad laltra coaceruate, cum inæquale, o uero rude deformatura, lepidiſſimamente il mōticulo ſcrupeo rendeuano, cū corruſcatiōe di uarii fulgetri di colore, cum proportionata eminētia. Nel uertice, o uero cacumine di queſto monticulo, naſceua uno arbuſculo di mali punici, di tronco, o uero ſtipite & di rami, & ſimilmente tutto queſto compoſito di oro prælucente. Le foglie appoſitie di ſcintillāte Smaragdo. Gli fructi alla granditudine naturale diſperſamente collocati, cum il ſidio doro iſchiantati largamente, & in loco degli grani ardeuano nitidiſſimi rubini, ſopra omni paragonio nitidiſſimi di craſſitudine fabacea. Poſcia lo ingenioſo fabro di queſta inextimabile factura & copioſo eſſendo del ſuo diſcorſo imaginario haueа diſcriminato, in loco di Cico gli grani cum tenuiſſima bractea argentea. Oltra di queſto & ragioneuolmente haueа ficto & alcuni altri mali crepati, ma di granelatura immaturi, oue haueа cōpoſito cum improbo exquiſito di craſſi unione di candore orientale. Ancora ſolertemente haueа fincto gli balauſti facti di perfecto coralio in calici pieni di apici doro. Vltra di queſto fora della ſummitate del ſiſtulatamente uacuo ſtipite uſciua uno uerſatile & libero ſtylo, il cardine imo delqua le, era fixo in uno capo peronato, o ue ramente firma to ſopra il medio dellaxide. & aſcendeua per il peruio & inſtobato trunco.

785

Who hath woe? Who hath sorrow? Who
hath contentions? Who hath wounds
without cause? Who hath redness
of eyes? They that tarry long
at the wine! They that
go to seek mixed wine!
Look not thou upon the
wine when it is red,
when it giveth
its color
in the
cup,
when it
moveth itself
aright.
At
the last it
biteth like a serpent
and stingeth like an adder!

7

This is the bait
the fisher-
men take,
the fishermen take, the fishermen take, when they start out the fish to
wake, so early in the morning. They take a nip before they go — a good one, ah! and long and slow,
for fear the chills will lay them low, so early in
the morning. Another — when they're on the
street, which they repeat each time they meet
for "luck" — for that's the way to greet a
fisher in the morning. And when they are
on the river's brink again they drink without a wink — to fight malaria they think
it proper in the morning. They tip a
flask with true delight when there's a
bite; if fishing's light they "smile"
the more, till jolly tight all fishing
they are scorning. Another nip as
they depart; one at the mart and
one to part; but none when in
the house they dart expecting
there'll be mourning. This
is the bait the fishermen try,
who fishes buy at prices
high, and tell each one
a bigger lie of fishing
in the morning.

790

There was an old decanter, and its mouth was gaping wide; the rosy wine had ebbed away and left its crystal side: and the wind went humming humming up and down: the wind it blew, and through the reed-like hollow neck the wildest notes it blew. I placed it in the window, where the blast was blowing free, and fancied that its pale mouth sang the queerest strains to me. "They tell me—puny conquerors! the Plague has slain his ten, and war his hundred thousand of the very best of men; but I"—'twas thus the Bottle spake—"but I have conquered more than all your famous conquerors, so feared and famed of yore. Then come, ye youths and maidens all, come drink from out my cup, the beverage that dulls the brain and burns the spirits up; that puts to shame your conquerors that slay their scores below; for this has deluged millions with the lava tide of woe. Tho' in the path of battle darkest streams of blood may roll; yet while I killed the body, I have damn'd the very soul. The cholera, the plague, the sword, such ruin never wro't, as I in mirth or malice on the innocent have brought. And still I breathe upon them, and they shrink before my breath, and year by year my thousands tread the dusty way of death."

791

Aux amys des Muſes.

BOVTEILLE
Sommeille
Chez tes Vices,
Dōt les abbois
Iapēt ma terre
Dās cete guerre
Que Lucifer
Forma d'enfer:
E' dōt ma gloire
Eut la victoire
Par deux Accets divers
Contre ces lous pervers
Q... ...aux Muſes la chaſſe
Iuſqu'en leur ſacré Parnaſſe:
Bouteille donc ne manque pas
De ſommeiller dans leur repas,
E... que que attraict qu'ils te faiſent
Fuy ces Loups qui te pourchaſſent.
Que plut aux Dieux: que BACCHVS
Quand ils ſeront de ſoif vaincus,
Les puiſſe tant ſouler de boire
Qu'ils crevent d'eau dedans le Loire
... les flots du Cocyte, ou le Styx
Ou leur deſtin pour iamais ait prefix
Pour ſubir la peine fatalle
Ou de Syſiphe, ou de Tantale
Qui pour mile crimes divers
Sont expoſez dans
les Enfers.

INTVS MELIORA RECONDIT.

BOVTEILLE
Reveille
Ces ESPRITS:
QVI cheris
Des MVSES
Dōtent les ruſes
De ces plédeurs
Qui picoreurs
Nōt l'induſtrie
Qu'à tricherie
Pour meler au leur
Le bien d'vn mineur
Qui loin de toute aſſiſtēce
N'a que Dieu pour ſa deffēce
Et qui m'euſſent du tout perdu
Si le Ciel ne m'euſt deffendu
Muſe, chantons la gloire de ce Sage
Dont la faveur m'a ſauvé de ce p...
Qu'ils m'ont ... dans cet affreux ...
Ou mon Eſprit qui ne ſe plaît qu'aux ...
Trouve en cerchant des libres ſolitu...
Vn triſte Enfer d'horribles ſervitu...
D... ... le bien ... que ie vous
Face bien toſt la vengeance des Cie...
Que iamais ce meſchant HYD...
Ne puiſſe boire de STYX
De tabac, de biere ou de vin
Iuſqu'au dernier iour
de ſa fin.

Cypridis eſto, lagena merobiba Cypridis, eſto.
Donum, chara ſoror nectarei calycis:
Bacchum oriſona blandæ comes.inclyta menſæ,
Colli anguſta dapis filia ſymbolicæ.

7

Apollinaire used the term) has recently been brought to light by Berjouhi Barsamian Bowler. These motifs blossom against a biblical background which is not always specifically Hebrew – with the exception of certain themes such as Jonah and the whale or Balaam and his astrolabe; they take on the shapes of a bestiary which properly belongs to the Middle Ages – griffins, unicorns, horses with eagle's heads, etc. But sometimes the image casts off its fabulous quality and depicts instead a nobleman setting off for the chase with his falcon, or a knight in armour returning to his castle.

Nous ne pouvons rien trouver sur la terre
Qui soit si bon ni si beau que le verre.
Du tendre amour berceau charmant,
C'est toi, champêtre fougère,
C'est toi qui sers à faire
L'heureux instrument
Où souvent pétille,
Mousse et brille
Le jus qui rend
Gai, riant,
Content.
Quelle douceur
Il porte au cœur!
Tôt,
Tôt,
Tôt,
Qu'on m'en donne,
Qu'on l'entonne;
Tôt,
Tôt,
Tôt,
Qu'on m'en donne
Vite et comme il faut:
L'on y voit sur ses flots chéris
Nager l'allégresse et les ris.

787

Buvons, amis, et buvons à plein verre.
Enivrons-nous de ce nectar divin!
Après les Belles, sur la terre,
Rien n'est aimable que le vin;
Cette liqueur est de tout âge:
Buvons-en!... Nargue du sage
Qui, le verre en main,
Le haussant soudain,
Craint, se ménage,
Et dit: holà!,
Trop cela!
Holà!
La!
La!
La!
Car
Panard
A pour refrain:
Tout plein!
Plein!
Plein!
Plein!
Fêtons,
Célébrons
Sa mémoire;
Et, pour sa gloire,
Rions, chantons, aimons, buvons.

788

Du vase en cristal de Bohême
Du vase en cris
Du vase en cris
Du vase en
En cristal
Du vase en cristal de Bohême
Bohême
Bohême
En cristal de Bohême
Bohême
Bohême
Bohême
Hême hême oui Bohême
Du vase en cristal de Bo Bo
Du vase en cristal de Bohême
Aux bulles qu'enfant tu soufflais
Tu soufflais
Tu soufflais
Flais
Flais
Tu soufflais
Qu'enfant tu soufflais
Du vase en cristal de Bohême
Aux bulles qu'enfant tu soufflais
Tu soufflais
Tu soufflais
Oui qu'enfant tu soufflais
C'est là c'est là tout le poème
Aube éphé
Aube éphé
Aube éphémère de reflets
Aube éphé
Aube éphé
Aube éphémère de reflets

789

Que mon
Flacon
Me semble bon!
Sans lui,
L'ennui
Me nuit,
Me suit;
Je sens
Mes sens
Mourans,
Pesans.
Quand je le tien,
Dieux! que je suis bien!
Que son aspect est agréable!
Que je fais cas de ses divins présens!
C'est de son sein fécond, c'est de ses heureux flancs
Que coule ce nectar si doux, si délectable,
Qui rend tous les esprits, tous les cœurs satisfaits.
Cher objet de mes vœux, tu fais toute ma gloire.
Tant que mon cœur vivra, de tes charmans bienfaits
Il saura conserver la fidelle mémoire.
Ma muse, à te louer, se consacre à jamais.
Tantôt dans un caveau, tantôt sous une treille,
Ma lyre, de ma voix accompagnant le son,
Repétera cent fois cette aimable chanson:
Règne sans fin, ma charmante bouteille;
Règne sans cesse, mon cher flacon.

793

Bouteille,
Merveille
De mon cœur,
Ta liqueur
Vermeille
Me séduit,
M'enchaîne,
M'entraîne,
Agrandit
Mon esprit,
L'enflamme
Et produit
Sur mon ame
Le bien le plus doux!
Au bruit de tes glouglous
Quelle ame ne serait ravie!
Tu sais nous faire supporter
Les plus noirs chagrins de la vie,
Et des tourmens (plus affreux) de l'envie
Par des chemins de fleurs tu sais nous écarter.
Loin de toi qui pourrait encor trouver des charmes?
A tes coups séduisans qui pourrait résister,
Quand le puissant Amour à tes pieds met ses armes,
Pour accroître sa force, et mieux blesser après
Les cœurs indifférens qui bravent ses succès
Et les heureux effets que produit ton génie?...
Mais combien de mortels ont chanté mieux que moi,
Mieux que moi célébré ta puissance infinie,
Et fait de te chérir leur souveraine loi!
Piron, Collé, Panard, Vadé, Favard, Sedaine,
En adorant ton culte, ont illustré la scène,
Et nous ont tous appris à n'oublier jamais
Que le feu des plaisirs qui circule en nos ames;
Besoin d'aimer, d'éteindre douces flammes,
Sont les moins grands de tes bienfaits.

794

DIVINE TO EAT, EASY TO MAKE, AND
BEAUTIFUL TO LOOK ON: ELEGANT PAR-
FAITS. THERE ARE TWO TYPES: THE
FRENCH, WHICH IS A CREAMY, DEL-
ICATE, COOL (BUT NOT ICY) MIX-
TURE WITH A BASE OF SUGAR,
EGGS, CREAM, FRUIT AND/OR
FLAVORINGS; AND THE AMERI-
CAN, MADE WITH COMMERCIAL
ICE CREAMS OR SHERBETS OR
BOTH WITH A SURPRISE INGRE-
DIENT, SUCH AS FRUITS, COR-
DIALS, COGNAC, NUTS, SAUCES
(SEE McCALL'S FINE SAUCE
RECIPES ON PAGE 00). WITH
AMERICAN PARFAITS, YOUR
IMAGINATION CAN HAVE FREE
REIN. WITH THE FRENCH, HOW-
EVER, YOU MUST FOLLOW REC-
IPE DIRECTIONS TO THE
LETTER. PARFAIT MEANS, OF
COURSE, PERFECT, AND WE
CAN IMAGINE FEW MORE PER-
FECT DESSERTS, ESPECIALLY
IF YOU WANT TO SHOW OFF.
FOR THESE ARE TRULY SHOW-
OFF RECIPES! FROM THE
COOK'S STANDPOINT, THERE
IS A REAL ADVANTAGE IN SERV-
ING FROZEN DESSERTS. FOR
THE OBVIOUS REASON, THEY
MUST BE MADE WELL AHEAD
AND REFRIGERATED. THUS,
THE BIG DESSERT PROBLEM
IS OUT OF THE WAY WHEN IT'S
TIME TO PREPARE THE MAIN
PART OF THE MEAL. AT FAR
RIGHT, YOU SEE AN AMER-
ICAN PARFAIT, VANILLA
ICE CREAM LAYERED
WITH PISTACHIO
AND TOPPED
WITH WAL-
NUTS AND
WHIPPED
CREAM.
THE STRAW-
BERRY AND
APRICOT
PARFAITS
ARE BOTH
CLASSIC
FRENCH.
FOR THE RECIPES,
TURN TO PAGE 00, WHERE
YOU WILL FIND THE FRENCH AS WELL
AS GOOD VARIATIONS OF THE QUICK
AND POPULAR AMERICAN PARFAITS.
THEN, PLAN A PARTY.

795

Ter Eere van de Oranje
Prins FRISO.

A Vous Hertog van Vendôme
'k Wensch het moet u wel bekomen,
g'Hebt nu braaf te gast geweest;
hy vat aan w. est niet bevreest,
Denkt om 't spreekwoord van de Fransen
Ongelukken zyn kwaê kansen.
Kyk hoe zuynig ziet de Man,
Of hy 't niet gebeet'ren kan.

A vous Brugge en Gentenaars;
Ba Goêliens dat is wat raars,
Wel wie Duyvel zou dat droomen,
Dat den Hertoog van Vendômen
Dat so wel heeft afgelapt;
Daar de kan op vol getapt.

Daar leyt de Franse magt en hoogmoed nu vertreên,
Door Vrieslands jonge Prins, door Marlbourg en Eugeen
Nu, al de Kannen, tot de kim toe volgeschonken,
En op de welvaard van die Helden uytgedronken:
Drink vrye Vriesen, drink, drink tot de grond toe uyt;
En dan geroepen, lang leefd Frizo met zyn Bruyd;
Dan Marlbourg, dan Eugeen dan al de Generalen,
Die Vrankryks magtig Heyr aan piesjes hielpen malen.
Zoo Vrienden dat is uyt; nu schenkt terstond wêer in
Op de gezondheyd van Brittanjens Koningin;
Die op de welvaard van de Vrygevogte Staaten,
Held Ouwerkerk, en al zyn dappere Zoldaaten.

Ba zoo, dat smaakt ha, ha, dat kan men voelen,
Zoo kan men 't hart als Vrankryks hoogmoet koelen,
Dat doed een mens zyn beeten dorst vergaan,
Gelyk Lowys de lust om meer te slaan,
Drink niet te schoon de glaasjes uyt maar spaar,
Wat grondzop voor bedroogen Bellevaar.

't Is uyt en zitten wy omtrend,
Gelyk de Fransjes onder Gent,

Nu zyn wy onder in de voet,
hy kyk daar zit de Franse moet,

Var my by, 't oorgelyk Eugeen en Malboroug de Franse deên

Kyk hoe dat het door ce tuyt, als Vendême lo opt voor uyt. kluk, kluk, kluk.

Dit Jaar van Wonder,
Doen ging ten onder,
Louys Boerbon,
Zyn Lelizon.

1708.

lang leven de Helden

Gedrukt t'Amsterdam
by Corn. v. Hoogenbuyzen.

796

SINCLAIR
ALKOHOL
Dem
Malik-Verlag
wird bei Vermeidung
einer Geld- oder Haft-
strafe verboten, die
deutsche Ausgabe von
Upton Sinclair „Alko
hol" mit einem Titelbild
zu vertreiben, auf dem
sich neben einem Be-
trunkenen eine Whisky-
Flasche mit der Aus-
stattung befindet, die
die Firma
London
ihrem Whisky
gibt.

797

THE
BIG
DRINK
THE STORY OF
Coca-Cola
E.J. KAHN JR

798

842

843

the gramophone'. At any rate, in the same lecture, which he delivered in the middle of the war when the state of mind of his audience made him repudiate the 'magic cast-offs of the colossal Romanticism of Wagner's Germany', Apollinaire personally set the limits of this emancipation and this new spirit, which he saw as 'full of danger, full of pitfalls'. He had once been associated with the demonstrations organized by the Futurists, (though we might put forward the theory that his sole reason for pursuing their theories to extremes was an urge to ridicule the movement); but he now appealed to his audience to fight against 'cosmopolitan lyricism' and spoke of his aversion to disorder and chaos. It is important that we should stress the fact that, unlike the poets of today, Guillaume Apollinaire was not particularly concerned with the way his calligrams were presented typographically. So their final shape is merely a typographic transcription by a third party – the anonymous type-setter – of a hand-written poem. For instance all we know of the poem '*Il pleut*' ('It's Raining') is that, according to Pierre Albert-Birot, it was composed in a single night by the printer Levé, who, already semi-retired, was fired with enthusiasm when he saw the manuscript.

Apollinaire's work was influenced by that of the Cubist painters – '*Les Demoiselles d'Avignon*' dates from 1907 – and exercised in its turn an equally strong influence on the plastic art of his period, rather than on actual poetry (with the exception of what is known as 'spatialist' poetry). The only people to imitate his *Calligrammes* were those who admired his work so much that they were eager to pay him homage by offering a
892-893 pastiche of his work. Bertrand Guegan's menus appear to make direct allusions to his work; and in the same way, the seven

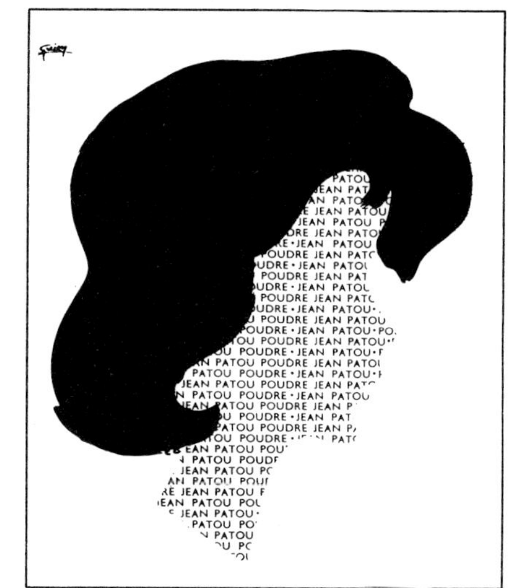

847

850

851

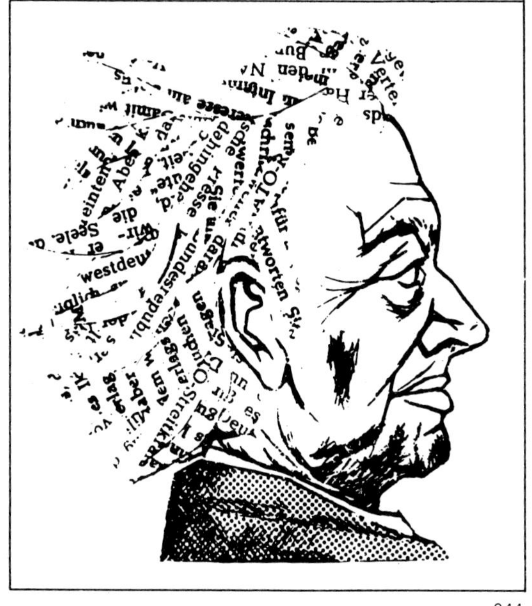

844

845

846

Photosia, la solution
de vos problèmes de reproduction. Pho
tosia, la solution de vos problèmes de repro
duction. Photosia, la solution de vos problèmes de
reproduction. Photosia, la solution de vos problèmes de
reproduction. Photosia, la solution de vos problèmes de re
production. Photosia, la solution de vos problèmes de repr
duction. Pho
tosia, la solu
tion de vos
problèmes de
reproduction.
Photosia, la solu
tion de vos pro
blèmes de repro
duction. Photosia
la solution de vos
problèmes de re
production. Pho
tosia, la solution
de vos problè
mes de reproduc
tion. Photosia, la solution de vos problèmes de reproduc
tion, Photosia, la solution de vos pro blèmes de reproduction.
Photosia, la solution de vos problèmes de reproduction. Pho
tosia, la solution de vos problèmes de reproduct
Photosia, la solution de vos problèmes
de reproduction. Photosia, la solution
de vos problèmes de reproduction. Pho
tosia, la solution de vos problèmes de
reproduction. Photosia, la solution de
vos problèmes de reproduction. Pho
tosia, la solution de vos problèmes
de reproduction. Photosia, la solu
tion de vos problèmes de reproduc
tion. Photosia, la solution de vos
problèmes de reproduction.
Photosia, la solution de vos
problèmes de reproduction. Photosia la
solution de vos problèmes
de reproduction. Photosia,
la solution de vos problèmes de
reproduction. Photosia, m
la solution de vos pro vo
blèmes de reproduc tion
Photosia, la solution de vos
problèmes de reproduc tion.
Photosia, la solution de vos problè
mes de reproduction. Photo sia, la solution
de vos problèmes de reproduction. Photosia, la solu
tion de vos problèmes de reproduction. Photosia, la
solution de vos problèmes de reproduction. Photosia,
la solution de vos problèmes de reproduction. Photosia,
la solution de vos problèmes de reproduction. Photosia
la solution de vos problèmes de reproducion. Photosi

848

FUNNY GIRL

849

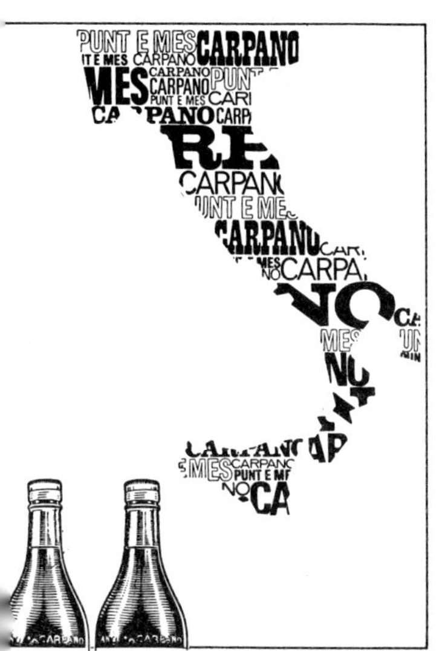

852

L'Italie : une certaine
manière de voir, de pen-
ser, de vivre. Ce particula-
risme italien se manifeste
aussi bien dans l'équilibre de
la nature que dans l'ordon-
nancement des jardins et
des villas ou dans les différents arts où
le génie la-
tin s'est
exercé.
En voici
toutes les
richesses.
Un magnifique
ouvrage 25x32 cm.
de 352 pages 420
photographies
dont 60 hors-
texte en cou-
leurs reliure
pleine toile
sous jaquette
en rho-
doïd illus-
trée en
cou-
leurs,
72
NF

853

The
HEEL,
said Chris-
topher Marlowe,
was invented by a
woman who was al-
ways being kissed on
the forehead. Undeniably,
it raises her stature, giving her footing and ele-
vation. This is done not
by inches alone, but
with a sizable meas-
ure of savoir faire.
A DELMAN heel is
a trompe-l'oeil par
excellence. It abbreviates the foot,
lengthens the body, lightens the car-
riage, takes inches off the hips, and gives
the costume altogether new dimension. She
who walks in beauty, walks in DELMAN heels.

854

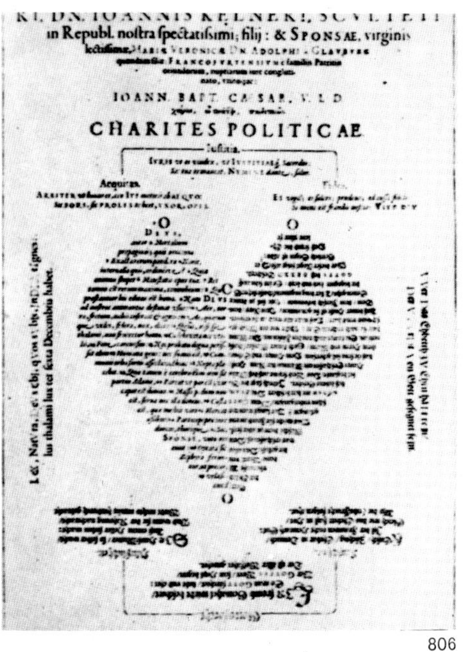

806

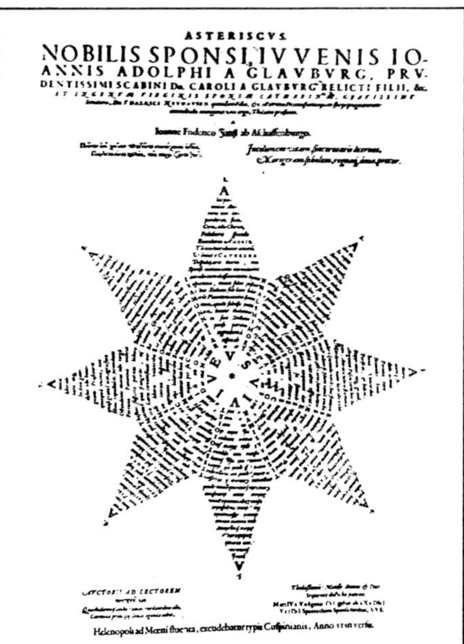

807

Springet
Und klinget
Vergesset der Schmertzen/
Singet
Und bringet
Dem gütigsten Gott/
Nach seinem Gebott
Danck-Opffer von Hertzen.
Es kommet und scheinet die fröliche Zeit/
Die alles auff Erden von neuem erfreut.
Wecket die Andacht/ entzündet die Flammen/
Kommet zum Lobe des Höchsten zusammen/
Welcher in manchem gefährlichen Jahr/
Hunger uñ Seuchen und Kriegesgefahr.
Gewaltig von hinnen getrieben/
Damit wir gefreyet geblieben/
Ohne Betrübnuß u Plag/
Biß auff dẽ heutigẽ Tag/
O hertzlichs Erbarmẽ
Wie köñen wir Armẽ
Die liebliche glück/
Dz gute geschick
Des Mächtigsten preisen!
Uns danckbar erweisen!
Die Wohlthat und Treu ist zu gros!
Und unser Gedancken zu blos!
Doch gleichwol so sollen wir heute nicht schweigen/
Uns unserem Vermögen nach danckbar erzeigen/
Singen und klingen das Himmel und Erden
Mit uns von neuem erfrölichet werden

808

Geistliche Waldfaren oder Engelsüß/ von der Bitterkeit dieses und Süßigkeit des zukünfftigen Lebens. Infallen-den und steigenden Reimen.

Ach! ach wie muß ein Mensch auff dieser Welt sich leiden

Dein Rei ö Welt/
Das Sch arem Gezelt/
Mir n t gefällt/
In der ist tel Leit/
Betrübnuß ü ch und Streit/
Unmuht Kre und Schmertzen/
Nagen un re Hertzen/
Bald ist Traur n bald Gefahr/
Also daß w r immerdar
Schweres Ele nd kläglich leiden/
Und in Kum er täglich weiden/
Biß wir von d r Erden scheiden/
Da wir in er wü schten Freuden/
Von dem Holtz de Lebens essen/
Und der bittern S mach vergessen/
Drum Welt h gute Nacht/
Ich geh e s eines ach

Zu all n Zeiten
Mit Feinde n streiten.

Erinnerung.
Liese erstlich den Stengel von oben bis an die Wurtzel/ u. hernach die Wurtzel also: Ach! ach wie muß ein Mensch auf dieser Welt sich leiden zu allen Zeiten mit Feinden streitẽ. Nach diesem fange wider oben an: dein Reich ö Welt! das Schwarm-Gezelt/ mir nit gefällt u. s. w.

809

Ein Seufftzer zc.

Wann Wann
Streit/ Leid
Und Noht mein H ertz berükket
Wann Angst mich sch ertzlich drükket
So schwinget sich mein G ist hinauff zum Herrn/
Der ist mein Liecht und T ost und Glantz und Stern/
Er neigt sein Ohr und h ret auff mein flehen
Die meine Seel gen immel läßet gehen/
Gibt frische Hertzens-K afft/ ja Muht und Fried
Und lindert Mir mein Weh und Leid,
Er stärkket me ine Seele
Und heilet i re Fehle
Er ist mein Hülff mein Heil/
Mein Erbgut und mein Theil/
Da kann ich haben
Was mich mag laben/
Drum acht ich nicht
Wan gleich mich sticht
Schmertz und Weh
Von der Höh,
Komt Raht
Vnnd
That

810

O we! O was für!
Im Himmel ists gut.

Hier Hier
hitzet ritzet
auch Ehrl ches Hertz
g Jammer vnnd Schmertz
gst / Elend unnd Grämen
agen unnd nehmen
Uns offters den Muth/
entzünden die Glut/
brennende Pfeil
rennen in eil/
durch Ad'n unnd Blut.

hier vor bitteres Elend sehen!
r Pein und Quaal außstehen!
r Ungemach durchgehen!

Sollen doch die Stücker springen
Und vom Knallen
abwerts fallen
Wann die Pfeile so durchdringen:
Doch erfolget auf die Qual
In dem blau-gewölbten Saal
Von deß Lämmgens güldnem Thron
Krohn und Lohn
Freud und Muth
Wie der Seufftzer lehret
Und erklärer:
In dem Himmel sey es gut

811

Du Schöpffer halte sie/ wann Noth und Unfall wehet/
Du Heyland rette sie/ wann ihnen Leid zustehet/
Du Tröster tröst sie in Creutz und Ungemach/
Regier Hertz und Sinn und führ all ihre Sach
Zu deines Namens Ehr. Laß deinen Segen fliessen/
Glück Heyl und Wolfahrt sich wie eine Fluth ergiessen/
Daß sie gesegnet seyn an Gut/ an Leib/ an Seel/
Und leben lange Jahr ohn Kummer/ Noth und Fehl.
Bencket diesem Wunsch/ den ich euch zugeschrieben/
Laß euch verliebtes Paar noch diese Wieg belieben/
Und dencket wie ihr euch mit Lust und Liebe labt/
Daß nach dreyviertel Jahr ihr was zu wiegen habt.

Kunst-Wiege/
Derer sich das wolvertraute Paar/ (wann sie der gütige Gott mit einem jungen Söhngen segnen wird) nach Belieben bedienen kan.

1. D u zartes Reiß
2. A uff diesem Kreiß
3. D iß ist die Zeit zur Ruh
4. A ch schlaff und ruhe wohl du güldner Schatz
5. Schlaff sanfft/ so will ich dir ein schöne Ra ...
6. Kin Vielgeliebtes Hertz/ thu deine Li ...
7. ... daß wir sein in stiller Ru ...

10. HOE ...
11. DA ...
8. NUN ...
9. ...

12. der ... Herr Josephs der mächtige Pfleger
13. behüte dich immer fürm höllischen Jäger.

Wird nach den Zahlen gelesen.
1 Du zartes Reiß
2 Auff diesem Kreiß
3. Diß ist die Zeit zur Ruh/
4 Ach schlaff und ruhe wol du güldner Schatz du und so fort an.
Schluß

812

Grab- und Trauer-Kreutz.

I. Hans Gerhard Ruland sitzt in Ehren/ kein eitle Lust kan Ihn bethören.

II. Der Himmel ist Ihm bald erschienen/ Er herrschet bey den Seraphien.

1. Hier Ach! hier vermeset die Gebein/ die der Sammler dürrer Knochen
2. aufgeraufft/ und nit ohn Pein/ Hertz/ und alles/ Ihr zerstochen/
3. Daß ein Hanß nur an Gesicht/ unverschäms lag Lust und Leben/
4. Daß die Rose/ die Edle war/ ihre Blätter ihm must geben.

5. Diese Rose wird und werth geschätzet/
6. Uñ gefällt Auch Gott er Sie versetzet/
7. IN Das Paradeis/ d n wieder offeN/
8. Da die Glaubigen und EHR zu hoffEN.

III. Er hat der Mutter/ wie im Leben/ so nach dem Tod/ Gesellschafft geben.

IV. Die Leiber/ in der Erden-Kammer/ sind frey von Unglück/ Noth und Jammer.

9. Nun/ Ihr Edlen Nimfen kompt/ werft die schöne Kräntz und Kronen
10. Diesem Knaben in die Grufft/ seine Unschuld zu belohnen;
11. Werft den grünen Rosmarin und die Blumen all' hinein/
12. und gedencket daß Ihr müst auch deß Würgers Beute sein.

813

Das
Glücke
Berücke
Kein Unfall der Zeit
Schmücke
Beglücke
Ach Himmel! die Freud
Und segne die seelige Stunden
Da Weißheit und Tugend in Liebe verbunden
Laß Hertzen und Seelen vereiniget seyn
Doch laß die Beliebten nicht immer allein
Laß grünende Zweige erquicken
Und cröne mit zartesten Blicken
Das Hoch- und Wohl-Edele Hauß
Und weñ deñ die Sterblichkeit aus
So baue
Die Aue
Der Englischen Lust
Und labe die Brust
Mit Himmels-Ergetzen
Und ewig beständigen Schätzen.

814

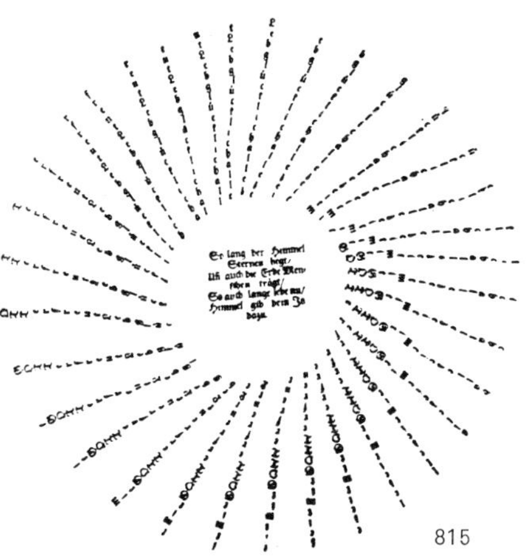

815

816

817

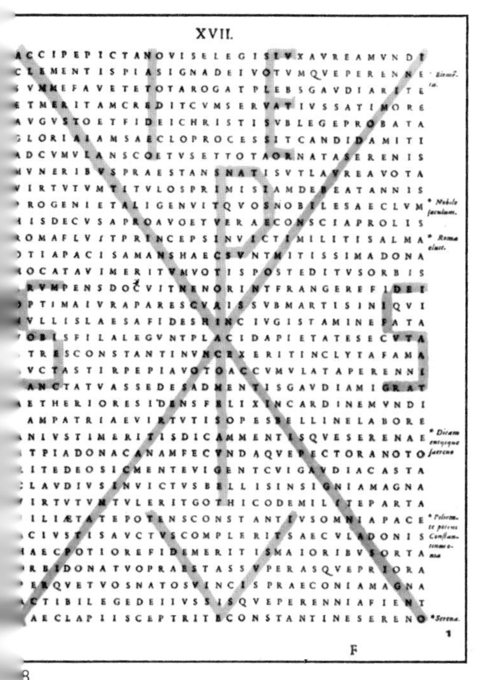

8

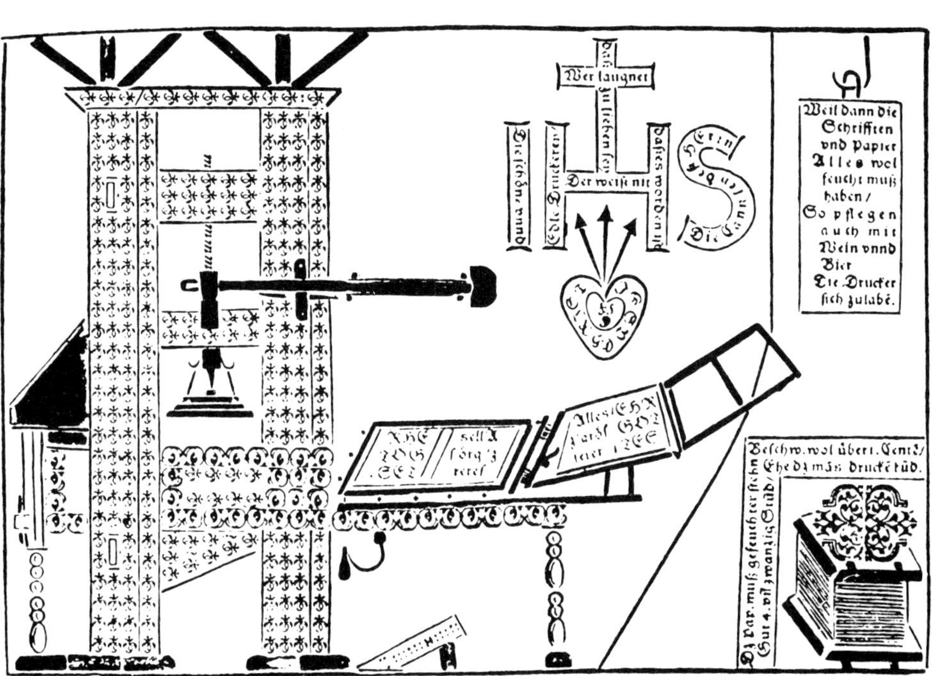

819

820

8

82

The vogue for writing-portraits, which had been in existence for several centuries, testifies to an equal degree of skill and dexterity in their authors: some of them such as President
832 833 Lincoln or Marshal Foch are virtually photographic likenesses. From 1693 onwards, an English printer succumbed to urgent pleas from several quarters by drawing a portrait of King William and Queen Mary, and in the eighteenth century John Stuart composed a portrait of George I out of the Lord's Prayer, the Ten Commandments, the thirty-one Psalms and prayers for the King and the royal family. There is also a portrait of Queen Victoria made up of 173,000 words which relate the historical details of her reign; it took the author, a man called D. Israël, four years and seven months to complete it. In 1889 a poet called André Bourgade composed a poem in homage to the Eiffel Tower with the title 'A Tower 300 metres high constructed in 300 lines'. A manufacturer of
834/836 typewriter ribbons recently distributed a series of portraits inspired by famous paintings which had been typed with a variety of coloured ribbons, the idea being to demonstrate the 'micrometric' precision of his method of registering an impression. It was a way of reinventing both cross-stitch and tapestry work, and the screen in half-tone engraving and the

VIEUX MÉTÉORE EMPORTÉ PAR L'ORAGE!.. L'ÉCLAT QU'IL RÉPANDIT BRILLERA D'AGE EN AGE

2

823

825

Nous voici enfin arrivés à l'époque où l'historien, appuyé sur des documents sérieux et authentiques, peut, à l'aide du talent et de la concision, devenir clair, suivi, je dirai même intéressant.

Les Essklwons, ou Esclavons, ou Sclavons, et plus tard Klaws, Slaves ou esclaves, du mot *slavia* qui, dans leur diome, signifie gloire, étaient les mêmes que ces Wepdrognwiens ou Wolpolodrgswliens ou mieux Petchenègues que nous avons vus si souvent infester les régions septentrionales, et que nous verrons plus loin sous le nom de Golwsphriens ou Snsplglpdswiths (et par corruption Poldniwgkariksss) passer la Dwlarzwirrwka (aujourd'hui Deneper ou Dniéper), où 56,813 restent engloutis, sans compter les femmes, les vieillards et les petits enfants, et se confondre avec les races Threrwpnmdplwisses ou Prtwpdnckgniennes, connues vulgairement sous le nom de Vogoulles, Tchermisses, Touwaches, Permiens, autrefois Biarmiens, Finois, Lapons, Estoniens, Roussalki, Pollowtzi, Hossars, Kiwiwthes, Whgptstv, Huns, Bulgares, Ougriens, Krwngpthgntklss (car c'est par erreur qu'on écrit Hragnwkpstwsklmtsss), etc., etc., etc., etc. Ces hommes vagabonds menaient la vie pastorale; ils étaient *pastores*, *pastyri* ou *pastovkli*. Ils portaient ce nom parce qu'ils faisaient paître leurs troupeaux (*pascere*, *pasti*, πταομαι, qui en grec signifie posséder. Mais revenons à notre sujet. La fortune de ces pasteurs consistait en brebis, *oves*, *ovsti*, οις et avec le digamma οϝις; en bœufs, βος, βιξ, βους [illegible] Ils devaient se garantir des bêtes féroces, *fera*, *wer*, ζηρ et chez les attiques φηρ [illegible] αι. Aussi trou[illegible] t'on dans le dialecte slavon beaucoup de [illegible] facio, λεγομαι; cubo, facere [illegible] dormio [illegible] dopnovites, du mot [illegible] rete [illegible] *plyt*, *plyvou* (naviguer[illegible] t πλειν, πλειω, πεπτω (je plai [illegible] et dans le mot dolgor il n'y a [illegible] ucc [illegible] de radical que le mot [illegible] es on le voit par la simple comparaison.

[illegible] monde ce diterran[illegible] tique éclairci, entrons courageusement dans l'histoire

Ce point de [illegible] vous [illegible] chose quitvan tout mcummomɔuɔcum

et remarquons a [illegible] tce Oriswsptchwts ομαι,

gagne la rive op [illegible] par suite de

ne sait plus où [illegible] mert aoon ectutc.

Mes empesmhdi

826

827

'lines' in television; it was also a way of emulating the 'ready-
made hypergraphics' produced by the letterists. Last year,
a computer was 'programmed' to produce a naked woman,
whereupon it constructed a body with really very graceful 838
contours.

Compared with these products of the electronic age, typographic calligrams seem mere child's play; it is true that the
use of certain photo-mechanical processes cancels out the need
for the laborious collages of the past. Calligrams can depict
man in his entirety, from head to foot, along with objects and
the whole world which surrounds him. We can have head-gear,
a head of hair, faces, bodies, a dress, arms, a shoe, boots shaped
to look like Italy, cigarette-smoke, sun and rain; or else a
Morris pillar plastered with posters, an image depicting
strength and war, a flag, familiar objects, a bridge, a motor car,
streets, towns full of letters . . . 842/872

The pictorial poems which make up Apollinaire's *Calligrammes*
are too well-known to be dwelt on at length; sometimes the
figured object is inserted in the text, as in the bugle; or alterna- 879
tively the pictorial composition involves the whole poem and
corresponds to the title, examples being 'The tie and the 876
watch', 'Heart, crown and mirror', 'Mandoline, carnation and
bamboo', 'The stabbed pigeon and the fountain'; or again, the 875
'Ocean-letter' spreads its dual sun over several pages. But
other collections of Apollinaire's work – found after his
death – also contain calligrams which are still at the manuscript
stage. In his *Poèmes à Lou*, we find a fig, a cigarette, a brandy
flask, a mirror, a 75-millimetre gun, a temple, a bust of a
woman wearing a hat, an orange still joined to its leaves, a heart
pierced by an arrow; sometimes the verse will flicker like a
flame or spiral downwards like a dead leaf; or sometimes it will
describe the curves of a pair of breasts. Among the poems
found after the poet's death, or in his correspondence, we will
come across spectacles, clocks, a vase of flowers, a Twelfth- 877
cake, the fore-quarters of a horse plus the words '*Tout terrible-
ment*,' and then also some birds, Picasso's thumb, various little
human figures including a boxer, a dancer, and the last of the 880
Mohicans; and then again a bottle, a pipe, a hand, a swastika . . .
and, as an illustration of an attempt to fit a square peg into a
round hole, a square table and a pedestal table.

A calligram dedicated to Pablo Picasso and depicting one 878
of the master's paintings – we can pick out a guitar – appeared
in 1917 in the magazine *Sic*, which was run by another poet
called Pierre Albert-Birot. Albert-Birot is the underrated
author of *Grabinoulor*, a saga novel in the epic style and without 883 885/887
punctuation, who also composed a number of his own calli-
grams; he specialized in 'placard-poems' and 'poster-poems' 922
which were surrealist in inspiration. He thus caught up with the
simultaneity of vision in Apollinaire, who prayed for an art of

828

expression which would allow the reader 'to read a whole poem at a single glance, just as a conductor reads the superimposed notes in a musical score all at once, so one can see these plastic and printed elements'.

But Apollinaire never put the theories he expressed in his *L'Esprit nouveau et les poètes* into practice, either because he died before he could do so, or simply because he didn't want to. He wrote: 'Typographic gimmicks handled with great daring have the advantage of giving rise to a visual lyricism which was virtually unknown to previous generations. These tricks and devices can go even further and achieve a synthesis of the arts, of music, painting and literature.'

These visions of a future where 'poets will have a freedom they have never known up to now' were voiced at a time 'when typography had reached the last brilliant phase of its career, at the dawn of the new methods represented by the cinema and

830

83

83

829

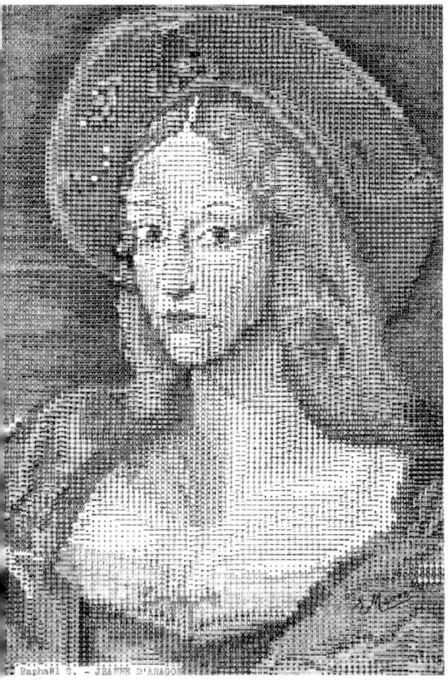

835

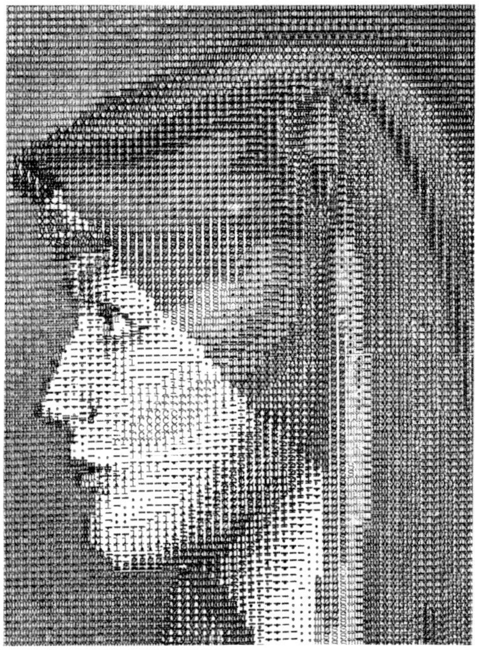

836

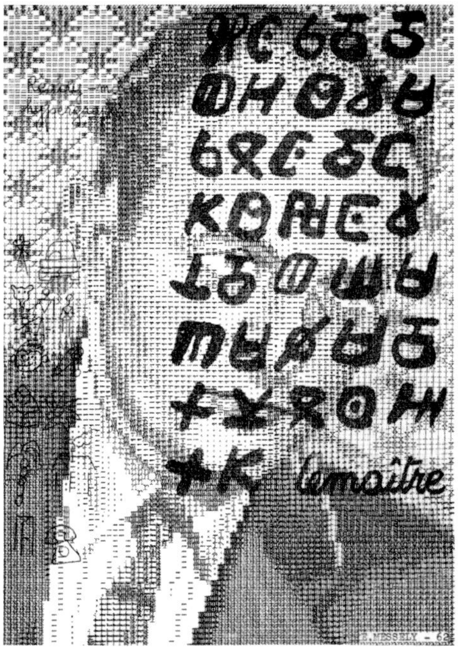

837

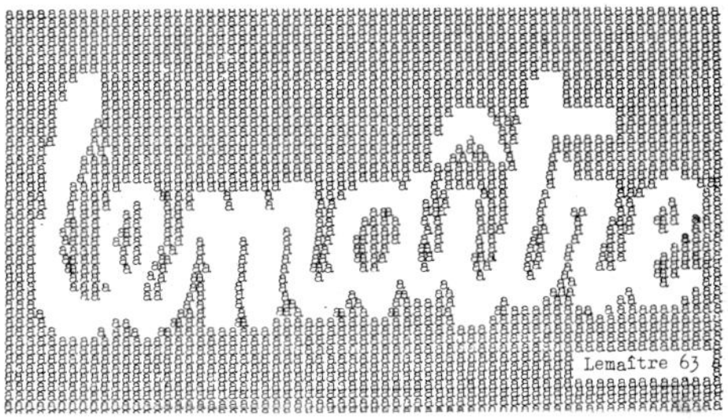

839

838

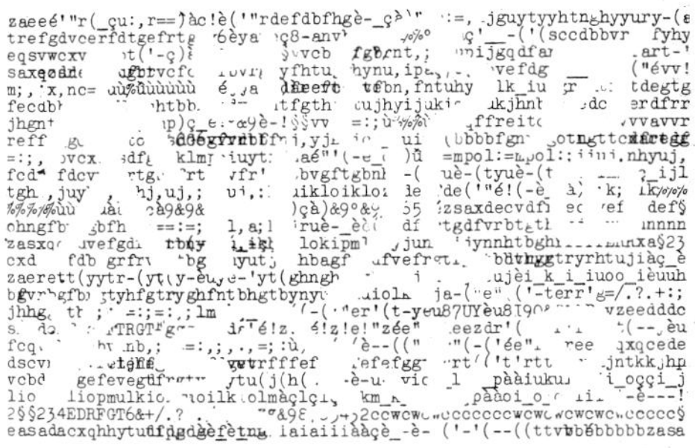

840

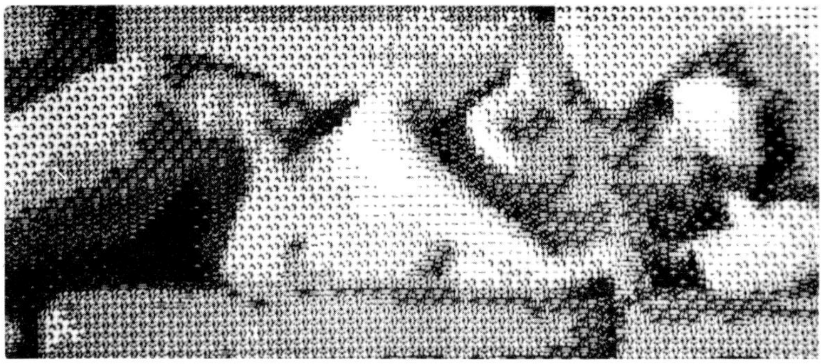

841

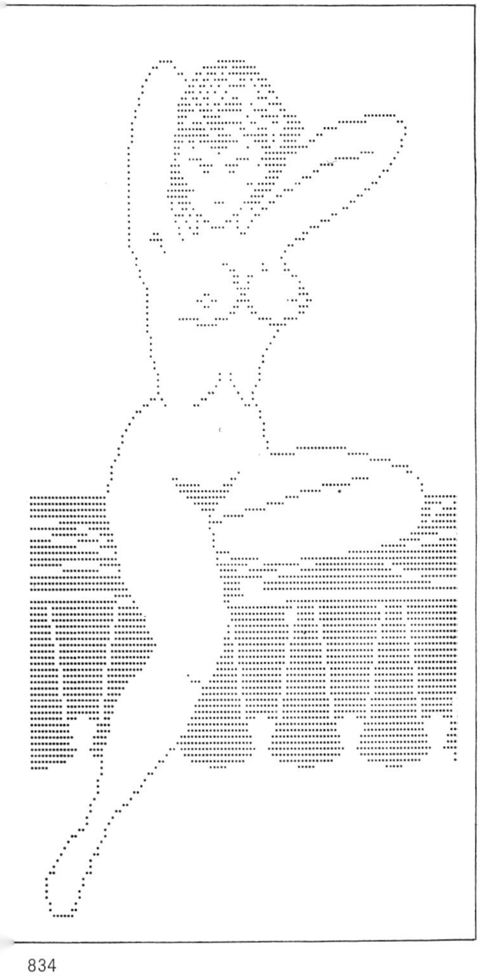

834

842

8

the gramophone'. At any rate, in the same lecture, which he delivered in the middle of the war when the state of mind of his audience made him repudiate the 'magic cast-offs of the colossal Romanticism of Wagner's Germany', Apollinaire personally set the limits of this emancipation and this new spirit, which he saw as 'full of danger, full of pitfalls'. He had once been associated with the demonstrations organized by the Futurists, (though we might put forward the theory that his sole reason for pursuing their theories to extremes was an urge to ridicule the movement); but he now appealed to his audience to fight against 'cosmopolitan lyricism' and spoke of his aversion to disorder and chaos. It is important that we should stress the fact that, unlike the poets of today, Guillaume Apollinaire was not particularly concerned with the way his calligrams were presented typographically. So their final shape is merely a typographic transcription by a third party – the anonymous type-setter – of a hand-written poem. For instance all we know of the poem '*Il pleut*' ('It's Raining') is that, according to Pierre Albert-Birot, it was composed in a single night by the printer Levé, who, already semi-retired, was fired with enthusiasm when he saw the manuscript.

Apollinaire's work was influenced by that of the Cubist painters – '*Les Demoiselles d'Avignon*' dates from 1907 – and exercised in its turn an equally strong influence on the plastic art of his period, rather than on actual poetry (with the exception of what is known as 'spatialist' poetry). The only people to imitate his *Calligrammes* were those who admired his work so much that they were eager to pay him homage by offering a
892-893 pastiche of his work. Bertrand Guegan's menus appear to make direct allusions to his work; and in the same way, the seven

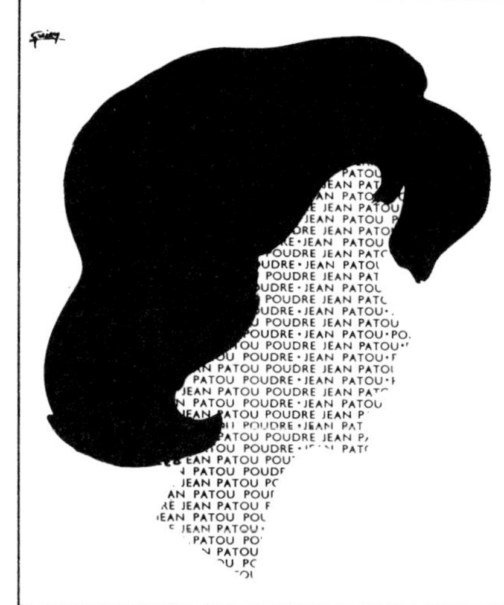

84

850

85

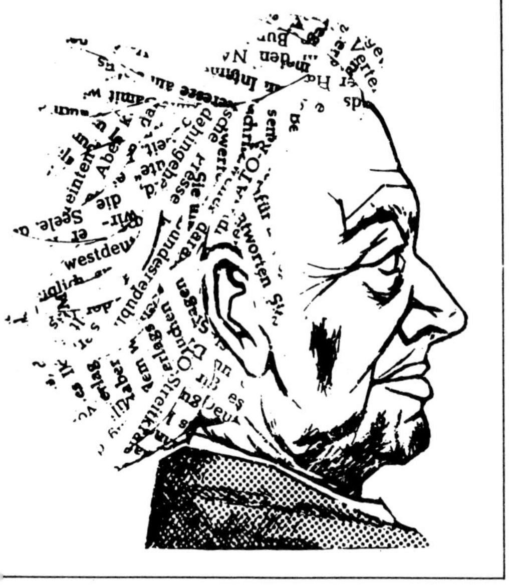

844

845

846

Photosia, la solution
de vos problèmes de reproduction. Pho
tosia, la solution de vos problèmes de repro
duction. Photosia, la solution de vos problèmes de
reproduction. Photosia, la solution de vos problèmes de
reproduction. Photosia, la solution de vos problèmes de re
production. Photosia, la solution de vos problèmes de repr
duction. Pho
tosia, la solu
tion de vos
problèmes de
eproduction.
otosia, la solu
n de vos pro
mes de repro
ction. Photosia
olution de vos
blèmes de re
duction. Pho
ia, la solution
vos problè
s de reproduc
Photosia, la solution de vos problèmes de reproduc
Photosia, la solution de vos pro blèmes de reproduction.
sia, la solution de vos problèmes de reproduction. Pho
la solution de vos problèmes de reproduct
sia, la solution de vos problèmes
production. Photosia, la solution
s problèmes de reproduction. Pho
, la solution de vos problèmes de
oduction. Photosia, la solution de
problèmes de reproduction. Pho
ia, la solution de vos problèmes
reproduction. Photosia, la solu
ion de vos problèmes de reproduc
tion. Photosia, la solution de vos
problèmes de reproduction.
Photosia, la solution de vos
problèmes de reproduction. Photosia la
solution de vos problèmes
de reproduction. Photosia,
la solution de vos problèmes de
reproduction. Photosia, m
la solution de vos pro vo
blèmes de reproduc tion
Photosia, la solution de vos
problèmes de reproduc tion.
Photosia, la solution de vos problè
mes de reproduction. Photo sia, la solution
de vos problèmes de reproduction. Photosia, la solu
tion de vos problèmes de reproduction. Photosia, la
solution de vos problèmes de reproduction. Photosia,
la solution de vos problèmes de reproduction. Photosia,
la solution de vos problèmes de reproduction. Photosia
la solution de vos problèmes de reproduction. Photosi

848

FUNNY
GIRL

849

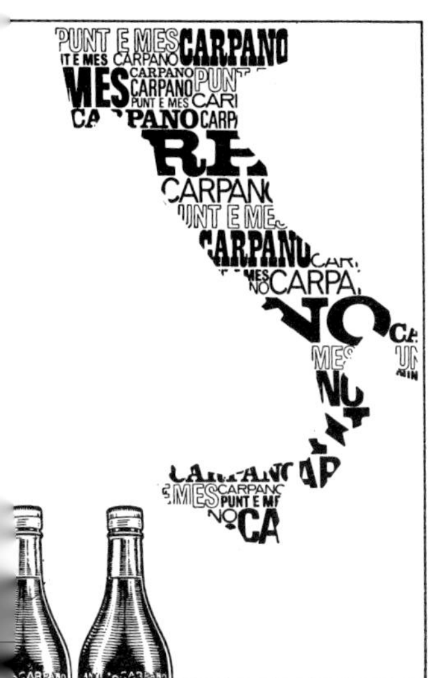

852

L'Italie : une certaine
manière de voir, de pen-
ser, de vivre. Ce particula-
risme italien se manifeste
aussi bien dans l'équilibre de
la nature que dans l'ordon-
nancement des jardins et
des villas ou dans les différents arts où
le génie la-
tin s'est
exercé.
En voici
toutes les
richesses.
Un magnifique
ouvrage 25x32 cm.
de 352 pages 420
photographies
dont 60 hors-
texte en cou-
leurs reliure
pleine toile
sous jaquette
en rho-
doid illus-
trée en
cou-
leurs,
72
NF

853

The
HEEL,
said Chris-
topher Marlowe,
was invented by a
woman who was al-
ways being kissed on
the forehead. Undeniably,
it raises her stature, giving her footing and ele-
vation. This is done not
by inches alone, but
with a sizable meas-
ure of savoir faire.
A DELMAN heel is
a trompe-l'oeil par
excellence. It abbreviates the foot,
lengthens the body, lightens the car-
riage, takes inches off the hips, and gives
the costume altogether new dimension. She
who walks in beauty, walks in DELMAN heels.

854

888/891 calligrams invented by Louise de Vilmorin to adorn her *Alphabet des aveux* ('Alphabet of Confessions') – a barrel, a broom, a pomegranate and fig, a shoe, a dagger, a window and a *képi* – owe quite as much to traditional prosody as to the pleasant distractions begun long ago by Simmias of Rhodes.

It was Raymond Queneau who unearthed some pamphlets by Nicolas Cirier in the Bibliothèque Nationale during the course of his search for 'literary lunatics'. He revealed his discovery, which should really be called 'typographical frenzy', in his book, *Lines, Numbers and Letters.* Announcing that he was being persecuted by his boss, Pierre Lebrun, poet, academician and a director of the Royal Printing Works, where Cirier was employed as a reader, our poet composed his *L'Apprentif administrateur* in 1840. This is a sort of Dadaist brochure *avant la lettre* and is printed on ordinary paper, folders or proof paste-ons in a variety of colours. Why L'Apprentif? Merely for the sake of producing a symmetrical title-page, explains the author. This 'picturesque and literario-typographico-bureaucratic pamphlet' does include a few figured
905 texts, the most notable being a trowel and an eye composed in Latin.

858

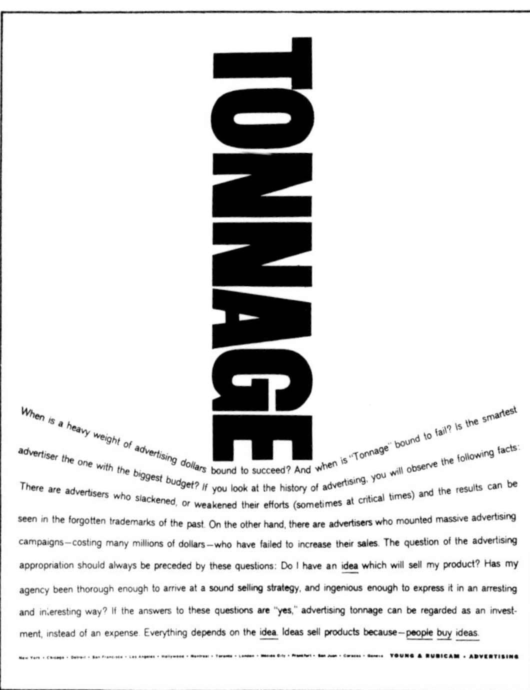

855

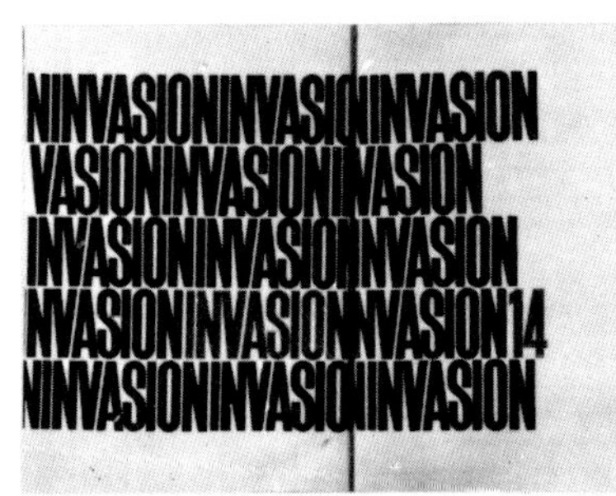

856

857

85

860

861

862

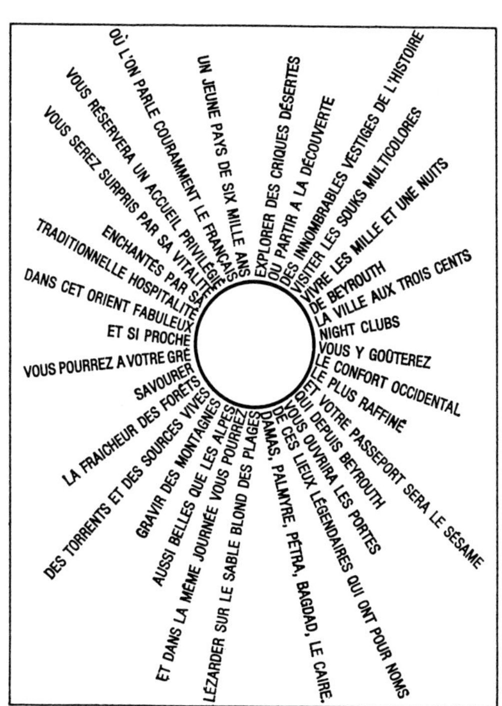

863

864

865

c'est en amérique que tout a co
mmencé d'autres pays poussent le
nationalisme jusqu'à vouloir l'annexer mais
le rock'n'roll est né aux états-unis sans qu'o
sache exactement comment à partir de formes
musicales qui existaient bien avant que bill hale
et ses comets décrochent vers la fin de 1954 le
gros titres de la première page des journau

866

En 1956 l'Angleterre vit à l'heure du Skiffle. Tout avait commencé quelques temps auparavant avec l'orchestre "Trad" de Chris Barber qui tenait regulièrement le sommet du Hit-Parade – le Melody Maker et le New Musical Express, revues de jazz, existaient déjà depuis plusieurs années – grâce aux classiques du jazz Nouvelle-Orléans : *"Sweet Georgia Brown", "Bourbon Street"*... Or parmi les musiciens de Chris Barber, se trouvait un joueur de banjo dont les goûts personnels étaient plus proches du Folk et du Country & Western que du Traditionnel. Lonnie Donnegan, car c'est de lui qu'il s'agit, était originaire de Glasgow; à l'âge de 17 ans, il avait appris à jouer de la guitare et du banjo. Il s'était engagé ensuite dans l'armée et avait vécu deux ans à Vienne où il s'était mis à chanter pour des copains de chambrée. A son retour dans la capitale, Chris Barber l'avait engagé dans son orchestre. C'est précisément en 1956 que Lonnie décida de former son propre groupe. Presque immédiatement, ce fut le succès avec *"Rock Island Line"* qui était, au départ, une des plages d'un 33 tours de Chris Barber. Couplé avec *"John Henry"*, ce morceau se vendit à plus d'un million d'exemplaires des deux côtés de l'Atlantique. Le Skiffle était né, et Lonnie en était devenu le roi. Au fait, qu'entendait-on exactement par Skiffle? Essentiellement un "compromis du folk-blues, de la chanson cow-boy, le tout accompagné de certains relents de New Orleans". Le créateur de ce genre musical insistait surtout sur l'origine noire et le blues; *"John Henry"* est un vieux worksong du Texas. Et Lonnie Donnegan de rappeler le personnage légendaire de Lonnie Johnson, son guitariste de blues favori. Le phénomène Skiffle vit aussitôt des milliers de groupes se former : il suffisait d'une guitare, d'un banjo, d'une caisse en bois; d'une de ces fameuses contrebasses fabriquées avec des boîtes de thé, un manche à balai et un peu de ficelle, pour se lancer dans la grande aventure. Partout en Angleterre, jusque dans les villages les plus reculés, les jeunes s'entraînaient dans le style nasal et aigu de Lonnie Donnegan. De nos jours le Skiffle a gardé bon nombre de fans; dans notre pays, Hughes Auffray lui doit sa réussite... Mais à quoi ressemble la jeunesse anglaise de cette époque? C'est loin d'être la folie. Seule une minorité fait vraiment parler d'elle et en général de manière assez péjorative : les Teddy Boys. Teddy, Ted, Edouard, ils ont reçu cette appellation en raison des habits édouardiens qu'ils affectionnent tout spécialement : vestes cintrées, longues redingotes, pantalons étroits et sans revers (une vraie révolution!); issus de la classe ouvrière, ils n'hésitent pas à investir 20 guinées (environ 300 F) dans un costume, somme considérable alors! Leur coiffure diffère aussi de celle de l'anglais moyen; celui-ci arbore la "short back and sides" qui tient plus de la tonte militaire que d'une véritable coupe de cheveux; les Teddy Boys sont coiffés à la Tony Curtis, cheveux mi-longs, rejetés en arrière, et pattes. Hollywood est passé par là. Dernière caractéristique vestimentaire, les Winkle Pickers, d'immenses souliers aux extrémités très pointues. Le Teddy Boy est un violent. Il vit en bande et sur une moto. Il passe ses nuits dans les "all-night cafés". Son passe-temps favori "the coin in the juke-box", la pièce dans le juke-box. Après avoir glissé quelques pennies et sélectionné un disque, il lui faut bondir sur sa moto, effectuer un parcours déterminé puis revenir à plein gaz vers son point de départ avant que le disque ne soit terminé. Le parcours devient de plus en plus long et de plus en plus dangereux : le premier à échouer est désigné comme le "chicken", le dégonflé de la bande. Autre amusement du même type : le jeu consiste à aligner une dizaine de motos à un carrefour et à démarrer en trombe lorsque le feu s'allume au rouge. Là aussi, celui qui hésite à la dernière seconde devient le "chicken". De 1954 à 1956, les Teddy Boys instaurèrent un climat d'insécurité qui atteint son paroxysme lors des émeutes raciales de Notting Hill Gate, auxquelles ils participèrent activement. Néanmoins ce ferment de révolte allait s'avérer propice à l'implantation du rock'n roll en Angleterre. Il fallait des fans pionniers : ce furent les Teddy Boys. Le premier événement majeur dans l'épopée du rock anglais, l'étincelle qui déclenche la folie générale, ce fut la sortie du film "Rock around the clock" et la première tournée de Bill Haley. Le Daily Mirror organisa un service de cars et fréta un train spécial pour emmener ses fans voir à Southampton le timide Américain et son groupe, les Comets. En dépit d'un succès triomphal, les critiques restèrent partagés quant à ses possibilités musicales. C'est que quelque mois auparavant, un chanteur bien de chez eux avait fait dresser l'oreille aux Anglais : Tommy Steele leur semblait nettement supérieur au créateur de *"See you later, alligator"* et de *"Razzle Dazzle"*. Fin 1956, Tommy Steele faisait ses premières apparitions en public en Grande-Bretagne. Un Hit, *"Rock with the caveman"* et Tommy était passé des soirées à cinq shillings dans les sous-sols de Soho aux cachets les plus élevés de tout le pays. Peter Jones, journaliste au Record Mirror, nous raconte l'un des premiers shows de Tommy Steele : "A gauche du public, un jeune garçon, Dennis Price, est debout au piano. Debout, notez bien : l'influence de Little Richard se fait sentir dans le jeu de scène. Il porte une chemise blanche, un pull noir et des jeans noirs. Près de lui, le saxo-ténor Alan Stuart, le contrebassiste Allan Weighell et le batteur Léo Pollini. Dans la salle, une foule de bras se tendent, des programmes déchirés volent dans tous les coins, des filles s'évanouissent, le cri de guerre "Tommy, Tommy, Tommy" retentit. Tommy entre alors en scène; les hurlements montent en un crescendo continu. Il chante *"Giddy up a ding dong"*. Ses cheveux se balancent à droite et à gauche. Ses jambes semblent être en caoutchouc; ses membres ne restent pas un instant immobiles. Il chante

"Dont be cruel", "Rock with the caveman", "Singing the blues". Il tient une guitare en bandoulière, la d
tel un fusil vers la partie la plus bruyante de l'auditoire. Tommy présente ses morceaux avec un fort accent cockn
Il explique à la salle qu'il ne réalise pas très bien lui-même ce qui lui arrive. Le show se termine en émeu
Comme tous les jeunes Anglais de cette époque, Tommy aimait fréquenter Soho, le quartier pittoresque animé
étrangers, des boîtes de strip-tease et des cinémas, du show-business en général. Il existait à l'époque d
Old Compton Street, un coffee-bar appelé *"The Two I's"* dirigé par deux ex-catcheurs australiens, Paul Lincoln
Ray Hunter. Le commerce marchait mal, mais lorsque les deux propriétaires se décidèrent à livrer leur sous-sol
"guitaristes itinérants", tout alla beaucoup mieux. Par la même occasion, les Two I's entraient dans la légende
la Pop-Music anglo-saxonne. Depuis quelques temps y jouait un groupe de Skiffle, les Vipers, ensemble déjà popul
grâce à un morceau : *"Pick a bale of cotton"*. C'est là qu'un jour Tommy descendit, sa guitare sous le b
et que le plus naturellement du monde, il fit le bœuf avec les Vipers. Les choses en restèrent là, mais, lors
trois mois plus tard, Tommy se retrouva en présence du groupe, un homme vint le contacter après le specta
John Kennedy, ex-photographe de presse à Fleet Street, lui proposa ses bons offices en tant que mana
Tommy, qui n'avait rien à perdre, accepta. Et Kennedy allait s'avérer être "the right man, in the hight pla
En 1957, Tommy Steele s'imposa comme le seul chanteur de rock anglais capable d'atteindre le numéro un à
coup. *"Singing the blues"* fut un Hit massif que les seules vedettes britanniques à réussir dans leur
étaient des chanteurs à voix, comme Frankie Vaughan ou Jimmy Young. Le reste des charts était bloqué
Elvis Presley, Bill Haley, Little Richard, l'Alan Freed Big Band et une multitude de rockers américains. Bie
John Kennedy s'associa à Larry Parnes et la carrière de Tommy prit un nouvel essor. "The Tommy S
Story" fut le premier film ayant pour vedette un chanteur de rock'n'roll britannique. Terminé en mars 1957
ne fut pas une production très inspirée; néanmoins, elle remplit à bloc tous les cinémas. C'est à cette ép
qu'il faut noter la première grande émission "pop" à la télévision, le "Six Five Special" de Jack G
Jack, un producteur et animateur de talent, adorait la Beat-Music; beaucoup de vedettes d'alors lui do
leur réussite. Son show hebdomadaire était très varié; il présentait à la fois des chanteurs de rock,
chanteurs noirs de Rhythm & Blues, des groupes de Skiffle et de jazz New Orleans. Le "Six Five Special" étai
événement attendu dans la fébrilité par des millions de teenagers, et leur rêve à tous était d'obtenir
autorisation de la BBC pour danser devant les caméras pendant l'enregistrement de l'émission. Quant à la n
elle avait beaucoup évolué; les Teddy Boys avaient abandonné leurs oripeaux édouardiens pour se barder de c
la manière des rockers venus des Etats-Unis : Gene Vincent, Vince Taylor. Ils portaient désormais des casqu
en cuir constellées de badges métalliques à l'exemple de Marlo Brando dans "L'Equipée sauv
L'apparition des chaînes qu'ils portaient autour de la ceinture ou du cou est égale
typique de cette époque. D'ailleurs, par assimilation aux forçats américains, on les
surnommés les "chain gangs". Cependant on peut encore difficilement associer
partie de la jeunesse aux Rockers, avec un R majuscule, parce que la notion de Ro
n'interviendra que beaucoup plus tard, vers 1961-1962, à une époque où, les pion
du rock étant retombés dans l'oubli, une minorité qui aura gardé les vêtements
goûts et les attitudes sociales de 1957 viendra prendre la défense d'ex-g
noms tels Eddie Cochran, Buddy Holly, Carl Perkins et Bill Haley. Face aux ro
ex-Teddy Boys, on trouve pêle-mêle deux types de teenagers : les Trads amateurs de
Orleans et de Skiffle; ils sont habillés d'une manière assez bohème, blue-jeans délavés à fra
chemises flottantes et cheveux bouclés; les Mods, sophistiqués, dont les prédilections vont au jazz mod
Ceux-ci fréquentent plus particulièrement le Flamingo dans Wardour Street et les Two I's devenus désorma
clubs "in" d'où sortent les idoles. A l'heure du lunch dans Old Compton Street, vous étiez certair
rencontrer des jeunes musiciens, la guitare sur le dos, qui entraient dans la boîte où Tommy Steele ava
ses débuts, avec l'espoir secret que le même conte de fées se reproduirait pour eux. Pour revenir à la
un problème majeur se posait alors : Lonnie Donnegan et Tommy Steele venaient de recevoi
récompenses de l'Industrie du disque, décernées chaque année aux meilleures ventes nationales, ma
Compagnies voulaient savoir maintenant qui allait faire le prochain gros boom. Depuis quelques mois, les no
venus étaient de simples étoiles filantes, un 45 tours ou deux, puis ils retombaient dans l'oubli. Main
tout le monde attendait. Et une fois de plus ce fut Larry Parnes qui trouva la solution. Depuis son asso
avec John Kennedy, Larry avait monté une écurie assez incroyable de "pop singers". Il prospectait un peu p
à Londres et ailleurs, prenait de jeunes chanteurs en main et créait une image autour d'eux. Il insistait
tout à ce qu'ils aient un nom qui frappe... Marty Wilde, Georgie Fame, Duffy Power, Vince Eager, Billy Fur
Marty Wilde fit une entrée très remarquée dans la profession avec *"Endless Sleep"*, resté depuis un classique du rock a
Marty se spécialisa surtout dans les chansons tristes et dans les ballades; beau garçon, ses passages à la télévis

867

868

869

La circulation
est dense malgré
l'heure matinale. L'air
n'est pas encore trop surchauffé.
Les lourds tapis aux points noués, les
populaires moquettes, les confortables descentes
de lit, les rapides carpettes se croisent dans
des chuchotements laineux. Seuls, quelques clochards
circulent sans façon sur de minables
nattes effilochées qui claquent au vent .

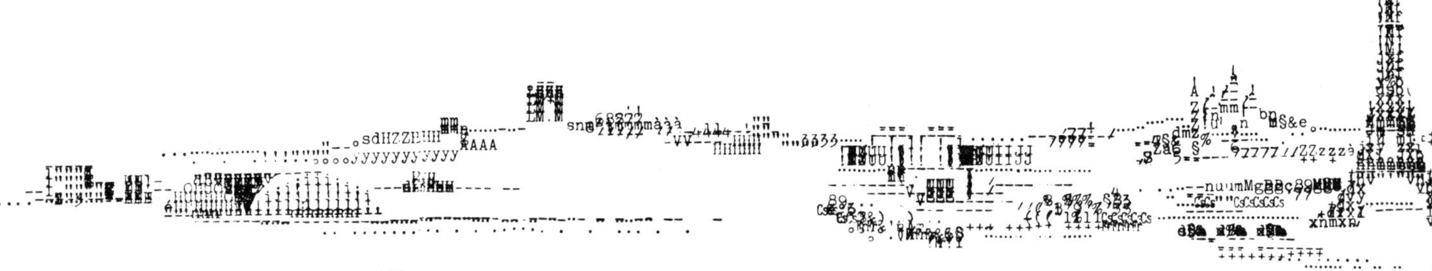

870

871

872

873

874

A play on words involving 'a long and a sad tale' and 'a long tail' led to the tale shaped like a mouse's tail which appears in 903
Alice in Wonderland and is probably one of the most famous and popular figured poems in England. In Lewis Carroll's original manuscript, the mouse's tale was identical in design but seemed 904
to fit in better with the narrative because it depended on the mouse's hatred for dogs and cats. The tail may have originated with Alfred Lord Tennyson, who told Carroll of a dream he had had, in which he imagined that he had written a long poem about fairies, beginning with extremely long lines and then tapering down to lines of no more than two syllables each.

In this connection we might also refer to a famous poem by Victor Hugo called 'Les Djinns' which appeared in his 897
Orientales (1829). It consists of 120 lines divided up into octets, each of which has a different metre; the poet has used an arrangement of rhopalic lines which grow first longer and then shorter for his description of the djins as they emerge from the depths of the night, fly past in a tumultuous roar of noise and then fade away into the distance. If we take the trouble to place the stanzas end to end – which is never done on the printed page – the poem takes on the shape of an elongated diamond and thus has a doubly descriptive quality, for as well as the *image* traced by the lines of the poem we have a superimposed *sound* which starts up, grows, is amplified, dies down and then fades away altogether. The choice of rhymes, some whispering, some shatteringly loud, and the skilful use of alliteration and assonance strengthen the sound image contained in the poem.

On parle
d'interdire
ces vieux tacots
inusables venus
tout droit de Perse en
contrebande...

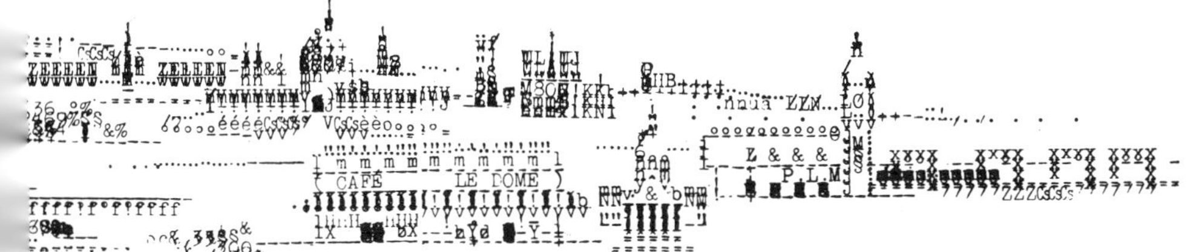

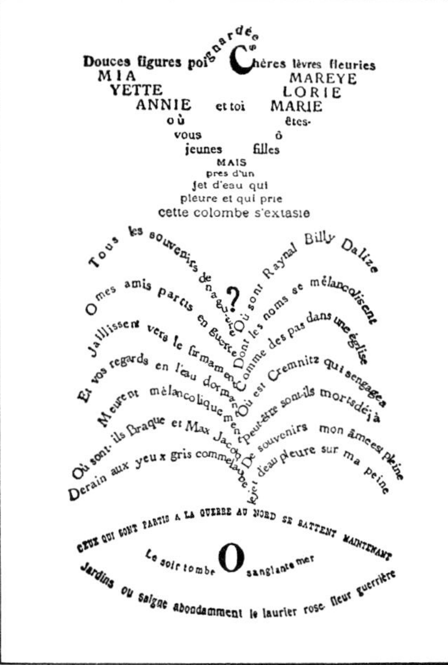

875

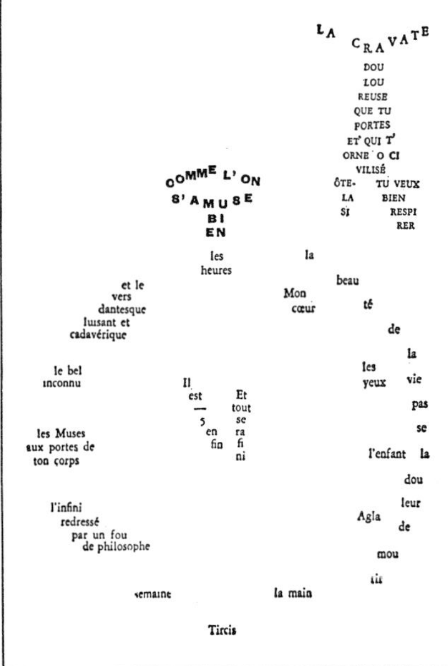

876

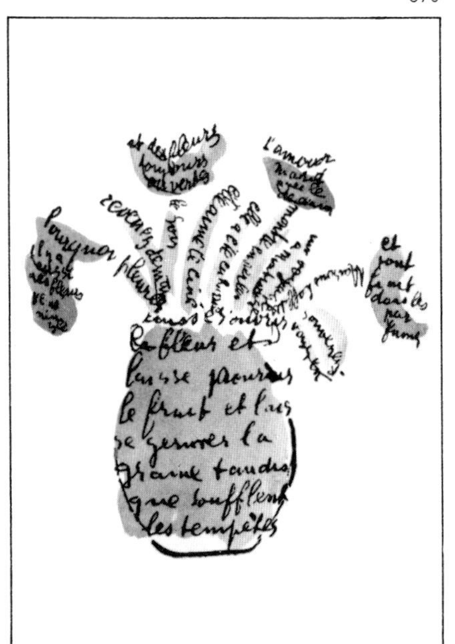

877

PABLO PICASSO

Voyez ce peintre il prend les choses avec leur ombre aussi et d'un coup d'œil sublimatoire
Il se déchire en accords profonds et agréables à respirer tel l'orgue que j'aime entendre
Des Arlequines jouent dans le rose et bleus d'un beau-ciel Ce souvenir revit
les rêves et les actives mains Orient plein de glaciers L'hiver est rigoureux
Lustres or toile irisée or loi des stries de feu fond en murmurant.
Bleu flamme légère argent des ondes bleues après le grand cri
Tout en restant elles touchent cette sirène violon
Faons lourdes ailes l'incandesce quelques brasses encore
Bourdons femmes striées éclat de plongeon-diamant
Arlequins semblables à Dieu en variété Aussi distingués qu'un lac
Fleurs brillant comme deux perles monstres qui palpitent
Lys cerclés d'or, je n'étais pas seul! fais onduler les remords
Nouveau monde très matinal montant de l'énorme mer
L'aventure de ce vieux cheval en Amérique
Au soir de la pêche merveilleuse l'œil du masque
Air de petits violons au fond des anges rangés
Dans le couchant puis au bout de l'an des dieux
Regarde la tête géante et immense la main verte
L'argent sera vite remplacé par tout notre or
Morte pendue à l'hameçon... c'est la danse bleue
L'humide voix des acrobates des maisons
Grimace parmi les assauts du vent qui s'assoupit
Ouis les vagues et le fracas d'une femme bleue
Enfin la grotte à l'atmosphère dorée par la vertu
Ce saphir veiné il faut rire!
Rois de phosphore sous les arbres les bottines entre des plumes bleues
La danse des dix mouches lui fait face quand il songe à toi
Le cadre bleu tandis que l'air agile s'ouvrait aussi
Au milieu des regrets dans une vaste grotte.
Prends les araignées roses à la nage
Regrets d'invisibles pièges l'air
Paisible se souleva mais sur le clavier musiques
Guitare-tempête ô gai trémolo
O gai trémolo ô gai trémolo
Il ne rit pas l'artiste-peintre
Ton pauvre étincellement pâle
L'ombre agile d'un soir d'été qui meurt
Immense désir et l'aube émerge des eaux si lumineuses
Je vis nos yeux diamants enfermer le reflet du ciel vert et
J'entendis sa voix qui dorait les forêts tandis que vous pleuriez
L'acrobate à cheval le poète à moustaches un oiseau mort et tant d'enfants sans larmes
Choses cassées des livres déchirés des couches de poussière et des aurores déferlant

GUILLAUME APOLLINAIRE

878

AS-
TU CON
NU LA QUI
PU TAIN A FOUTU LA VXXXXX A TOUTE L'ARTILLERIE
DE N
ANCY L'ARTILLERIE ne s'est pas aperçu qu'elle avait au mal

879

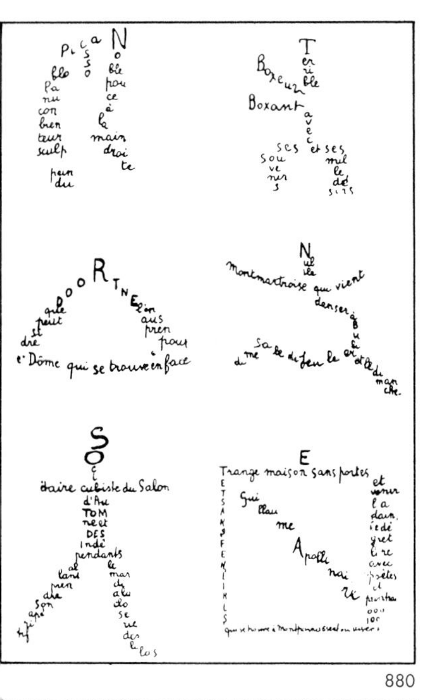

880

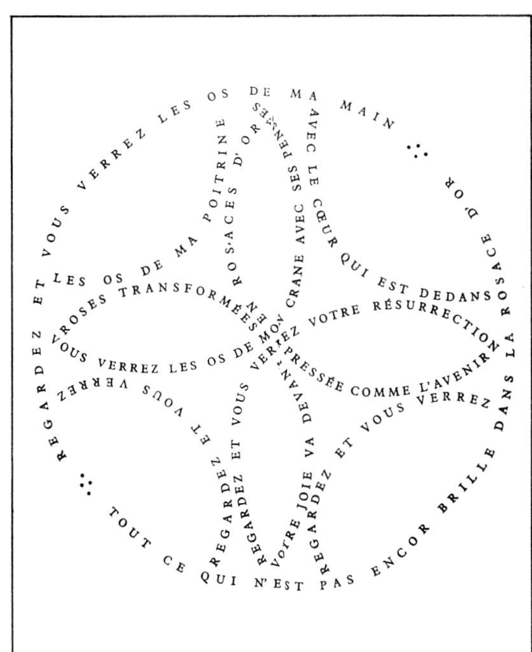

883

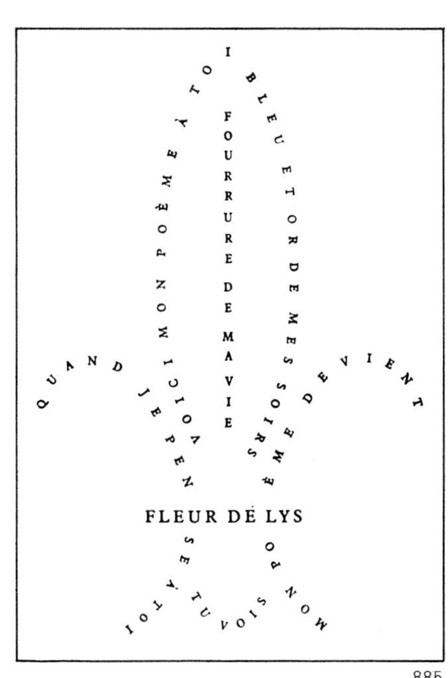

885

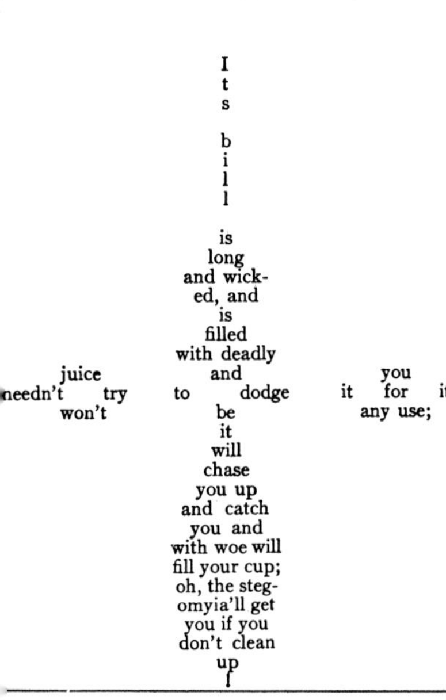

881

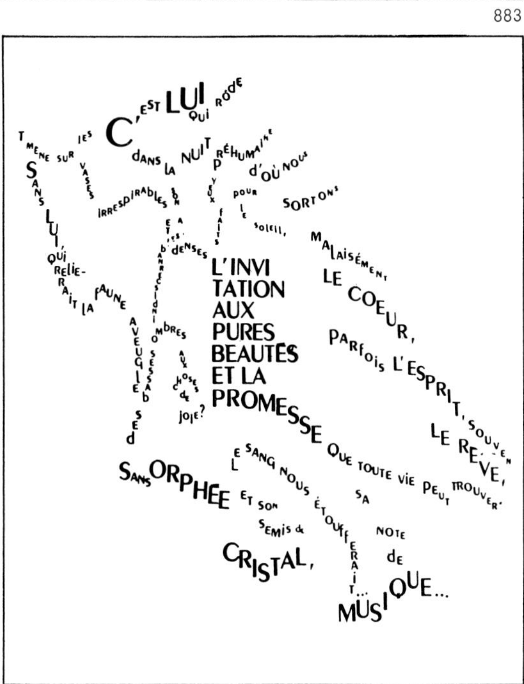

884

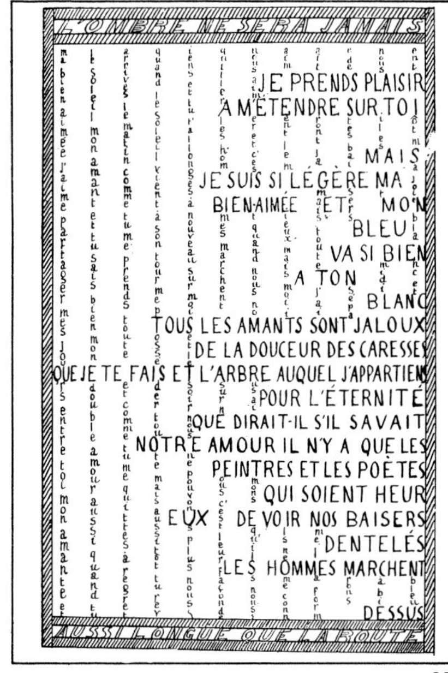

886

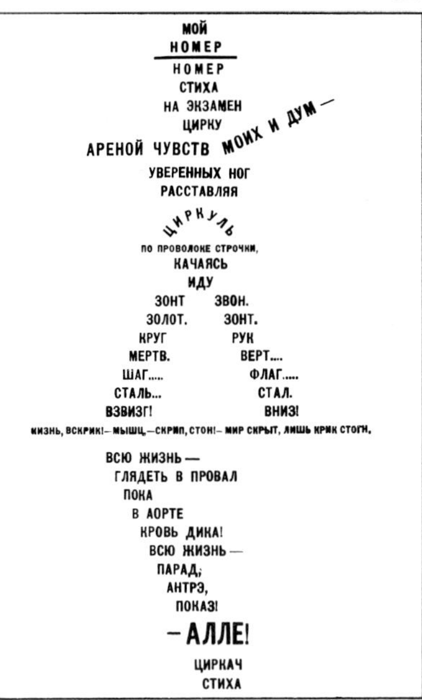

882

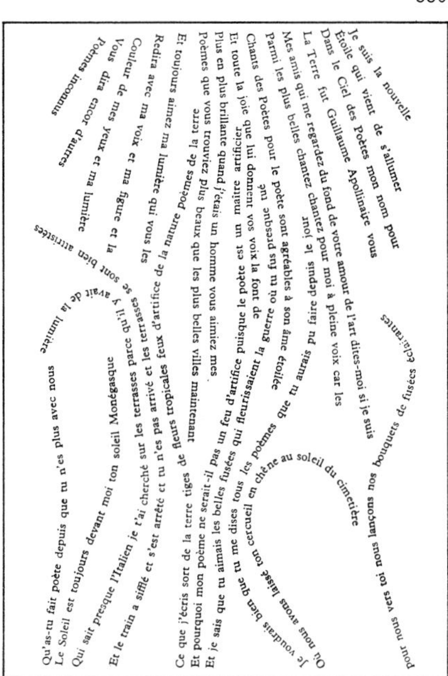

887

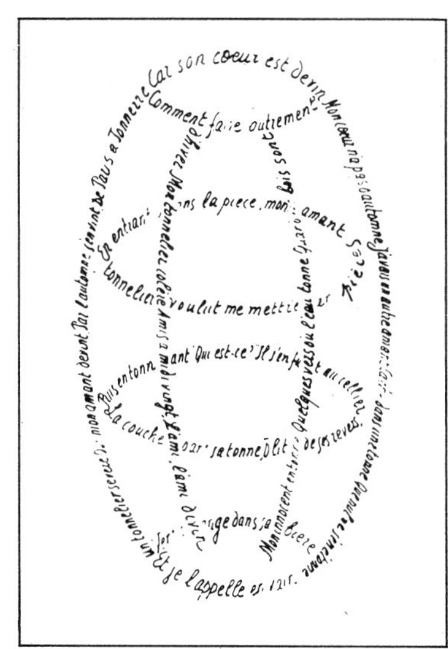

888

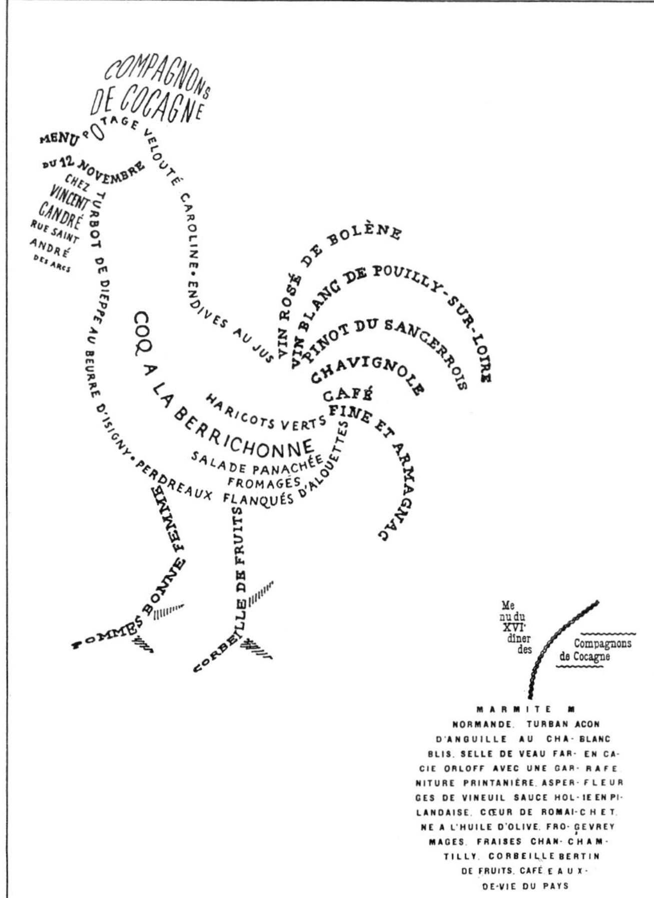

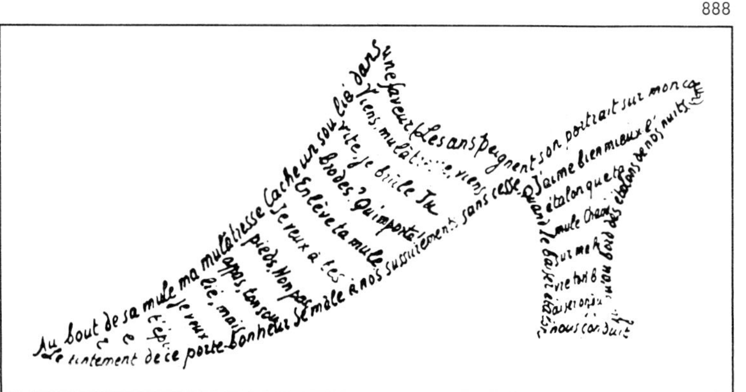

889

892

890

891

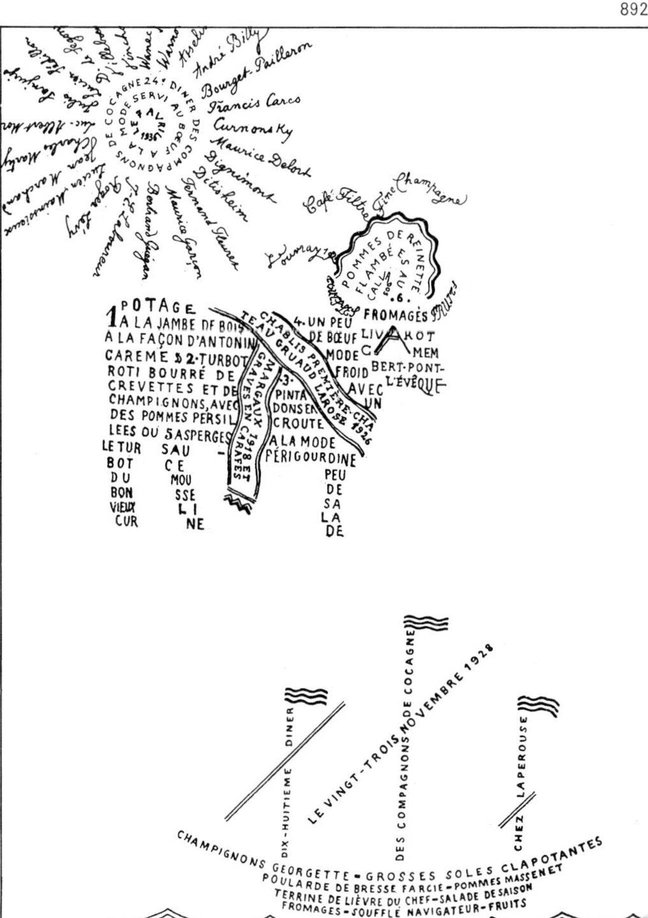

893

STEINBERG

894

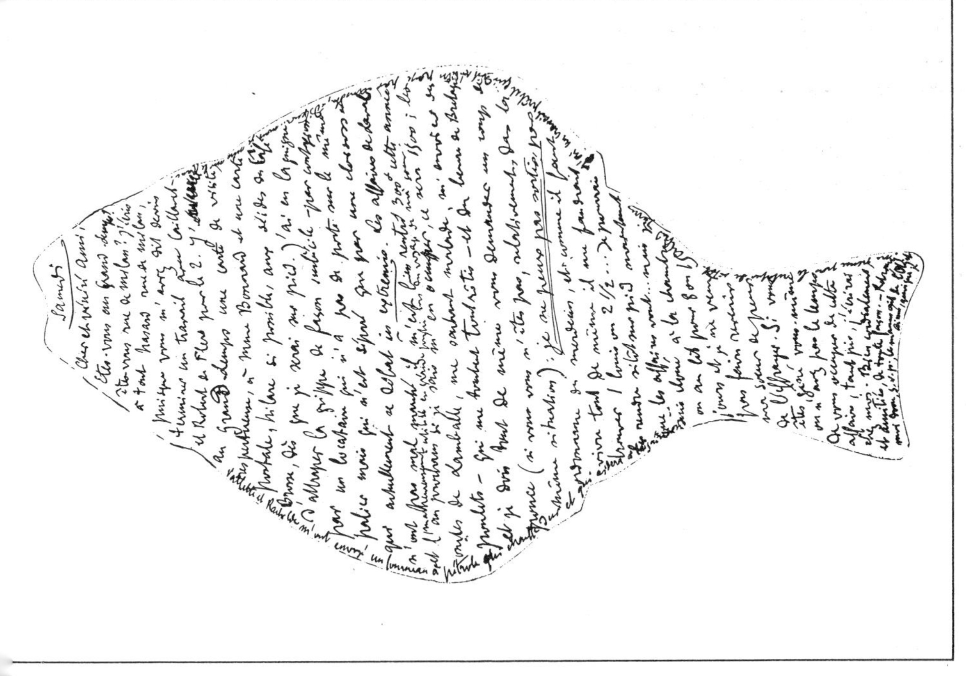

895

les "prima donna" aiment
beaucoup les bandes ma-
gnétiques car en s'écoutant,
elles perfectionnent à loisir
cet art que Stendhal disait
divin... Vous n'êtes peut-être
pas une grande cantatrice,
pourtant les bandes ma-
gnétiques peuvent vous être
d'un grand secours : courrier
conférences, répétitions ou chants
d'oiseaux, les bandes magné-
tiques Kodak enregistrent tous
les sons possibles, sur tous les
magnétophones possibles et les
reproduisent avec la plus
rigoureuse, la plus constante
la plus envoutante fidélité. Elles
ne s'usent jamais, tiennent peu de
place, s'effacent pour de nouveaux enregistrements selon
votre bon plaisir. Elles sont pour
vous une seconde mémoire toujours pré
sente, objective et fidèle. * * * * * * * * *

896

A small piece in English by an anonymous author who gave it the French title, *Avoirdupoids,* makes use of an image to express an abstract idea.

The length of this line indicates the ton of coal as dug by the miner.
This one indicates the ton shipped to the dealer.
The small dealer gets a ton like this.
This is the one you pay for.
This is what you get.
The residue is:
Cinders and
Ashes.
And this line will give you some conception of the size of the BILL.

Gabriel Martin's *Les Psaumes de la Beauté* (*Psalms of Beauty*)
898 includes a poem called 'Le Dos' ('The back') which has the same curving shape as its subject-matter. Jules de Rességuier, another French nineteenth-century poet, wrote a monosyllabic sonnet which runs: *Fort / Belle / Elle / Dort / Sort / Frêle / Quelle / Mort! / Rose / Close / La / Brise / L'a / Prise!;* an image on the brevity of existence makes itself felt automatically.

One is tempted to see embryo calligrams in certain types of poems which have a rigid structure, such as those with alternate rhymes, iambics for instance. And surely even La Fontaine's supple prosody conjures up the idea of an 'abstract' calligram? And as for free verse, surely it too is reduced to a pictorial design, since it has had its traditional sound supports amputated? Remy de Gourmont notes that typography 'has too often played a preponderant role in the history of free verse', but he does recognize that 'true free verse is conceived as such, i.e. as a musical fragment, the design of which is modelled on the emotive idea underlying it and is no longer governed by the rigid rule of number', for 'we do not read with our eyes alone; we read with our ears, we have the memory of words in our mind as we read'. And he draws our attention to Gustave Kahn's 'care in making his thought poetic both in visual terms and in musical terms; the images sing and the music depicts'.

The same type of calligraphic aims could be found in French classical verse, the most notable example of this being the way oblique and vertical lines appear when Alexandrines are broken up into a series of short rejoinders. This process of dislocating a line was of course accentuated by Victor Hugo.

Authors have even managed on occasions to produce pictorial images in prose, without the help of the open-work pattern offered by verse. When Charles Nodier makes his
907 readers go down the five steps of a staircase, he is simply introducing a genuine calligram in the very middle of his text. But the linear overcrowding of a text, especially if it is carried to exaggerated lengths and is accompanied by a total lack of punctuation – as in the interior monologues in Faulkner or Joyce, or by strings of proper names in Blaise Cendrars, or of adjectives in Céline – creates a sort of dynamic overload and leads us to see the page in a particular way.

Murs, ville,
Et port,
Asile
De mort,
Mer grise
Où brise
La brise,
Tout dort.

Dans la plaine
Naît un bruit.
C'est l'haleine
De la nuit.
Elle brame
Comme une âme
Qu'une flamme
Toujours suit !

La voix plus haute
Semble un grelot.
D'un nain qui saute
C'est le galop.
Il fuit, s'élance,
Puis en cadence
Sur un pied danse
Au bout d'un flot.

La rumeur approche
L'écho la redit.
C'est comme la cloche
D'un couvent maudit;
Comme un bruit de foule,
Qui tonne et qui roule,
Et tantôt s'écroule,
Et tantôt grandit.

Dieu ! la voix sépulcrale
Des Djinns !... Quel bruit ils font !
Fuyons sous la spirale
De l'escalier profond.
Déjà s'éteint ma lampe,
Et l'ombre de la rampe,
Qui le long du mur rampe,
Monte jusqu'au plafond.

C'est l'essaim des Djinns qui passe,
Et tourbillonne en sifflant !
Les ifs, que leur vol fracasse,
Craquent comme un pin brûlant.
Leur troupeau, lourd et rapide,
Volant dans l'espace vide,
Semble un nuage livide
Qui porte un éclair au flanc.

Ils sont tout près ! — Tenons fermée
Cette salle, où nous les narguons.
Quel bruit dehors ! Hideuse armée
De vampires et de dragons !
La poutre du toit descellée
Ploie ainsi qu'une herbe mouillée,
Et la vieille porte rouillée
Tremble, à déraciner ses gonds !

Cris de l'enfer ! voix qui hurle et qui pleure !
L'horrible essaim, poussé par l'aquilon,
Sans doute, ô ciel ! s'abat sur ma demeure.
Le mur fléchit sous le noir bataillon.
La maison crie et chancelle penchée,
Et l'on dirait que, du sol arrachée,
Ainsi qu'il chasse une feuille séchée,
Le vent la roule avec leur tourbillon !

Prophète ! si ta main me sauve
De ces impurs démons des soirs,
J'irai prosterner mon front chauve
Devant tes sacrés encensoirs !
Fais que sur ces portes fidèles
Meure leur souffle d'étincelles,
Et qu'en vain l'ongle de leurs ailes
Grince et crie à ces vitraux noirs !

Ils sont passés ! — Leur cohorte
S'envole, et fuit, et leurs pieds
Cessent de battre ma porte
De leurs coups multipliés.
L'air est plein d'un bruit de chaînes,
Et dans les forêts prochaines
Frissonnent tous les grands chênes,
Sous leur vol de feu pliés !

De leurs ailes lointaines
Le battement décroît,
Si confus dans les plaines,
Si faible, que l'on croit
Ouïr la sauterelle
Crier d'une voix grêle,
Ou pétiller la grêle
Sur le plomb d'un vieux toit.

D'étranges syllabes
Nous viennent encor;
Ainsi, des arabes
Quand sonne le cor,
Un chant sur la grève
Par instants s'élève,
Et l'enfant qui rêve
Fait des rêves d'or.

Les Djinns funèbres,
Fils du trépas,
Dans les ténèbres
Pressent leurs pas;
Leur essaim gronde :
Ainsi, profonde,
Murmure une onde
Qu'on ne voit pas.

Ce bruit vague
Qui s'endort,
C'est la vague
Sur le bord;
C'est la plainte,
Presque éteinte,
D'une sainte
Pour un mort.

On doute
La nuit...
J'écoute : —
Tout fuit,
Tout passe;
L'espace
Efface
Le bruit

Régulier, souple et long, fermé dans le corset,
Sur les hanches, en roi, tu balances, coquet,
Ta forme si flexible. Et ta large carrure,
Descend, s'amincissant jusqu'à la ceinture,
Afin qu'on puisse aisément dans les bras
Enlacer tes séduisants appas.
Mais que faut-il pour qu'on te pince?
Tu t'évanouis si mince,
Que le plus petit doigt,
Dans son angle étroit,
Comme une paille,
Te reçoit,
O taille!
Dos!
Puis, très à propos,
Vont, s'élargissant, les hanches.
Sur chacune, tour à tour, tu penches.

898

Rabelais, on the other hand, resorted to piling up words, expressions or subordinate clauses and grouping them into parallel columns so as to make his lists seem exhaustive, which 899
makes them look like the pages of a dictionary. This arrangement conceals a very special kind of typographic humour, which is peculiar to Rabelais and involves interrupting the flow of the narrative and making exaggerated use of quotations; he thus takes the reader right out of his depth, stunning him with the fruits of his erudition, the mechanics of which finish up by merely ticking over in neutral, as it were.

Raymond Queneau sometimes uses similar methods in an 901
attempt to call language into question altogether. In his *Life and Opinions of Tristram Shandy* a tale without (or virtually without) a hero, and without a moral, Lawrence Sterne indulges in a parody of Romanticism, but of Romantic composition and writing rather than the actual language of Romanticism. The text is interrupted by endless digressions or overloaded with crossings-out; whole passages are replaced by a series of asterisks, and some pages are left blank, while others are completely blacked out or marbled all over, as endpapers tended to be at that period. Sometimes the author breaks off after a comma; or else he calls on the reader himself to continue the narrative; elsewhere he will try to make him aware of the passing of time by giving him certain data concerning space and distance. For the first time, typography visibly plays an active part throughout the book.

58. Rabelais.

aux eschetz[4],
au renard,
au marelles,
au vasches,
à la blanche,
à la chance,
à trois dez,
au tables,
à la nicnocque,
au lourche,
à la renette,
au barignin,
au trictrac,
à toutes tables,
au tables rabatues,
au reniguebieu,
au forcé,
au dames,
à la babou,
à *primus*, *secundus*,
au pied du cousteau[5],
au clefz,
au franc du carreau,
à pair ou non,
à croix ou pille[6],
au martres,
au pingres,
à la bille,
au savatier,
au hybou,
au dorelot du lievre,
au fault villain,
au cailleteaux,
au bossu aulican,
à Sainct Trouvé,
à *pinse m'orille*,
au poirier,
à pimpompet,

à la tirelitantaine,
à *cochonnet va devant*,
au pies,
à la corne,
au beuf violé,
à la cheveche,
à *je te pinse sans rire*,
à picoter,
à deferrer l'asne,
à laiau tru,
au *bourry*, *bourryzou*,
à *je m'assis*,
à la barbe d'oribus,
à la bousquine,
à *tire la broche*,
à la boutte foyre,
à *compere*, *prestez moy vostre sac*,
à la couille de belier,
à boute hors,
à figues de Marseille,
à la mousque,
à l'archer tru,
à escorcher le renard,
à la ramasse,
au croc madame,
à vendre l'avoine,
à souffler le charbon,
au responsailles,
au juge vif et juge mort,
à tirer les fers du four,
au pyrevollet,
à clinemuzette,
au picquet,
à la blancque,
au furon,
à la seguette,
au chastelet,

899

DU ROI DE BOHÈME. 529

« saviez comme ses palefreniers l'ont travaillée!...
« Comme ils l'ont chamaillée!...
« Comme ils l'ont tiraillée!...
« Comme ils l'ont éraillée!...
« Comme ils l'ont bataillée!...
« Comme ils l'ont bretaillée!...
« Comme ils l'ont ferraillée!...
« Comme ils l'ont harpaillée!...
« Comme ils l'ont tenaillée!...
« Comme ils l'ont fouaillée!...
« Comme ils l'ont dépenaillée!...
« Comme ils l'ont encanaillée!...
« Comme ils l'ont appareillée!...
« Comme ils l'ont habillée!...
« Comme ils l'ont étrillée!...
« Comme ils l'ont toupillée!...
« Comme ils l'ont écouvillée!...
« Comme ils l'ont gaspillée!...
« Comme ils l'ont grapillée!...
« Comme ils l'ont mordillée!...
« Comme ils l'ont pointillée!...
« Comme ils l'ont tortillée!...
« Comme ils l'ont houspillée!...
« Comme ils l'ont déguenillée!...

900

— Les voilà qui s'empoignent, dit Pierre.
— Ils en sont quand même venus aux mains.
— Ils doivent être d'égale force.
— L'un et l'autre semblent redoutables.
— Ils sont tombés à terre.
— Ils se cognent la tête.
— Ils se tordent les bras.
— Ils se mordent les yeux.
— Ils se déchaussent les dents.
— Ils se frottent les oreilles.
— Ils s'écrasent les doigts de pied.
— Ils se saignent le nez.
— Ils se heurtent les tibias.
— Ils se noircissent les paupières.
— Ils se tapent sur le ventre.
— Ils s'arrachent les cheveux.
— Ils se cassent les reins.
— Ils se tirent les joues.
— Ils se retournent les jointures.
— Ils se compriment le larynx.
— Ils se brisent les omoplates.
— Ils se couronnent les genoux.
— Ils s'aplatissent les parties génitales.
— Ils se démettent les articulations.
— Ils se claquent les muscles.
— Ils s'épilent les sourcils.
— Ils se broient le menton.
— Ils se luxent les testicules.
— Ils se démanchent la verge.
— Ils se malaxent les côtes.
— Ils se grignottent les intestins.
— Ils se pilent le foie.
— Ils se sanguinent la face.
— Ils se dépiautent.
— Ils se mutilent.
— Ils s'émiettent.
— Affreux combat!
— Horrible conjoncture!

901

Or venue est la saison
Que la belle Pleiade erre,
Qui nous fait rire la terre,
Iettant ses fruits à foison.
Sus sus qu'on delaisse
De sombre tristesse
Les ennuyeux laqs:
Et que rien on n'oye
Resonner que joye,
Ieux, ris, & soulas.
Laissons donques en ce jour
Et reputons comme vile
La tumultueuse vile,
Et son avare sejour.
Ores fait bon estre
En plaine champestre,
Allons donq pour voir
Les biens dont nature
Par songneuse cure
Nous veut tous pourvoir.
A ce plaisir savourer
La terre aussi nous convie
D'une gracieuse envie
Qu'elle ha de nous bienheurer.
Elle ha pour parure
De fine verdure
Manteau façonné,
De maintes florettes
(Apats d'amourettes)
Richement orné.
De son plus aymable honneur
La forest ha revestue:
Brief à tout nostre bon-heur
Entierement s'esvertue.
Sur le champ fertile
Va la vague utile
Des barbus espics,
Donnant apparence

902

"Fury said to
a mouse, That
he met
in the
house,
'Let us
both go
to law:
I will
prosecute
you.——
Come, I'll
take no
denial;
We must
have a
trial:
For
really
this
morning
I've
nothing
to do.'
Said the
mouse to
the cur,
'Such a
trial,
dear sir,
With no
jury or
judge,
would be
wasting
our breath.'
'I'll be
judge,
I'll be
jury,'
Said
cunning
old Fury;
'I'll try
the whole
cause,
and
condemn
you
to
death.'"

903

We lived beneath the mat,
Warm and snug and fat.
But one woe, and that
Was the cat!
To our joys
a clog, In
our eyes a
fog, On our
hearts a log
Was the dog!
When the
cat's away
Then
the mice
will
play.
But, alas!
one day (so they say)
Came the dog and
cat. Hunting
for a
rat
Crushed
the mice
all flat,
Each
one
as
he
sat
Underneath the mat, Warm and snug and fat. Think of that.

90[4]

Lucer-
na corporis tui, est
oculus tuus... Vide ergò ne lumen quod
in te est tenebræ sint. Luc. XI, 34, 35. — Et
adducunt ei cæcum, et
rogabant eum
ut illum tan-
geret.
Tunc
ap-
prehensâ manu cæci.... interrogavit e-
um (Jesus) si quid videret. — Et as-
piciens ait : Je vois marcher des
hommes qui me paraissent des arbres.
Marc. VIII, 22...24...

τί θέλεις;.... ἵνα ἀναβλέψω

לב

Marc. X, 51.

ANDRES
ARBRES

A WORD TO THE WISE

Plagiaire ! moi, plagiaire ! — Quand je voudrois trouver moyen pour me soustraire à ce reproche de disposer les lettres dans un ordre si

N O U V E A U,

ou d'assujettir les lignes à des règles
de disposition si bizarres,
ou pour mieux dire
si follement
hétérocl-
ites ! ! !

906

DU ROI DE BOHÈME. 107

Et s'il me plaît de m'ennuyer ce soir, pensai-je en traversant le carré, n'est-ce pas jour de Bouffes et séance à l'Athénée? D'ailleurs, repris-je en
descendant
les
sept
rampes
de
l'escalier.

— D'ailleurs, la semelle de Popocambou n'étoit pas de liége. Elle étoit de cabron.

Que dit monsieur? demanda le portier en ouvrant son vasistas, ou was ist das de verre obscurci par la fumée, et en y passant sa tête grotesque illuminée de rubis d'octobre.

— Je dis qu'elle étoit de cabron.

907

It was from Sterne that Nodier borrowed the title for his
Histoire du roi de Bohême et de ses sept châteaux ('A tale of the
King of Bohemia and his Seven Castles'), which in fact has
very little to do with castles, since the reader merely reaches
the first of them, after considerable difficulty, right at the end of
the book. 'It's genuine Sterne! A mere pastiche!' admits the
author at the outset, before introducing three figures to
represent himself: 'Théodore' (imagination), 'Don Pic de
Fanferluchio' (the scholar's memory) and 'Breloque' (reasoning
reason). But Nodier also borrows Rabelais's interminable lists 900
of names and succeeds in reviving, in Sterne's footsteps, a form
of typographic humour which involves printing a text upside
down (Lewis Carroll was to prefer mirror-writing) and introducing 'placards' into his narrative which heralds those in
Aragon's *A Paris Peasant* or the proverbs of the Surrealists.
Finally, the chapter called 'Protestation' – which we should not 906
take any more seriously than the author did himself – and
where Nodier claims the freedom to arrange the letters as he
fancies, contains the seeds of the preoccupations of his age and
also those of the following century.

UN COUP DE DÉS

JAMAIS

QUAND BIEN MÊME LANCÉ DANS DES CIRCONSTANCES ÉTERNELLES

DU FOND D'UN NAUFRAGE

908

UN COUP DE DÉS

A toutes celles et à tous ceux qui auront vécu,
A toutes celles et à tous ceux qui seront morts
pour tâcher de porter remède au mal universel;

Ce poeme est dédié.

Prenne à présent sa part de la dédicace qui voudra.

Marcel et Pierre Baudouin.

914

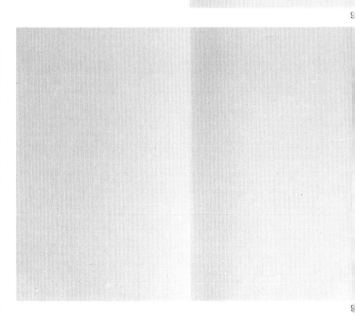

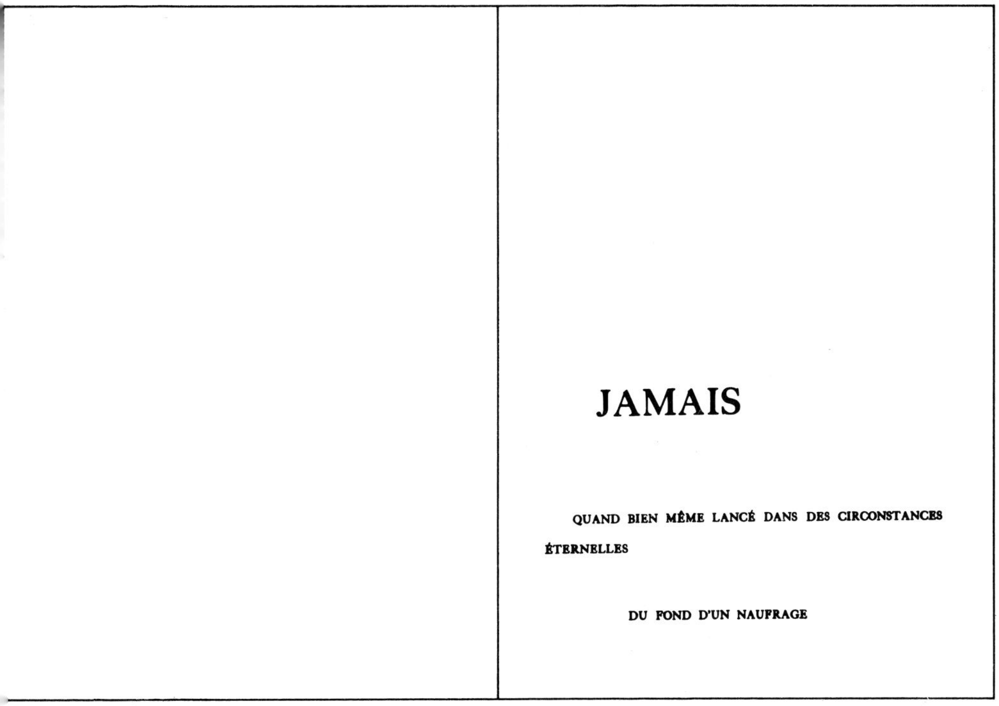

JAMAIS

QUAND BIEN MÊME LANCÉ DANS DES CIRCONSTANCES ÉTERNELLES

DU FOND D'UN NAUFRAGE

910

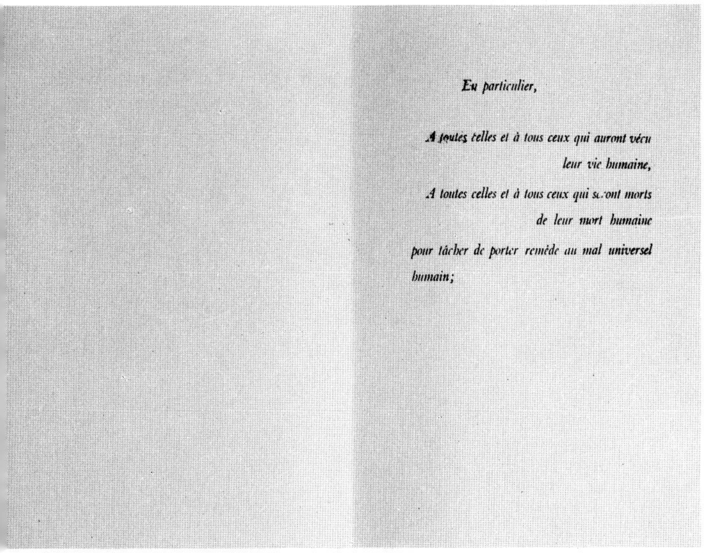

En particulier,

A toutes celles et à tous ceux qui auront vécu
leur vie humaine,
A toutes celles et à tous ceux qui seront morts
de leur mort humaine
pour tâcher de porter remède au mal universel humain;

912

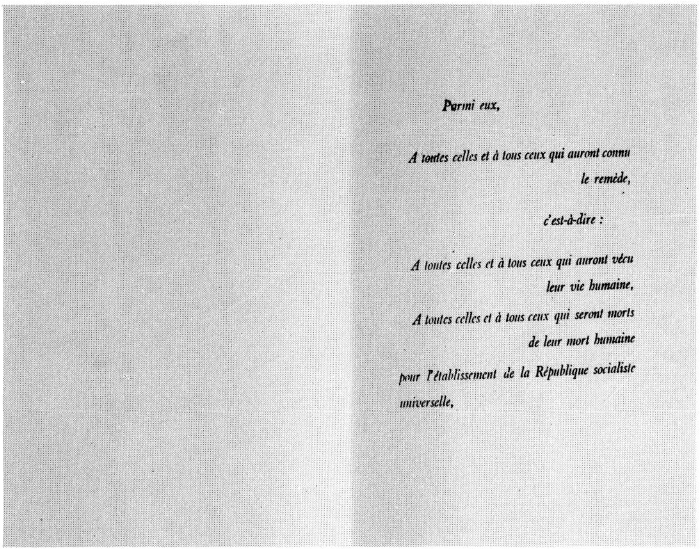

Parmi eux,

A toutes celles et à tous ceux qui auront connu
le remède,

c'est-à-dire :

A toutes celles et à tous ceux qui auront vécu
leur vie humaine,
A toutes celles et à tous ceux qui seront morts
de leur mort humaine
pour l'établissement de la République socialiste universelle,

913

916

Jeanne d'Arc

917

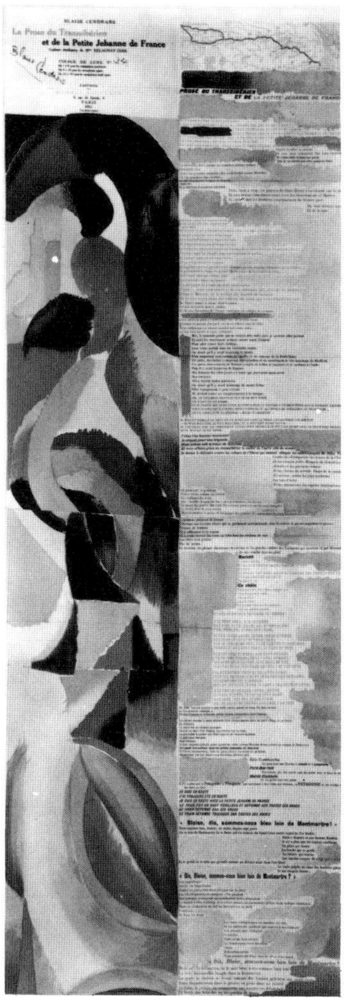

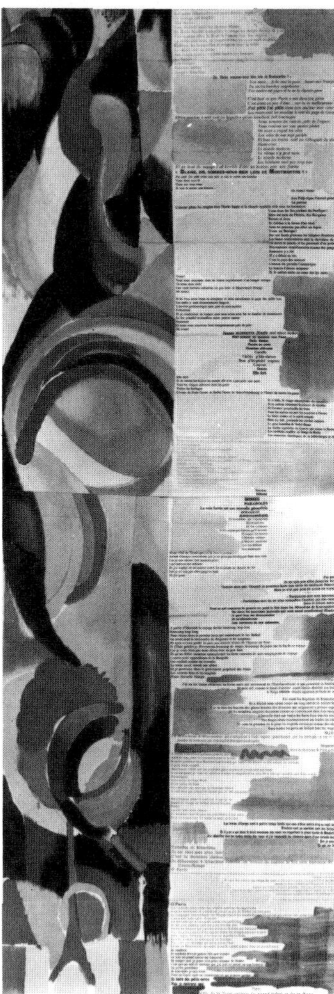

918

J'AI TOUJOURS ÉTÉ EN ROUTE
JE SUIS EN ROUTE AVEC LA PETITE JEHANNE DE FRANCE
LE TRAIN FAIT UN SAUT PÉRILLEUX ET RETOMBE SUR TOUTES SES ROUES
LE TRAIN RETOMBE SUR SES ROUES
LE TRAIN RETOMBE TOUJOURS SUR TOUTES SES ROUES

« Blaise, dis, sommes-nous bien loin de Montmartre? »

Nous sommes loin, Jeanne, tu roules depuis sept jours
Tu es loin de Montmartre de la Butte qui t'a nourrie du Sacré-Cœur contre lequel tu t'es blottie
Paris a disparu et son énorme flambée
Il n'y a plus que les cendres continues
La pluie qui tombe
La tourbe qui se gonfle
La Sibérie qui tourne
Les lourdes nappes de neige qui remontent
Et le grelot de la folie qui grelotte comme un dernier désir dans l'air bleui
Le train palpite au cœur des horizons plombés
Et ton chagrin ricane...

« Dis, Blaise, sommes-nous bien loin de Montmartre ? »

Les inquiétudes
Oublie les inquiétudes
Toutes les gares lézardées obliques sur la route
Les fils téléphoniques auxquels elles pendent
Les poteaux grimaçants qui gesticulent et les étranglent
Le monde s'étire s'allonge et se retire comme un harmonica qu'une main sadique tourmente
Dans les déchirures du ciel les locomotives en furie
S'enfuient
Et dans les trous

Les roues vertigineuses les bouches les voix
Et les chiens du malheur qui aboient à nos trousses
Les démons sont déchaînés
Ferrailles
Tout est un faux accord
Le *broun-roun-roun* des roues
Chocs
Rebondissements
Nous sommes un orage sous le crâne d'un sourd...

« Dis, Blaise, sommes-nous bien loin de Montmartre ? »

Mais oui, tu m'énerves, tu le sais bien, nous sommes bien loin
La folie surchauffée beugle dans la locomotive
La peste le choléra se lèvent comme des braises ardentes sur notre route
Nous disparaissons dans la guerre en plein dans un tunnel
La faim, la putain, se cramponne aux nuages en débandade
Et fiente des batailles en tas puants de morts
Fais comme elle, fais ton métier...

« Dis, Blaise, sommes-nous bien loin de Montmartre ? »

Oui, nous le sommes, nous le sommes
Tous les boucs émissaires ont crevé dans ce désert

918*b*

919

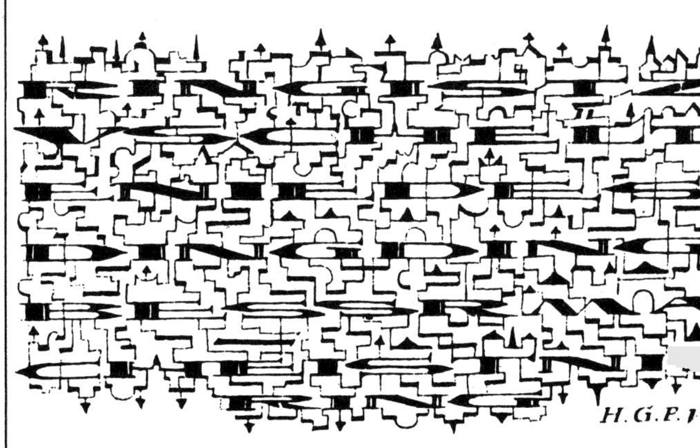

921

POÈME – PANCARTE
PAR ICI
PAR LÀ
1 K. 500
PARADIS
Suivez jusqu' au bout
Ensuite vous demanderez aux Anges

922

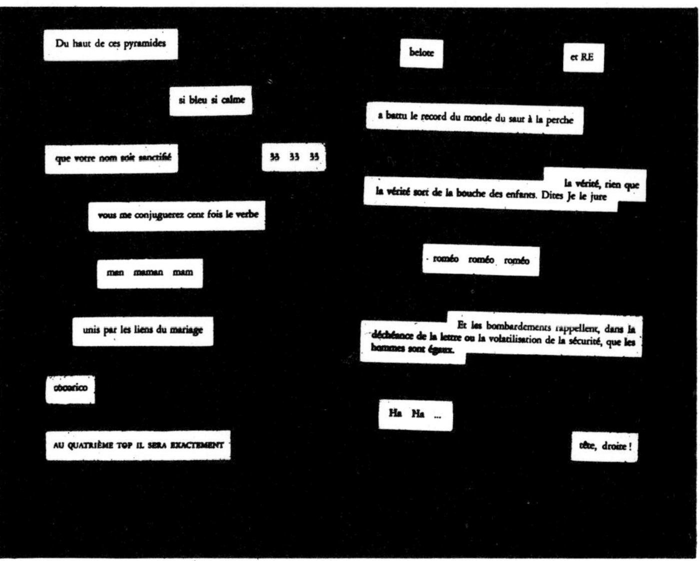

923

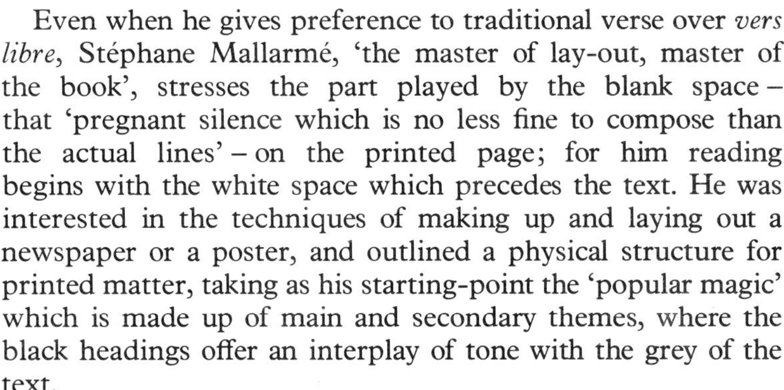

Even when he gives preference to traditional verse over *vers libre*, Stéphane Mallarmé, 'the master of lay-out, master of the book', stresses the part played by the blank space – that 'pregnant silence which is no less fine to compose than the actual lines' – on the printed page; for him reading begins with the white space which precedes the text. He was interested in the techniques of making up and laying out a newspaper or a poster, and outlined a physical structure for printed matter, taking as his starting-point the 'popular magic' which is made up of main and secondary themes, where the black headings offer an interplay of tone with the grey of the text.

Mallarmé did not compose any calligrams. Yet what would his *Coup de dés* ('The Throw of a Dice'), which after all consists of a mere two phrases, look like if it were arranged into compact rectangular blocks? Even if we were to add enough punctuation to isolate the 'prismatic subdivisions' of the basic idea underlying it, the essence of the poem would be lost and we would no longer be able to watch a language in the process of creation, as we can now. For what we have here is a genuine calligram (in Latin the same word denotes 'form' and 'beauty'). 'I seemed to see the figure of a thought, which had been set down in our space for the first time', reported Paul Valéry, to whom Mallarmé had just shown the final draft of his poem. 'Here, truly, space itself spoke, thought, gave birth to temporal forms.' This attempt at explaining the world in Orphic terms means of course that the whole page – or even a double page – is taken in at a single glance. It 'is taken as a single unit, as the perfect line is also'. The phrase '*Un coup de dés jamais n'abolira le hasard*' ('Chance will never be abolished by the throw of a dice') represents a musical score composed of words, a visual symphony and, to Valéry, the orchestration of a poetic idea.

The text is divided up into a central theme and a series of secondary or adjacent motifs which respond to each other through the interplay of different type-faces and type-sizes, italic and roman, upper and lower case, in the same way that the orchestral instruments in an orchestra are endowed with their own individual timbre. The tonality is also conveyed, on a rising or falling scale. At the same time, pictorial notation also plays a part in the *Coup de dés,* even though it is not immediately obvious: we can see a ship heeling over from the top of one page to the bottom of another, a feather fluttering, a movement speeding up or slowing down. What is more, space and time are contained within the poem: space is represented by a starry sky with the constellations (along with the marker points on the dice) offering an image of upside-down writing; and time is represented by the symphony in its role as an enactment of a period of time.

This poetic reconstruction of the universe is accompanied by an attempt at giving material existence to the idea underlying speech. For Mallarmé, the text represents 'chance conquered word by word'. And yet, far from abolishing chance altogether, his own denial contributes to the process of putting the finishing touches to the Idea of it, just as elsewhere the poet will try to give some idea of the object by linking the memory of it with its own absence.

In fact, the ideal vehicle for this poem in which Infinity is finally nailed down once and for all might have been a circular book without a beginning or an end and paraphrasing the movement of the planets, the text ending on the same words with which it began. This venture at producing 'The Book' obsessed Mallarmé, but he was never able to follow it right through; it still exercises a fascination today over the poets involved in the search for the Total Book. Some of them feel that if they take up even one of Mallarmé's ideas, they will finish up with a pack of cards with endlessly interchangeable pages. Others, such as Raymond Queneau, believe that the
921 never-ending book can take the form of his *Cent mille milliards de poèmes* ('A hundred thousand thousand million poems') which is made up of ten sonnets with each line printed on a detachable slip of paper, which allows the reader to choose what he fancies from 10^{14} different poems; this makes a hundred thousand thousand million of them, representing, according to the author's calculations, more than a million centuries' worth of reading . . .

We should note here that the *Coup de dés* did not receive
909-910 its final form until fifteen or so years after its author's death and that at the time it was set from the manuscript which Valéry had seen. The first version had been published in London in
908 1897 in *Cosmopolis,* the international magazine, and Mallarmé had been forced to bow to the demands of the magazine by abandoning the idea of getting the reader to read across two pages at once, and also on the blank 'expanses' in between.

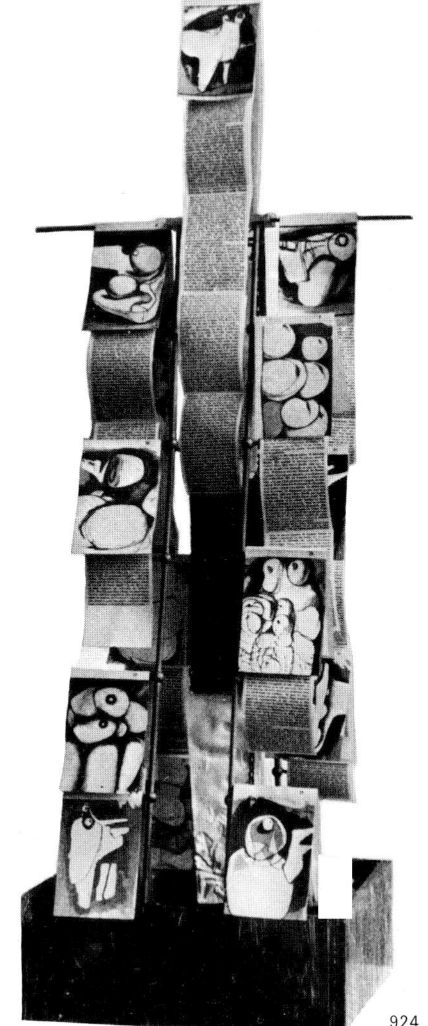

924

92

926

927

CH
EEEEEEEèèèèèèèèèèèèèèèèèèèèèèèèèèèèèèèèèèèèèèè
+ Je t'aime + − × 29 caresses + la lune et les ruisseaux
chantent sous les arbres.... paradis de mes bras Viens
chance + − × + − 3000 par mois +
vanité eeeeeeeeeeeeeee bague rubis 8000 +
6000 frs. chaussures
Demain chez moi
AlRrrrrrr R Suis sérieuse Trois
baisers futuristes
R

928

B
Da forchte
sich der Hut-Schapo
da forchte sich der Frack
da forchte
sich der
ACH so
schöne Spitzenschal

930

931

UNE NUIT D'ÉCHECS GRAS

PagE composée par Tristan TZara ✱

HIHIHIHIHIHIHIHIHIHIHI

Réclame pour la

VENTE DE PUBLICATIONS dada

du 10 au 25 Décembre 1920

chez **POVOLOZKY**, 13, rue Bonaparte, Paris

JÉSUS-CHRIST RASTAQUOÈRE PAR FRANCIS PICABIA PARAIT AUJOURD'HUI

DA DA DADADALINE DADADADASTE P DADAPHONE DADADADA VA CHOSE DADA

391 N° 6 2 Frs New-York

mettez le Brodway à Besançon et un petit parfum dans New-York Saluez le timbre poste

391 N° 8 2 Frs ZURICH rose

feu économique rose

l'art est mort

Picabia, Gabrielle Buffet, Arp, Tzara, Alice Bailly, Pharamousse et le VAGIN MYSTIQUE de Zurich

Francis PICABIA

UNIQUE EUNUQUE

Préface par Tr. TZARA

COLLECTION DADA

Au Sans-Pareil, Paris : 3 fr. 50

La pierre s'exprime par la forme, et parfois la luminosité des facettes, - vibration de l'air parcouru. Je hais la nature Picabia n'aime pas le métier. Ses poèmes n'ont pas de fin, ses proses ne commencent jamais. Il écrit sans **travailler**! présente sa personnalité, ne contrôle pas ses sensations. Pousse dans la chair des organismes

FRANCIS PICABIA :

La Fille née sans Mère

4 Fr.

Pensées sans langage

3 Fr. 50

La parole fertilise le métal : ba..ade ou urubu ouragan ourlé et ouvert — il laisse dormir ses sentiments dans un garage. 3 Fr. 50.

IL Y A DADA ET DADA............

Un livre de GEORGES RIBEMONT-DESSAIGNES est sous presse. — Lequel ? Ah !..

L'AMOUR dans le Cœur

Parlez-lui de moi

Jne homme dessin. cub. ou tr. bureau très bon. réf. Tout le monde collabore. Tout le monde lit. Tout le monde mange. Personne ne vous met l'amour dans le cœur parlez-lui de moi. Lisez Cannibale. Le secret de Rachilde de Foch de la Mercer les origines secrètes de Dada-band. La tête sur le chapeau. Exempl. de luxe à 10 frs. Garantis.

N° 1 1 Fr. **N° 2** 1 Fr.

Directeur : Francis PICABIA

CANNIBALE

La Revue

BLEU

de Mantoue, courageusement dirigée par Cantarelli et Fiozzi va devenir l'organe dada italien. Mme Renée Dunan la célèbre philosophe, écrit que Dada n'est pas une métaphysique mais une ypopsychie. Bleu ... meilleure explication de

L'YPOPSYCHIE

! ! ! Je ne vous conseille pas D'ACHET R l'anthologie Dada. ELLE est épuisée LES exempl. de luxe coûtent 25 Fr.

DIVORCE RAPIDE 90 à l'heure

I II III IV V VI VII VIII IX X XI XII XIII

Ne vous pressez pas

les 25 poèmes de Tristan Tzara sont épuisés

Il ne reste que quelques exemplaires sur hollande. (*tirage 10 exemplaires*) A 150 FR.

XIV XIII XII XI X IX VIII VII VI V IV III II I

MATCH

391

13

Achetez-le dans votre intérêt

PROVERBE

5 numéros Fr. 2.50

Directeur : PAUL ELUARD

Tout est dans tout. Partout casse-cou

Max Ernst, vous voilà célèbre.

Max Ernst

Max Ernst

Max Ernst, vous voilà célèbre.

et BAARGELD

MAX ERNST

et la flore dada arrangée par

cryptogramme de l'amour de la faune

(Cologne, 7 frs.)

DIE SCHAMADE

Serner :

DERNIER DÉRANGEMENT

(Steegmann, Hannovre)

3 Fr.

manifeste Dada

par Francis

PICABIA

Chez POVOLOZKY 5 FR. 1000 exemplaires de luxe et un seul sur papier ordinaire il y a un tirage spécial sur papier doux et transparent pour décalquer la Sainte VieRge.

Vient de paraitre : **HÉLAS**

CINÉMA CALENDRIER DU CŒUR ABSTRAIT

par TRISTAN TZARA

19 Bois par ARP

Collection Dada

tirage limité

10 exempl. sur Japon 150 Frs.

200 exempl. sur papier à la forme 25 Frs.

Adresser les commandes au " Sans Pareil " 37, Av. Kléber, Paris

Réclame pour moi Tristan tzara

Paul Bourget écrit sur ce livre : Il faut absolument lire ce livre merveilleux

Henri Lavedan écrit sur ce livre : Il faut lire ce livre. Tzara est un sinistre farceur

Henri Bo deaux écrit : Il faut lire ce livre sur un champ de violettes

Picasso écrit : Arp est le plus grand graveur sur bois

Anatole France écrit : Tzara est un idiot, son livre un attentat aux mœurs

FRENCH CANCAN

RIO TINTO

MERCI

I LOVE YOU

La solution de tous les mystères de l'univers

Des recettes contre :
la famine,
la blennhoragie
les indispositions de l'estomac cérébral,
le dadaïsme de l'Académie Française,
les bordels mal exploités.
la peste de Constantinople et les expositions de peinture de Paris.

Un écrivain qui n'a pas de machine à écrire n'est pas un écrivain mais un parfum en vogue

DADA 3

Fr. 1.50

Edition de Luxe

20 Fr.

Occasion, Situation, Expropriation

ARP :

La Pompe à nuages

(Steegemann Hannovre)

3 Frs

voici le célèbre Arp
le voici venir
voici le célèbre Arp
le voici venir venir venir

BRAVO ! BRAVO ! BRAVO !

DADAPHONE

Prix 1 fr 50

messieurs mesdames achetez entrez achetez et ne lisez pas vous verrez celui qui a dans ses reins la clef du niagara l'homme qui boite dans une boite les hémisphères dans une valise le nez enfermé dans un lampion chinois vous verrez vous verrez vous verrez la danse du ventre dans la seringue de massachussets celui qui enfonce le clou et le pneu se dégonfle les bas de soie de mademoiselle atlantide la malle qui fait 6 fois le tour du monde pour trouver le destinataire monsieur et sa fiancée son frère et sa belle-sœur vous trouverez l'adresse du menuisier la montre à crapauds le nerf en coupe-papier vous aurez l'adresse de l'épingle mineure pour le sexe féminin et de celui qui fournit les photos obcènes au roi ainsi que l'adresse de l'action française.

J. EVOLA

ARTA ASSTRATTA

Collection DADA. ROME. 2 Frs.

Théorie Poèmes, dessins.

Bulletin Dada

2 Frs 2 Frs

2 Frs 2 Frs 2 FR 2 fr 2 FR 2 FR 2 Frs 2 Frs 2 frs 2 FR. 2 FR. 2 fr 2 fr. 2 Fr. 2 FR. 2 Fr. 2 Fr. 2 Fr. 2 fr. collaborateurs collaborateurs collaborateurs Ribemont Ribemont Ribemont Picabia Eluard Eluard Eluard, Picabia Serner Serner Breton Breton Serner Breton Tzara Dermée Dermée Aragon Soupault Aragon Jacques Edwards Aragon Aragon Arp Picabia Schad Arp Arp

933

934

In spite of these restraints, which took away part of the poem's visual unity, it was still a remarkable innovation; from now on the blank space, 'the nuptial proof of the idea', could play a role on the page no less important than that played by the line.

It is pertinent to compare this publication with that of the first edition of Charles Péguy's *Jeanne d'Arc*, which was set in the same year by the author, with the help of twenty typographers at his printer's; their names were listed at the back of the book among the details about the edition. The relevance of the comparison becomes clear if we notice that Péguy, too, introduces duration of time in a spatial form through the lay-out of his play. The book comprises 752 unnumbered pages, including a large number of blanks, and opens in the same way as the sequence showing the credit titles in a film; the full 911/917
title does not appear until page 25 and the actual text of the play begins on page 40. There are four pages between each act, and ten or so pages between each part; instructions concerning a variety of different time-lapses (ranging from fifteen seconds to twenty minutes) appear every time the word CURTAIN is set, and in the body of the text other information concerning the passing of time is sometimes scattered among the blank pages.

It is true, of course, that Péguy, whose manuscripts reveal a curious sort of writing with wide gaps between the lines of the text, took a good deal of trouble over the presentation of his *Cahiers de la quinzaine* and was rather more than an enlightened amateur; for instance, he expressed his regret at not being able to make use of 'colours for marking the different layers of a poetic structure, as in geology: the strata; the structure; primary, secondary, tertiary matter; level surfaces and curving surfaces; horizontal areas and corrugated areas; contour-lines and the lie of the land; isometries and planimetries; rocky matter and humus, lodgment, curve, peat or fertile slime.'

New poetic techniques began to emerge which tended to accentuate the expressive quality of a word (to the extent of turning it into an object) by allowing typography to play a larger and larger part in a book. In Barzun's view, the poet must convey 'by means of sight, sound and feeling the actual impressions of life and of the universe'; Sébastien Voirol composed a poem for two voices at once based on Stravinsky's *Rites of Spring*, for which he used five differently coloured inks. Blaise Cendrars's *La Prose du Transsibérien et de la petite Jeanne de France*, is the first 'simultaneous' book, which takes the 918
form of a fold-out album $6\frac{1}{2}$ ft long and was printed, according to the publisher, in an edition large enough to reach as high as the top of the Eiffel Tower. The author used all the different characters he could find in the cases at the Crété printing-works, while the splodges of colour which Sonia Delaunay painted to 'bathe the poem with light' were reproduced by means of eighty different coloured inks . . .

Marinetti, the leader of the Futurist movement, who had

MONSIEUR-NICOLAS!

SECONDE ÉPOQUE.

Je ſuis Enfant-de-cœur. 1746—1747.

Fœlices quibus uſus adeſt! Ego neſcia rerum *Ovid.*
Difficilem cu'pæ ſuſpicor eſſe viam. *P. Helen. Paridi.*

ICÊTRE est un hôpital, dont le nom deshonoré frappe toujours desagreablement l'oreille. On ſait que de mes 2 Frères du 1er lit, l'Un était Prêtre, depuis 5 ans, ét depuis 2 ou 3 curé de Courgis, à 1 lieuë de Chablis, 3 d'Aucerre: Mon autre Frère, ſimple clërc, était alé à Paris, en ſortant du Seminaire, pour être précepteur. Il trouva une place, chéz des Janſeniſtes: Mais il ne put ſuporter les contradicçions du Père, les petiteſſes de la Mère, les caprices *adorés* de 1746

935

Seconde ÉPOQUE. 309

RONS CE QU'IL SERA A-PROPOS DE FAIRE DE CET ENFANT: LE FOND EST PROPRE A L'ÉTUDE, VOUS ME L'ASSURÉZ? „Je vous l'aſſure„. 1746

C'est tout ce que je pus entendre de leur converſacion, que je compris à-peine alors; mais qui depuis m'est revenue, come je la raporte ici.

Le lendemain, je fus obligé de conduire aux champs le Bergér Larivière, qui ne conaiſſait pas notre finage: Celui-ci ne m'entretenait que de la manière dont On arrange le bois des trains qui viénnent à Paris; des dangérs de la rivière & des pertuis; de la pêche, &c^a. Mon Cousin *Jean-Merrat*, neveu de ma Mère, était ſon heros: Il me racontait de lui, p^{our} la pêche, des choses étoñantes! Il plongeait dans les foſſes, formées dans les petites rivières par la chute d'Un courant: Il m'aſſura que Jean reſtait ſous l'eau des temps aſſés conſiderables, pour prendre de gros Poiſſons dans les ſinuosités des roches, les attacher à ſa jambe, & remonter avec ſa pêche. Eneffet, ce bon Garſon, ſa Mère & ſa Sœur Babet nous aportaiét pluſieurs-fois l'au- Dern^{re} Bergerie.

A 3

936

LE PÈRE JÉSUITE

Il est attaché au mât et tient dans ses mains liées un crucifix de bois. Il dit:

Seigneur, je vous remercie de m'avoir ainsi attaché!
Et parfois il m'est arrivé de trouver vos commandements péuibles.
Et ma volonté en présence de votre règle
Perplexe-rétive
Mais aujourd'hui il n'y a pas moyen d'être plus serré à VOUS que je ne le suis et j'ai beau vérifier chacun de mes membres, il n'y en a pas un seul qui de Vous soit capable de s'écarter si-peu.
Et c'est vrai que je suis attaché à la croix, mais la croix où je suis n'est plus attachée à rien — ELLE FLOTTE SUR LA MER
o . . . . . o
La mer libre à ce point où la limite du ciel connu s'efface
Et qui est à égale distance de ce monde ancien que j'ai quitté
Et de l'autre nouveau.
Tout-a-ex-pi-ré autour de moi, tout-a-été-con-som-mé sur cet étroit autel qu'encombrent les corps de mes sœurs l'une sur l'autre,
La vendange sans doute ne pouvait se faire sans désordres,

937

been worshipping the cult of *velocità* since 1909, announced his intention of using 'three or four inks of different colours on a single page and twenty different type-faces if necessary'. He was searching for some entirely new methods of expression which would give modern man an opportunity to read synthetically, and at the same time give him a visual shock. Marinetti
930 and his disciples, Soffici, Boccioni, Carrà, Russolo, Cangiulo, etc., aimed to destroy syntax by arranging the nouns 'according to where they happened to have originated', to do away with the adjective and the adverb, to replace punctuation with mathematical and musical signs, to throw the orchestration of the images into confusion, indicate the weight of objects and their smell, to invent 'untrammelled imagination', to kill solemnity and 'brazenly to make literature ugly'. They prepared to hate cleverness and 'to tighten up thought', to reject the curved line and condense metaphors. This Futurist revolution was to reject 'the idiotic and nauseating concept of the old-style book of verse' and, by making use of graphic analogies and abstract onomatopeia, to forge a new type of expressive typography which, together with a sort of lyrical
926/928 intoxication, was destined to 'liberate words'.

Nowadays the poetry of such authors as Michel Butor (*Mobile, 6 810 000 litres d'eau par seconde*) or Henri Pichette
923 (*Les Epiphanies*) could no more forget what it owes to these 'anti-traditionalist' manifestos – which were soon supplanted by the provocative statements of the Dadaïsts – than it could deny itself the typographic methods which it brings into play as a means of expression. The poetry of Dylan Thomas calls

POÈME À CRIER ET À DANSER

Chant III

êêêê èèè éé
a ouou a ouou êê
(1) bing————bing————
(1) brrrrr————brrrrrrrrr tzinnn
(1) ô————ô————ôôô
a iii a iii a iii i i i
âo âo âo âo âo âo âo tzinnn
âo âo âo âo âo âo âo tzinnn
rrrrrrrrrrrrr rrrrrrrrrrr
rrrrrrrrrrrr
(2) ouououououououououououououououou
(3) uuuuuuuuuuuuuuuuuuuuuuuuuuuuuuuuuu
i

939

insinuations, il faut savoir ce qu'el
sont. Donne-moi la définition de
l'insinuation; je réclame la
définition de l'insinuation.
Tu vois qu'ils sont descendus. Ils ont emmené ceux
palier. Ils ne crient plus. Qu'est-ce qu'on leur a f
On les a égorgés, probablement.
Quelle drôle d'idée, ah non, ce n'est pas
drôle d'idée, mais pourquoi les a-t-on égorgés?
peux tout de même pas aller leur deman
C'est pas le moment. On les a peut-être pas égo
Après tout, on en a peut-être fait autre chose.

kp'erioUM lp'er ioum

Nm' periii PERno

bprEtiBerreeeRREbee

ONNOo gplanpouk

kontnpout PERIKOUL

RAEEe e EEee

oapAerrre EEE

mgl ed padANou

M'TNOU tnoum t

938

ah ! oh ! ah ! oh !
allons
laissez-moi grincer des dents
caïman
Ulysse
je m'en vais habiter ma
cagna dans mes cacaoyers
les cacaoyers des cacaoyères donnent pas des cacahuètes
donnent du cacao !

941

c'est pas par là

c'est par ici

c'est pas par là

c'est par ici

c'est pas par

c'est par ici

c'est pas par

c'est par ici

942

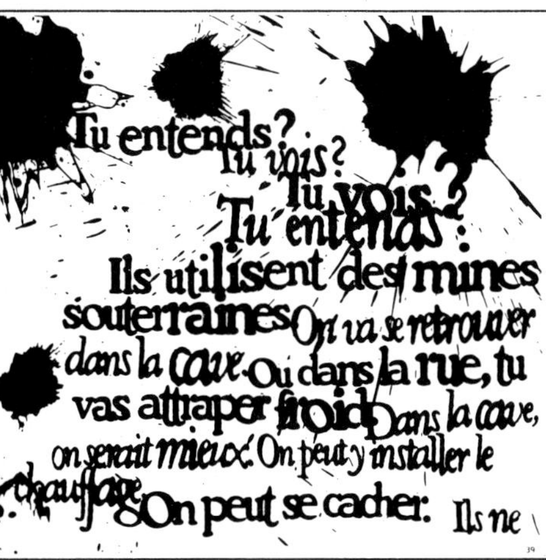

Tu entends?
Tu vois?
Tu vois?
Tu entends?
Ils utilisent des mines souterraines. On va se retrouver dans la cave. Ou dans la rue, tu vas attraper froid. Dans la cave, on serait mieux. On peut y installer le chauffage. On peut se cacher. Ils ne

940

This edition is composed of characters from the Fonderie Monotype and were set and prepared by Paul Dupont and printed by photolithography in Great Britain by Lowe and Brydone (Printers) Ltd. The characters of the "anecdotes" were obtained from the Fonderies Deberny and Peignot. The typographical drawings are from Union-Elysees. The binding was done by Mansell Bookbinding Co. Ltd.

943

on similar methods, in that it sketches geometric shapes
modelled on a virtually respiratory rhythm.
We also have in our own day a number of typographic
creations which have an entirely independent existence,
without the help of a text, or even an argument. For instance
Eugenio Carmi has worked out a book of sounds called
944 *Stripsody* and made up of nothing but onomatopoeic words.
Similarly, Winifred Gaul has taken some texts written by
Hölderlin when his mind was beginning to go, pulled them
apart and put them together again in the shape of a 'visible
poem'. Another example of a 'visible' text is the typographic
941/943 interpretation of Ionesco's *La Cantatrice chauve* (*The bald
Primadonna*), which offers a new style of play-reading. The
designer who laid it out has combined the techniques of the
cinema and the strip-cartoon and has used the actual faces of
the actors, which have acquired the importance of an ideogram
in the hands of the photographer Henry Cohen; acting as a
sort of stage-director, the designer aims to translate the
atmosphere, the movement, the speeches and the silences in
the play, trying at the same time to convey an idea of duration
of time and space on the stage by the simple device of the
interplay of image and text. This attempt was not the first
of its kind: we will recall in this context the case of Restif de la
935-936 Bretonne, who personally set *Monsieur Nicolas* and was
described in the following terms by Nerval in *Les Illuminés:*
'His system entailed using type-faces in various different
sizes within the same book, varying them according to what
he took to be the importance of such and such a phrase.
Twelve-point type was used for passion, for passages where a
strong emotional effect was intended, eight-point for the basic
narrative or moral remarks, bourgeois type for the boring but
necessary details, which could thus be squeezed into a small
space . . . Often he would use either caps or letters a point or
two down to indicate long and short syllables.'
When Jean-Louis Barrault decided to produce Claudel's
The Satin Slipper during the last war, he prepared a 'typescript
937 -cum-elocution' for his actors, the idea being to make it
easier for them to find the incantatory rhythms and vocal
modulations of Claudel's prose. Long before Antonin Artaud,
Pierre Albert-Birot had invented his 'poem for shouting and
939 dancing' where the typography glorifies the shout. More
940 recently, a 'sound calligraphy' based on Ionesco's *Délire à deux*
has attempted to transcribe the human voice and sound in
general; this means that the writing is used to reconstruct the
volume, pitch, length, timbre and tonic accent of the voices of
the two actors, along with the sounds all round them, by
means of unevenly spaced typography, splodges, and ink-blots
which represent so many custard pies in terms of sound. In
951/955 Jean Tardieu's *Conversation-sinfonietta,* the designer has
adopted Mallarmé's angle of vision as seen in his *Coup de dés,*
arranging the voices of a vocal sextet on the actual level of

944

945

L'amiral cherche une maison à louer

Poème simultan par R. Huelsenbeck, M. Janko, Tr. Tzara

HUELSENBECK — Ahoi ahoi Des Admirals gwirktes Beinkleid schnell zerfällt Teerpappe macht Rawagen in der Nacht
JANKO, chant — Where the honny suckle wine twines ilself arround the door a swetheart mine is waiting patiently for me I
TZARA — Boum boum boum Il déshabilla sa chair quand les grenouilles humides commancèrent à bruler j'ai mis le cheval dans l'âme du

HUELSENBECK — und der Conciergenbäuche Klapperschlangengrün sind milde ach verzerrt in der Natur chrza prrrza chrrrza
JANKO, chant — can hear the weopour will arround arround the hill my great room is
TZARA — serpent à Bucarest on dépendra mes amis dorénavant et c'est très intéressant les griffes des morsures équatoriales

HUELSENBECK — prrrza chrrrza prrrza Wer suchet dem wird aufgetan Der Ceylonlöwe ist kein Schwan Wer Wasser braucht find
JANKO, chant — mine admirabily confortabily Grandmother said I love the ladies
TZARA — Dimanche: deux éléphants Journal de Genève au restaurant Le télégraphiste assassine

Intermède rythmique

HUELSENBECK	hihi *ff*	Yabomm	hihi *p*	Yabomm *cresc ff*	hihi	hihi *cresc* hihiiiii *ff f*
TZARA	rouge bleu *p*	rouge bleu	rouge bleu *f cresc*	rouge bleu *ff*	rouge bleu *cresc fff*	
SIFFLET (Janko)	———. *p*	————. *cresc*	——. *f*	— — .	————. *ff*	— — —. *fff*
CLIQUETTE (TZ)	rrrrrrrrr *f decrsc*	rrrrrrrrr *f*	rrrrrrrrr *cresc*	rrrrrrrrr *fff*	rrrrrrrrr *uniform*	rrrrrrrrr
GROSSE CAISE (Huels.)	O O O *ff*	O O O O O *p*	O O O O O *f*	O O O O *fff*	O O *p*	

HUELSENBECK — im Kloset zumeistens was er nötig hätt ahoi iuché ahoi iuché Find was er nötig
JANKO (chant) — I love the ladies I love to be among the girls And when it's five
TZARA — la concièrge qui m'a trompé elle a vendu l'appartement que j'avais loué Dans l'église après la messe le pêcheur dit à la comtesse: Adieu Mathilde

HUELSENBECK — hätt' O süss gequollnes Stelldichein des Admirals im Abendschein uru uru uro uru uru uro uru uru uru uro pataclan patablan pataplan uri uri uro
JANKO (chant) — o'clock and tea is set I like to have my tea with some brunet shai shai shai shai shai shai shai shai Every body is doing it doing it doing it Every body is
TZARA — Le train traîne la fumée comme la fuite de l'animal blessé aux intestins ecrasés

HUELSENBECK — Der Affe brüllt die Seekuh bellt im Lindenbaum der Schräg zerschellt tara-tata taratata tatatata In Joschiwara dröhnt der Brand und knallt mit schnellen
JANKO (chant) — doing it doing it see that ragtime coupple over there see that throw there shoulders in the air She said the raising her heart oh dwelling oh
TZARA — Autour du phare tourne l'auréole des oiseaux bleuillis en moitiés de lumière vis-sant la distance des batteaux Tandis que les archanges chient et les oiseaux tombent Oh! mon

HUELSENBECK — Peitschen um die Lenden Im Schlafsack gröhlt der alte Oberpriester und zeigt der Schenkel volle Tastatur L'Amiral n'a rien trouvé
JANKO (chant) — oh yes yes yes yes yes yes yes yes yes yes yes oh yes oh yes oh yes oh yes yes yes oh yes sir L'Amiral n'a rien trouvé
TZARA — cher c'est si difficile La rue s'enfuit avec mon bagage à traves la ville Un métro mêle son cinéma la prore de je vous adore était au casino du sycomore L'Amiral n'a rien trouvé

NOTE POUR LES BOURGEOIS

Les essays sur la transmutation des objets et des couleurs des premiers peintres cubistes (1907) Picasso, Braque, Picabia, Duchamp-Villon, Delaunay, suscitaient l'envie d'appliquer en poésie les mêmes principes simultans.

Villiers de l'Isle Adam eût des intentions pareilles dans le théâtre, où l'on remarque les tendances vers un simultanéisme schématique; Mallarmé essaya une reforme typographique dans son poème: Un coup de dés n'abolira jamais le hazard; Marinetti qui popularisa cette subordination par ses „Paroles en liberté"; les intentions de Blaise Cendrars et de Jules Romains, dernièrement, ammenèrent Mr Apollinaire aux idées qu'il développa en 1912 au „Sturm" dans une conférence.

Mais l'idée première, en son essence, fut exteriorisée par Mr H. Barzun dans un livre théoretique „Voix, Rythmes et chants Simultanés" où il cherchait une rélation plus étroite entre la symphonie polirythmique et le poème. Il opposait aux principes succesifs de la poésie lyrique une idée vaste et parallèle. Mais les intentions de compliquer en profondeur cette t e c h n i q u e (avec le Drame Universel) en éxagerant sa valeur au point de lui donner une idéologie nouvelle et de la cloîtrer dans l'exclusivisme d'une école, — echouèrent.

En même temps Mr Apollinaire essayait un nouveau genre de poème visuel, qui est plus intéressant encore par son manque de systême et par sa fantaisie tourmentée. Il accentue les images centrales, typographiquement, et donne la possibilité de commancer à lire un poème de tous les côtés à la fois. Les poèmes de Mrs Barzun et Divoire sont purement formels. Ils cherchent un éffort musical, qu'on peut imaginer en faisant les mêmes abstractions que sur une partiture d'orchestre.

* * *

Je voulais réaliser un poème basé sur d'autres principes. Qui consistent dans la possibilité que je donne à chaque écoutant de lier les associations convenables. Il retient les éléments caractéristiques pour sa personalité, les entremêle, les fragmente etc, restant tout-de-même dans la diréction que l'auteur a canalisé.

Le poème que j'ai arrangé (avec Huelsenbeck et Janko) ne donne pas une description musicale, mais tente à individualiser l'impression du poème simultan auquel nous donnons par là une nouvelle portée.

La lecture parallèle que nous avons fait le 31 mars 1916, Huelsenbeck, Janko et moi, était la première réalisation scénique de cette estéthique moderne.

T R I S T A N T Z A R A

946

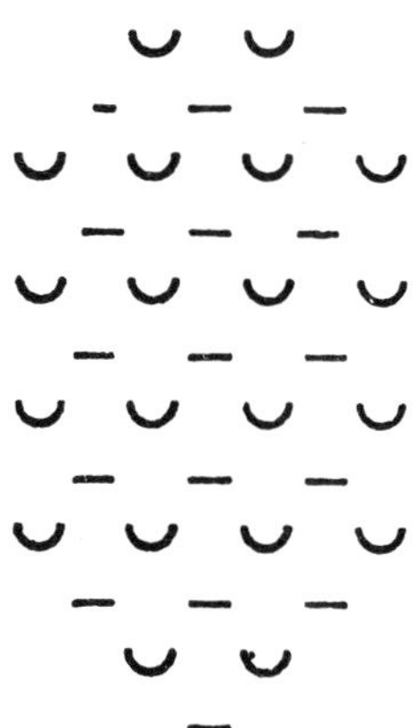

47

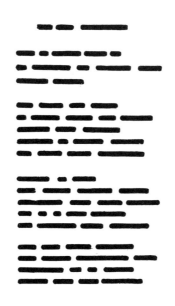

948

KARAWANE
jolifanto bambla ô falli bambla
grossiga m'pfa habla horem
égiga goramen
higo bloiko russula huju
hollaka hollala
anlogo bung
blago bung
blago bung
bosso fataka
ü üü ü
schampa wulla wussa ólobo
hej tatta gôrem
eschige zunbada
wulubu ssubudu uluw ssubudu
tumba ba- umf
kusagauma
ba - umf

949

Blikken trommel
Blikken trommel
Blikken trommel
RANSEL
BLikken trommel
Blikken trommel
Ransel
Blikken trommel
Ransel
Blikken trommel
RAN

Rui schen
Rui schen
Rui schen
Rui schen
Ruischen
Ruisch . . .
Rui . . .
Ru . . .
Ru . . .
R . . .
R . . .
r . .
.

950

conversation-sinfonietta
conversation-sinfonietta
conversation-sinfonietta
conversation-sinfonietta
conversation-sinfonietta
conversation-sinfonietta

par Jean Tardieu essai d'orchestration typographique collection la lettre et l'esprit Gallimard

95

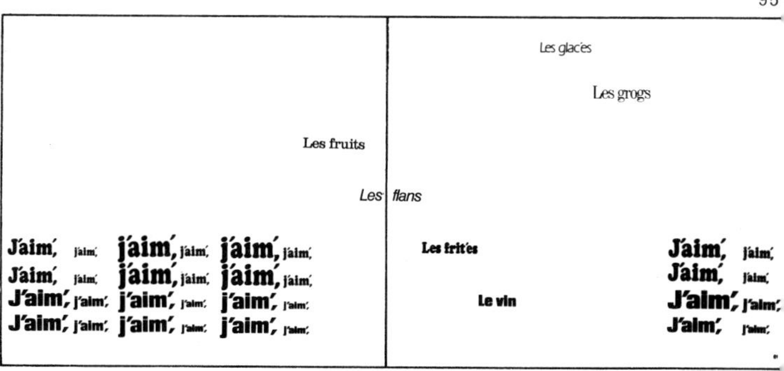
Les glaces
Les grogs
Les fruits
Les flans
J'aim' j'aim' j'aim'
Les frites
Le vin
J'aim' j'aim'

95

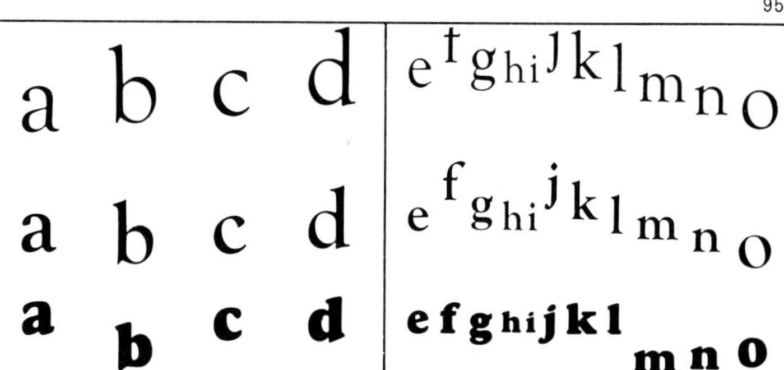
a b c d
e f g h i j k l m n o
a b c d
e f g h i j k l m n o
a b c d
e f g h i j k l m n o

95

959

son de ma voix s'étouffe

960

rage et je pleu re et traî née par la fou le qui s'éla

Quoi donc?

Quoi donc?

J'ai rencontré, je vous le donne en mille, un bateau à voile!

Quoi donc?

donc?

Un bateau à voile en plein dans la rue
Quelle étrange chose!

Un bateau à voile en plein dans la rue
quelle étrange chose!

Mais c'était un bateau-réclame
ah ah ah ah ah! ah! ah! ah!
en carton et en bois peint,
porté sur une automobile.

Un bateau à voile en plein dans la rue
Quelle étrange chose!

Un bateau à voile en plein dans la rue
Quelle étrange chose!

Un bateau à voile en plein dans la rue
Quelle étrange chose!

952

Et ça s'embrasse au fond des bois! oh oh oh oh oh oh oh oh oh oh oh oh oh

oh oh oh oh oh oh oh oh oh oh oh oh

oh oh oh oh oh oh oh oh oh oh oh oh

oh oh oh oh oh oh oh oh oh oh oh oh

oh oh oh oh oh oh oh oh oh oh oh oh nos jeunes gens sont bien entreprenants **Parlons bas, Parlons bas,**

oh oh oh oh oh oh oh oh oh oh oh

953

Et tout et tout Et tout et tout Et tout et tout

ut Et tout et tout Et tout et tout

Et tout et tout **Et tout et tout**

Et tout et tout Et tout et tout Et tout et tout *Et tout*

Et tout et tout Et tout et tout Et tout et tout Et tout

Et tout et tout Et tout et tout Et tout et tout Et tout

955

m n o p l l l m n o p q r s t u v x i i gre c

m n o p l l l m n o p q r s t u v x i gre c

m n o p l l l m n o p q r s t u v x igrec

957

Z a a a a a a a b b b b b b b c c c c c c c d d d d d d d e f

Z a a a a a b b c c c c c c d d e f

Z **abcd**

958

s le rir' des autres et je crie de douleur de fureur et de

qui danse une folle farandole je suis emportée au loin et

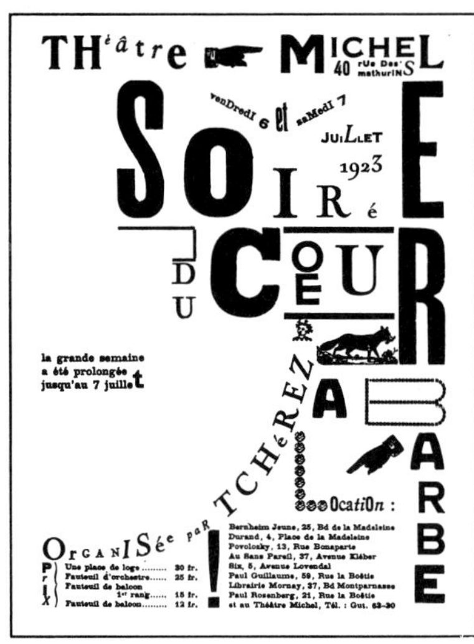

961

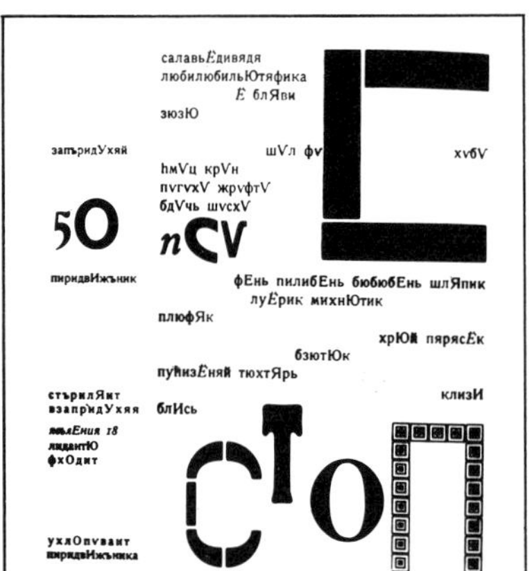

962

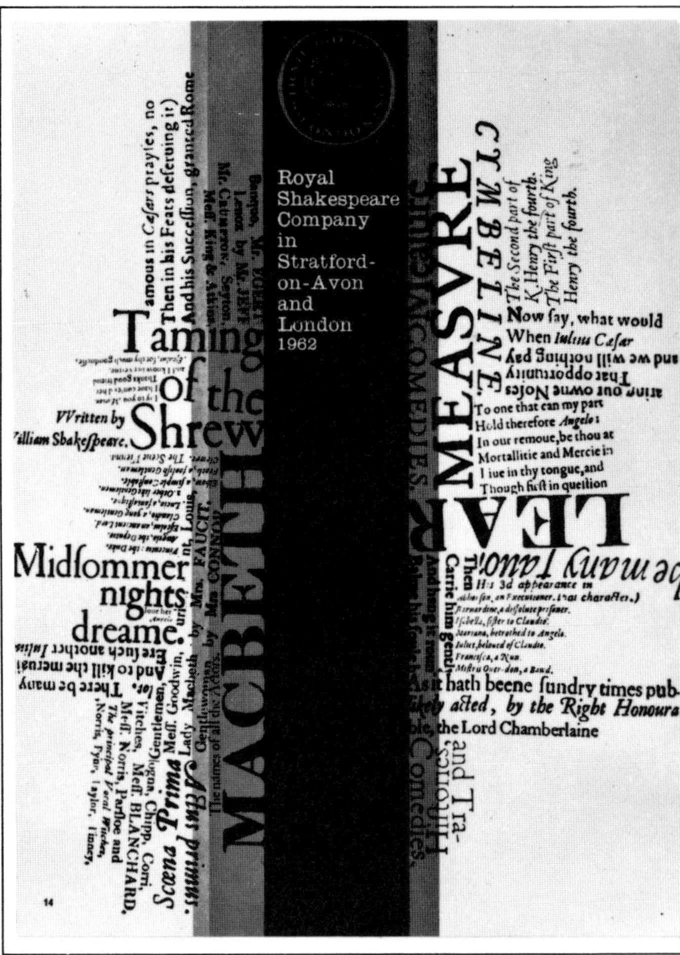

96

963

96

their regiṣter, and as it were making the reader act as conductor.
This experiment was taken a stage further in the musical field
by a typographic transcription of Mozart's *Alphabet*, and also 956 958
by one of Edith Piaf's songs offered as a vocal calligram. 959–960
This method had already been exploited, particularly in
'phonetic poems'. The 'Fish's Nightsong' ('*Fisches Nacht-* 947
gesang') is made up of a series of symbols denoting long and
short syllables, and its shape vaguely conjures up an image of a
fish. The author, Christian Morgenstern, was also the inventor
of a language called 'laloula', which he would use for telling of
such things as the crow's love-duet. Man Ray also composed
a special 'noisy song' which was rather like a conversation 948
conducted in morse code, while Hugo Ball juxtaposed imagin-
ary words set in various different type-faces in his *Karawane*. 949
Raoul Hausmann broke his words up into groups so that he 938
could get at the heart of the letter more easily; in *Le Courrier
Dada* he explains how he treats 'letters, sounds, bunches of
consonants and vowels by declaiming them at a high or low
pitch', expressing this by his choice of letters, which are 'big
or small, thick or thin, thus making them seem like musical
notation.' On the other hand, in a 'note for the bourgeois'
which goes with the text of Tristan Tzara's *The Admiral* 946
searches for a house to let, a simultaneous poem for several
voices written in collaboration with Richard Huelsenbeck and

966

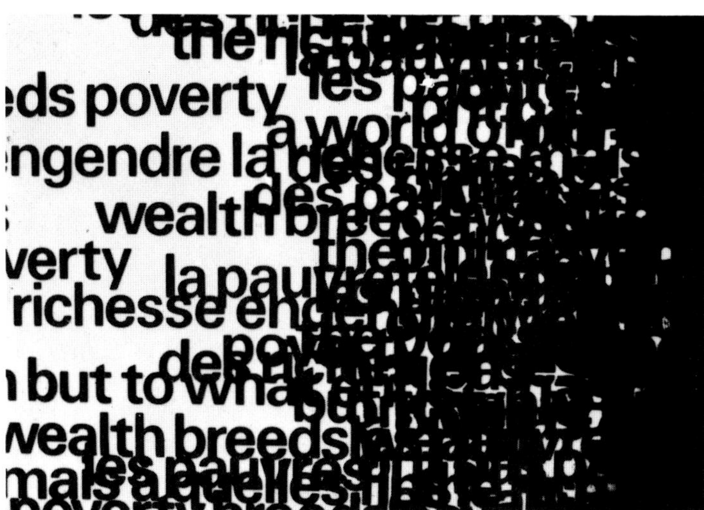

967

968

969

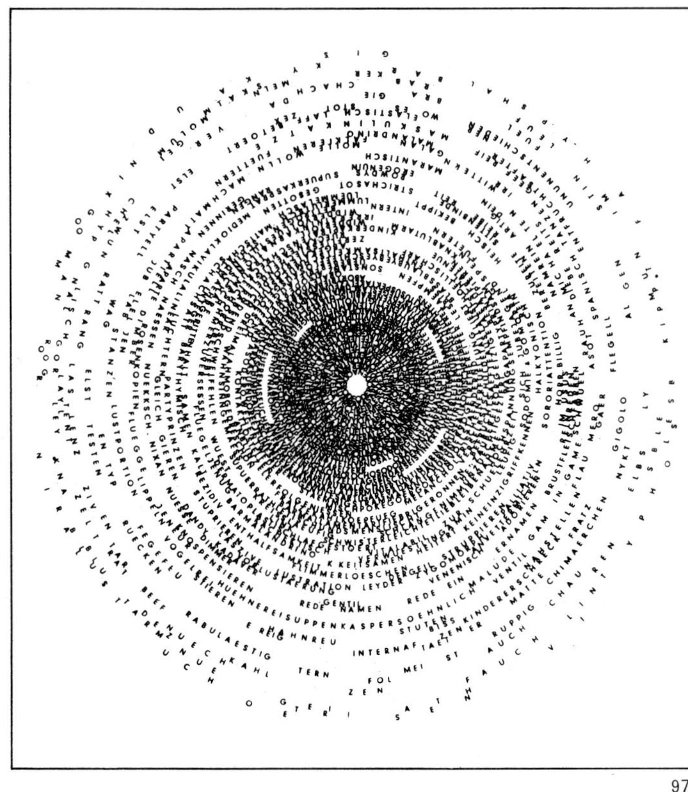

97

Marcel Janco, the author refrains from giving a description in musical terms; he wants to offer each listener absorbed in his 'parallel reading' the possibility 'of linking the appropriate associations' and retaining 'the elements which are characteristic of his personality . . . , yet remaining within the path which the author has laid down for him'.

In the chapter called 'Invention' in his *King of Bohemia*, Nodier offers us a curious item which foreshadows letterist poetry. It is concerned quite simply with recounting the arrival of a stage-coach at a castle with the help of various onomatopoeic words of his own invention, as he explains in the following chapter, which is called 'Interpretation'. According to him, this page, 'unique among all the written monuments to the word, conceals, beneath what appears to be a mere witticism, the extremely powerful effort of a creative imagination'. The reader *hears* the horses neighing and pawing the ground, the crack of the whip, the shouts of the coachman, the wheels creaking, the paving-stones trembling, right down to the final shout of 'hurrah!' from the people living in the castle. We can only be sorry that Nodier did not have the appropriate modern methods at his disposal to enable him to *see* these sounds with the help of a type of letterpress printing modulated down to the last paroxysm of a shout.

Iliazd was another 'letterist' before his time who invented
his own language, known as 'zaoum' this time and used for his
962 *Ledentu le phare* (Ledentu the Lighthouse); meanwhile Kurt
929 Schwitters made rhythmic capital out of his groups of letters.

97

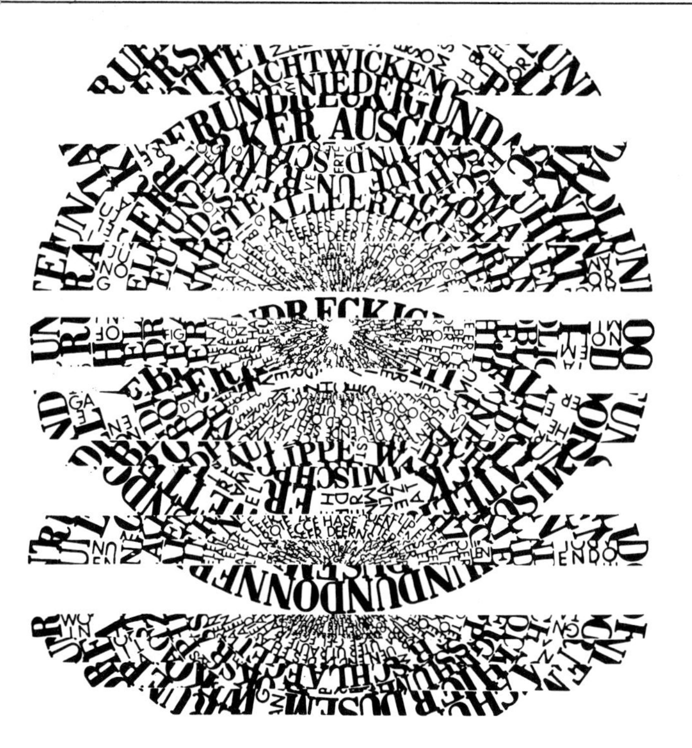

971

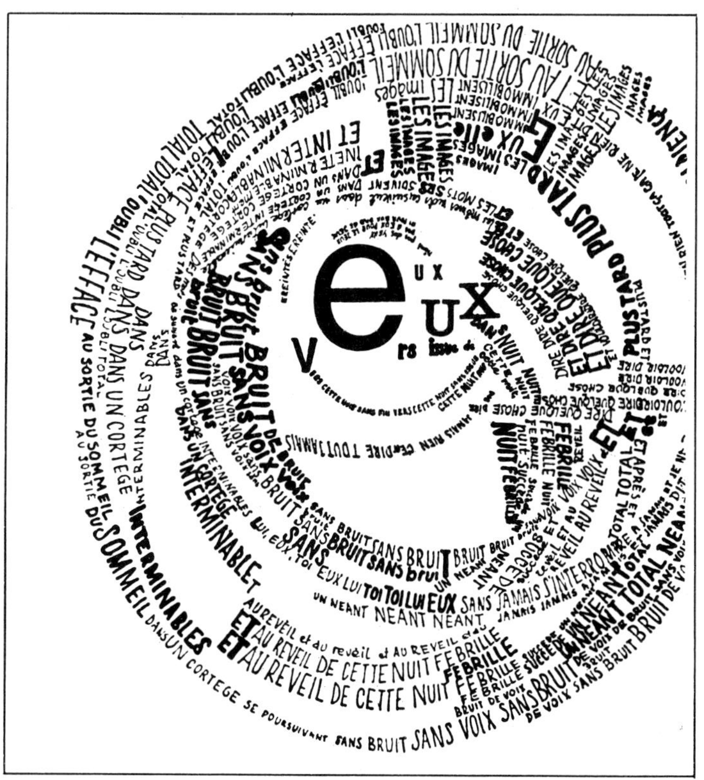

972

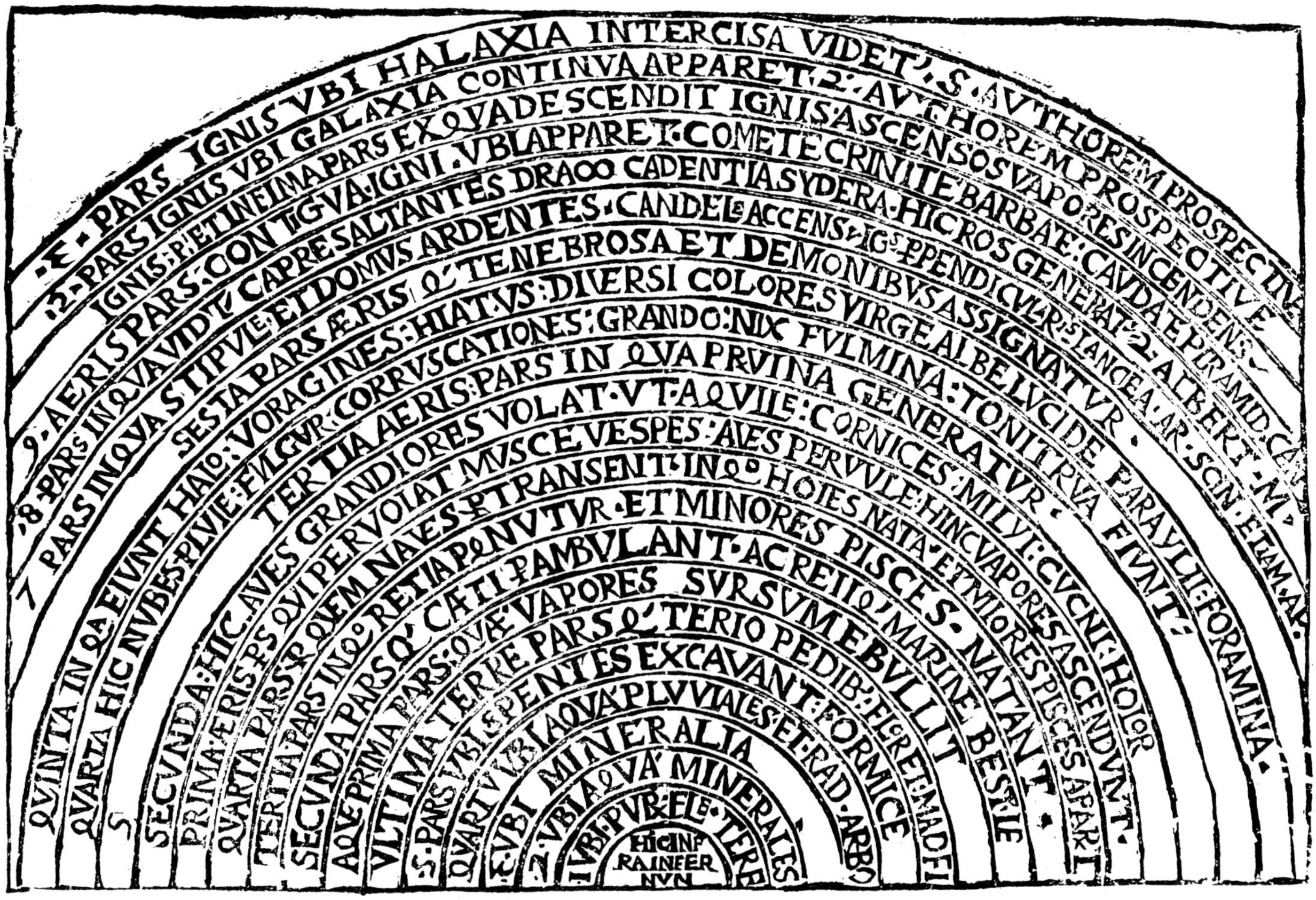

974

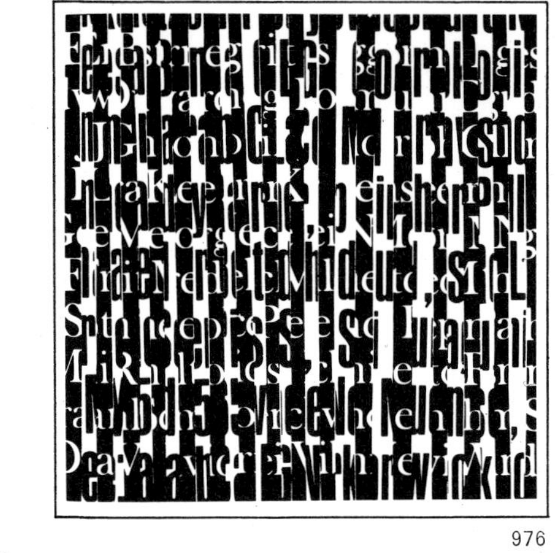

976

977

975

978

979

Partez sur une nouvelle base :

VOTRE DEMARCHE 64
SUR TALONS 4 CM

par Alice Chavane

Par où commencer pour vous mettre à la mode ! Mais par le bas ! Cet hiver, pas de problème : bas tricotés et talons bas, voilà le B.A... Bas de la nouvelle silhouette... et une bonne nouvelle pour toutes les femmes qui aiment trotter, bouger, danser en oubliant une fois pour toutes qu'elles ont des pieds. Ne vous dites pas « Je vais au moins perdre 2 ou 3 cm ». Pensez à tout ce que vous allez gagner : pieds bien assis, démarche plus libre, plus jeune. Vous allez réapprendre à vous tenir bien droite, à sortir le cou, et finalement, tout ça, ça grandit. Si vous avez des jambes trop fortes : bas de laine fins mais talons un peu plus hauts (jamais plus de 5 cm). Si vous avez des jambes fluettes, torsadés ou grosses côtes. Et quelles que soient vos jambes, si vous avez de la tête, vous calculerez que d'ici le temps des bas de laine, vous avez largement... le temps de vous faire... de belles jambes. Cette mise à pied des talons hauts est bien la mode la plus salutaire et la plus intelligente...

980

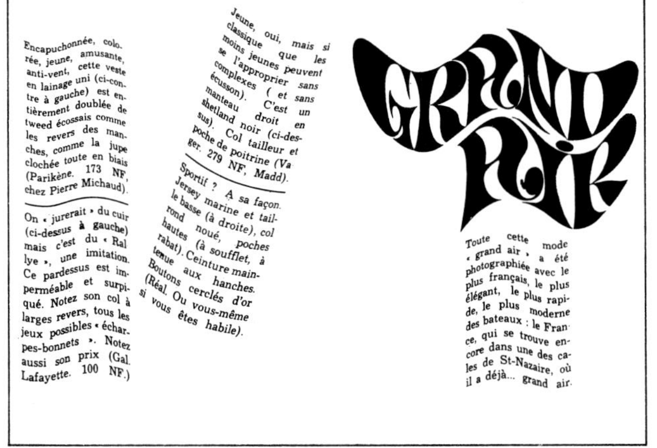

Encapuchonnée, colorée, jeune, amusante, cette veste anti-vent, en lainage uni (ci-contre à gauche) est entièrement doublée de tweed écossais comme les revers des manches, comme la jupe clochée toute en biais (Parikène. 173 NF, chez Pierre Michaud).

On « jurerait » du cuir (ci-dessus à gauche) mais c'est du « Rallye », une imitation. Ce pardessus est imperméable et surpiqué. Notez son col à larges revers, tous les jeux possibles « écharpes-bonnets ». Notez aussi son prix (Gal. Lafayette. 100 NF.)

Jeune, oui, mais si classique que les moins jeunes peuvent se l'approprier sans complexes (et sans écusson). C'est un manteau droit en shetland noir (ci-dessus). Col tailleur et poche de poitrine (Vager. 279 NF, Madd).

Sportif ? A sa façon. Jersey marine et taille basse (à droite), col rond noué, poches hautes (à soufflet, à rabat). Ceinture maintenue aux hanches. Boutons cerclés d'or (Réal. Ou vous-même si vous êtes habile).

Toute cette mode « grand air », a été photographiée avec le plus français, le plus élégant, le plus rapide, le plus moderne des bateaux : le France, qui se trouve encore dans une des cales de St-Nazaire, où il a déjà... grand air.

981

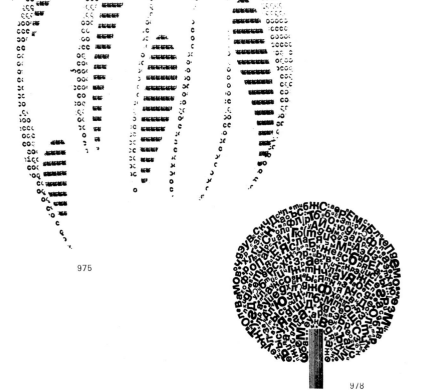

FOOTBALL FORM-I

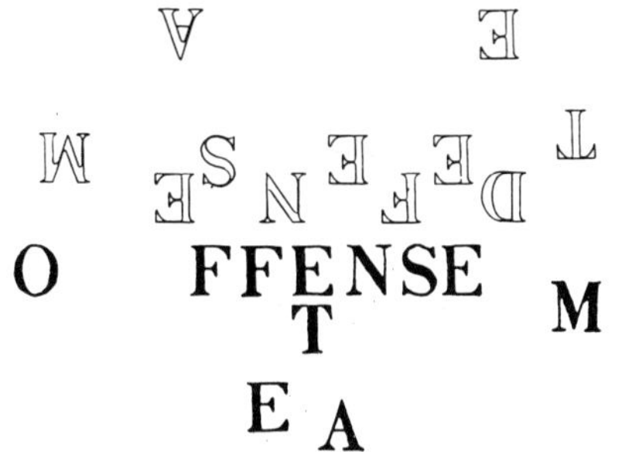

FOOTBALL FORM-II

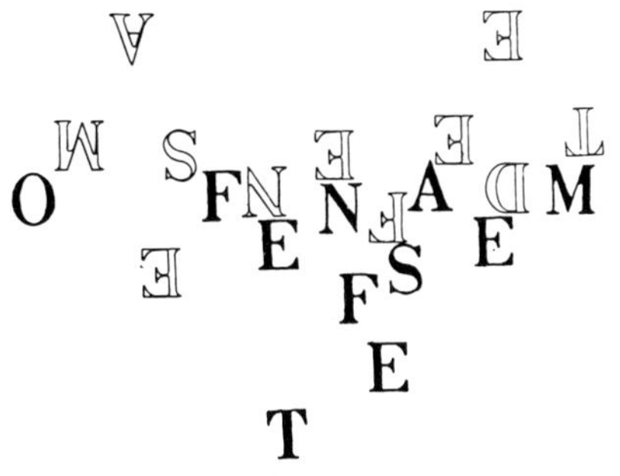

FOOTBALL FORM-III

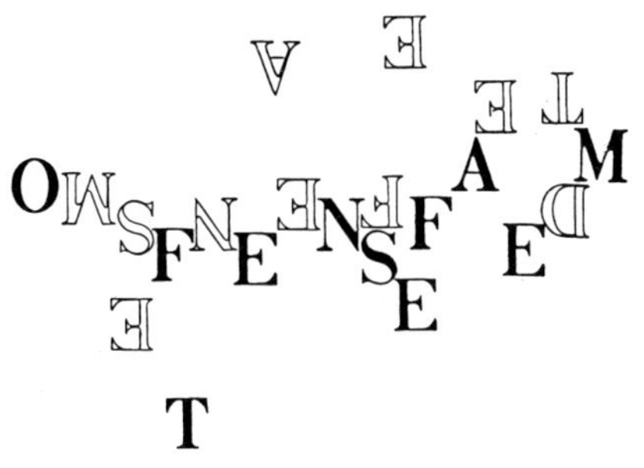

FOOTBALL FORM-VI

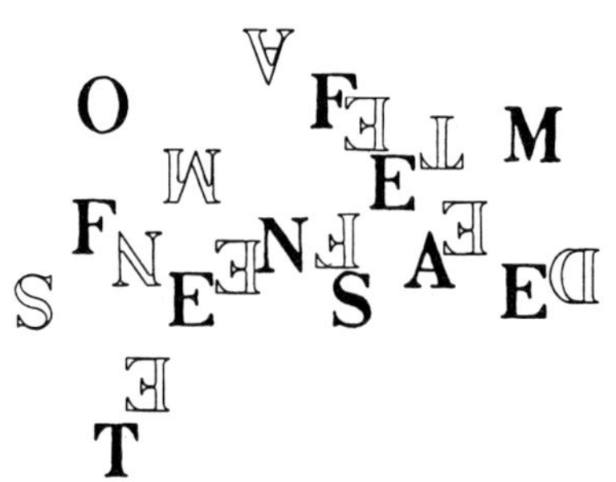

982/985

But it is when we come to the field of space, where the surface arrangements of a word, or even of a letter, gives the written passage a multi-dimensional aspect, that we come across the largest number of examples. *Une nuit d'échecs gras*, a page 932 designed by Tristan Tzara for the magazine *391*, has remained an archetype of this genre. This disorganized muddle of words, a deliberate jumble, a real old rag-bag of typefaces which must have made the typographers of the period sit down and weep, is not without beauty and attracts the eye while discouraging us from actually reading it.

The first visual poems can no doubt be found in modern advertising. Posters, hand-outs, newpaper advertisements, book-jackets, glossy magazines, animated cartoons in the cinema and on television, 'audio-visuals' – all these transform marvellous, ubiquitous, irrational, absurd elements into things which seem, thanks to the phenomenon by which familiarity breeds contempt, banal and trivial. Typographers have become poets, while poets, who once used to leave the printer to look after the business of designing what they had written, are discovering that the essential element in a poetic message emerges by way of its typographic presentation. So,

986

987

the process of creation automatically includes 'visualizing' a poem; and it thus becomes itself the subject-matter of poetry.

Pierre Garnier, a French representative of 'Spatialism' 975 saw the movement as 'the poetic animation of all linguistic elements. Spatialism endeavours to be a general linguistic art, an art of inspirations with signs which have not yet been catalogued.' This movement, which is sometimes known as 'concrete poetry', links the concepts of time, structure and energy to the concept of space; these activities are concerned with visual poems, phonetic poems, tactile poems, mechanical

le livre
roman
fiction
sordide

souffre
d orgueil
repu

d efforts
féroces

d autres
arts
friands

de scènes
d images
qui
dévorent

l évince

le mot
y gagne
senti

rendu
au vide
qui
l émousse

il
redevient
lentement

l étamine
qui mène
la brigue

988

IBM

98

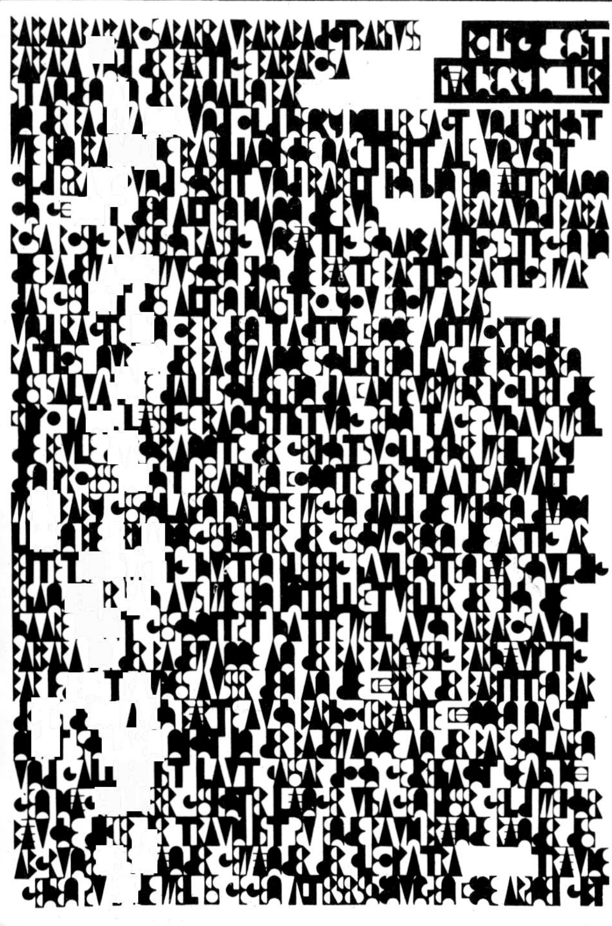

990

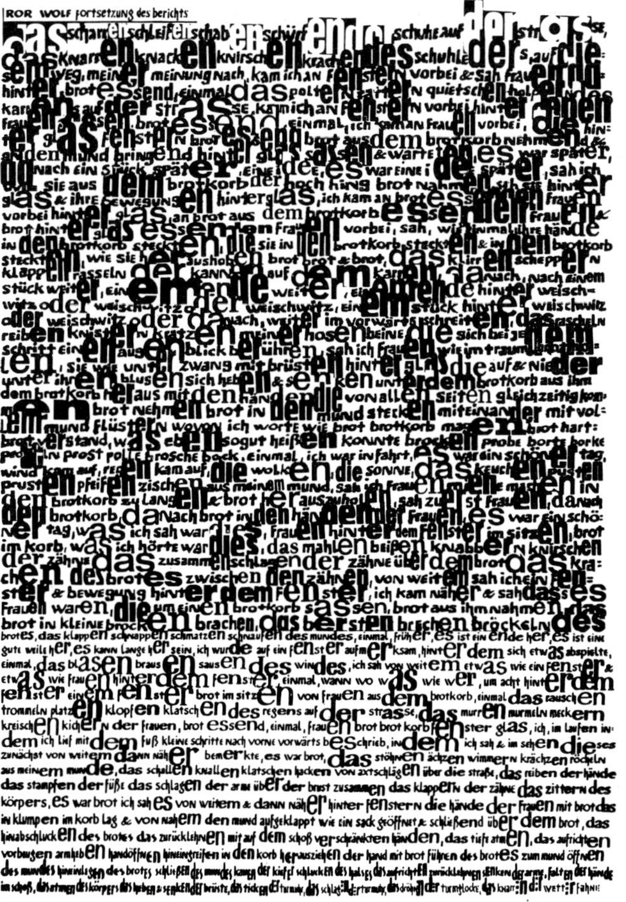

991

992

993

994

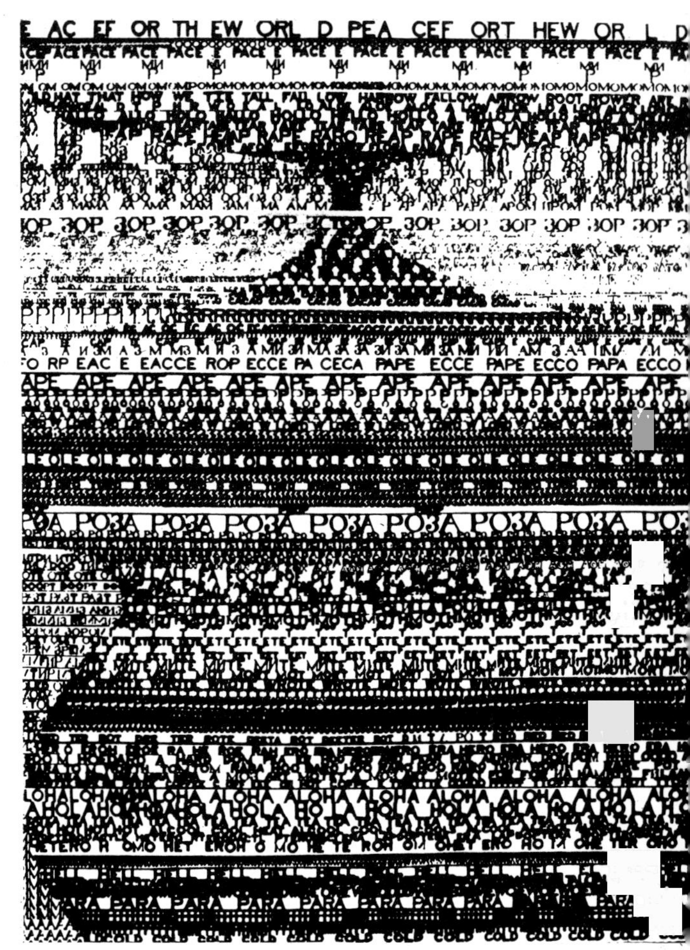

99

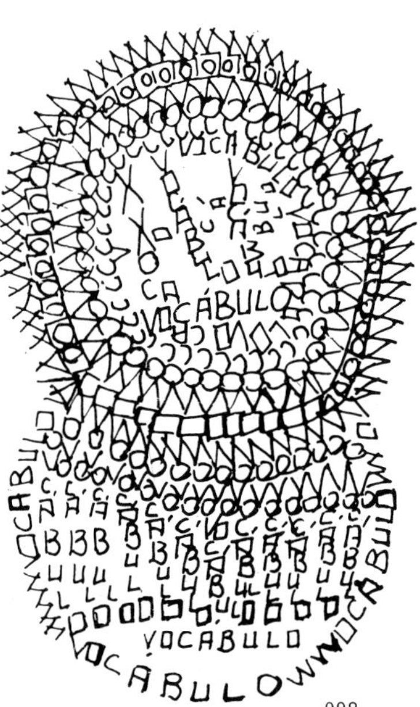

998

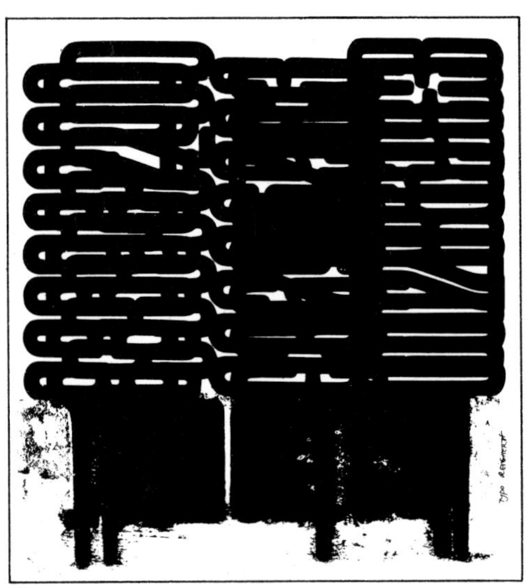

999

1

996

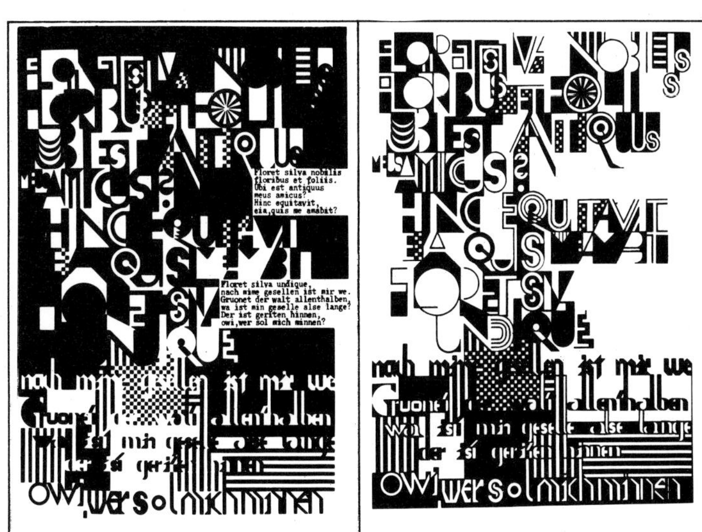

997

poems (composed on a typewriter and illustrated by Ilse
Garnier), semantic poems, and even stretch as far as objective
poetry, (which is formulated by musicians, painters or typographers) and to cybernetic poetry, serial poetry, permutational
poetry, etc. Eugen Gomringer, Diter Rot, Emmett Williams,
Gerhard Rühm and the Noigandres Group of São Paolo
founded the movement, and over the last fifteen or so years its
adherents have been scattered all over the world: in Germany
(Carl Friedrich Claus, Ferdinand Kriwet, Franz Mon, Timm 969/971 976
Ulrichs, Hansjörg Mayer), Italy (Carlo Belloli), England (P.S. 993 986
Houedard, who is the author of some calligrams which are
mystical in inspiration), France (Jean-François Bory), the 972
United States, Japan, etc. Some poets, although they do not
actually belong to the movement, work along parallel lines but
in isolation, examples being Henri Chopin, or Wolfgang 1001/1032
Schmidt, the Dienst brothers, who founded the journal 990-991 997
Rhinozeros with its revival of the art of calligraphy, and who see
the letter as a means of information just as well as an aesthetic
object; the Swiss poet Jean-Claude Grosjean, a recent discovery, is the author of four books of poetry grouped together
under the title *Poésie*, in which the letter is arranged according 988
to certain mathematical or biological laws. In the field of music,

1033

10

1035

10

1037

1038

Karl-Heinz Stockhausen has organized a sound universe governed by the laws of space with his *Groups for Three Orchestras* or *The Adolescents' Song*.

The poet and engraver Camille Bryen, with Raymond Hains and Jacques de la Villeglé, is the author of 'the first frenzied/non-
994 read poem'* It is called 'Hépérile éclaté' and is executed with the help of corrugated glass-frames which take away the original meaning of what is written and create a new form of writing in which words splinter into 'ultra-words'. Isidore Isou is the inventor of 'unheard-of' letters and the champion of the letterist movement; its members or sympathizers (Maurice Lemaître, Jacques Spacagna, Jean-Louis Brau, François Dufrêne and others) reinvent the alphabet and compose what they call 'hypergraphics' which attempt to bring together the letter and the image, rather in the same way that Schönberg tried to unite music and words in his *Pierrot Lunaire*.

1033/1038 Adolf Hoffmeister's collages hover on the borderline between image and writing in much the same way; they depict *legible* landscapes and are the products of collaboration between the artist's talent, his sense of humour (which is an instrinsic ingredient of the collage process) and pure chance. About ten years ago Hoffmeister was travelling in the southern provinces of the Soviet Union; he had neither paintbrush nor paints with him, and could not find any in the places where he stayed, so he had the idea of cutting up the local newspapers and making pictorial reconstructions of the countryside of Georgia or Abkhasia. In doing so he illustrated anew and in his own way the old process which tends to give language an aesthetic value, and to merge, in the *expression,* the type of concepts which Western handwriting holds at arm's length by its very nature, even to the extent of making them totally contradictory. As Mallarmé wrote to Gide in connection with his *Coup de dés:* 'The rhythm of a phrase concerning an act, or even an object, is meaningless unless it imitates them, and unless, when pictorially represented on paper and taken back by the letter to the original impression, it knows how to give back something, in spite of everything.'

We should specify here that in his compositions Hoffmeister takes a step in the opposite direction by setting out himself, this time, to meet the letter.

*The French is *'premier poème à délire',* which offers a deliberate play on words: *'délire'* meaning 'delirium' or 'frenzy' can be read as 'dé-lire' = 'to unread' (translator's note).

IV The letter and the written symbol in painting

1039

At various periods illuminators, painters and engravers have all incorporated letters into their work. They have rarely made them the basic theme of their compositions. In painting, letters generally have a purely anecdotal role, forming part of the backcloth, as in Utrillo's street scenes, or jostling each other in closely serried ranks on the open pages of a book, as in medieval illumination. Sometimes the part they play is imbued with an emblematic or magical quality; or otherwise, when we come to the Impressionists, we find lettering on signboards or on the headline of a newspaper which the model is holding. In some of Bernard Buffet's canvases, the artist's signature is unfurled bang in the middle of the sky and invades the composition to such an extent that it even gives it its framework: it thus extends the range of pictorial writing, revealing the actual movement of the hand which traced it and disclosing secrets which figurative painting keeps hidden. But the 'subject-matter' remains, in spite of the surface lay-out, which is closely related to the way the hand-written dedication on the blank page at the front of a book is arranged, or the way a hand-written letter is presented.

It seems that the first piece of work by a painter to give pride of place to the letter was Fernand Léger's illustrations to a
text by Blaise Cendrars called *The End of the World filmed by* 1039-1040
the Angel of Notre-Dame, in which God the Father, sur- 1042
rounded by telephones, directs a Hollywood-style production of planetary dimensions. Léger mingles objects, faces and letters in a kaleidoscopic vision which reflects the aesthetic preoccupations of his age. Here the letter breaks right away from any element of picturesqueness and sheds the last vestige of figurative representation; instead it is superimposed over the text in many places, and takes on its shape or, alternatively,

1040

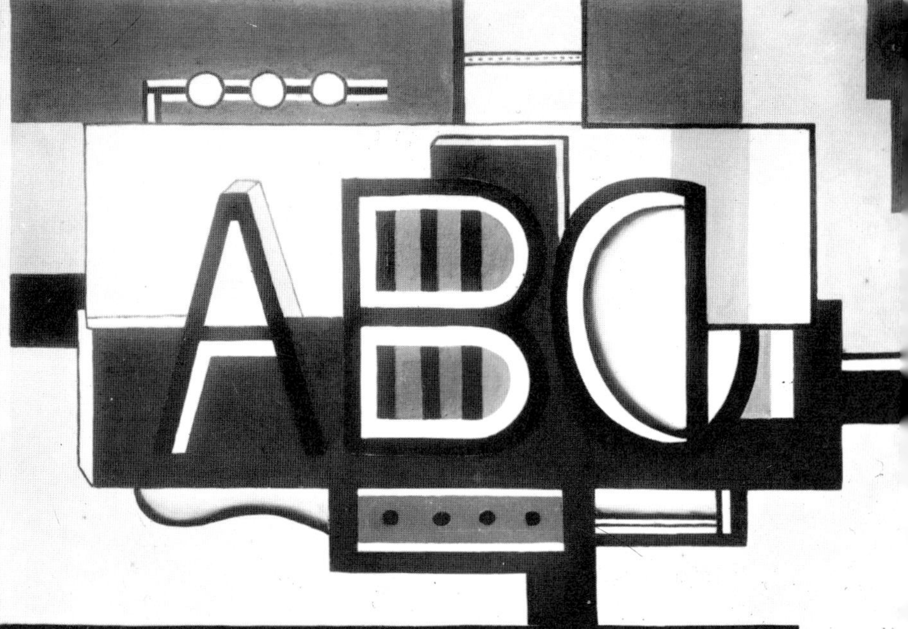

104

drives the text out altogether, taking over the whole of the
space on the page and making a solo appearance resplendent
in brilliant colours. On other occasions, Léger will make sure
that the letter plays this type of solo part and treath it as an
1041 object: in his *Still Life*, for instance, we have the first three
letters of the alphabet, seen in contrasting perspective; another
1043 canvas will depict the letter R back to front and looking as if it
is hanging down from the top of the composition. (The same
letter—right way round this time—stands stiffly at the side of the
1044 road in Paul Klee's *Villa R.*) Finally, Fernand Léger introduces
letters into a film called *The Mechanical Ballet* which he made
in 1924 with Dudley Murphy; this time we are restricted to the
rather more austere register of black-and-white only, but the
speed of the image inscribed on the film makes up for this.

There are several reasons for the sudden interest displayed by painters in the letter and the written symbol. In the first place, the structural quality of the letters in the Latin alphabet gave a painter such as Léger first-class material at a period when he was preoccupied with geometric shapes. On the other hand, at the beginning of the century the paintings of the Nabis heralded the later fashion for *japonaiseries* by drawing their inspiration from the calligraphy of the Far East, in which writing and drawing are readily combined. A decade or two earlier, Gauguin's wood-cuts gave the letter its own special destiny by suggesting a new type of decorative writing which would later come into full flower with the arrival of *art nouveau*. (Incidentally, it was Degas, fascinated as he was by letters, who recalled a sign-board which can still be seen today in the rue

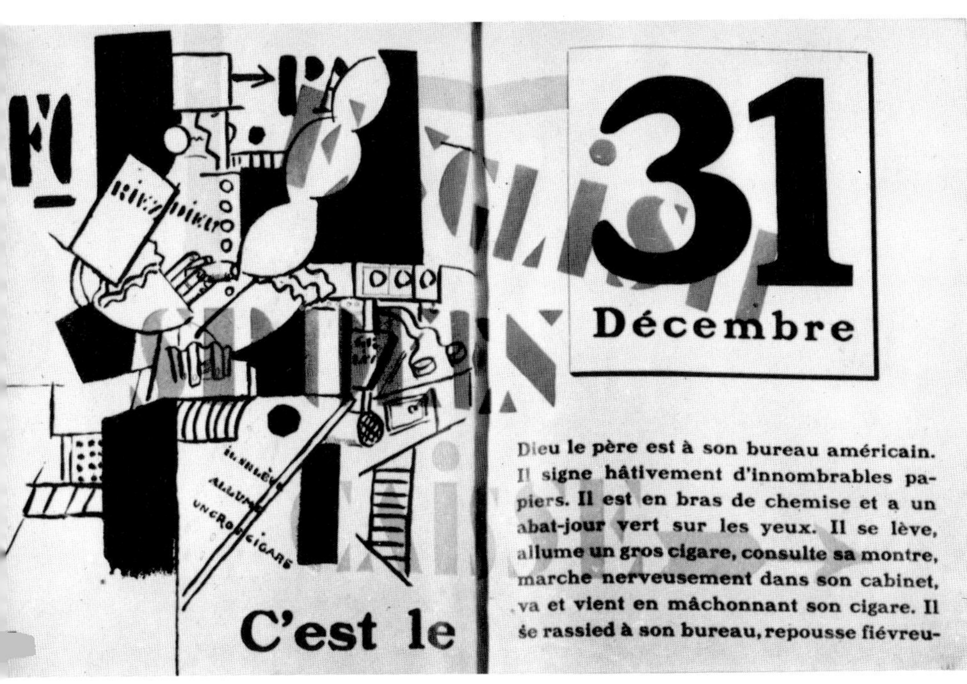

C'est le

31 Décembre

Dieu le père est à son bureau américain. Il signe hâtivement d'innombrables papiers. Il est en bras de chemise et a un abat-jour vert sur les yeux. Il se lève, allume un gros cigare, consulte sa montre, marche nerveusement dans son cabinet, va et vient en mâchonnant son cigare. Il se rassied à son bureau, repousse fiévreu-

1042

1043

1044

Jacob in Paris and said that he knew of nothing which was more perfect than these four words: *Typographie de Firmin-Didot*.) But the strongest influence on painting has come from the various art movements which have shared the limelight over the last fifty years: Cubism, Orphism, Futurism, Suprematism, Constructivism, Unanimism – not to mention Dadaïsm, Surrealism or other more recent movements – and we should also add to this list the attraction exercised by the Bauhaus. Painters, poets and musicians offered us a new and transformed way of looking at things, partly in their own work, partly in proclamations and manifestos. This means that the barriers which were once erected between literature and the graphic arts, between poetry, calligraphy or typography, painting and imagery are now disappearing. Picabia and Marcel Duchamp are poets as much as painters; (the most frequent common denominator among contemporary artists is their humour – a type of humour inherited from Lichtenberg and Swift, Lautréamont and Kafka, Edward Lear and Alphonse Allais). Both Dubuffet and Arp have produced a considerable amount of literary work. The Italians who wrote those thundering Futurist manifestos were all painters or sculptors. Jean Cocteau classifies all his activities under the heading of poetry, referring to his 'theatre poetry', 'novel poetry', 'cinema poetry', etc. The poems of Picasso, Michaux, Kandinsky or Klee, the 'hypergraphies' of the letterists, Camille Bryen's experiments, are so many pieces of evidence to prove the existence of a form of artistic impression which from now on makes use of all the methods at its disposal, or even invents new ones.

1045

1046

1047

In a review of Picasso's painting written in 1913, Guillaume Apollinaire emphasizes that 'numbers and moulded letters insistently make their appearance as picturesque elements which are new in art and have long since been impregnated with humanity'. Although in this instance the letters are likened to objects (which are so abstract that they would have been banished from still-lifes in an earlier age), and although they do not contain any clearly *legible* message and are not saddled with any particular meaning, they do tend nevertheless to introduce linguistic elements into pictorial space – though these may take the form of mere allusions to jog one's memory. So these snatches of speech, these scattered props for thought proceed to take root in painters' canvases, even to the point of looking, on occasions, like relics of a dead language. No artist was to use them so lavishly and so exhaustively as Paul Klee: for the first time – if we except certain types of illumination and calligraphy – whole texts invade the canvas, uniting 1045/1048
rhetoric and image. Klee assigns patches of modulated colour to letters or to syllables, or occasionally to whole words; these letter-images or drawn words spread out over a flat surface as in tapestry or in a child's drawing, their humour and their poetic

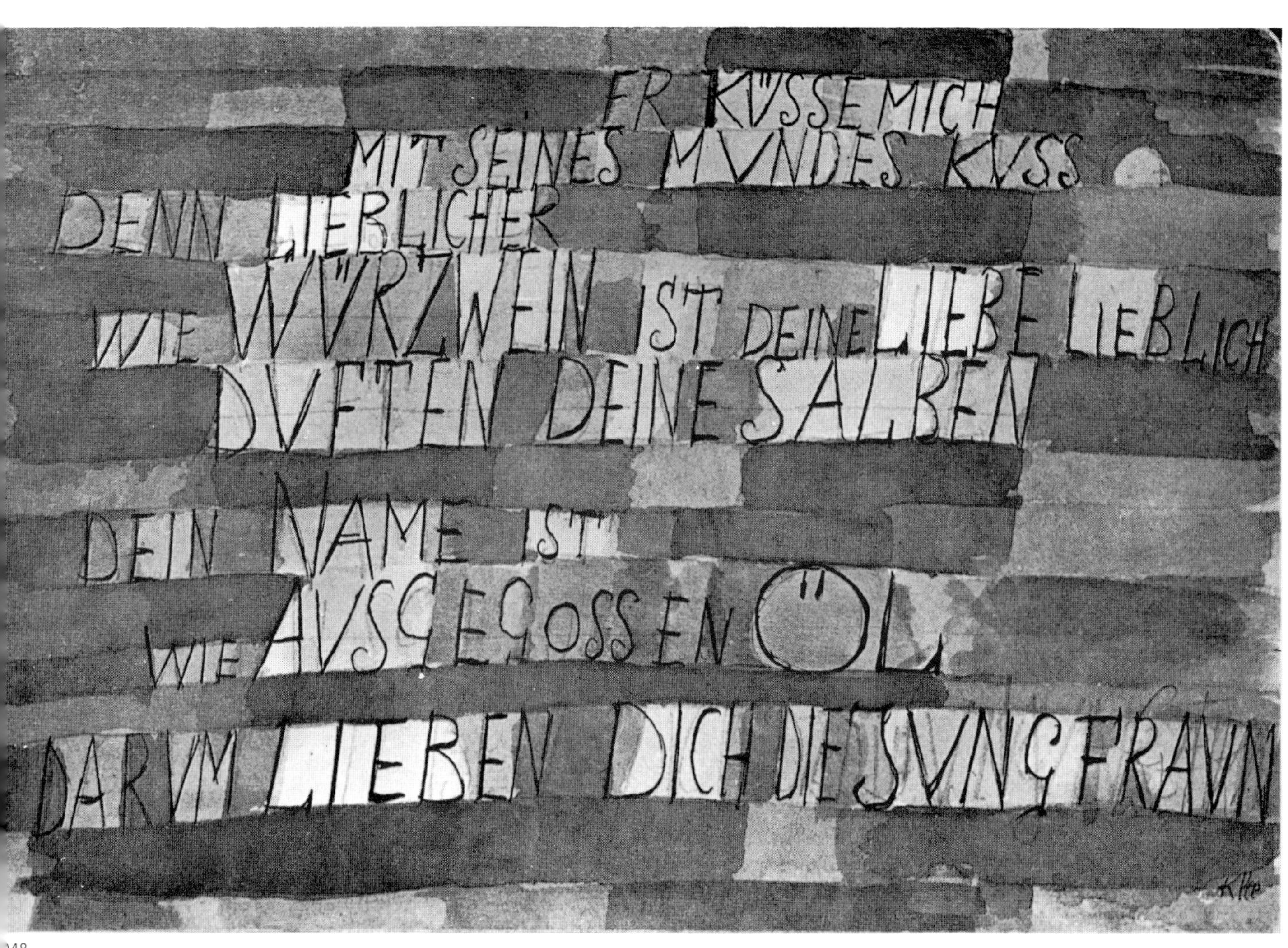

1049

1053

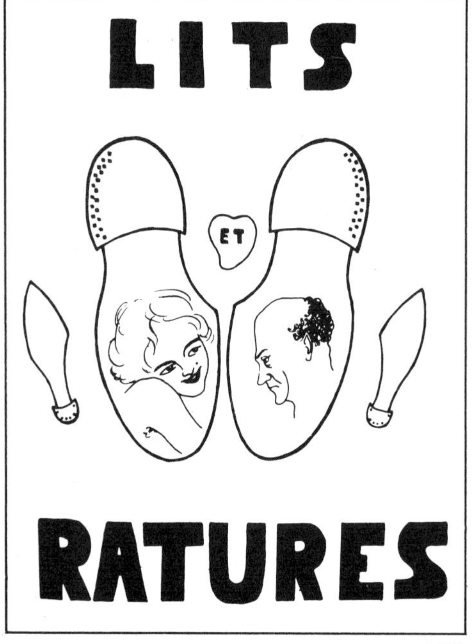

1054

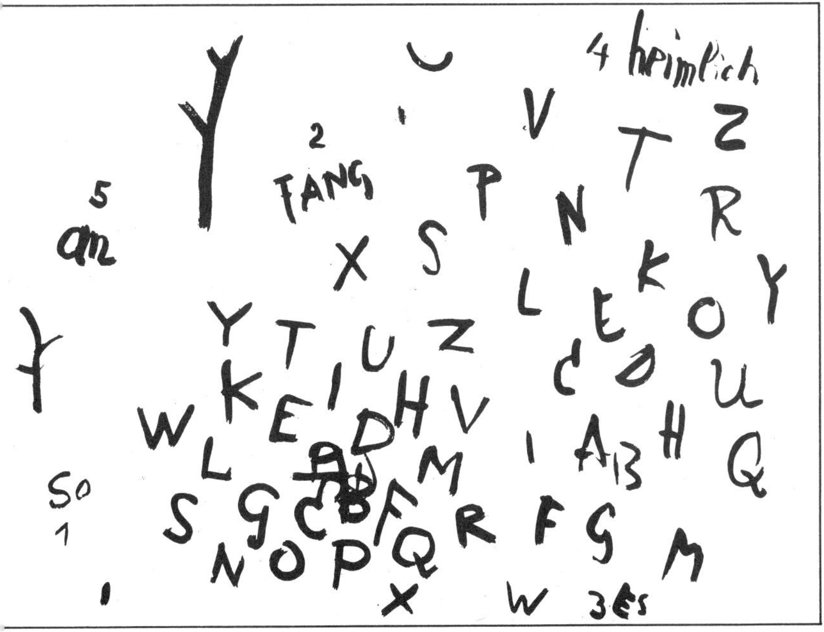

1051

1052

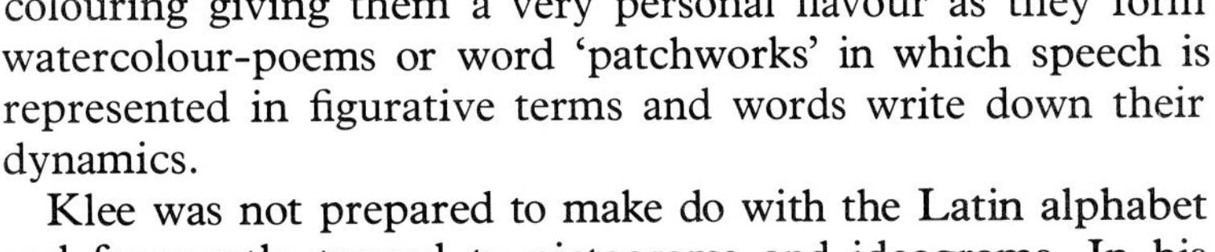

colouring giving them a very personal flavour as they form watercolour-poems or word 'patchworks' in which speech is represented in figurative terms and words write down their dynamics.

Klee was not prepared to make do with the Latin alphabet and frequently turned to pictograms and ideograms. In his youth he had been interested in these age-old methods of expression, and particularly in the way the outlines of the various symbols have developed over the centuries, generally progressing from realistic notation to abstraction. He began to invent pictograms for his own use, and would skilfully mix these with all sorts of borrowings from early forms of writing. So we can find a child, some trees, an animal and letters from the Etruscan alphabets facing in all directions, all grouped together on a patch of green representing a meadow, some of the letters being upside-down, sideways, back to front or whatever.
Elsewhere two figures are treated in two different ways: 1050
partly according to a figurative schema, partly in ideograms. Other drawings reveal various signs derived from hieroglyphics, with scarcely any degree of stylization. Finally, in one of his last works Klee composed the face of Death by using the three
letters TOD – which spell out the German word for 'death'. 1052

Klee's painted poems should be compared with a painting by Yves Laloy – the ambiguous reality inherent in this painting, taken together with its caption, forms an untranslatable
Surrealist proverb which reads: *Les petits pois sont verts – Les* 1055
petits poissons rouges. And we will also recall Chagall, who worked for a sign-painter in his youth and sometimes gives his figures the shape of Hebrew characters.

L.H.O.O.Q

1056

With the advent of Cubism, the hidden face of objects is revealed for the first time, via the thousand facets which make up a stubborn reconstruction. When it had reached the final stage of its development, it substituted plane surfaces for the volumes which had already gradually grown flatter and lost their thickness to a remarkable degree. It was thanks to this metamorphosis that the *printed word* made inroads into contemporary painting. From 1912 onwards, Braque and Picasso
1060-1061 introduced the first collages into their paintings; before using newspaper, Braque had resorted to using paper printed to imitate wood: he had been amazed at this discovery, which reminded him of his early years as a journeyman-painter when he would spend hours trying to create the same effect. Both painters were probably merely aiming to introduce into their paintings the neutral qualities and stable elements offered by the grey and uniform letterpress printing seen in the daily newspapers of the period. At any rate, the collages were more than mere subsidiaries or accessories: on numerous occasions they constitute the essential theme – or even the sole theme – of the composition and, by virtue of the way they have been cut, take on the actual shape of the objects concerned (just as a calligram would). This means that they offer the illusion that the objects are actually there. At the same time, they are a fragmented notation of thought, which is scattered in the image; these scraps of figurative representation, detached as they are from reality, finally give a haphazard form of truth to the image. Ever since Lautréamont told of a meeting between an umbrella and a sewing-machine on a dissecting-table, we have known that humour often borrows certain elements from chance.

Long after he had abandoned collages, Picasso was to allow letters – which would generally be stencilled – to enter his paintings now and then in the form of titles: *Valse, Ma jolie,*
1062 etc. In Juan Gris's work we can very often see the name of a newspaper, either only half of it or the whole thing, depending on where the fold comes, but always carefully drawn on a flat white tint. Meanwhile Schwitters prefers bus-tickets, cheques and hand-outs, and sometimes newspapers again as well; he
1057-1058 produced various *assemblages,* all of which bear the title *Merz,* from the name of his own movement and the review which he enlivened and which published photomontages. In fact this mode of expression was invented in about 1919 by some of the
1066 Berlin Dadaïsts – Raoul Hausmann, Georg Grosz and John Heartfield. Photomontage was therefore the achievement of painters, and not of graphic artists working in advertising, as is too often thought to be the case. It was not until later that advertising, the press and political propaganda got hold of the process and put it to the uses with which we are now so familiar. As a matter of fact photomontage is derived from the first collages, and the note of originality which we find in the Dadaïsts' *assemblages* stems mainly from the violence of their

10

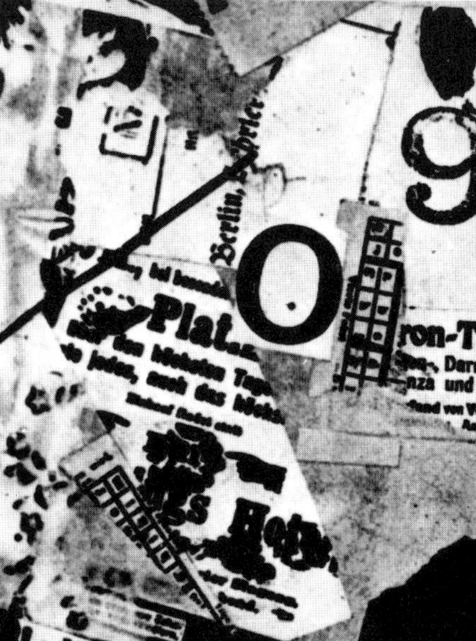

10

10

060

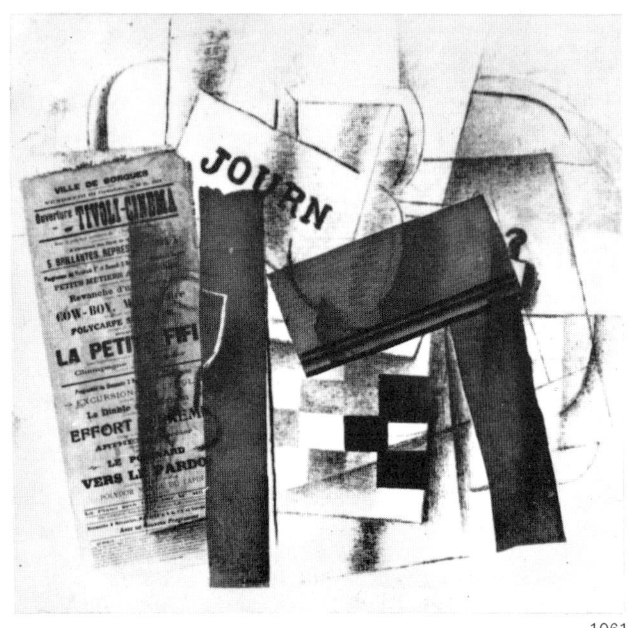

1061

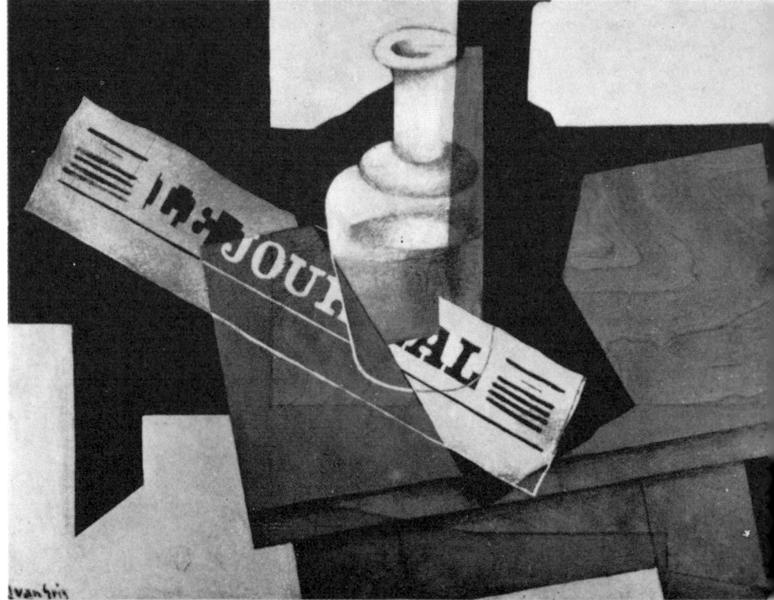

1064

1065

106

1063

expression, which is obtained with the help of typographic material arranged in strongly contrasting groups; what is more, these are fairly closely related to the material used in the Futurist Manifestos.

In the same way, defaced posters, laying bare as they do the stratifications where shapes and colours meet or cause a sudden break, seem to be a legacy inherited from collages (even if they do adopt the reverse process of 'un-sticking').

A systematic study of all the artists who may have been pre-occupied with the different ways of introducing lettering into their pictorial space does not come within the scope of this book; still less would we be justified in analysing the various forms such attempts took, or measuring their importance. So we will limit ourselves to giving a few names and examples which demonstrate the variety of the methods used, and at the same time illustrate various attempts which were based on the common objective of transfiguring lettering into pictorial images or giving writing a pictorial dimension. We will also note that none of the various art movements which have come and gone since Cubism has neglected the problem of the relationship between the letter and the image. This is true
of 'Simultaneism' with Robert Delaunay's prismatic mirrors 1070

which he handed down to modern advertising; it is also true of
Futurism and the Futurist Manifestos – Carrà's paintings 1059
developed within the framework of an accurate reading of these manifestos; and in our own day, with Pop Art and the young American school . . On the other hand, some painters seem to be working along their own individual lines of research;

1068

1069

1070

1071

1072

1073

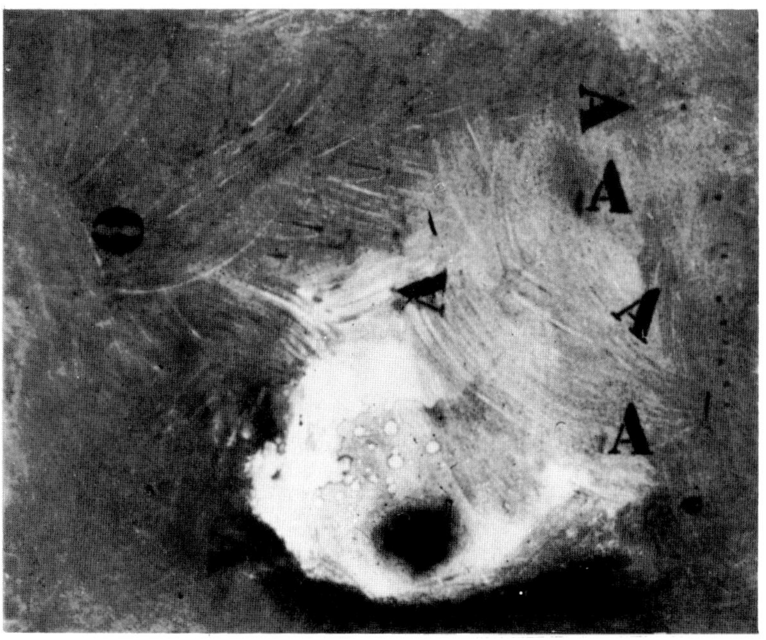

1074

1075

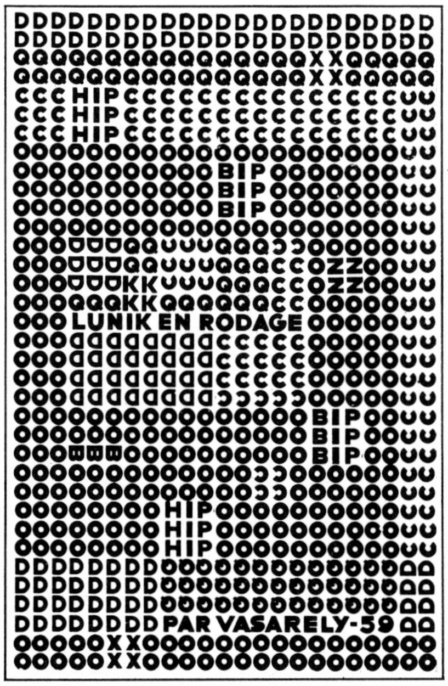

HIP
BIP
LUNIK EN RODAGE
BIP
HIP
PAR VASARELY-59

1076

1077

10

1079

most of the canvases which Mirò recently showed at Venice offer variations on a single theme: the interplay of a few
1074 letters against stripes of colour, on a white ground. As early as 1919 Pougny had conjured up a similar universe in his *La*
1064 *fuite des formes* (Flying Forms). Werkman used a hand-press, and this made him all the more interested in the typographic
1075 material which gives his compositions their solidly constructed
1072 outlines. Ben Shahn sometimes superimposes writing on to the neutral letterpress of newsprint, while Vasarely, abandoning his cross-hatching on this occasion, takes the cosmos and
1076 computers as the keynote of his lettering. Even photographers tend to fall under the spell of lettering: for instance, a few years ago William Klein, fascinated by the 'typographic' countenance of a town like New York, lived surrounded by gigantic
1077 letters which were plastered all over the walls and floor of his studio.

108

1081

Aragon considers that 'the importance of an artist can be measured by the number of new signs he has introduced into the language of the plastic arts'. As he sees it, the sign is 'the physical appearance of meaning' and the language of painting, or even the 'language of language'. He points to various object-signs in Matisse, particularly his armchairs, mentions the
mouth-sign drawn in the shape of the figure 3 or the letters S, 1089
Z or M, and conjures up a vision of the painter at the age of seventy-six spending night after night drawing letters, relearning the alphabet and *painting* lines of verse. Matisse himself was confident that the sign can 'be religious, priestlike, liturgical, or quite simply artistic'. 'I am conscious' he wrote to Aragon, 'of having attributed dramatic passions to armchairs, foliage, to the utensils in a still-life or in a *face*.'

We know that in his letters Van Gogh changed over instinctively from writing to drawing, either by interjecting a
sketch of a painting or specifying colours, or simply because he 1078
needed to supplement speech by an image. As, conversely, he changes over equally naturally from an image to a written text, we are entitled to think that not only does he see these two modes of expression as complementary, but they can also on occasions become confused and bound up with the same type of writing and appear as a manifestation of its personality. As a matter of fact, many of Van Gogh's paintings are more *written* than painted. His whirling suns, his scorching heaths, his crackling corn are so many magnetic fields, so many groups of symbols interlinked by the rhythm of the composition.

Pollock's canvases are overrun with vast and tangled net- 1080
works flooded with the painter's personality, while Capogrossi lays bare the vertebrae of his tortuous compositions. The 1086

1082

1083

1084

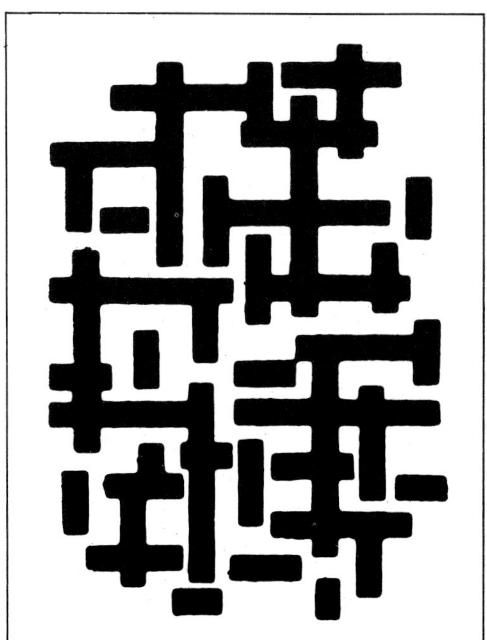

1085

10

1089

1085 signs in Theo van Doesburg's work, on the other hand, are as
disjointed and steady as letters, and are always upright. There
1084 is no point in looking for any trace of letters in Mondrian, who
transforms Cubism into total abstraction, but his bare lines,
paying homage to geometry, take over the space, thus paving
the way for the despotic reign of the innumerable 'lineals' in
typography today.

In the work of most contemporary painters, plastic truth
is a concept which is quite independent of legibility; very often
nowadays, if we want to 'decode' a painting we must go beyond
the global vision it offers. Although the truth of the signs is
more immediate, it can happen that some of them belong to a
language which remains unknown and secret. In a passage in his
Lines, Numbers and Letters in which he refers to 'Mirò or the
prehistoric poet', Raymond Queneau gives an excellent
1087 analysis of the rudiments of the painter's ideogrammatic
1082 language. Kadinsky, too, has his own vocabulary of images and
signs.

In a general way, it is tempting to liken any transcription of a foreign language we do not speak to an abstract form of writing. Christian Dotremont demonstrated this with his *Le Train Mongol;* his text does not become intelligible until we have turned over the tracing-paper on which it is reproduced and turned the text round through 90°.

1088 1083 In both Mathieu's and Masson's work the act of painting and
the act of writing are inextricably linked, and the sign is con-
stantly being modulated by writing; even the gesture of the
hand as it traces out the sign becomes visible, while the
thought, which is normally more fleeting and swifter than

1087

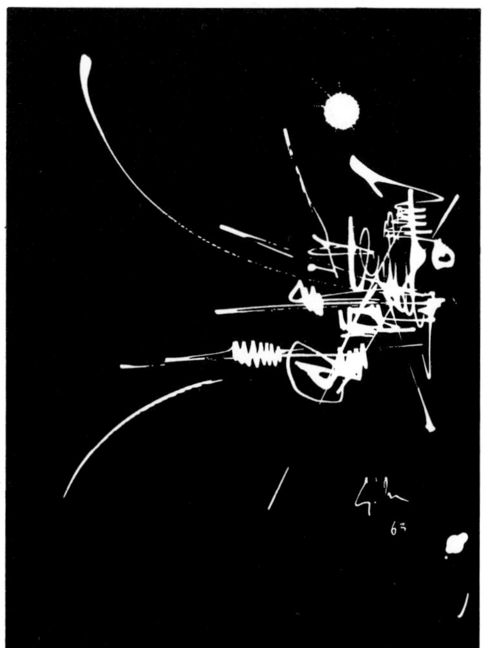
1088

writing, seems to have been arrested in mid-flight. These calligraffiti (as John Willett would call them) are slightly reminiscent of the writings of the Zen priests in the importance 1079
they give to gestures. Thus in many a composition we find that the painter has made use of a symbol or an ideogram but has not acknowledged this. Some artists, such as Alcopley, go even 1094
further and take us back to the early period of writing. It is interesting at this point to juxtapose various pieces of graphic evidence which are poles apart historically and geographically: there is no fundamental difference between the rock-drawing in 1092

1090

1091

1096 figure 1092 and the stabile designed by Calder for Expo in
1093 Montreal, or between the Chinese ideogram in figure 1093 and a
1095 graphic piece by Michaux; the structure is identical in each case, just as the reference to the human image is equally visible.

Henri Michaux has been preoccupied ever since 1927 (*Narration*) by a type of writing which can no longer make
1097/1099 do with mere words; in his *Mouvements* he invites us to use a new method of reading and arranges the choreography of an ink-blot as it seeps out in all directions and is activated by a series of tremors from within. The various phases of this mime-play merge into each other like frames of film, and tell of the endless vicissitudes of spiritual adventure. Michaux is at pains to 'draw the moments which, when put end to end, form a person's life; he would like 'to reveal the phrase within, the phrase without words'. *Mouvements* seems to conform equally well to these words of Michaux: 'to draw the awareness of existence and the passage of time'. 'I was infatuated with movements, filled with tension by these shapes which came hurtling towards me at top speed, and with their own rhythm', he wrote. 'A rhythm would often dominate a page, or sometimes several consecutive pages, and as the number of symbols grew, their vividness also increased . . .' 'It is because they have freed me from words, those clinging partners', adds Michaux, 'that my drawings soar upwards and are almost joyous . . . I therefore see them as liberators, a new language, turning its back on words.'

In the space of a few years, Jean Dubuffet added a third dimension to the flat and even writing of *L'Hourloupe*. His hatchings underwent a cellular proliferation and became statues and, more recently, houses – which are no doubt as unsuitable for habitation as *le facteur* Cheval's 'ideal palace'. In
1090 *Parade Funèbre pour Charles Estienne* the amoebic writing is crowded in on some pages as if we were caught up in the rush hour in the Underground.

One of the most important merits of this osmosis between the image and the written word is the way it banishes the divorce produced in the majority of illustrated books because two different temperaments have been doomed to live together on thoroughly artificial terms. The extent to which the two personalities of author and artist emerge distinctly from their work governs the autonomy of their expression and the distinctness of the register; this means that the lack of unity generally leads to misunderstanding. Yet if we accept the advisability of illustrating a book, the image ought then to take over from the text, to reveal what the text turns out to be incapable of describing; on the other hand, the written word could transcend the image by integrating it into a higher language, in which there would be enacted a poetic transmutation, which the image turns out to be intrinsically incapable of performing. Any

1092

1093

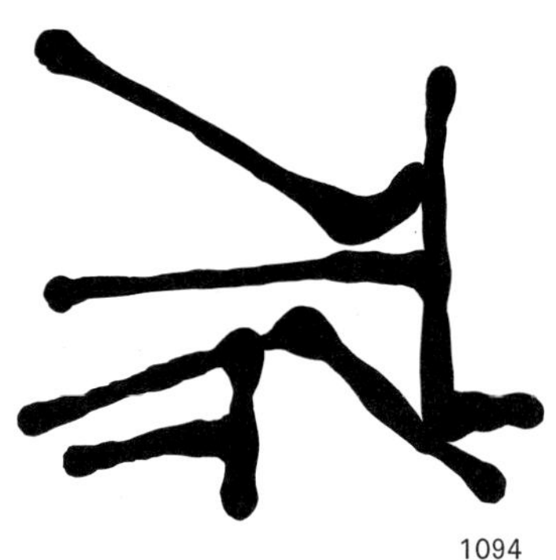

1094

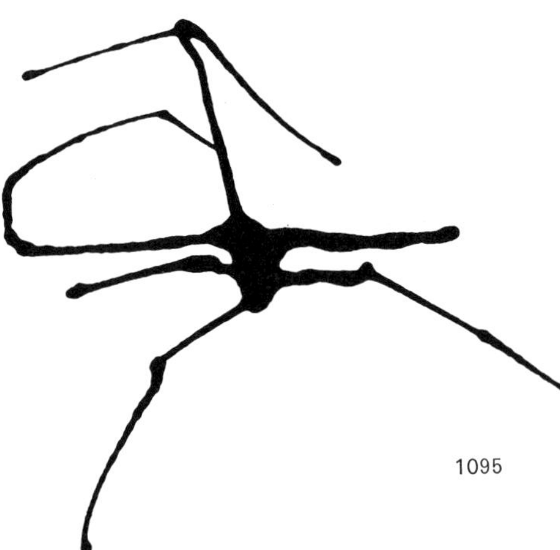

1095

1096

7

1098

1099

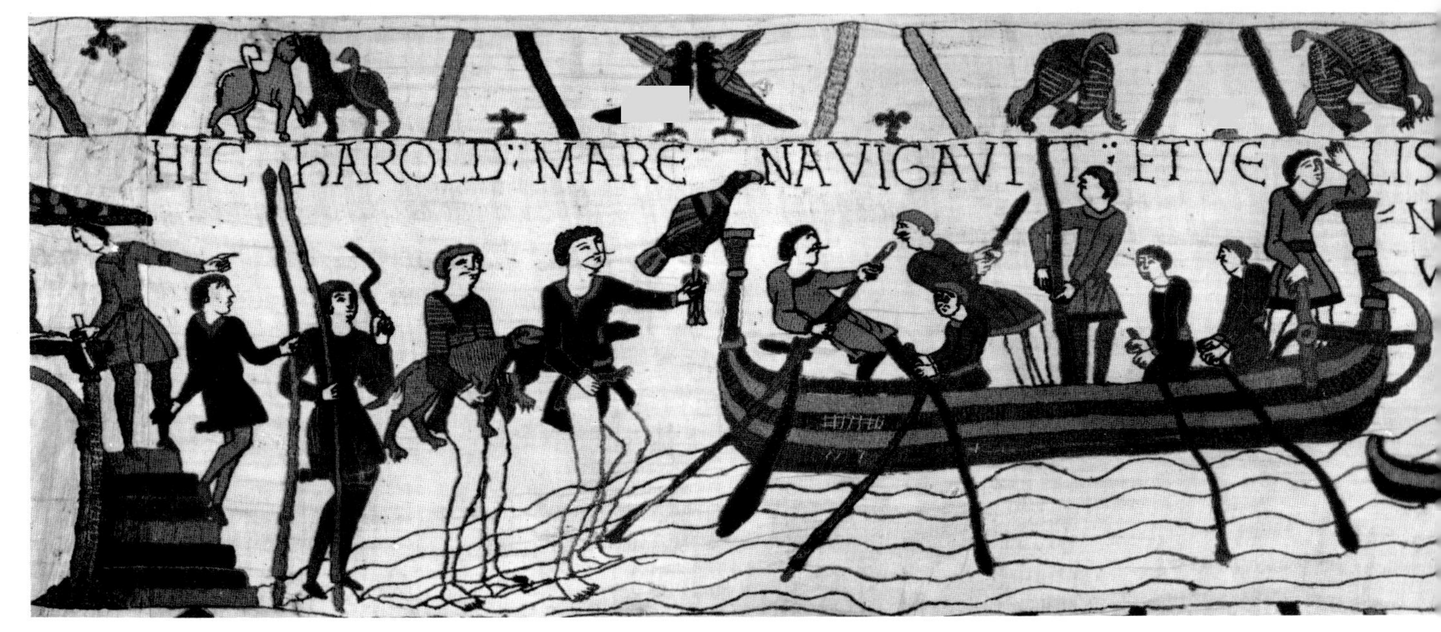
HIC HAROLD: MARE NAVIGAVIT: ET VE LIS

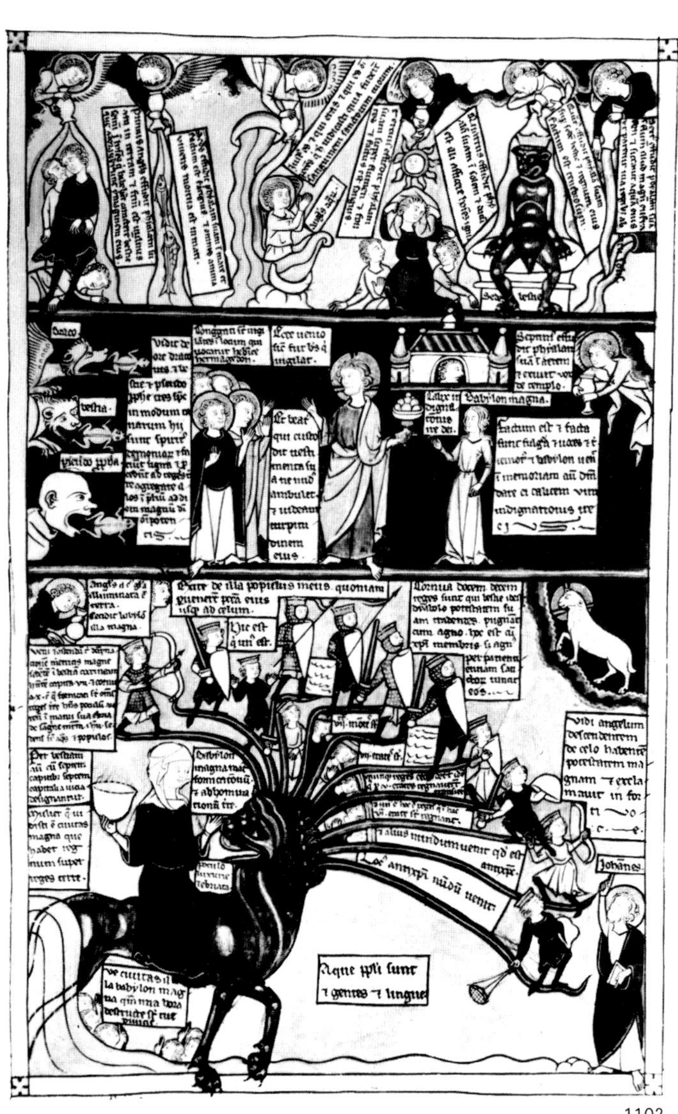

1102

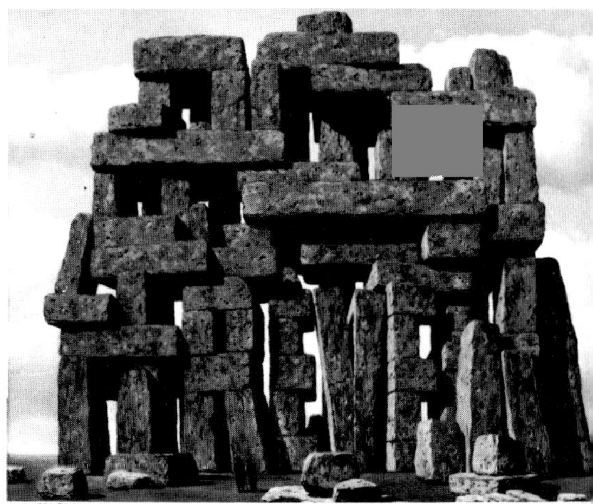

1

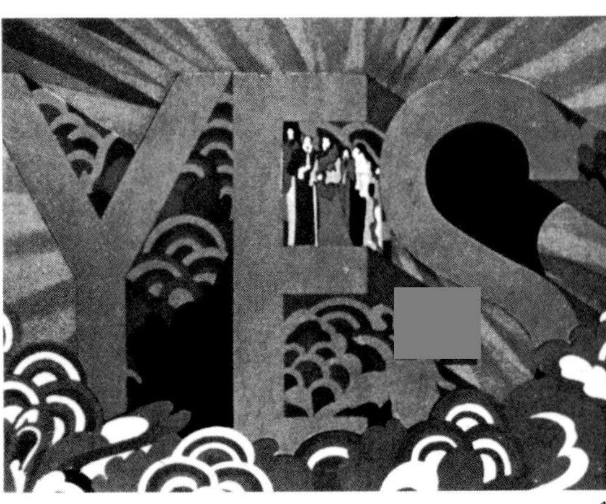
YES

1

1100

1101

'literal' form of illustration, even when it occurs on the pretext of remaining faithful to the text, implies even in the most successful cases a straight-forward tautology. For these reasons, successes are extremely rare in the field of illustration. (We would be hard put to it to find more than a few examples in each century; Bonnard's illustrations to Verlaine's *Parallèlement* are one of these rare exceptions, uniting as they do two like-minded sensitive temperaments.) What is known as 'bibliophilism' is only really interesting in that it allows the original work of an artist to reach a wider public, but the attraction which results from this usually works to the detriment of the written word (hence the common expression *livres de peintres*). On the other hand, it is true that the text has often been published beforehand and has therefore won a reputation of its own – which may be why it was selected for such treatment in the first place.

Although it rarely happens, a case where the author illustrates his own work ought to represent the ideal solution; but this would also mean that the author must not be put off at the outset by the need to acquire the requisite skills, knowledge of techniques, etc. and must be able to express himself just as successfully on two different planes at once. Which means that to all intents and purposes that type of miracle rarely happens. Where Edward Lear and Victor Hugo are successful, Grandville goes astray.

It is true that some ventures in this field cannot be classified into any of the traditional categories. Think of Marcel Duchamp's *The bride laid bare by her bachelors, even,* which is made up of ninety-four different items (notes, sketches, rough versions, plans, etc.) all put together in a box: surely this is tied up with Mallarmé's attempt to produce 'The Book'? Doesn't poetry sometimes look like a painted composition? When Steinberg rewrites the façade of the Opéra in Paris or takes the art of drawing an ellipse to extremes, isn't he nullifying the efforts demanded by the ritual forms of speech?

Nowadays the strip cartoon, that modern version of the old-style story-without-words, has won a vast audience. This narrative form, which makes reading more immediate, could never become a universal language. And yet it does manage to reconcile graphic representation with speech, though admittedly the image comes out of it best.

Besides, there is no real difference between a narrative
1100 account of William the Conqueror's exploits in his attempt to
1105 conquer England and the tale of Jodelle's adventures or the
1104 film called *The Yellow Submarine*, which tells the epic story of the Beatles. In these cases, the letter is not a shameful accessory, which will only be resorted to in desperation when the image turns out to be incapable of transcribing a phrase in its
1101 entirety; instead, as we can see in Matisse's *Jazz*, it is a rhythmic element which precedes, introduces or accompanies the image, supplying information about its potential meanings and guaranteeing its continuity. It is also a plastic element which sometimes assumes a monumental aspect.

This means that the same story could be told twice with a gap of a thousand years between the two versions, if it were not for two essential features which throw external appearances into confusion: style and writing. But that is another story and will be dealt with in a later study.

11

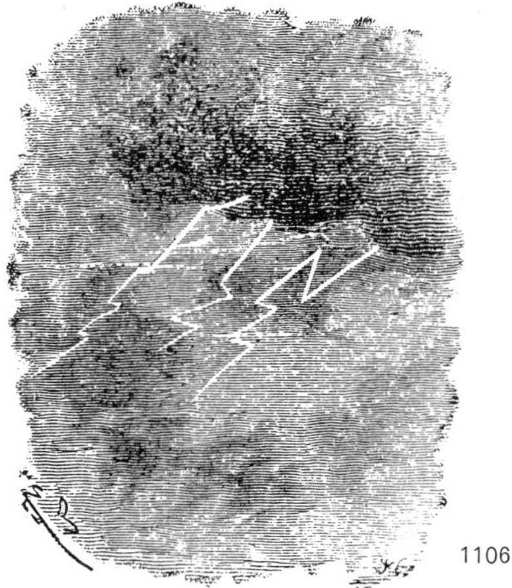

1106

Captions to illustrations

1 Chinese writing. From a manuscript by Tsen Yen-Tung.

2 Design by Jerome Snyder. From *Fact* review, New York, 1965.

3 Times Square, New York. Photograph by Massin.

4 Broadway, New York. Photograph by Massin.

5 Paris, Photograph by Massin.

6 A Paris Morriss pillar. Photograph by A. Ackerman.

7 Advertising on a curtain (?), *c.*1900. From the author's collection.

8 Placards at the edge of the Alaska Highway in the Yukon (Canada). The workmen of different nationalities who worked on this new road left these behind, and they have been kept because of their originality. Photograph by Yves-Guy Bergès.

9 A poster by Villemot for Bally shoes.

10 Hong Kong. Photograph by Henry Steiner.

11 A design by Folon for *Agenda Olivetti* 1969.

12 Paris. Photograph by Harold Chapman.

13 Las Vegas. Photograph by Thomas Höpker.

14 Classified advertisements from the *Boston Globe*, 1967.

15 A 'no entry' sign. Photograph by Massin.

15a General view of typographic wall in the restaurant of the CBS building, New York. Photograph Keith Murgatroyd.

16 A design by Folon for a survey of structuralist grammar. In *Le Monde*, 1968.

17 A photographic illustration from a folder showing letters 'specially designed for large buildings, publicity on roofs, shops and factories, etc. They can be seen a mile away'. All rights reserved.

18 A double-page advertisement by Giusti, for Fiat cars. In *Life*, 1968.

19 A plate from *Praxis Perspectivae*, by Lucas Brunn. Nuremberg-Leipzig, 1615.

20 An illustration showing an exhibition at the Louvre, from Grandville's *Un autre monde* Paris, 1844.

21 Two plates from *Praxis Perspectivae* (*op. cit.* 19).

22 An advertisement for Pakistan International Airlines. All rights reserved.

23 An extract from *Rébus charivariques*, Paris, *c.*1840.

24 The day before the opening of the Paris Fair. Photograph by permission of *Jours de France*.

25 A Nazi parade at night. © Benoist-Méchin.

26 The name letters for the steamship *France*, before completion. Photograph by Ervino Puchar (1960).

27 The poster for the film *Casino Royal*.

28 An invitation to the Max Ernst exhibition in 1930 © S.P.A.D.E.M.

29 Paris in May 1968. All rights reserved.

30 Tokyo. Photograph by Nicolas Bouvier.

31 Paris. Photograph by Massin.

32 New York. Photograph by Massin.

33 Newspaper vendor announcing the outbreak of war, in Great Britain in 1939. Copyright Radio Times Hulton Picture Library.

34 From *Rébus charivariques* (*op. cit.* 23).

35 From Geoffroy Tory's *Champ Fleury, In which can be found the art and science of the true proportions of Attic letters, which are otherwise called Antique letters, or vulgarly Roman letters - proportioned in accordance with the human body and face.* Paris, 1529.

36-40 Stills from the James Bond film *From Russia with Love*. These letters projected on to a dancer's body were designed by Robert Brownjohn.

41 A design by Jerome Snyder, from *Fact* review.

42 Graffito on a Paris wall. Photograph by Massin.

43 From Tory's *Champ Fleury* (*op. cit.* 35).

44 Design by Jerome Snyder, from *Fact* review.

45-63 From *Champ Fleury* (*op. cit.* 35).

64 A manuscript of the French *Corbie* School, showing the first page of Saint-Ambroise's *Hexaemeron*. Illumina-

tion on parchment, second half of the eighth century. *Bibliothèque Nationale,* Paris.

65-66 A prayer-book from the north-east of France. Middle of the eighth century. In the *Biblioteca Apostolica Vaticana.*

67 The initial B from Saint Gregory's *Commentary on Job.* End of the seventh century. In the *Bibliothèque Nationale,* Paris.

68-70 The initials H, A and D from a Gallican lectionary. Luxeuil, seventh or eighth century A.D.

71-73 Initials P, Q and D from Saint Gregory's *Commentary on Job* (*op.cit.* 67).

74 Initial R from Eugyppius, *Excerpta ex operibus sancti Augustini.* Eighth century. In the *Bibliothèque Nationale,* Paris.

75 Initial E from Saint Augustine's *Quaestiones in Hepateuchon.* From the north of France; middle of the eighth century. In the *Bibliothèque Nationale,* Paris.

76-77 Initial P from a collection of treatises on grammar, including those by Servius and Asper. Ninth century. In the *Bibliothèque Nationale,* Paris.

78-79 Initials N and A, then QU and DI, from the *Book of Kells.* End of the eighth century. In Trinity College Library, Dublin.

80-107 The Gellone prayer-book. Between 755 and 787 A.D. Initials A, A, A, D, D, D, D, E, E, E, E, I, I, K, K, K, K, L, O, O, D, P, P, P, T, T, T, (crucifixion). In the *Bibliothèque Nationale,* Paris.

108-123 Initials D, A, A, T, N, N, I, D, P, V, P, Q, M, N and A, from the *Corbie* Psalter. Beginning of the ninth century. In the *Bibliothèque Municipale,* Amiens.

124 The initial I from *The Gospel According to St. John,* in the Gospel-book of the Church of Metz. In the *Bibliothèque Nationale,* Paris. Tenth century.

125 The initial I from *The Gospel According to St. Mark, ibid.*

126 The initial Q from *The Gospel According to St. Luke, ibid.*

127 The initial L from *The Gospel According to St. Matthew, ibid.*

128 Initial E from *The Wedding of Mercury and Philology* by Martiamus Capella. Fleury (?) Tenth century. In the *Bibliothèque Nationale,* Paris.

129 Initial R, *ibid.*

130 Initial B from the lectionary of Saint Martial, Limoges. End of the tenth century. In the *Bibliothèque Nationale,* Paris.

131 Initial B from the *Tropaire-prosier* of Saint Martial, Limoges. First part of the eleventh century. In the *Bibliothèque Nationale,* Paris.

132 Initial F, *ibid.*

133 Initial M, *ibid.*

134 Initial I. Saint Martial, Limoges. Eleventh century. In the *Bibliothèque Nationale,* Paris.

135 Initial V from the beginning of an eleventh-century Bible. Moissac (?) School. In the *Bibliothèque Nationale,* Paris.

136 Initial P. Saint Martial, Limoges. Eleventh century. In the *Bibliothèque Nationale,* Paris.

137 Initial H from Saint Gregory's *Moralia in Job.* Cîteaux, beginning of the twelfth century. In the *Bibliothèque municipale,* Dijon.

138 Initial I, *ibid.*

139 Initial P, *ibid.*

140 Initial Q, *ibid.*

141 Initial S, *ibid.*

142 Initial A with 'caprichos' from *Antiquités judaïques* by Josephus. Canterbury; first part of the twelfth century. In the University Library, Cambridge.

143 Initial U from the *Book of Job.* Winchester(?); middle of the twelfth century. In the Bodleian Library, Oxford.

144 Initial S. Stephanus Laugton, Eadmerus Cantuariensis, S. Anselmus Cantuariensis. Seventh to eighth century. In the *Bibliothèque Nationale,* Paris.

145 Initial T. *ibid.*

146 Initial D, from a Bible. End of the twelfth, or thirteenth century. In the *Bibliothèque Nationale,* Paris.

147 Initial M, *ibid.*

148-152 Gothic alphabet, called the 'Bergamo' Alphabet, by Giovannino de' Grassi. *c.*1390. In the *Biblioteca Civica,* Bergamo. Photography by Wells.

153 The Berlin Alphabet,*c.*1400. In the *Kupferstich-Kabinett,* Berlin. The original was destroyed during the last war.

154-157 The Romanesque alphabet called the 'Basle' Alphabet. 1464. Origin: the Netherlands (?). The original wood-engraving – now in Basle – inspired the copper-plate engraving by the Master of the Banderoles (Germany, 1478).

158-160 Gothic alphabet by the Master E.S. Southern Germany, 1499. Engravings on copper.

161 Charles d'Angoulême's *Paris Book of Hours.* End of the fifteenth century. In the *Bibliothèque Nationale,* Paris.

162-163 Alphabet by Noël Garnier. *c.*1540-1545. From left to right and from top to bottom: B, C, D, E, F, G, H, I, K, L, M, N, O, P, R, S, T, U, X, Y, Z. In the *Bibliothèque Nationale,* Paris.

164-165 Another Alphabet by Noël Garnier. *c.*1540-1545. From left to right and from top to bottom: A, B, C, D, E, F, G, H, I, K, Z, (I, according to Robert Dumesnil and André Linzeler) M, N, O, P, Q, R, S, T, U, Y, (or X ?) Z, D and Y. In the *Bibliothèque Nationale,* Paris.

166-172 Initials from the *Buch der Weisheit.* Urach, 1482.

173 Architectonic alphabet, by an unknown author. Second half of the fifteenth century (?) Reproduced in Jaro Springer's *Alphabets gothiques,* 1897.

174-183 Letters from an alphabet by Paulini. Italy, *c.*1570. In the *Bibliothèque Nationale,* Paris.

184 Letter from an alphabet by Paulini. In the author's collection.

185 *Ibid.* In the Metropolitan Museum of Art, New York.

186 *Ibid.* In the *Bibliothèque Nationale,* Paris.

187 Alphabet by Abraham de Balmes, in *Grammatica hebraea* (Venice, Bomberg, 1523). Reproduced by Geoffroy Tory in his *Champ fleury* in 1529. *op.cit.*35.

188-189 Alphabet by Jacobus Publicius, in *Artes orandi, epistolandi, memorandi.* Venice, 1482.

190-199 Mnemotechnic alphabets by Cosmas Rossellius, in *Thesaurus artificiosae memoriae.* Venice 1579.

200-202 Mnemotechnic alphabets by Trithemius, in *The Magazine of Sciences or the True Art of Memory discovered by Schenkelius.* Paris, 1623.

203 An alphabet and numbers by Robert Fludd, in *Utriusque cosmi Historia* (Oppenheim, 1619).

204 Hieroglyphic alphabet by C. V. Noorde. Netherlands, 1751.

205-206 Giuseppe Maria Mitelli's *Alphabeto in sogno exemplare per disegnare.* Bologna, 1683. In the New York Public Library.

207 New-year card by an unknown artist. *c.*1960.

208 'Human Alphabet' by Peter Flötner, engraved on wood. Germany, *c.*1534.

209 *The A-Z line,* by D. L. May – in *Punch* (23 March 1955).

210 An alphabet by Richard Daniel, in *Copy-book: or a Compendium of the most usual hands.* London, 1663. This was one of the many copies of Peter Flötner's 'Human Alphabet'.

211 Another copy of Flötner's 'Human Alphabet'. This one, by Martin Weygel was engraved at Augsburg about 1560. In the *Hofbibliothek,* Munich.

212 An alphabet designed by Joseph Balthazard Silvestre. dated October 1834. It was engraved by Girault, and reproduced in *The Alphabet Album, a Collection of Sixty Pages of Historiated and Decorated Alphabets from the Principal Libraries of Europe, or designed by Sylvestre, Teacher of Calligraphy to Princes.* A contemporary of Jean Midolle from Strasbourg, Sylvestre probably knew the many copies of the 'Human Alphabet' which were available in German-speaking countries. But his alphabet is very personal in conception and design. The original has seventy plates, designed in pen and ink, some of them richly illuminated. (In a private collection.)

213 *An Alphabet of People,* in *A new Collection of Letters of the Various Kinds of Letters Used by Painters and Engravers,* by A. Caulo. Paris, 1856.

214-215 An alphabet designed by Daumier. Paris, 1836. An announcement in the copies of the *Charivari* for 1837 praises the 'illustrated alphabets (comic, grotesque etc.) by Bernard, Bouchot, Bourdet, Challamel, Daumier, Forest, Lassalle and Traviès'.

216 *A Chimpanzee Alphabet for the Amusement of Children.* Paris, 1825. 'We hope to please our young readers with a complete collection of all the monkeys in the Menagerie of the *Jardin des Plantes',* writes the author, who, finding himself unable to supply primates for the letters F and K, presented a Finn and an inhabitant of Kamtchatka instead.

217 *An alphabet of people,* published in Germany in the first half of the nineteenth century, n.d. Columbia University, New York.

218 A lithograph figured alphabet, 1836. The letters are arranged as in the original.

219 A lithograph figured alphabet, 1836. As in the preceding plate, the arrangement of the letters is as in the original. Perhaps a game or cut-out alphabet was intended.

220 *Grotesque Alphabet.* This title appears on the preceding plate, but it is however not certain that it applies to this particular alphabet.

221 Lithograph alphabet designed by Bourdet. Paris, 1836.

222 Chromolithographic alphabet. France (Vosges), 1891. In the *Bibliothèque Nationale,* Paris.

223 A devil alphabet. Lithograph. Paris, 1836. With a few variations (the letters A, I, J, L, M, N, S, U), this alphabet resembles one published the preceding year. There are also other copies, notably that of Marquet (Metz, 1837).

224 *Alphabet of Devilry* by A. Caulo, *op.cit.* 213. The theme is still popular, twenty years after the preceding example.

225 *Devil Alphabet* by Jean Midolle, in *Works by Jean Midolle engraved on stone and published at the lithographic press of Emile Simon the younger,* Strasburg, 1834. The originality of this work lies in the gothic writing. Its creator shows a skill and sense of fantasy reminiscent of the Master E.S.

226 *Animal Alphabet* from Silvestre, *op.cit.* 212. From the original manuscript. This alphabet inspired that of Giuseppe Palermo in *Grande Album di Calligraphia . . .,* Naples, 1852.

227 Alphabet of people, in *A Collection of Alphabets dedicated to Artists, by Jules Blondeau and Mès (?), published and edited by Veuve Turgis.* Paris, *c.*1840.

228 Animal alphabet, *ibid.*

229 Silhouette alphabet, *ibid.*

230 An animal alphabet from A. Caulo. *op.cit.* 213.

231 An alphabet of vegetables *op.cit.* 217.

232 *Thistle Alphabet* ('en forme de chardons'). *op.cit.* 217.

233 An alphabet by Vespasiono Amphiareo (Venice, 1565) reproduced by George Henri Paritio.

234 Another alphabet by Vespasiono Amphiareo. Silvestre reproduced it exactly, three hundred years later.

235 *Woodland* by Jean Midolle, *op.cit.* 225. There are several versions of this alphabet (which has also been fairly widely reproduced during the last twenty years), originally deriving perhaps from a classical and Germanic model. Silvestre reproduced it also, without modifications, in his collection.

236 An alphabet by A. Caulo, *op.cit.* 213.

237 Alphabet by Boussenot. Paris, 1836.

238-239 Architectonic alphabet, by Johann David Steingruber. Schwabach, 1773.

240-241 *Picture alphabet created by Professor Antonio Basoli, published with historical and artistic notes by G. C. Lossada.* Lithographs; Bologna, *c.*1850. Harvard College Library, Dept of Printing and Graphic Arts.

242 Architectonic alphabet by A. Caulo. *op.cit.* 213.

243-244 *Gothic Composition* from Jean Midolle, *op.cit.* 225.

245 *Inventive ways of showing Arithmetical Figures with Comic Positions.* Italian print. Beginning of the nineteenth century. In the author's collection.

246 Animated figures. Coloured copperplate-engraving. France, 1834.

247-249 Pages from *The wacky world of Numburrs*, by Sheldon Wasserman. The Citadel Press, New York. 1965.

250 Child's drawing.

251 Greetings card by the graphic artist Alfred Mattauch, 1966.

252 Magic alphabet, 1861. In the *Bibliothèque Nationale*, Paris. A piece of card makes the letters appear, changing A into B, C into D, and so on.

253 *Useful puppets or the origin of letters. An alphabet dedicated to the inimitable Jacko the Chimpanzee and to all Young Children who want to learn to read quickly*. 1826. In the *Bibliothèque Nationale*, Paris.

254 *New Alphabet*. Paris, 1838.

255 *Comic Alphabet*. Coloured lithograph. *c.*1850. In the author's collection.

256-257 Children's drawings.

258 Drawing by Steinberg, from *The Labyrinth*. © Saul Steinberg.

259 *Alphabet of Metamorphoses*. Lithograph. Paris, *c.*1850.

260 Coloured lithograph *Grotesque Alphabet*, Paris, *c.*1850. In the collection of the author.

261 *The Orient Express ABC*. Paris, *c.*1890. In the author's collection.

262 Illustration by Folon for a study on modern linguistics and French grammar, in *Le Monde*, Paris, February, 1968.

263 Building blocks with sculpted and coloured letters. In the author's collection.

264 Signed manuscript by Arthur Rimbaud *(Voyelles)*.

265 Soup with letters. Moli, *pâtes alimentaires supérieures*. Thonon, France.

266-269 *Amusing Grammar Lesson*, in *Almanach des Enfants pour* 1886, Paris. In the author's collection.

270-294 *Trim ABC. Magic Alphabet*, by Bertall. Hachette, Paris, 1861. *No more children reciting their letters incorrectly! In an hour they will know the alphabet and a hundred verses!* – note on the title-page.

295 Letter A in *Wonderful Stories – Tales from every land collected and arranged by P. Christian*. Paris, 1844.

296 Letter A from *The Amorous Devil, a fantasy novel by J. Cazotte*. Engraved on wood by Edouard de Beaumont. Paris, 1845.

297 Letter A from *Wonderful Stories op.cit.* 295.

298 Letter A from *Alphabetic Charades* by Victor Adam. *c.*1835-1840.

299 Letter A from *A New Alphabet in Riddles*, by Victor Adam, 1833.

300 Letter A from *The Book of Snobs* by William Thackeray. Extracts were published in *Punch* from 1846-1847, and were published in book form in 1848.

301 Letter A from an alphabet reproduced in *An Abridged specimen of Printing Types made at Bruce's Son and Co.* 1869.

302 Letter B from *A New Alphabet in Riddles, op.cit.* 299.

303 Letter B from *The Amorous Devil. op.cit.* 296.

304 Letter B from *An Abridged Specimen op.cit.* 301.

305 Letter B from *Wonderful Stories, op.cit.* 295.

306 A letter B from an alphabet reproduced in *An Abridged Specimen . . . op.cit.* 301.

307 Letter C, from *Wonderful Stories, op.cit.* 295.

308 Letter C from *A New Alphabet in Riddles, op.cit.* 299.

309-310 Letter Cs from *An Abridged Specimen . . . op.cit.* 301.

311 Letter D from *Wonderful Stories, op.cit.* 295.

312 Letter D from *A New Alphabet in Riddles, op.cit.* 299.

313-314 Letters D and E from *An Abridged Specimen . . .op.cit.* 301.

315 Letter E, from *Wonderful Stories, op.cit.* 295.

316 Letter F, from *An Abridged Specimen . . . op.cit.* 301.

317 Letter F, from Thackeray's *Miscellaneous Sketches from Punch*.

318 Letter F from *Wonderful Stories, op.cit.* 295.

319 Letter F from *A New Alphabet in Riddles, op.cit.* 299.

320 Letter F from *Wonderful Stories, op.cit.* 295.

321-322 Letters G and H, from *An Abridged Specimen, op.cit.* 301.

323 Letter I from *The Amorous Devil. op.cit.* 296.

324-325 Letter J from Thackeray's *Miscellaneous Sketches from Punch. op.cit.* 317.

326 Letter K from *A New Alphabet in Riddles, op.cit.* 299.

327 Letter K from *An Alphabet of Arts and Trades*. Moulins, 1832.

328-330 Letter Ls from *The Amorous Devil, op.cit.* 296.

331 Letter M from Balzac's *Petites Misères de la vie conjugale*. Wood-engraving by Bertall. Chlendowski, Paris, 1845.

332 Letter M from *A New Alphabet in Riddles, op.cit.* 299.

333-335 Letter N from *The Amorous Devil, op.cit.* 296.

336 Letter O from a rébus. *c.* 1840.

337 Letter O from *Petites Misères de la vie conjugale, op.cit.* 331.

338 Letter P from *Wonderful Stories, op.cit.* 295.

339 Letter P from *A New Alphabet in Riddles, op.cit.* 299.

340 Letter P, from *Animated Letters, An Alphabet with recreational exercises. A new work dedicated to children*, by Houx-Marc. Paris, s.d. (*c.* 1840).

341 Letter Q from *The French – Painted by Themselves*. *c.*1840.

342 Letter R from *Wonderful Stories, op.cit.* 295.

343-344 Letter Ss from *The Amorous Devil, op.cit.* 296.

345 Letter S, from *A New Alphabet in Riddles, op.cit.* 299.

346 Letter S from *Wonderful Stories, op. cit.* 295.

347 Letter S from *The Book of Snobs, op.cit.* 300.

348 Letter T, *ibid.*

349 Letter U, from *The Amorous Devil, op.cit.* 296.

350 Letter U from *Vere Foster's Copy Book,* n. 10; n.d. (*c.* 1840-1850).

351 *The Letter Hunt, a scene from Ancient French History.* Lithograph, *c.*1836.

352 Letter U from *Alphabetical Charades. op.cit.* 298.

353 Letter V from *Wonderful Stories, op.cit.* 295.

354 Letter V from *Petites Misères de la vie conjugale, op.cit.* 331.

355 Scottish advertisement, 1865. In the collection of the author.

356 A popular song. Lithograph, *c.*1850. In the collection of the author.

357-358 Letters W and X, in *A New Alphabet in Riddles, op.cit.* 299.

359 Letter X, from *Alphabetical Charades, op.cit.* 298.

360 Letter X from *Vere Foster's Copy Book, op.cit.* 350.

361-362 Letter Xs from *Alphabetical Charades, op.cit.* 298.

363 Letter X from *Animated Letters, op.cit.* 340.

364 Letter X from *Alphabetical Charades, op.cit.* 298.

365 Wood-engraving by Castelli for *A Good Little Devil,* by the Comtesse de Ségur. *Bibliothèque rose Illustrée,* Hachette, Paris, 1865.

366 The titles of popular leaflets showing an alphabet called 'Devilries', N. Gallay and Guignon. 1842.

367 *The Hunt,* a satirical print on the freedom of the press. In *La Caricature,* Paris, 1832.

368 *Théâtres des Pupazzi,* by Lemercier de Neuville. Lyons, 1876. In the author's collection.

369 Chinese puzzle, or game. *c.*1900. In the author's collection.

370 Letters X and Y from the *Alphabet of Trades, op.cit.* 327.

371 Letter Y from *An Abridged Specimen op.cit.* 301.

372 Letter Y from *Alphabetical Charades, op.cit.* 298.

373 Letter Y, from *A New Alphabet in Riddles, op.cit.* 299.

374-375 Letter Y, from Thackeray's *Miscellaneous Sketches from Punch, op.cit.* 317.

376-377 Letter Ys, by Victor Adam, *c.*1836.

378 Letter Z, from *A New Alphabet in Riddles, op.cit.* 299.

379-381 Letter Zs from *Alphabetical Charades, op.cit.* 298.

382 Letter Z from *An Alphabet of Trades, op.cit.* 327.

383-390 Letters C, D, E, F, G, H, I and J. Wood-engravings by Théophile Schuler. France, 1865.

391 Pen drawing by Franz Christophe for an (unpublished) edition of the works of Baron Münchhausen. Graphic Arts Collection; University Library, Princeton.

392-395 A puzzle – coloured lithographs on pieces of wood. Second Empire(?). In the author's collection.

396-432 Animated letters from rebuses, mostly taken from *Rébus charivariques,* (*op.cit.* 23) *c.*1840 and from the *Petit Journal pour Rire,* Paris, 1856.

433 An English chromolithograph (printed in Germany). End of the nineteenth century (?). In the author's collection.

434 'A, B, C' by C.S. Calverley. From *A Whimsey Anthology,* edited by Carolyn Wells. Dover Publications, New York, 1963.

435 One of the alphabets written and illustrated by Edward Lear.

436 A fragment of a 'nonsensical' alphabet, by an anonymous wood-engraver. Beginning of the nineteenth century. In the Lehmann-Haupt collection.

437 'The Alphabetical Constitution of Young America'. Second half of the nineteenth century.

438 *The Sunday Fisherman* by A. W. Bellaw, from *A Whimsey Anthology, op.cit.* 434.

439 The title-page of *A New Alphabet in Riddles,* by Victor Adam, *op.cit.* 299.

440 From *The Works of Jean Midolle, op.cit.* 225.

441 *A Comic Alphabet,* designed, engraved and published by George Cruikshank. Pentonville, 1936. Harvard College Library Dept. of Printing and Graphic Arts.

442 An illustration by Stanley Mack for *The ABC of Bumptious Beasts,* a book of verse by Gail Kredenser. Harlin Quist, 1966.

443 *M is for mountain,* in *A is for anything, an ABC book of pictures and rhymes,* by Katharina Barry. Rupert Hart-Davis Ltd, London, 1961.

444 An alphabet designed by Alice Horodisch-Garman, reproduced in a folder of the 'Voor het Kind' society ('for children'), Amsterdam, Christmas 1957. In the collection of H. Lehmann-Haupt. By permission of the Nederland and Stichting Comité voor Kinderpostzegels. Stichting 'Voor het Kind'.

445 Animated letters. Watercolour. From the Primary School, rue Delambre, Paris.

446-450 *ABC.* Frederick Warne and Co, London and New York, *c.*1880. Colour lithography on linen. Cover and various pages. In the author's collection.

451-454 *Once Upon a Time* – text by Marcelle Marquet, illustrations by Suza Desnoyer. Lithograph by B. Grosser, s.l.n.d. (*c.*1957). There is a striking similarity in conception and theme between this and the previous example, in spite of the fact that several generations of teachers, pupils and methods separate one from the other.

455 A Steinberg drawing in *The New World,* 1960.

456 A design by Nadar in *Petit Journal pour rire,* Paris, 1856.

457 The back of the jacket of the *ABC* shown previously. *op.cit.* 445-450.

458 'A fantasy alphabet' in *Madamoiselle Lili's Alphabet Book* by L. Froelich and 'a father', Hetzel, Paris. *c.*1875. In the author's collection.

459 Two initials drawn by Renoir in 1879. Reproduced in *Renoir Drawings* by John Rewald. Bittner, New York, 1946.

460-464 Drawings by Pierre Bonnard for *Père Ubu's illustrated almanac,* by Alfred Jarry. Dated 1st January 1901.

465 *Peace, the Hope of Europe.* An anonymous caricature published in Frankfurt. End of the eighteenth, beginning of the nineteenth century.

466 *Danse macabre.* Title-page of *The Great Danse*

Macabre of Men and Women. Baillieu, Paris, *c*.1865. The text and wood-engravings from the *Danse Macabre de Troyes* (1486) are reproduced in this book.

467 The title-page of *Popular Songs*, by Norman McLaren, Jim Mackay, Laurence Hyde, George Dunning, Jean P. Ladouceur and Maurice Montgrain n.d.

468 *Merry Christmas*. A greetings card by the New York architect Greville Rickard, 1950.

469 *Cuisine*. Press advertisement. *c*.1840.

470 *Live a pious and good life*. A popular German print (second half of the nineteenth century) shown by Armin Haab and Walter Haettenschweiler in *Lettera II* 1961.

471 'Nancy'. A postcard from *The Golden Age of Postcards* by Ado Kyrou. André Balland, Paris, 1968.

472 *Roberts Piere ist nuntod schenck den frieden uns O Gott dieses winscht die gantze welt weil die handlung eingestelt*. (Robespierre is now dead, send us peace O God, the whole world desires it because trade has come to a standstill.) A satirical print of German origin. July 1794. In the *Bibliothèque Nationale*, Paris.

473 *To Smokers*. (Notice to Smokers and Chewers). A fragment of a lithograph by Currier and Ives, New York, after 1854. From a reproduction in the Arrents Tobacco collection, New York Public Library.

474 April 1st. Postcard from *The Golden Age of Postcards, op.cit.* 471.

475 *1915*. A postcard from a private collection.

476 *Thank you*. ('Thank you – Ballet Ruse'). A greetings card with a pun on 'ballet russe', issued by Ten Bamboo Studio, New York. By an unknown designer.

477 A detail of the title-page of *L'écho de la mode*, a Paris weekly magazine. Whereas most designers who work with French texts find accented letters an embarrassment, and usually use only slight horizontal or vertical lines, the designer of this headline has put the accent on a coiffure, showing an é well dressed.

478 A detail from an Italian poster for Kappa socks. 1968.

479 *Happy birthday*. Part of a folder issued by Inkweed Arts, New York. Unknown designer.

480 Press advertisement designed by Alain Duperron for the Alain Brieux Bookshop, Paris. *c*.1965.

481 A detail from publicity for the film *Birds die in Peru* directed by Romain Gary. Frankfurt, 1968.

482 *Génie*. Press advertisement for a detergent.

483 *Peace*. Spanish greetings card, 1963.

484 Sign for oyster-bar of the Paris restaurant, *La Coupole*.

485 *La Palette*. A Paris restaurant sign.

486 Wall reinforcement letter used by builders in the French countryside. Besides S, one sometimes sees an H, I, N, T, V, X, Y or Z. It is worth noting here also, the number of shutters, doors and barriers which may be reinforced with a letter Z.

487 Two-headed skeleton or letter Y?

488 Letter N or plate from a book on grasses?

489 Silhouette X. French corset advertisement.

490 The Bonhomme à Laigle buildings in France. Did the round windows precede the inscription, or did this determine the architect's design? Photography by Massin.

491 One of the countless street signs in Boston (Massachusets), in 1967. Photograph by Massin.

492 In 1945, Norwegian patriots wrote 'Long Live the King' with their bodies, against the snow. All rights reserved.

493 Japanese pavilion at Montreal in 1967. Photograph by Massin.

494 The front of *Le Monocle* cabaret club in France. Photograph by Massin.

495 A poster by Robert Brownjohn for the film *Obsession and Fantasy*.

496 Publicity by Calberson Transport, printed on stamp-book covers.

497 *La Voie Buccale*. The monthly journal of the students at the *École Dentaire*. Rennes, 1961. In the collection of R. J. Ségalat.

498 A press advertisement for a gunsmith's. France, 1966.

499 Title for a column in the French magazine *Elle*.

500 Press advertisement. Boston, 1967.

501 Headline in *France-soir* (December 1962).

502 Advertisement for Miko ices.

503 A headline in *France-soir* (July, 1964).

504 A press advertisement. United States, 1967.

505 An advertisement by André François for Pirelli tyres.

506 A poster advertising *Time* magazine. 1967.

507 A press advertisement for an estate agency. France.

508 Headline in *Elle* magazine.

509 French press advertisement. 1969.

510 A label designed by Pierre Gauchat for the Denzler ropeworks at Zurich.

511 Press advertisement for car oil. 1968.

512 A French press advertisement, 1966.

513 A press advertisement for a Paris restaurant, 1968.

514 Advertisement for Cypris shoes, Paris.

515 Headline from *Elle* magazine.

516 Press advertisement for the film *Crossing the Rhine*, *c*.1961.

517 A headline from *Elle* magazine.

518 A headline in the magazine (designed by Siné) edited by Jean-Jacques Pauvert in May and June 1968.

519 Extract from a folder showing camping equipment.

520 A headline in *Elle* magazine, by J. F. Clair, Studio Chevalier. *c*. 1960.

521 *Crédit Populaire de France* poster, 1968.

522 Press advertisement for a brand of mattress, 1968.

523 Display unit, *c*.1925-1930.

524 An advertisement for dairy products.

525 A detail from a travel agency brochure.

526 *Ibid.*

527 Paris-New York. A detail from an airline advertisement.

528 A detail from a press advertisement for a language tuition method (Language Studies France). 1968.

529 A label of a brand of wool.

530 A press advertisement for a film.

531 A detail from the press advertisement for the comedy *Fleur de cactus.* Paris, 1968.

532 An advertisement in *Elle* magazine.

533 A newspaper advertisement. *c.*1965.

534 A heading for a column in *Elle* magazine.

535 An advertisement by Gene Federico for *Woman's Day* magazine.

536 A cover design by Louis Dorfsman for a brochure on radio publicity.

537 A label for a French brand of women's underwear.

538 Magazine column heading.

539 Label on a brand of coffee.

540 Poster by Paul Colin for the *Loterie Nationale* in France, 1936.

541 Advertisement for a Paris magazine, 1967.

542 The sign of the Paris restaurant 'Jacob's Ladder'.

543 A headline in a popular magazine – *Charlie Chaplin's Greatest Films.* 1930.

544 Heading in a picture-strip magazine.

545 Press advertisement. Boston, 1967.

546 Press advertisement for a winter sports resort.

547 A press advertisement for a film.

548 A press advertisement for a lighter.

549 Press advertisement for Grayline.

550 A cover design by Herb Lubalin for a New York Life Insurance Co brochure.

551 The colophon of the *Nouvelle Revue Française* modified for an advertisement for a collection of adventure stories. 1936.

552 Jacket design by Pierre Faucheux for *The Anthology of Black Comedy,* by André Breton. Le Sagittaire. Paris, 1950.

553 Some chapter heads from *d'Exercises de style* by Raymond Queneau. Dummies by Massin. Gallimard, Paris, 1963.

554 Chapter titles of the English edition of *Exercises de style,* designed by Stefan Themerson. Gaberbocchus Press, London, 1960.

555 A fold-out page from *Exercises de style,* designed by Pierre Faucheux. *Club des Libraires de France,* 1956.

556 A double-page spread from *Cahiers du Collège de Pataphysique* portfolio 17 ('Exercise in potential literature'), 1961, showing chess problems, each one forming one of the letters of the word *pataphysique.*

According to François Le Lionnais, the elaboration of these figurative problems – which must conform to the rules of the game and must not contain any extra pieces – is a real tour de force.

557 A composition which is reproduced in *Surrealist Manifestoes* by André Breton. Le Sagittaire, Paris, 1955.

558-561 Letters G, P, Q and Y designed by Jacques Carelman for *L'Anthologie du Rire.* Editions Planète, Paris, 1955.

562 A press advertisement for a brand of tyres. *c.*1965.

563 A poster by Paul Colin for a theatre magazine. Spectators form the letters of the title *Bravo. c.* 1928.

564 An advertisement by Cassandre for a large Paris shop. *c.*1928.

565 A design by Jerome Snyder from *Fact* review, New York, 1965.

566 The jacket of Claude Lévi-Strauss's book *La Pensée Sauvage.* The illustration, which stresses the ambiguity of the title by showing the flower which bears this name in France (*pensée* or pansy), was chosen by the author.

567 A riddle: 'What is my name?' The answer is Max, formed by treetrunks, if the illustration is turned round. Designed by Epinal, at the beginning of the twentieth century.

568 *Mother and child.* A composition by Herb Lubalin and Allan Peckoclide for an American review.

569 The back of a Greek postcard. *c.*1960.

570 A part of a press advertisement for a brand of Scottish whisky.

571-573 The titles of maps showing the French *départements,* in the *Atlas Migeon,* Paris, 1871.

574-575 *Licht* (light) and *dunkel* (dark). Examples of expressive typography from the course by André Gürtler at the Kunstgewerbeschule in Basle.

576 'Gagalphabet', a game described in the French magazine *Formidable* in June 1967.

577 A detail of a stand in the pavilion of Industrial Design at the Montreal Exhibition, 1967.

578 One of the series of Pixies by the designer Jack Wom. From *The Boston Globe.* ©1967. United Features Syndicate, Inc.

579-580 Two pages from *Watching Words Move* by Brownjohn, Chermayeff and Geismar.

581 Title-page from Grandville's *Fleurs animées.* Paris, 1847.

582 The number 48, painted by Grandville on the pilaster of his country house at Chatou. From *l'Illustration.*

583 'The old high C's from the chest'. A design by Bertall in *Petit Journal pour rire* (1856).

584 From Grandville's *Un autre monde, op.cit.* 20.

585 Title-page of Grandville's *Métamorphoses du jour.* Paris, 1829.

586 The title-page of *Scènes de la vie privée et publique des animaux,* by Grandville. Paris, 1842.

587 *Waltz.* Four dancing-partners in full evening dress ask some ladies for a waltz . . . The various groups of people dash into the ballroom . . . One of the ladies falls over, to her partner's horror . . . The other couples dance past them, turning their heads to look . . . The lady and her clumsy partner start waltzing again . . . Ahead of them, a bench collapses beneath the weight of three people . . . A lady injures her knee slightly; her partner is most anxious on her behalf and hovers attentively round her . . . An enormous fly (sharp) has flown into the ballroom, attracted by the lights: one of the ladies tries to chase it away with her handkerchief, and almost faints; her partner attempts to reassure her, and then offers her a chair (natural) . . . The waltz gets livelier . . . Everybody sits down: one of the gentlemen wipes his forehead; one of the ladies is quite out of breath and leans on her elbow. *Le Magasin pittoresque.* 1840.

588 *Oriental march.* The march of the Turks and the Negroes . . . The Turks move forward slowly and solemnly, bearing standards or axes (crotchet-rests) . . . The Negroes go swiftly up and down the steps; the ones coming down are carrying large boxes or various musical instruments, while the ones going up are holding pikes or light spears . . . We can see a prisoner on his knees with an axe being raised above his head; another prisoner is being dragged along in chains . . . Booty or gifts (flats, sharps or naturals) are being carried on stretchers. *Ibid.*

589 *Religious music.* The choir-boys kneel, sing and wave their censers . . . The priest holds up the communion cup (pause mark) . . . More singing and prayer . . . The sacristan puts out the candles. *Ibid.*

590 *Barcarole.* Negro fishermen (crotchets) bid farewell to their wives and sisters; a woman entrusts her child to her husband . . . It is a fine day; the boats glide gently under huge arches (phrase marks) . . . But the weather changes: clouds begin to cover the sky, the sea becomes angry; the boats rise and sink with the waves; one man falls overboard . . . alas! . . . The anchors are useless . . . Then the storm seems to die down . . . A fisherman has saved the child; he blows a horn (pause mark) . . . But the wind begins to blow violently again . . . The fishermen raise their hands to heaven in despair . . . The storm grows angrier: a boat capsizes; six of the fishermen are engulfed; their lifeless bodies float past . . . Seagulls (crotchet-rests) skim over the surface of the sea . . . A few boats hurry back to port, using the lighthouse as their guide . . . The mother waits weeping on the shore; her child is handed to her. *Ibid.*

591 *Round, Tarantella.* Dance of the Negroes and the crotchets . . . Acrobats, funny faces, spirited dumb-show . . . The speed increases every time the refrain recurs . . . The sharps are represented by spiders or tarantulas. *Ibid.*

592 *Masked gallop.* A witch . . . Pierrette with a lantern (sharp) . . . Everyone rushes forward . . . Wild dancing . . . The masked figures collide, fall, and roll along helter-skelter head over heels. *Ibid.*

593 *Grand march.* This first piece is in E major: four sharps (quavers) in the clef (banner) . . . This is a spirited presto . . . The action begins with a short and lively fugue . . . An officer is hurrying his soldiers towards a bridge . . . There is a violent onslaught on the bridge . . . A clashing of swords; some sturdy defensive fighting; one of the warriors is stabbed through and through . . . The bridge is attacked a second time . . . The mighty commander harangues his soldiers (pause mark) . . . On hearing his words, his gallant men fling themselves on the enemy, who take to their heels in panic; some of them throw down their arms and appeal to heaven for help . . . One of the warriors is wounded in the heel, just like Achilles . . . The standard-bearer tries to prevent his fellow-soldiers from running away . . . Final efforts at recapturing the bridge. It is attacked with great ferocity and defended with equal ferocity . . . One of the leaders and his young son are killed and drowned in front of the fortress, which issues a constant stream of shells (pauses) . . . They have paid a high price for their victory. *Ibid.*

594 *Pastoral* in D major: two sharps (double crows) in the clef (boa constrictor) . . . Triple time . . . This scene takes place in an English colony . . . A coloured girl wants to leave her native hamlet to go into service in the town. *A minister tries to persuade her to abandon her plan* . . . It is a long journey: she will have to travel through a dangerous forest. What is she looking for so far away? happiness? she can find it just as easily in her village as in the town. She will get married; she will be a happy wife and mother. In an attempt to illustrate his point, the minister shows her *a young shepherd kissing the hand of his betrothed, a young shepherdess who is a Negress* . . . But the girl takes no notice of the minister's advice; one morning she starts out. In the forest, *fatigue and the cold encourage her to take a rest beneath a sycamore. Some runaway Negro slaves who have learnt that she is passing through the forest draw near with the idea of robbing her. She is rescued by an emancipated slave with a dog.* She returns to the hamlet, and, full of gratitude, *gives her hand to her rescuer for him to kiss; a Negress complains to the minister.* Fearing a reprimand, the girl goes away again. This time, *the runaway slaves steal her purse* (flat), which is all she has in the world, while she is asleep; then they rape her. *Her screams are heard by her father and mother,* who were out looking for her . . . her old father is furious (pause mark)! . . . and her old mother is stricken with grief as she follows behind, moving with difficulty and overcome with despair! They bring their daughter back to the village. The poor child no longer has a dowry. *The young men greet her with jeers and banter, and leave her alone. She bewails her sin with bitter tears. Even her girl-friends sing mocking songs to her. She goes to implore the minister to forgive her and to beg for God's grace.*

The French for 'crotchet' is *noire,* which means 'black' when used as an adjective; so the Negro or 'black' slaves naturally become crotchets, or *noirs-noires*! *(Translator's note.) Ibid.*

595 Animated music, by Gustave Doré, from *Histoire pittoresque, dramatique et caricaturale de la Sainte Russie.* J. Bry the elder, Paris, 1854.

596 *Scottish music,* by Peynet.

597 *Joco Seria* – a drawing by Grandville in *Petites misères de la vie humaine.* Paris, 1843.

598 Animals in ornamental foliage, by Wolfgang Hieronimus Van Bömmel, Nuremberg, 1660. Reproduced in *Vieux Papiers, Vieilles Images, Cartons d'un Collectionneur* by John Grand-Carteret, Paris 1896.

599 A composition by Arcimboldo.

600 An anti-Napoleon cartoon. April 1814. In the author's collection.

601 *Ballet apocalypse,* by Grandville, in *Un autre monde, op.cit.* 20.

602 Kiki of Montparnasse. Photograph by Man Ray.

603 *'Mascarades à la grecque'*, from *Le Magasin pittoresque,* 1840 From an anonymous cartoon of 1761.

604 Landscape with figures. A lithograph of the restoration period. Reproduced in *Vieux Papiers, Vieilles Images. op.cit.* 598.

605 *The Tower of the Day.* A popular print made at the time of the building of the Eiffel Tower. 1889. *Ibid.*

606 An apsarasa mounted on a camel made of figures of apsarasas, heavenly dancers and animals. From an Indian miniature. In *Le Magasin pittoresque,* 1838.

607 A coloured composition by Nadar for the *Petit journal pour rire* (1856).

608 Organ tiles at Oaxaca (Mexico). Beginning of the eighteenth century. Photograph by John Dominis.

609 Transformation card of the General Baron Athalin. Restoration period. From *Vieux Papiers, Vieilles Images, op. cit.* 598.

610 Transformation card. Second Empire. *Ibid.*

611 *Numbskull concert.* Transformation card of the Restoration period. *Ibid.*

612 Illustration by John Tenniel for *Alice's Adventures in Wonderland* by Lewis Carroll. Macmillan, 1865.

613 Alice and Humpty-Dumpty. An illustration by John Tenniel for *Through the Looking-Glass and What Alice Found There,* by Lewis Carroll. Macmillan, 1871.

614 'Fish', from *Words and Calligraphy for Children* by John W. Cataldo; Reinhold, New York, 1969.

615 Publicity for a large Paris shop. 1969.

616 Anonymous design referred to by Aaron Burns in his *Typography;* Reinhold, New York, 1961.

617 'It's raining': poem by Guillaume Apollinaire from *Calligrammes, Poèmes de la Paix et de la Guerre (1913-16);* Paris, Mercure de France, 1918.

618 A page from the French magazine *Elle* (*c.*1960).

619 *'La Dive Bouteille'* ('wine that maketh glad the heart of man!') from the 1605 edition of Rabelais's *Pantagruel (Le cinquiesme et dernier livre des Faicts et des dicts heroiques du Bon Pantagruel, composé par M. François Rabelais, Docteur en Medecine . . .)* From 1565 onwards, the publishers gave this 'drinking song' the form of a gourd.

620 Advertisement for a type of mineral water which appeared in *Elle* (1960).

621 'A type of beauty', anon., from *A Whimsey Anthology, op.cit.,* 434.

622 Poster for the French film *Une ravissante idiote.*

623 'Wings' by Simmias of Rhodes, from *Analecta veterum poetarum graecorum,* Argentorati, 1772-6.

624 'Egg' by Simmias of Rhodes, *ibid.*

625 'Axe' by Simmias of Rhodes, *ibid.*

626 'Jason's altar' by Diosadas of Crete, from *Analecta . . . , op.cit.,* 623.

627 'The altar of the Muses' by Diosadas of Crete, *ibid.*

628 Theocritus' 'Pipe of Pan'.

629 'Organ' by Publius Optatianus Porphyrius, from *Poetae latini minores,* Altenburg, 1780.

630 'Altar' by Publius Optatianus Porphyrius, *ibid.*

631 'Pipe of Pan', by Publius Optatianus Porphyrius, *ibid.*

632 Two-colour design by Venance Fortunat (sixth century) from *Venantii Honorii Clementiani Fortunati* (1603).

633-5 *Ibid.*

636 Acrostic poem by Abbon, Abbot of Fleury, who died *c.* 1004, the year the poem was dedicated to the Emperor Otto; from *Biblioteca Latina* by Fabricius (1784).

637 Hrabanus Maurus (784-856): *De Laudibus sanctae Crucis,* a manuscript belonging to the Fulda School (836-40). It depicts Louis le Pieux, son of Charlemagne, Emperor of the West and King of the Franks. *(Vienna, Staatsbibliothek).*

638 *Ibid.* Another version from the Carolingian period.

639-68 Hrabanus Maurus : *De laudibus sanctae Crucis* (Pforzheim, 1503).

669-80 Figured texts from a tenth-century Greek manuscript of the *Acts of the Apostles,* with commentaries, now in the *Bibliothèque Nationale* in Paris. The manuscript comprises nearly a thousand of these figures, the most frequent motif being the Orthodox cross.

681-701 Pages from an astronomical manuscript comprising the poem 'Phenomena' by Aratus, translated by Cicero, and figured texts by Julius Hyginus. Illuminated on parchment; tenth century; British Museum.

702 Eagle or sparrow-hawk formed from the invocation 'in the name of the mild and merciful God'.

703 A talisman formed from the names of the twelve Imams: Ali, Hassan, Hossein, Ali, Mohammed, Giafar, Noussa, Ali, Mohammed, Ali, Hassan and Mohammed.

704 A lion built up from lines in honour of Ali, Mohammed's son-in-law and the fourth person to succeed him.

705 A face composed from the names of Allah, Mohammed, Ali and Hassan, repeated in a symmetrical pattern.

706 Arabic calligram dating from the nineteenth century.

707 The Moslem creed ('There is no God but God, and Mohammed is His prophet') in the Cufic alphabet; it is repeated twice in the opposite direction, so that it can be read from the left or from the right and forms the silhouette of the seven main minarets and the cupolas of Mecca.

708 Poster designed by Ryuichi Yamashiro for a re-afforestation campaign.

709 The symbol for 'death' written by the Japanese Philosopher Hakuin (1685-1768). It is referred to by Philippe Schuwer in *Nature et formes des messages visuels,* Techniques graphiques, Paris 1967.

710 Calligram of an ox reproduced in *Recherches sur les superstitions en Chine* (A study of Chinese superstitions) by Father Henri Doré. (18 vols, Shanghai, 1911-38).

711-32 *Recherches de plusieurs singularités, par Françoys Merlin, Contrôleur général de la maison de feu madame Marie-Elisabeth, fille unique de feu roy Charles dernier . . . portraictes et escrites par Jacques Cellier demeurant à Reims,* 1583-1587.

(A study of several strange things, by Francoys Merlin, Comptroller-General of the household of the late madame Marie-Elisabeth, only daughter of the late king Charles the last . . . portrayed and written by Jacques Cellier, living in Rheims, 1583-1587.) The remainder of the extremely long title describes the work in the following terms: 'A collection of pen-and-ink drawings, patterns for writing and architecture, versions of the Lord's Prayer and alphabets in several languages, a drawing of the cathedral church and Saint-Rémy in Rheims, Notre-Dame in Paris and other Paris monuments, and of geographical and astronomical instruments, etc. *Followed by several portraits traced out in writing.'* (The manuscript is in the *Bibliothèque Nationale* in Paris.)

733 Title-page from *Sylvae, quas vario carminum genere primarri scholastici Collegii Dolani Societatis Jesu, in publica totius Civitatis gratulatione, laetitiaque ex tempore obtulerunt . . . ,* , Dôle, 1592. (Paris, *Bibliothèque Nationale*).

734 A pipe of Pan modelled on Theocritus's, *ibid.*

735 A Greek altar, by Antoine Tabet, *ibid.*

736 A Latin altar, by Philippe Merceret, *ibid.*

737 Nine Greek and Latin eggs, *ibid.*

738 Greek axe, by Antoine Besancenot, from Vesoul, *ibid.*

739 Latin axe, by Antoine Besancenot, from Vesoul, *ibid.*

740 Greek wings, by Frédéric de Chaviré, *ibid.*

741 Latin wings, by René Chevreton, *ibid.*

742 Greek spectacles, by Pierre Dolet of Baume, *ibid.*

743 Latin spectacles, by François Outhenin from Jussieu, *ibid.*

744 Latin labyrinth, by Claude Rougement from Baume, *ibid.*

745 Concentric circles made up of Latin verses, by Claude Sachot of Dôle, and a Greek triangle, by Armand Desprez, *ibid.*

746 Latin triangle by Antoine Rousselet of Vesoul, *ibid.*

747 Latin hexagon, by François Cornu of Charoles, *ibid.*

748 Greek parallelogram and rectangle by Claude Gillabod of Arbois, *ibid.*

749 Greek square and Latin rhombus, both by Claude Gillabod of Arbois, *ibid.*

750 Greek *pons asinorum* by Claude Gillabod, *ibid.*

751 'Easter eggs for the French' by Jehan Grisel, in *Premières Œuvres Poetiques,* Raphaël du Petit-Val, 1599. *(Paris, Bibliothèque Nationale).*

752 'The wings of love for virtuous women' by Jehan Grisel, *ibid.*

753 'Old-style battle-axe' by Jehan Grisel, *ibid.*

754 A laurel bough by Robert Angot de l'Eperonnière in *Chef-d'oeuvre poétique, ou première partie du Concert des Muses françoises* (Masterpiece of poetry or the first part of the Concert of the French Muses'), Caen, Jacques Brenouset and Julien de Boulanger, 1634. *(Paris, Bibliothèque Nationale).*

755 A lute by Robert Angot de l'Eperonnière, *ibid.*

756 A calligram by Geoffroy Tory in *Champ fleury, op.cit.,* 35.

757 Tiara by Fortunio Liceti in *Allegoria Peripatetica de generatione . . .* 1640.

758 A cross, also by Fortunio Liceti, *ibid.*

759 Another cross, this time by Geoffroy Tory in *Champ fleury, op.cit.,* 35.

760 A third cross, by Robert Angot de l'Eperonnière in *Chef-d'Oeuvre poétique, op.cit.,* 752.

761 'Easter eggs' by Robert Angot de l'Eperonnière, *op.cit.,* 752.

762 A map of the world by Simon Bouquet, from *Bref et sommaire recueil de ce qui a esté faict, et de l'ordre tenüe à la joyeuse et triumphante Entrée de très-puissant, très magnanime et très-chrestien Prince Charles IX . . .* ('A short and concise collection of all that which has been done, and of the arrangements made for the joyous and triumphant Entry of the most-powerful, most-magnanimous and most-Christian Prince Charles IX . . . '), Paris, 1572.

763 A design in the form of a cross, based on a medieval model, and quoted in Charles Bombaugh's *Gleaning for the Curious from the Harvest-fields of literature,* Hartford, Connecticut, 1875.

764 A cross, after Robert Herrick, *Hesperides* (1648).

765 The most common geometric shapes used for figured verses and enumerated in *The Art of English poesie,* thought to be by George Puttenham, London, 1589.

766 An altar by George Herbert from *The Temple, sacred poems and private jaculations,* Cambridge, 1641.

767 *'Wings'* by George Herbert, *ibid.*

768 Dedication shaped like a pyramid, from an English translation of Guillaume du Bartas: *Sepmaine ou La Création du Monde* (published in France in 1579) by Josuah Sylvester.

769 *Ode to an old violin,* anon., from *Handy-book of Literary Curiosities,* by William S. Walsh, London, 1892.

770 A bow and arrow: an English version of a triplet composed by a Hindu poet. Quoted by Charles Bombaugh in his *Gleanings for the curious . . . , op.cit.,* 761.

771 A rhombic funeral chant composed by George Wither (1588-1677), *ibid.*

772-83 Pages from the English translation of *Sepmaine, op.cit.,* 768.

784 Composition in the shape of a glass in Rabelais' *Le Cinquiesme Livre.*

785 A glass: Aldus Manutius, Venice, 1499.

786 A glass of wine, as referred to in *Proverbs* XXIII, 29-32; from *A Whimsey Anthology, op.cit.,* 434.

787 Another glass, this one by Panard (d. 1765), as reproduced in *Œuvres Choisies,* published by Armand Gouffe, Paris, 1803.

788 A glass by Pierre Capelle, from *Contes, anecdotes, chansons et poésies diverses de Capelle, fondateur-sociétaire du Caveau moderne* ('Tales, anecdotes, songs and various items of poetry by Capelle, founder-member of the cabaret called *'Le Caveau Moderne')* Paris, 1818.

789 Calligram by André Breton, 1920.

790 'Bait of the average fisherman' by H. C. Dodge, from *A Whimsey Anthology, op.cit.,* 434.

791 'The song of the decanter', anon., *ibid.*

792 *'Aux amys des Muses'* ('To the friends of the Muses'): twin bottles by Robert Angot de

l'Eperonnière, from *Chef d'oeuvre poétique, op.cit.*, 752.

793 A bottle by Panard, from *Œuvres Choisies, op.cit.*, 787.

794 Another bottle, this one by Pierre Capelle, from *Contes, anecdotes . . . , op.cit.*, 788.

795 A vase by Otto Storch and Bill Cadge, *McCall's*.

795 A teapot and vase; from *De Nieuwe Nassouwse Princelyke Schenkhan . . . ,* Amsterdam, 1708.

797 A photograph by John Heartfield for Upton Sinclair's *Alcohol*, 1932.

798 An advertisement for *The big drink: the story of Coca Cola*.

799-805 Compositions extracted from medieval texts in Hebrew brought to light by Berjouhi Barsamian Bowler in *Typographica*, London.

806 A composition in honour of the marriage of Christoph Kellner (1587). It is reproduced in Robert Diehl's *Figurensatz in Frankfurter Drucken der Renaissance und des Barocks*, 1591.

807 A composition for the marriage of Johann Adolf von Glauburg, 1591, *ibid.*

808 'Cup', by J. R. Karst, 1667, *ibid.*

809 'Fern', by J. R. Karst, *ibid.*

810 'Heart', by J. R. Karst, *ibid.*

811 'Heart pierced by an arrow', by J. R. Karst, *ibid.*

812 'Cradle', by J. R. Karst, *ibid.*

813 An elegy in the form of a cross by Anna Sibylla Ruland (1699), *ibid.*

814 Compositions designed in honour of the marriage of Town Councillor Nikolaus von Uffenbach (1721), *ibid.*

815 Greetings card, mid-eighteenth century, *ibid.*

816 Labyrinth from *L'art d'écrire* by Christoph Weigel, Nuremberg, 1716.

817 Urban Wyss: 'Labyrinth' (1692).

818 A manuscript by Paulli Velseri, Augsburg, 1595.

819 A composition by a sixteenth-century German typographer.

820 *Lettre Ecrite par le Reine de France Marie-Antoinette à la soeur de Louis XVI, Madame Elisabeth . . . A la Concièrgerie, le six octobre Mil sept cent quatre vingt treize, a 4 heures ½ du matin* ('Letter Written by the Queen of France Marie-Antoinette to the sister of Louis XVI, Madame Elisabeth . . . In the Concièrgerie, the sixth october One thousand seven hundred and eighty-three, at half past four in the morning'). (This was the day of her execution.) A composition by A. Pélicier *(Collection R. J. Ségalat)*.

821 'Bonaparte, First Consul of the French Republic', a popular print *(Collection R. J. Ségalat)*.

822 'The Colonne Vendôme': a popular print of about 1830 *(Collection R. J. Ségalat)*.

823 'The Constitutional Charter': a popular print of 1830. *(Collection R. J. Ségalat)*.

824 'The tax return': as seen by Siné in *L'Express*, 1961.

825 'The gentleman who struggles to write 1000 words on the back of a postage-stamp when he gets back from the office of an evening, just for the fun of it . . . ' From *L'Européenne illustrée*, some time in the second half of the nineteenth century and reproduced in *Vieux Papiers, Vieilles Images, op.cit.*, 598.

826 Drawing by Gustave Doré, in *Histoire de la Sainte Russie, op.cit.*, 595.

827 *'Les toiles du Nord'* by Gustave Doré, *ibid.*

828 *Le farceur de* 1834, a popular almanac, from *Vieux Papiers, Vieilles Images, op.cit.*, 598.

829 'The Bell of Freedom' is composed with the help of the text of the Declaration of Independence of the United States of America. Even the crack which spoils the appearance of the bell has been reproduced in this calligram.

830 A sixteenth-century portrait of Martin Luther *(Bibliothèque Nationale, Paris)*.

831 Early nineteenth-century version of 'Doctor Martin Luther', now in the Bibliothèque Nationale in Paris.

832 A portrait of Abraham Lincoln composed from the text of the 'Proclamation of Emancipation'.

833 A portrait of Marshal Foch by Georges Tcherukine, © 1930 from 'The Pantheon of Glories' (*c.* 1930). The text retraces the principal episodes in the career of the military leader and the almost photographic likeness in the portrait is obtained purely by writing. *(Author's collection)*.

834 François Premier, after Clouet: a 'typewritten painting' on canvas by E. Messely, using Korès ribbons and duplicated with Korès Drytype Super stencils. The original is 20 cm × 30 cm (approx. 7¾ ins × 11¾ ins) and consists of 24,000 touches; it took thirty to forty hours to do. For the reproduction there had to be a series of seven or eight printings, in a different colour ink each time. The marking of the lay is micrometric.

835 Jeanne d'Aragon, after Raphael, by E. Messely.

836 'Typewritten Composition' by E. Messely.

837 Typewritten portrait of Maurice Lemaître by E. Messely. It was completed by Lemaître himself.

838 A calligram composed with a computer, reproduced in *Paris-Match* (1968).

839-40 Typewritten compositions by Maurice Lemaître (1963).

841 Design produced by a computer (1968).

842 Newspaper advertisement by Rochas for a toilet-water.

843 Advertisement put out by Fonderies Deberny et Peignot for the Univers type-face.

844 A composition by Victor Otto Stomps which appeared in *Privatpressen in Deutschland* by Dorothea Grunenberg, Paul Eckhardte (*c.* 1964).

845 Poster for *Elle* magazine (Paris, 1967).

846 Newspaper advertisement for Lempereur dresses (*c.* 1960).

847 Newspaper advertisement for Jean Patou scent (*c.* 1960).

848 Newspaper advertisement for Photosia.

849 Detail from a newspaper advertisement for the film *Funny Girl*.

850 Newspaper advertisement by Robert Delpire for Citroen cars (1963).

851 Heading from the magazine *Elle* (1961).

852 Newspaper advertisement for an aperitif called Carpano.

853 Details of a newspaper advertisement for a book published by Hachette.

854 A design by Reba Sochis for Bergdoff Goodman shoes.

855 Advertisement designed by Donald Egensteiner for the advertising agency Young & Rubicam.

856 Double-spread title page for *Invasion 14,* a novel by Maxence Van der Meersch; dummy by Georges Bracher; Club du meilleur livre, Paris, 1955.

857 Book jacket; Knopf, New York, 1968.

858 Newspaper advertisement for Franklin Typographers, New York; from *Print, America's graphic design Magazine* (1966).

859 Advertisement for the Galeries Lafayette.

860 Advertisement by Gouju and Almaric for Gitanes cigarettes.

861 A drawing by Jerome Snyder which appeared in *Fact,* New York, 1965.

862 Advertisement by Steiner-Herkner-Beck of Stuttgart for Peddy & Co.

863 Advertisement for the Lebanese Tourist Office (1968).

864 Invitation-card designed by Patrick Ferrey.

865 Heading from *Elle* magazine designed by Bernard Cretin.

866 A double-spread from *Spécial Pop,* issue No. 1 (special issue), published by Albin-Michel in Paris in 1967.

867 Another double-spread from *Spécial Pop, ibid.*

868 Page heading from *Elle* magazine.

869 Label for a film-distributing company.

870 Composition by René Fauconnet in *R.F. 301,* a satirical story, *s.l.* 1961.

871 Cover designed for the magazine *Fortune* by Lustig (1952).

872 Cover designed by Gerard Finel for the gazette of the I.N.I.A.G.

873 Advertisement for Olivetti typewriters (1960).

874 Advertisement for Mont Saint-Michel, designed to be stamped on envelopes.

875 *'La Colombe poignardée et le jet d'eau'* ('The stabbed pigeon and the fountain') from Guillaume Apollinaire's *Calligrammes, op.cit.,* 617.

876 *'La cravate et la montre'* ('The tie and the watch') by Apollinaire, *ibid.*

877 Design in colour by Apollinaire for the catalogue to an exhibition of the work of Leopold Survage and Irene Lagut (1917).

878 'Pablo Picasso' : one of Apollinaire's compositions which appeared in the magazine *Sic* (issue no. 17) in May 1917.

879 Another of Apollinaire's designs from his *Calligrammes, op.cit.,* 617.

880 Unpublished designs by Apollinaire which were reproduced in his *Œuvres poétiques,* published by Gallimard in the Bibliothèque de la Pléiade series, Paris, 1956.

881 'The Stegomyia': an anonymous composition in *A Whimsey Anthology, op.cit.,* 434.

882 Compositions by Semion Kirsanov (1925).

883 *'Rosace'* ('Rose-window'): a design by Pierre Albert-Birot reproduced in *Poésie,* 1916-24, Paris, Gallimard, 1967.

884 *'Le Bestiaire Fabuleux'* (The Fabulous Bestiary') by Jean Lurcat and Patrice de la Tour du Pin, Paris, 1950.

885 'Fleur-de-lys': a design by Pierre Albert-Birot in *Poésie, op.cit.,* 883.

886 'The shadow will never be as long as the road': a design by Pierre Albert-Birot for a collection called *La joie de sept couleurs* (1918): reproduced in *Poésie, ibid.*

887 'Offering': a design by Albert-Birot from *La Lune ou Le Livre des Poèmes* (1924).

888-91 Calligrams by Louise de Vilmorin in her *L'Alphabet des aveux,* Paris, Gallimard, 1955.

892-3 Two figured menus designed by Bertrand Guegan and reproduced in the journal *Arts et métiers graphiques,* vol 32, Paris, 1932.

894 Drawing by Steinberg (1961). *(Frank Weil Collection, New York).* (© Saul Steinberg.)

895 Letter by Alfred Jarry to Claude Terrasse written on the back of a printed card and cut out into the shape of a fish (*c.* 1905). *(Private collection.)*

896 Drawing by André François for a Kodak publicity folder.

897 'The Djins' : a poem by Victor Hugo published in his *Les Orientales,* Paris, Bossange, 1829.

898 'The back': a 'poetic drawing' by Gabriel Martin from *Les Psaumes de la Beauté,* ('Psalms of Beauty') which he dedicated to 'all pretty women'; Paris, J. B. Ferreyol, 1891.

899 A page from François Rabelais's *La vie inestimable du grand Gargantua, père de Pantagruel . . . ;* Paris, Club français du livre, 1948.

900 A page from Charles Nodier's *l'Histoire du Roi de Bohême et de ses sept châteaux* ('A tale of the King of Bohemia and his seven castles') Paris, Delange Frères, 1830.

901 A page from Raymond Queneau's novel *Le Chiendent,* Paris, Gallimard, 1933.

902 Typography by the Lyons printer Jean de Tournes for Guillaume Guèroult's *L'Hymne du Temps et de ses parties,* 1560.

903 'The Mouse's Tail' in *Alice in Wonderland* is one of the most famous calligrams in English literature.

904 The first version of the same poem, as it appeared in the original manuscript.

905 'Typographic eye', from Nicolas Cirer's *L'Apprentif ɹnǝʇɐɹʇsᴉuᴉɯpⱯ, pamphlet pittoresque (!) littérario-typographico-bureaucratique . . .* Paris, published privately in 1840.

906 The beginning of the chapter called 'Protestation' in Nodier's *Histoire du Roi de Bohème . . . , op.cit.* 900.

907 A page from the *Histoire du Roi de Bohème . . . , ibid.*

908 The opening of Stéphane Mallarmé's poem *Un coup de dés jamais n'abolira le hasard* ('Chance will never be abolished by the throw of a dice') from the international review *Cosmopolis,* London, May 1897.

909-10 Opening of the same poem as it was finally set from the original manuscript; Paris, Gallimard, 1914.

911-917 Sequence of pages from Charles Péguy's *Jeanne d'Arc.* First edition, 752 octavo pages. Paris, Librairie de la Revue Socialiste, December 1897. The last of the pages shown here takes us no further than the half-title of the book; eight blank pages precede the first real page, which is where the envoy begins. This method of alternating text and blank pages introduces duration of time and space into the lay-out and thus gives the book a cinematic quality. The book's presentation is astonishingly bold and was deliberately planned as such by the author, who worked out the details of the lay-out himself; it is a forerunner of the credit sequences seen in films today.

918 *La Prose du Transsibérien et de la Petite Jeanne de France,* a poem by Blaise Cendrars. 'Simultaneous colours' by Sonia Delaunay. This is the sole edition and is known as *'The First Simultaneous Book'.* Paris, Editions des Hommes Nouveaux, 1913. *(Musée National d'Art Moderne, Paris).*

919 Poster for the drama group 'Art and Action' advertising a triple bill of Stéphane Mallarmé's *Un coup de dés jamais n'abolira le hasard,* Rene Ghil's *Le Pantoun' des Pantoun'* and Guillaume Apollinaire's *Le Larron.*

920 A composition by Giovanni Francesco Cresci from *Essemplare di piu sorti lettere* (1629).

921 Raymond Queneau : *Cent mille milliards de poèmes.* Mock-up by Massin. Paris, Gallimard, 1961. *(Photo: Andre Bonin).*

922 'Poster-poem' by Pierre Albert-Birot, in *Poésie, op. cit.* 883.

923 Double spread from Henri Pichette's *Epiphanies,* with typography by Pierre Faucheux. Paris, K. 1948.

924 'Book-object' produced by B. Meadows for Samuel Becket's *Molloy.* Editions Claude Givaudan, 1966.

925 'Book-object' by Vrindaban for poems by Octavio Paz. Editions Claude Givaudan, 1966.

926 F. T. Marinetti : *Les Mots en liberté futuristes;* Milan, 1919.

927 *Une assemblée tumultueuse: sensibilité numérique; id., ibid.*

928 F. T. Marinetti: *Lettre d'une jolie femme à un monsieur passéiste* ('Letter from a pretty woman to an old-fashioned gentleman'); *id., ibid.*

929 Kurt Schwitters, Kathe Steinitz and Theo van Doesburg: *Die Scheuche* (1925).

930 A Futurist 'typogram' by Ardengo Soffici in *Bif & ZF + 18* (1919).

931 A collage by Raoul Hausmann (1923).

932 *'Une nuit d'échecs gras'* a page designed by Tristan Tzara in 391, xiv, November 1920 (author's collection).

933 Cover for the first issue of *Der Dada,* attributed to Hausmann and Baader.

934 Cover for the *Club Dada;* Berlin, 1918.

935-6 Pages from *Monsieur Nicolas ou le Coeur Humain Dévoilé* ('Monsieur Nicolas or the Human Heart Unveiled') by Restif de la Bretonne, designed and printed by the author. The seventeen volumes of the original edition comprise 4,840 pages and were published in 1796 and 1797.

937 Opening of the text of Paul Claudel's *Soulier de Satin.* This *'typodiction'* is executed in various different type-faces in various sizes printed in black and red, and was prepared by Jean-Louis Barrault for the actors who were to appear in his production of the play for the Comédie Francaise in 1943. *(Author's collection).*

938 A phonetic poem by Raoul Hausmann (1919).

939 *'Poeme à crier et à danser'* ('Poem for shouting and dancing') by Pierre Albert-Birot, in *Poésie, op.cit.,* 883.

940 Double-spread from Eugène Ionesco's *Délire a deux.* Sound calligraphy by Massin, hand done and using the letterpress process. Paris, Gallimard, 1966.

941-3 Double-spreads from Ionesco's *La Cantatrice chauve* ('The Bald Primadonna'), with typographic interpretations by Massin and photographic interpretations by Henry Cohen based on Nicolas Bataille's production. Paris, Gallimard, 1964.

944 A page from *Stripsody* by Eugene Carmi. Arco d'Alibert, Rome and Kiko Galleries, Houston, USA, 1966.

945 Newspaper advertisement for a fizzy drink.

946 *'L'Amiral cherche une maison à louer'* by Richard Huelsenbeck, Marcel Janko and Tristan Tzara (1916). *(Private collection).*

947 Christian Morgenstern: *Fisches Nachtgesang* (1905).

948 Man Ray: *Lautgedicht* (1924).

949 Hugo Ball: *Karawane* (1917).

950 A poem by Theo van Doesburg, from *De Stijl,* xi, 1921.

951-5 Cover and double-spreads from Jean Tardieu's *Conversation-Sinfonietta.* With an attempt by Massin to provide a typographic orchestration. Paris, Gallimard, 1966. In this vocal sextet the voices are represented by different type-faces and arranged on the page at the actual level of their register.

956-8 Mozart's *Alphabet,* an attempt by Massin to offer a musical calligram. As in the previous examples, the voices are arranged in tiers according to their register; different thicknesses of the same type-face are used to indicate the tessituras of the voices; each letter is placed where the corresponding note would be, its size being governed proportionately by the value of the note; lastly, the variations are reproduced by means of an intermediate half-tone. (unpublished).

959-60 Part of a vocal calligram by Massin of Edith Piaf's song *La Foule.* The whole arrangement appeared in the *Evergreen Review* (New York, Grove Press, 1965) and included photographs of the singer by Emil Cado. The distortions were obtained by using sheets of latex printed in advance in Cheltenham bold. This attempt aims to offer a reconstruction both of the sound curve and of the volume, range and timbre of a voice.

961 Programme for the *'Soirée du Coeur à barbe'* at the Théâtre Michel, Paris (1923).

962 Page from *Ledentu le phare,* a one-acter written in *'zaoum'* by Iliazd. Paris, 1923.

963 A detail from the cover of the review *Mammoth* for March 1965.

964 Poster designed by George Mayhew for the Royal Shakespeare Company, 1962.

965 Two-colour advertisement for the aperitif Saint-Raphaël quinquina, designed by Atelier Loupot, *c.* 1950.

966-8 Luminous wall at Expo in Montreal, 1967.

969 Ferdinand Kriwet: 'Rolled up voyage', (1963). *(Museum of Modern Art).*

970 Ferdinand Kriwet: *Zuverspaetceterandfigurinnennenswertvollos* (1962).

971 Ferdinand Kriwet: a design which appeared in *Image* in October, 1965.

972 A design by Jean-François Bory.

973 A labyrinthine composition by the German calligrapher I. C. Hiltensperger; early eighteenth century.

974 Wood-cut from *Trithemius, op.cit.*

975 A composition by Pierre Garnier.

976 A composition by Franz Mon.

977 A composition by Theo Dimson (Toronto).

978 A composition by Valerian Valerianovitch Nerechtnikov (USSR).

979 A composition by Takahashi Shohachiro.

980-1 Two specimen lay-outs for *Elle* magazine by Peter Knapp (*c.*1960).

982-5 'Football Form I, II, III and IV' by Richard Kostelanetz (USA).

986 A composition by Hansjörg Mayer.

987 H. N. Werkmann: *The next call 4,* Groningen, 1924.

988 A page from *Poésie,* by Jean-Claude Grosjean; Paris, Gallimard, 1968.

989 A 'spatialist' composition produced with an IBM computer.

990 'Barbara': a piece of calligraphy by Klaus Peter Dienst and Rolf Gunter Dienst for *Rhinozeros* (1961).

991 *Ror Wolf. Fortsetzung des Berichts* a piece of calligraphy by Klaus Peter Dienst which appeared in *Rhinozeros* (1962).

992 Colour cover for an advertising brochure for the firm of Olivetti (*c.*1950).

993 Design by Timm Ulrichs.

994 *'Hépérile éclaté':* the first *'poéme à dé-lire',* produced by Camille Bryen, Raymond Hains and Jacques de la Villeglé using corrugated glass frames (1952).

995 John Furnival: *The fall of the tower of Babel.*

996 A composition by Seiichi Niikuni.

997 A double-spread from *Carmina Burana,* with calligraphy by Klaus Peter Dienst; Verlag Langer Peter Itzehoe, 1962.

998 Edgard Braga: *'Vocabulo'* (1966).

999 Joshua Reichert: 'The next call' (1962). This composition harks back to the title of a magazine published in about 1920 by H. N. Werkmann.

1000 Cover for the *Journal of Typographic Research* (Cleveland, Ohio).

1001-32 Wolfgang Schmidt: 'Série 6, Synthetic Script' (1962); Frankfurt, Typos Verlag, 1965. A series (reduced) showing most of the thirty-four pages which make up this cinematic book; it was used for a television film in 1964.

1033 'Abkhazia', a composition by Adolf Hoffmeister, (*c.* 1959).

1034 'Gagra'; *id.*

1035 'A view of Sotchi from the battery'; *id.*

1036 'The Jewish cemetry in Prague'; *id.*

1037 'Last summer in Carlsbad'; *id.*

1038 'Denradium at Sotchi'; *id.*

1039 Colour illustration by Fernand Léger for *La Fin du monde filmée par l'Ange Notre-Dame,* by Blaise Cendrars. Paris, Editions de la Sirène, 1919. © S.P.A.D.E.M.

1040 *Ibid.*

1041 Fernand Léger: 'Still-life ABC' (1927). *(Galerie Louise Leiris).* © S.P.A.D.E.M.

1042 Colour illustration by Fernand Léger (1939), *op.cit.*

1043 Composition by Fernand Léger (1927). © S.P.A.D.E.M.

1044 Paul Klee: 'Villa R' (1919) *(Kunstmuseum, Basle).* © S.P.A.D.E.M.

1045-6 Paul Klee: *'Einst dem Grau der Nacht enttaucht,* No. 3' (1918). Watercolour. *(Klee-Stiftung Kunstmuseum, Basle).* © S.P.A.D.E.M.

1047 Paul Klee: *'Und ach, was meinen Kummer . . .* (1916). Watercolour. *(Kunstmuseum, Berne).* © S.P.A.D.E.M.

1048 Paul Klee: *'Er küsse mich mit seines Mundes Kuss . . .'* (1921). Watercolour. *(Collection Angela Rosengart, Lucern).*

1049 Salvador Dali: *Les Ménines* © S.P.A.D.E.M. 1960 (Collection Mr and Mrs Levy-Bridgewater).

1050 Paul Klee: *'Tätlichkeiten'* (1940). *(© 1967 Cosmopress, Geneva).* © S.P.A.D.E.M.

1051 Paul Klee: *'Anfang eines Gedichtes'* (1938). © S.P.A.D.E.M. Watercolour. *(Kunstmuseum, Berne).*

1052 Paul Klee: *'Tod und Feuer'* (1940). *(Klee-Stiftung, Berne).* © S.P.A.D.E.M.

1053 Paul Klee: Groupe W. 1930. © S.P.A.D.E.M.

1054 Cover by Francis Picabia for the journal *Littérature* (1919). © S.P.A.D.E.M.

1055 Yves Laloy: *'Les petits pois sont verts . . . Les petits poissons rouges'.*

1056 Marcel Duchamp: 'L.H.O.O.Q.' (1919). Corrected ready-made. A reproduction of the Mona Lisa on which the painter has pencilled in a pair of moustaches. *(Pierre Matisse Gallery, New York).* © A.D.A.G.P.

1057 Kurt Schwitters: collage (1936-7) *(Marlborough Fine Arts).*

1058 Kurt Schwitters: collage (1920). *(Photo: J. D. Schiff).*

1059 Carlo Carrà: *'Manifestazione interventista'* (1914). Cut-out paper and pieces of newspaper. *(Collection Dr Gianni Mattioli, Milan).*

1060 Pablo Picasso: *'La Bouteille de Suze'* (1913). Cut-out paper, newspaper, wallpaper, etc. *(Washington University, Gallery of Art Saint Louis).* © S.P.A.D.E.M.

1061 Georges Braque: *'Le programme de cinéma'* (1913). Cut-out paper, charcoal and oil on canvas. *(Collection Mr and Mrs Bernard J. Reis, New York).* © A.D.A.G.P.

1062 Juan Gris: *'Carafe et journal'* (1916). Oil and pencil on wood. *(Norton Gallery and School of Art, West Palm Beach, Florida).* © A.D.A.G.P.

1063 Ardengo Soffici: 'Still-life with water melon' (1915).

1064 Jean Pougny: *'La fuite des formes'* (1919). Gouache. *(Private collection, Paris).* © A.D.A.G.P.

1065 Casimir Malevich: 'Lady at the Advertising Pillar' (1914). *(Stedelijk Museum, Amsterdam).*

1066 Raoul Hausmann: collage (1919).

1067 E. L. T. Mesens: *'Mouvement immobile'* (1960). Cut-out paper and ink drawing. *(Grosvenor Gallery, London).*

1068 Man Ray: 'Theatr' (1916). Collage and drawing. *(Galerie Rive Droite, Paris).* © A.D.A.G.P.

1069 Johannus Baader: 'Commemorative leaf for Gutenberg' (1919). Collage. *(Collection Frau Hannah Höch, Berlin).*

1070 Robert Delaunay: *'L'Equipe de Cardiff'* ('The Cardiff team') (1912-13). *(Stedelijk Van Abbe Museum, Eindhoven).* © A.D.A.G.P.

1071 Robyn Denny: 'Collage' (1957). Oil with torn paper, fabric, cardboard, etc.

1072 Ben Shahn: *'Sacco & Vanzetti'* (1958). Silk-screen. *(Stedelijk Museum, Amsterdam).*

1073 P. A. Gette: La Momie. Galerie Iolas. *Photo Serge Beguier.*

1074 Joan Mirò: composition. © A.D.A.G.P.

1075 Hendrik Nicolaas Werkmann: *'Komposition mit X'* (1927). Colour-printed on a hand-press. *(Stedelijk Museum, Amsterdam).*

1076 Victor Vasarely: *'Lunik en rodage'* ('Lunik running-in') (1959). Collage. *(Galerie Denise Rene, Paris).*

1077 The photographer William Klein at home *(Photo: William Klein).*

1078 Vincent Van Gogh: drawing taken from a letter to Emile Bernard written at Arles in June 1888.

1079 A piece of calligraphy by a Zen priest; Japanese, nineteenth century.

1080 Jackson Pollock: drawing (1950) *(Marlborough Gallery, London).*

1081 Jean Arp: *According to the rules of chance,* 1957. © A.D.A.G.P.

1082 Vassily Kandinsky: '30'. Oil. (1937). © A.D.A.G.P.

1083 Illustration by André Masson for André Malraux's *Les Conquérants* ('The Conquerors'). Paris, Editions Skira, 1948. *(© A.D.A.G.P.).*

1084 Piet Mondrian: Church façade (1912 or 1914). Charcoal. *(Harry Holzman Collection, New York).*

1085 A composition by Theo van Doesburg.

1086 Giuseppe Capogrossi: *'Superficie no.* 305*'* (1959). *(Gallerie del Naviglio, Milan).*

1087 Joan Mirò: *'Chiffres et constellations amoureux d'une femmea'* ('Numbers and constellations in love with a woman') (1940-1). Gouache, reproduced in the series of 22 plates of 'Constellations' with 'prose parallels' by André Breton (1959). *(Photo: Henry Cohen).* © A.D.A.G.P.

1088 A composition by Georges Mathieu.

1089 Drawings taken from a letter by Henri Matisse in which he demonstrates the shapes he frequently uses to describe the mouths of his figures. Quoted by Aragon in his *Henri Matisse roman,* Paris, Gallimard, 1970.

1090 Jean Dubuffet: double-spread from *Parade funèbre pour Charles Estienne* ('Funeral procession for Charles d'Estienne;) Paris, Editions Jeanne Bucher, 1967. © A.D.A.G.P.

1091 Pierre Bonnard: illustrations for *Tatane,* 'a song to make the Negroes blush and to glorify Father Ubu', from *Almanach illustré du Père Ubu (XXe siècle),* Paris, 1901.

1092 Cave drawing.

1093 The sign *chóu,* which means 'to entwine' or 'to bind'.

1094 Alcopley: drawing.

1095 Henri Michaux: Indian ink drawing used as a cover for the catalogue for the Galerie Motte in Paris in 1964.

1096 'Man': a stabile by Alexander Calder at the Montreal Expo, 1967. *(Photo: Massin).*

1097-9 Cover and pages from Henri Michaux's *Mouvements.* Indian ink drawings. Paris, Gallimard, in the *Point du jour* collection, 1952.

1100 A fragment from Queen Matilda's tapestry, which is known as the Bayeux Tapestry (*c.* 1066).

1101 An illustration by Henri Matisse for *Jazz.* © A.D.A.G.P.

1102 Lambert of Ardes: *Liber Floridus* (13th century); Paris, Bibliothèque Nationale.

1103 René Magritte: *The Art of Conversation* 1950. (Collection Mrs H. Robillart, Brussels). © A.D.A.G.P.

1104 A picture from the film *The Yellow Submarine.*

1105 A page from *Les Aventures de Jodelle* with drawings by Guy Peellaert and text by Pierre Bartier; Paris, Eric Losfeld, 1966.

1106 *Cul-de-lampe* or tail-piece by E. Bayard for *Après la pluie le beau temps* ('Fine weather after rain') by the Comtesse de Ségur. 'Bibliothèque rose illustrée' series, Paris, Hachette, 1871.

Bibliography

Communications, language, writing, images and signs

Aragon *Henri Matisse, roman* Gallimard, Paris, 1970

Marcel Cohen *La grande invention de l'écriture et son évolution* Paris, 1958

Etiemble *L'écriture.* Robert Delpire, Paris, 1961

Maurice Fabre *Histoire de la communication* Editions Rencontre and Erik Nitsche International, 1963

J. G. Février *Histoire de l'écriture* Paris, 1948

Ivan Fonagy, *Le language poétique: forme et fonction,* in *Problèmes du langage* Collection Diogène, Gallimard, Paris, 1966

Marcel Hignette *Du rôle respectif de l'alphabet, de l'image et des techniques audiovisuelles dans la diffusion de la culture,* in *Techniques graphiques,* no 74. Michel Brient, Paris, 1968

E. Javal *Physiologie de la lecture et de l'ecriture.* F. Alcan, Paris, 1905

Wolfgang Köhler *Gestalt Psychology*

Le langage Edited by André Martinet, Encyclopédie de la Pléiade, Paris, 1968

L'Homme et son langage Edited by Sir Gerald Barry, Dr J. Bronowski, James Fisher, Sir Julian Huxley. Tallandier, Paris, 1968

Marshall MacLuhan *The Gutenberg Galaxy* University of Toronto Press, Toronto, 1962

Marshall MacLuhan and **Quentin Fiore** *The medium is the massage. An inventory of effects* New York, London, Toronto, 1967

Roger Munier *Contre l'image* Gallimard, Paris, 1963

Erwin Panofsky *Studies in iconology* Oxford University Press, 1939

Jérôme Peignot *De l'ecriture à la typographie* Gallimard, Paris, 1967

François Richaudeau *La lettre et l'esprit* Planète, Paris, 1965

François Richaudeau *Le processus de lecture* Centre d'Etude et de Promotion de la lecture, Paris, 1968

F. de Saussure *Cours de linguistique générale* Paris, Lausanne, 1916

Philippe Schuwer *Natures et formes des messages visuels,* in *Techniques graphiques,* no 73 Editions Michel Brient, Paris, Nov/Dec 1967

William C. Seitz *The responsive eye* The Museum of Modern Art, New York, 1965

Sign, image and symbol edited by Gyorgy Kepes, Studio Vista, London; George Braziller, New York 1966

James Sutton *Signs in action* Studio Vista, London; Reinhold, New York, 1965

Peter Wildbur *Trademarks* Studio Vista, London; Reinhold, New York, 1966

Writing. The process and the image Exhibition catalogue for the Carpenter Center for the visual arts. Harvard University,1965

Symbolism in language and typography, figured alphabets and animated letters

One of the first comprehensive studies to be devoted entirely to 'human alphabets' was written by Dr Hellmut Lehmann-Haupt and Norman Petteway (cf. below) in 1958. Dietmar Debes has recently compiled an exhaustive list, with bibliographical references. It deals with anthropozoomorphic alphabets and, more generally, with all known 'figured' alphabets, cataloguing them according to century.

On the other hand, a very large number of studies by authors from various countries have discussed decorated or figured initials from the Byzantine period down to the Gothic period. We have no space here to mention all of them, so we have restricted our list to just a few titles.

Raymond Abellio *La Bible, document chiffré. Essai sur la restitution des clefs de la science secrète* 2 vols. Gallimard, Paris, 1950

Jurgis Baltrusaitis *Réveils et prodiges. Le Gothique fantastique* Armand Colin, Paris, 1960

Nadjm Oud-Dine Bammate *L'ordre alphabétique,* in *La Parisienne* no 42 (*L'Esprit et la lettre,* issue devoted to typography). Paris, March 1957

Robert Benayoun *Anthologie du nonsense* J. J. Pauvert, Paris, 1957

Bizarre, no 32-33. *Littérature illettrée ou la littérature à la lettre,* Edited by Noël Arnaud and François Caradec. Paris, 1964

Byzance et la France médiévale. Illuminated manuscripts from the 2nd to the 16th century. Bibliothèque Nationale, Paris, 1958. Exhibition catalogue

Aaron Burns *Typography* Reinhold, New York, 1969

Paul Claudel *La philosophie du livre, idéogrammes occidentaux Les mots ont une ame, L'harmonie imitative in Œuvres en prose* Bibliothèque de la Pléiade, Paris, 1965

Dietmar Debes *Das Figurenalphabet* Verlag Dokumentation, Münich-Pullach, 1968

S. M. Eisenstein *Structure, montage, passage* in *Le montage* Seuil, Paris, 1968

Etiemble *Le sonnet des voyelles. De l'audition colorée à la vision érotique* Gallimard, Paris, 1968

René Faurisson *A-t-on* LU *Rimbaud?* in *Bizarre,* no 21-22. J. J. Pauvert, Paris, 1962

Alan Fletcher, Colin Forbes and **Bob Gill** *Graphic design: visual comparisons.* Studio Vista, London; Reinhold, New York, 1963

Court de Gébelin *Histoire naturelle de la Parole ou Précis de l'origine du Langage et de la Grammaire universelle* 1776

René Ghil *Traité de verbe,* with a foreword by Stéphane Mallarmé, Giraud, Paris, 1886

Matila C. Ghyka *Sortilèges du verbe* Gallimard, Paris, 1949

John Grand-Carteret *Vieux papiers, vieilles images. Cartons d'un Collectionneur* Paris, 1896

Françoise Henry *L'Art irlandais* La Pierre-qui-Vire, Zodiaque, 1963-4. 3 vols

Jean Hubert, Jean Porcher and **W. F. Volbach** *L'Europe des invasions* Gallimard, Paris, 1967

Victor Hugo *France et Belgique. Alpes et Pyrénées. Voyages et excursions* Paris, 1910

O. Jennings *Early woodcut initials* 1908

Hellmut Lehmann-Haupt and **Norman Petteway** *Human alphabets,* in *Amor Librorum* Amsterdam, 1958

Max Lehors *Der Meister mit den Banderollen* Dresden, 1886

Victor Leroquais *Les Psautiers manuscrits latins des bibliothéques publiques de France* Protat, Paris, Mâcon, 1940

Victor Leroquais *Les sacramentaires et les missels manuscrits des bibliothéques publiques de France.* Protat, Paris, Mâcon, 1924

John Lewis *Typography: basic principles* Studio Vista, London; Reinhold, New York, 1963

Lively alphabets. The pictorial use of letter forms in the graphic arts Yale University Library, Conn., 1966. Exhibition catalogue

Manuscrits à peintures en France du VIIe au XIIe siècles Bibliothèque Nationale, Paris, 1954 Exhibition catalogue

Ruari McLean *Pictorial alphabets* Studio Vista, London; Dover, New York, 1969

Emile-A Van Moe *La lettre ornée dans les manuscrits du VIIe au XIIe siècle. Editions du Chêne, Paris, 1949*

Carl Nordenfalk *L'enluminure in Le Haut Moyen Age du quatrième au onzième siècle* Skira, Geneva, 1957

Carl Nordenfalk, *L'enluminure a l'époque romane,* in *La peinture romane* Skira, Geneva

Jean Porcher *L'enluminure cistercienne* in *L'art cistercien (France)* La Pierre-qui-Vire, Zodiaque, 1962

Ezra Pound *ABC of reading* Faber and Faber, London

Herbert Spencer *The visible word* Royal College of Art, London, 1968

Jaro Springer *Gotische Alphabete* Berlin, 1897

Etienne Tabourot *Bigarrures et Touches du Seigneur des Accords* Paris, 1583

Marcel Thomas *L'Enluminure parisienne à l'epoque de Charles V,* in *La Librairie de Charles V.* Exhibition catalogue, Bibliothèque Nationale, Paris, 1968

Fr. Wormald *The Miniatures in the Gospels of St Augustine (Corpus Christi College ms. 286)* University Press, Cambridge 1954

Zohar. Vol. I. Mantua, 1559

Figured poems, calligrams and lay-outs

Guillaume Apollinaire *L'Antitradition futuriste* Milan 1913

Guillaume Apollinaire *L'Esprit nouveau et les poètes* text of a lecture given at the Vieux-Colombier on 26 November 1917 and published in the *Mercure de France* (1 December 1918)

Aragon *Adolf Hoffmeister et la beauté d'aujourd'hui* in *Les collages* Hermann, Paris, 1965

Suzanne Bernard *'Le Coup de dés' de Mallarmé dans la perspective historique* in *Revue d'histoire littéraire de la France* April-June 1951

Charles Boultenhouse *Poems in the shapes of things* in *Art News Annual* New York, 1959

Berjouhi Barsamian Bowler *The word is ikon* in *Typographica* No 16. Lund Humphries, London, December 1967

Berjouhi Barsamian Bowler *Word as Image* Studio Vista, London, 1970

Charles Bombaugh *Gleanings for the curious from the harvest-fields of literature* Hartford, Conn., 1875

Aaron Burns *Typography* Reinhold, New York, 1961

Michel Butor *Répertoire II* Editions de Minuit, Paris, 1964

Lewis Carroll *The Annotated Alice. Alice's Adventures in Wonderland and Through the Looking Glass.* Edited by Martin Gardner, Penguin Books, Harmondsworth, 1965

Georges Charbonnier *Entretiens avec Michel Butor* Gallimard, Paris, 1967

Carl Dair *Design with type* University of Toronto Press, 1967

Jacques Damase *Révolution typographique depuis Stéphane Mallarmé* Galerie Motte, Geneva, 1966

Gardner Davies *Vers une explication rationnelle du ' Coup de dés'. Essai d'exégèse mallarméenne* Librairie José Corti, Paris, 1953

Michel Décaudin *A propos de Calligrammes* in *Guillaume Apollinaire, Calligrammes* Le Club du meilleur livre, Paris, 1955

Robert Diehl *Figurensatz in Frankfurter Drucken der Renaissance und des Barocks* 1951

Michel Foucault *Ceci n'est pas une pipe* in *Les Cahiers du Chemin,* No 2. Gallimard, Paris, 1968

Pierre Garnier *Spatialisme et poésie concrète* Gallimard, Paris, 1968

Raymond Gid *Célébration de la lettre* Robert Morel, 1962

Bertrand Guégan *Les vers figurés dans l'Antiquité et au Moyen Age* in *Arts et Métiers Graphiques* No 29, Paris, 1932

Bertrand Guégan *Vers figurés et calligrammes* in *Arts et Métiers Graphiques* No 32, Paris, 1932

Holbrook Jackson *Patterns in print* The Dolphin, 1941

Anne-Marie Lereboullet, *Les calligrammes dans l'expression littéraire* M. A. thesis under the direction of Professor Etiemble at the Institute of Comparative Modern Literature of the University of Paris, 1966-7

F. T. Marinetti *Les mots en liberté futuristes* Milan, 1919

Philomneste junior (*alias* Gabriel Peignot) *Amusements philologiques ou variétés en tous genres* Paris, 1808

George Puttenham *The Arte of English Poesie* London, 1589

Raymond Queneau *Bâtons, chiffres et lettres* Gallimard, Paris, 1950

Jean Roudaut *Michel Butor ou le livre futur* Gallimard, Paris, 1964

Jacques Scherer *L'Expression littéraire dans l'oeuvre de Mallarmé* Droz, Paris, 1947

Jacques Scherer *Le 'Livre' de Mallarmé premières recherches sur des documents inédits* Gallimard, Paris, 1957

Stefan Themerson *Idéogrammes lyriques* in *Typographica* No 14, Lund Humphries, London, December, 1966

Paul Valéry *Le Coup de dés, dernière visite a Mallarmé* in *Variété II* Gallimard, Paris, 1929

Carolyn Wells *A whimsey anthology* Dover Publications, New York, 1963

John Willett *Art, letters and the arrangement of ideas* Lectures given to the Slade School of Art and the Institute of Contemporary Arts and published in *Macabre,* No. 19-22 1966

The part played by letters and written symbols in the graphic arts

William C. Seitz *The art of assemblage* The Museum of Modern Art, New York, 1961

Beatrice Warde *The crystal goblet. Sixteen essays on typography* Sylvan Press, London, 1955

Herbert Bayer, Walter Gropius, Ise Gropius *Bauhaus, 1919-1928* Branford, Boston, 1959

Herbert Bayer *Herbert Bayer* Studio Vista, London; Reinhold, New York, 1967

Lettering by modern artists The Museum of Modern Art, New York, 1964

Lettering today edited by John Brinkley, Studio Vista, London; Reinhold, New York, 1969

Georges Mathieu *De l'image aux arts graphiques* Lecture given to the *Rendez-Vous Graphique* at Lurs-en-Provence and published in the *Cahiers de Lurs,* No. 2, 1965

James Smith Pierce *Pictographs, ideograms and alphabets in the work of Paul Klee* in *The Journal of Typographic Research* The Press of Western Reserve University, Cleveland, July 1967

José Piere, *Hannah Höch et le photomontage des Dadaïstes berlinois* in *Techniques Graphiques* No. 66, Michel Brient, Paris, Nov/Dec 1966

Schrift and Bild Catalogue published by the Staatlichen Kunsthalle Baden-Baden. Typos Verlag, Frankfurt, 1963

Philippe Schuwer *Typographie et arts d'aujourd'hui* in *Revue suisse de l'imprimerie* No 1, January 1958

Acknowledgements

We are greatly indebted to all those who have co-operated in the publication of this book, and in particular to Anne Ackermann and Roger-Jean Ségalat, also Noël Arnaud, Jean-Louis Barrault, Giuseppe Bisaccia, Pierre Bourgeade, Berjouhi Barsamian Bowler, Alain Brieux, François Caradec, Jacques Carelman, Robert Carlier, Eugenio Carmi, Joseph Chérel, Jean-Jacques Corre, Suzanne Duconget, Jean-A. Ducourneau, Germano Facetti, Patrick Ferrey, Jean-Marie Folon, André Francois, Pierre Garnier, Eleanor Garvey, Robert Giraud, Roger Grenier, Armin Haab, Adolf Hoffmeister, Eugène Ionesco, William Klein, Claude Labarre, Jean-Marie Lhote, Noël Lindsay, François Le Lionnais, Alfred Mattauch, André Parisot, François Peynet, Raymond Queneau, Victoria de Ramel, Roylance, Wolfgang Schmidt, Peter Schmitt, Philippe Schuwer, Siné, Hans Martin Spilkar, Henry Steiner, Peter Wick, Bernard Villemot, Louise de Vilmorin, John Willett.

We would also like to thank those firms that have helped us, including the Galerie Alexandre Iolas, Korès, Olivetti, La Gaine Scandale.

We have greatly benefited from the information supplied by Marcel Thomas, Head Keeper at the Bibliothèque Nationale, by the Carpenter Centre for the visual arts at Harvard, and by Trinity College Library, Dublin.

We are equally grateful to the following newspapers and periodicals: *The Boston Globe, l'Echo de la mode, Elle, L'Express, Formidable, France-soir, Life, McCalls, Le Monde, Fact, Fortune, Print* and *Typographica, Time, Woman's Day* and the publishers Albin Michel, André Balland, The Citadel Press, Gaberbocchus Press, Grove Press, Harlin Quist, Rupert Hart-Davies, Eric Losfeld, Merlin Verlag, Planéte, Van Nostrand Reinhold and in particular Dover Publications.

The quotations from Claudel (pages 119, 121, 124, 127) are taken from his *Ideogrammes occidentaux*, published by the Auguste Blaizot Library in 1927. The fragments of Zohar were translated by Nadjm Oud-Dine Bammate and reproduced in *La Parisienne* no. 42 March 1957. Both these texts have been reproduced by the kind permission of the publishers concerned.

Finally we thank Pierre Bruno for all his welcome advice and help.

Index of names

Erratum. *Page 131, line 12, read : « In Semitic writing » instead of semantic.*